SHAKESPEARE'S HISTORY PLAYS

This volume, with a foreword by Dennis Kennedy, addresses a range of attitudes to Shakespeare's English history plays in Britain and abroad from the early seventeenth century to the present day. It concentrates on the play texts as well as productions, translations and adaptations of them. The essays explore the multiple points of intersection between the English history they recount and the experience of British and other national cultures, establishing the plays as genres not only relevant to the political and cultural history of Britain but also to the history of nearly every nation worldwide. The history plays have had an astonishingly rich international reception tradition but critics and theatre historians abroad, those practising what has become 'foreign' Shakespeare, have tended to ignore these plays in favour of the comedies and tragedies. By presenting the British and foreign Shakespeare traditions side by side, this volume seeks to promote a more finely integrated world Shakespeare.

TON HOENSELAARS is Associate Professor in the English Department at Utrecht University. He is the author of *Images of Englishmen and Foreigners in the Drama of Shakespeare and His Contemporaries* (1992). He is also editor and co-editor of several collections including *Shakespeare's Italy* (1993, revised edition 1997), *Reclamations of Shakespeare* (1994), and *400 Years of Shakespeare in Europe* (2003).

SHAKESPEARE'S HISTORY PLAYS

*Performance, Translation and Adaptation
in Britain and Abroad*

EDITED BY
TON HOENSELAARS

WITH A FOREWORD BY
DENNIS KENNEDY

CAMBRIDGE
UNIVERSITY PRESS

PUBLISHED BY THE PRESS SYNDICATE OF THE UNIVERSITY OF CAMBRIDGE
The Pitt Building, Trumpington Street, Cambridge, United Kingdom

CAMBRIDGE UNIVERSITY PRESS
The Edinburgh Building, Cambridge, CB2 2RU, UK
40 West 20th Street, New York, NY 10011–4211, USA
477 Williamstown Road, Port Melbourne, VIC 3207, Australia
Ruiz de Alarcón 13, 28014 Madrid, Spain
Dock House, The Waterfront, Cape Town 8001, South Africa

http://www.cambridge.org

First published 2004

Printed in the United Kingdom at the University Press, Cambridge

Typeface Adobe Garamond 11/12.5 pt.   *System* LATEX 2$_\varepsilon$ [TB]

A catalogue record for this book is available from the British Library

Library of Congress Cataloguing in Publication data
Shakespeare's history plays: performance, translation and adaptation in Britain and abroad / edited by
Ton Hoenselaars; with a foreword by Dennis Kennedy.
p.   cm.
Includes bibliographical references and index.
ISBN 0 521 82902 X
1. Shakespeare, William, 1564–1616 – Histories.   2. Shakespeare, William, 1564–1616 –
Adaptations – History and criticism.   3. Shakespeare, William, 1564–1616 – Translations – History
and criticism.   4. Shakespeare, William, 1564–1616 – Dramatic production.   5. Great Britain –
History – 1066–1687 – Historiography.   6. Shakespeare, William, 1564–1616 – Stage history.
7. Historical drama, English – History and criticism.   8. Literature and history – Great Britain.
9. Kings and rulers in literature.   10. Middle Ages in literature.   I. Hoenselaars, A. J., 1956–
PR2982.S475   2004
822.3′3 – dc22   2004040752

ISBN 0 521 82902 X hardback

For Ieme

Contents

Acknowledgements

Preparing this collection of essays on the histories, I have enjoyed the generous support of colleagues and friends worldwide. My Utrecht colleague Paul Franssen was always there with advice or comments. I also owe a great debt of thanks to Graham Bradshaw (Chuo University, Tokyo), Michael Hattaway (Sheffield University), Wilhelm Hortmann (University of Duisburg), Saskia Kossak (University of Salzburg), Kristine Steenbergh (Utrecht University), Jozef de Vos (University of Ghent), and Sylvia Zysset (University of Basle). I am particularly grateful to Isabelle Schwartz-Gastine (University of Caen), for her generous advice and support.

This would not have been the same book without the encouragement and counsel of Mark Thornton Burnett (Queen's University, Belfast), both at our now historic lunch at the International Shakespeare Conference in Stratford, and in the time that followed.

The Utrecht Research Institute for History and Culture – personified by Wiljan van den Akker and Frans Ruiter – has been supportive of the histories project from the outset until its completion.

Sarah Stanton of Cambridge University Press was a welcome and efficient guide. Dennis Kennedy has been an unusual source of inspiration.

Utrecht, Summer 2003

Illustrations

Contributors

EDWARD BURNS is Senior Lecturer in English at the University of Liverpool. His books include *Restoration Comedy: Crises of Desire and Identity* (1987), *Character: Acting and Being on the Pre-Modern Stage* (1990), *The Chester Mystery Plays: A Modern Staging Text* (1987) and *William Shakespeare: Richard III* (2003). He has also edited *The First Part of King Henry the Sixth* for Arden 3 (1999) and *Five British Romantic Plays* (with Paul Baines, 2000).

JEAN-MICHEL DÉPRATS, both a scholar and a theatre translator, is Senior Lecturer in English and Theatre Studies at the University of Nanterre (Paris x). He has written many articles on Shakespeare, and has translated about thirty of Shakespeare's plays staged by prominent directors in France and abroad, including Stéphane Braunschweig, Irina Brook, Matthias Langhoff, Georges Lavaudant, Luca Ronconi and Peter Zadek. For the cinema he has done a dubbed version of *Henry V* and Franco Zeffirelli's *Hamlet*. He is currently preparing a new bilingual edition of *Shakespeare's Complete Works* for the Pléiade series published by Gallimard, the first two volumes of which (devoted to the *Tragedies*) appeared in 2002. His translations have won many prizes (Molière, Prix Osiris, Prix Halpérine-Kaminsky).

MANFRED DRAUDT is Professor of English Language and Literature at Vienna University and President of the Viennese Shakespeare Society. He has written numerous articles on Shakespeare, Renaissance drama and editorial matters. His interest in nineteenth-century popular literature and in travesties of Shakespeare is reflected in a series of articles, in his critical edition of Charles Matthews's *Othello, the Moor of Fleet Street* (1993) and in a forthcoming contribution to the new *Oxford Dictionary of National Biography*.

DANIEL GALLIMORE read English at Christ Church, Oxford, and took an MA degree in Japanese Studies at Sheffield University. He has taught English in Japan and Japanese at Oxford Brookes University. He is currently employed at Japan Women's University, Tokyo. He has written many articles on Shakespeare and Japanese culture.

DOMINIQUE GOY-BLANQUET is Professor of Elizabethan Theatre at the University of Amiens, a member of the CNRS Laboratoire des Arts de Spectacle, and a regular contributor to the *Times Literary Supplement.* Her books include *Shakespeare's Early History Plays: From Chronicle to Stage* (2003) and the essay collection *Joan of Arc, A Saint for All Seasons: Studies in Myth and Politics* (2003). She has also translated various works on the theatre, including John Dover Wilson's *What Happens in Hamlet* and W. H. Auden's *Lectures on Shakespeare* (2003).

KEITH GREGOR is Lecturer in English and Irish Literature at the University of Murcia, Spain. He is co-editor of *Teatro Clásico en Traducción*, and the author of numerous articles on Shakespeare and Renaissance culture. He is currently preparing a volume on the history of Shakespeare on the Spanish stage.

TON HOENSELAARS is Senior Lecturer in the English Department of Utrecht University. He is the author of *Images of Englishmen and Foreigners in the Drama of Shakespeare and His Contemporaries* (1992). He has edited, alone or with others, *Shakespeare's Italy* (1993), *The Italian World of English Renaissance Drama* (1997), *English Literature and the Other Languages* (1999), *The Author as Character* (1999), *Four Hundred Years of Shakespeare in Europe* (2003) and *Shakespeare and the Language of Translation* (2004). He is also the founding Chairman of the Shakespeare Society of the Low Countries, and managing editor of its journal *Folio.* He is currently writing a monograph on Shakespeare and Richard Wagner.

LISA HOPKINS is Professor of English at Sheffield Hallam University. She is the author of *John Ford's Political Theatre* (1994) and of many articles and notes on English Renaissance drama.

DENNIS KENNEDY is Samuel Beckett Professor of Drama and head of the School of Drama in Trinity College Dublin. His books include *Granville Barker and the Dream of Theatre* (1985), *Plays by Harley Granville Barker* (1987), *Looking at Shakespeare: A Visual History of Twentieth-century Performance* (1993; second edition, 2001) and *Foreign Shakespeare* (1993). He was an advisory editor for *The Oxford Companion to Shakespeare* (2001) and is the general editor of *The Oxford Encyclopedia of Theatre and Performance* (2003). He is currently writing a book on *Shakespeare and the Director* and researching another on the condition of the spectator in theatre, film and sports.

JAMES N. LOEHLIN is Associate Professor of English at The University of Texas at Austin. He is the author of *Henry V* in the Shakespeare in Performance series at Manchester University Press (1996), and has edited *Romeo and Juliet* for the Shakespeare in Production series of Cambridge University Press (2003). He has also published on teaching Shakespeare as well as Shakespeare and film. He is Director of the University of Texas Shakespeare at Winedale programme.

ANDREW MURPHY is Reader in English at the University of St. Andrews, Scotland. He is the author of *Shakespeare in Print: A History and Chronology of Shakespeare Publishing* (2003) and *But the Irish Sea Betwixt Us: Ireland, Colonialism, and Renaissance Literature* (1999). He is the editor of *The Renaissance Text: Theory, Editing, Textuality* (2000).

ALEXANDER SHURBANOV is Professor of English Literature at the University of Sofia. His books include *Renaissance Humanism and Shakespeare's Lyrical Poetry* (1980), *Between Pathos and Irony: Christopher Marlowe and the Genesis of Renaissance Drama* (1992), *Painting Shakespeare Red: An East-European Appropriation* (with Boika Sokolova, 2001) and *English Renaissance Poetics* (2002). He is the co-editor (with Vladimir Trendafilov) of *The Bulgarian Reception of English Literature through Translation* (2000), and has himself translated Chaucer's *Canterbury Tales* and Milton's *Paradise Lost* into Bulgarian verse.

BOIKA SOKOLOVA has for many years taught Shakespeare and English Renaissance literature at the University of Sofia (Bulgaria), and is currently a Visiting Fellow at Birkbeck College, University of London, and Adjunct Professor, University of California London Programme. She has written many articles on Shakespeare and other early modern writers. She is also the author of *Shakespeare's Romances as Interrogative Texts: Their Alienation Strategies and Ideology* (1992), and co-author (with Alexander Shurbanov) of *Painting Shakespeare Red: An East-European Appropriation* (2001). She is co-editor (with Derek Roper and Michael Hattaway) of *Shakespeare in the New Europe* (1994), and (with Evgenia Pancheva) of *Renaissance Refractions* (2001).

MARIANGELA TEMPERA is Professor of English at the University of Ferrara, Italy. She is the author of *The Lancashire Witches* (1981), *Feasting with Centaurs: 'Titus Andronicus' from Stage to Text* (1999), and many articles on Shakespeare and Renaissance drama. She is the editor of the series *Shakespeare: From Text to Stage* (1984).

Foreword: histories and nations

Dennis Kennedy

In the beginning there were four nations. That was what they called themselves, though at the time none of them was a sovereign state. They raised indigenous attack forces for a series of clashes, insisting on an absolute victor: the heroic, conquering, nation of nations. They did this every year, year after year, encouraged by national desires for glory, overwhelming public support, and a tradition of aggressiveness that reaches back to descriptions of war in the *Iliad* as a magnificent occupation for men, a thing of great beauty, triumph and overthrow in direct and undisguised antagonism. Despite their long-standing enmity and cultural and linguistic differences, they shared a lingua franca in combat, geographical proximity and a tattered political history. The rules of engagement, altered over time to suit changing circumstances, ultimately derived from a single source, a remote ascetic sanctuary located in the largest of the four, dedicated to the training of young men.

But then a fifth was admitted to the fray, a barbarian country with a history of enmity with the founding nation, equivalent in population, larger in area, contrary in custom, dissimilar in language and insufficiently aware, some therefore thought, of the true meaning of battle. If the addition struck those observers as bizarre, they would have been flabbergasted when nearly a century later a sixth challenger gained the right of combat despite its shadowy national history and uncertain martial qualifications. Perhaps more will join the struggle in future: there are no certainties in warfare. For now it remains six. In alphabetical order, England, France, Ireland, Italy, Scotland, Wales. The Six Nations Rugby Tournament.[1]

If these are all nations, they are so in different meanings of the word. Two British political entities now partially devolved from Westminster are matched with a fully independent one (yet whose northern six counties are not at this moment devolved from Britain at all). An ancient state whose borders shifted with regularity until 1945, often in the past trading soil with England. A nation formed only in the late nineteenth century out of highly disparate principalities and republics that continues to show severe regional stress. And the land of St George itself: nobody seems sure any longer what England means. Despite occasional confusion in common speech, England is hardly equivalent with the United Kingdom of Great Britain and Northern Ireland. While its borders are clear and its flag distinct, politically it is a little confused, since there cannot be complete devolution in the UK until England has its own parliament.

The six rugby nations are the countries that are most regularly referred to in Shakespeare, usually with some attention to governance; even Italy, which does not feature in the history plays (unless we count the Roman tragedies), is usually rendered on a political ground, as in *Romeo and Juliet*, *The Merchant of Venice* and *Othello*. The English sagas offer local versions of medieval polity on the way to becoming something more recognizable to the late sixteenth century. *Richard II* and the two parts of *Henry IV*, displaying rebellion in Ireland, Wales and the north of England, present arguments about the nature of an early modern nation, how it should be governed and who should govern it. Five of the rugby nations are represented in a single match in *Henry V*, the play which most probes the idea of nation, relying occasionally on sporting metaphors to do so, by getting four to gang up on one, so that Harry le Roy can become king of them all. Of course the France he conquered was hardly coterminous with the large hexagon that defines the borders of the country today. All his victories took place in Normandy and Picardy and his triumph was short-lived, as the *Henry VI* plays show; the Treaty of Troyes in 1420, which concludes *Henry V*, was in tatters at its hero's death two years later, a historical fact that makes the elevation of the play into a paean of English nationalism a strangely short-sighted move. (Henry would not have dreamed of war in Gasgoyne and Languedoc in the south-west, now the centre of French rugby. The residual nationalism of those regions is notorious, and there have even been moves to redesignate the fifth rugby nation as Occitania.)

What is a nation? What is a national history? In Shakespeare's chronicles these questions are intensely localized to England and England's provinces. With the major exceptions of grandiose or luxurious characters like Richard III and Falstaff, the history plays and their historical material have held relatively little interest for readers and audiences further afield. This is perfectly understandable. British colonial dominance encouraged a special connection in Anglophone theatre and criticism, but the endless genealogical patterns, the confusion of names and geography and the complicated dramatic actions have tended to diffuse their impact anywhere outside the originating nation. Why should France take to *Henry V* or rugby, two cultural products of its traditional enemy? Tom Lanoye and Luk Perceval, the recent adapter and director of the history cycles in Flanders, put it bluntly: the cycle plays are 'a baffling series of conspiracies, marriages, murder, and battles; a pandemonium of forty acts, two hundred scenes and three hundred characters'.[2] For Belgian and Dutch audiences, Lanoye said, Richmond and Kent are not historical figures or geographical place names, they are cigarette brands.

Correspondingly, the English have long taken a proprietary interest in the histories. It has often been noted that these plays constitute a national epic in dramatic form, and without doubt they have been significant in the project of nation building and nation maintaining. From the time of Elizabeth I to the time of Elizabeth II, from Burbage to Branagh, Shakespeare's nine dramas on the political development of England in the fifteenth century, through some nine kings, and occasionally with the addition of *King John*, have been drawn upon to define or redefine or query national identity. They cover almost half the list of monarchs in the breathless schoolchild mnemonic:

> Willy–Willy–Harry–Steve
> Harry–Dick–John–Harry 3
> 1–2–3 Neds–Richard 2
> Harry 4–5–6, then who?
> Edward 4 and Richard 3
> Thought I didn't know, tee-hee.

But the relative familiarity some English spectators have with their own history does not mean that the plays are easy, for in Stratford as well as Milan they are not routinely congenial in the way that most of the comedies and many of the tragedies are. Calling attention to this in an introductory manual, Russ McDonald writes that 'the chronicle play or history was also less familiar to Shakespeare and his audiences than comedy or tragedy because it was being invented at the very moment that Shakespeare began working in the form'.[3] We might add that the genre more or less died out in London immediately afterwards. There are predecessors and descendants but few examples of plays so directly conscious of public ideologies and private prerogatives, of dynastic and internecine angst or of the relationship of personality to power. Shakespeare's chronicles are complicated works that reach their conclusions through plots labyrinthine in bearing. If they can be thought of as a saga of the English nation, it is a tale of precarious preservation shot through with torture and distress.

Taken singly, the history plays can be impressive on a number of levels and individual scenes often reveal the inherent contradictions in the histories they relate. But it is the perception that they constitute a dramatic series with an internal logic and a grand overplot that gives them their special distinction in the world repertoire. Thinking of them as a cycle, or as two related cycles, makes possible large-scale showings that have substantially raised critical opinion of the plays, especially of the three parts of *Henry VI*, and liberated them from individual status through marathon experiences over a number of nights or in gruelling weekends. (For me, the most gruelling was Stuart Seide's production in French at the Avignon Festival in July 1994, outdoors in the Court of Honour of the Papal Palace, which began with the funeral of Henry V on a warm evening at 10 o'clock and ended with the crowning of Edward IV in a cool dawn at 6.30 the next morning.) Whether we accept Nicholas Grene's contention that the histories were written as 'serial' dramas, their exposition in serial fashion has indelibly affected how they are now viewed critically.[4]

But in the theatre this seriality is a recent idea. The notion of the Shakespeare cycle was the invention of a nineteenth-century theatre manager, Franz von Dingelstedt, who staged both cycles in Weimar for the tercentenary in 1864 and revived them in Vienna in 1875.[5] Also the translator-adapter of Shakespeare's works (Berlin, 1877), Dingelstedt was probably more interested in the amalgamation of the plays into a critical Shakespearian mass than he was in an extensive review of English history. Nonetheless his antiquarian productions, similar in nature to the historicism of Charles Kean in London in the 1850s, emphasized the particularity of period, attempting the display of a medieval authentic, an approach to the chronicles that continued with a number of directors well into the twentieth century. The theatrical methods differed over time, of course, as did the look of things, but the impulse to create a *mise-en-scène* in tune with current notions of the past has often been at the root of attention to these plays.

Wagner's *Ring* cycle, first seen entire in Bayreuth in 1876, was part of the trend to marathon performance of Shakespeare. Certainly the construction of the Bayreuth Festspielhaus, the first theatre in history dedicated to a single artist, greatly influenced the drive to build the Shakespeare Memorial Theatre in Stratford, which opened three years later, the first theatre in history dedicated to a single dramatist. Yet no history cycle was produced there, or anywhere else in Britain, until Frank Benson's production of the double tetralogy in 1906 (oddly, minus *1 Henry IV* because he could not find a sufficiently heroic part for himself). While his scenography was not lavish, the scent of English empire past and present was heavily in the air. It was so again at Stratford at the end of the empire when Anthony Quayle mounted the complete second tetralogy of histories in 1951, played on a unit set by Tanya Moiseiwitsch, the directing shared with Michael Redgrave and John Kidd. With almost a half century between them, serial performance had obviously not taken root in Shakespeare's nation. In fact the only other major cyclic presentation in the first half of the century was again in Germany, Saladin Schmidt directing all ten of the English chronicles in Bochum in 1927.

Nonetheless it was in Stratford that the Royal Shakespeare Company changed common notions of the histories. When in 1963 Peter Hall chose to use the first cycle to define the style of the newly created company, and to celebrate the writer's quatercentenary by adding the second cycle the following year, he deliberately sought hard-edged acting and visuals that had little to do with the historicist tradition. Yet he too was following foreign leads, particularly those of a German marxist and a Polish dissident. As James Loehlin shows here, by mid-century Bertolt Brecht had provided 'a model for historical theatre' in his own plays, in his analytical commentary and in his directing practice. Brecht's company visited London a few weeks after his death in 1956 with two history plays of a different type, *Mother Courage* and *The Caucasian Chalk Circle*; Hall was so impressed that when he founded the RSC in 1960 he based his organizational, social and aesthetic standards on the Berliner Ensemble. With his designer John Bury, Hall extracted from the Ensemble a Brechtian realism for the histories: the Middle Ages concocted from heavy clanging broadswords, grunting actors, sweaty leather and a rough-hewn approach that revealed glimpses of the social and class circumstances underneath Shakespeare's dramas.

But when unravelled a bit, many of the Brechtian motifs were stylistic rather than interpretive, for at the heart of the cycle was Jan Kott's decisive essay on the histories, 'The Kings', published in *Shakespeare Our Contemporary* in Polish in 1961, in French in 1962 and in English in 1964. Kott's essay comparing *King Lear* to Beckett's *Endgame* – the quintessential Cold War play – had already substantially affected Peter Brook's version of *Lear* for the RSC in 1962; theatrically speaking, Brook's dark vision was Hall's greatest influence. Kott was writing as a former marxist, disenchanted by the Soviet invasion of Hungary in 1956 and Stalinist authoritarianism in Poland. He saw in Shakespeare's chronicles a cycle of unending repression, political opportunism and murderous brutality that paralleled his view of life, a generalized application of the Eastern European condition. Using the central image of the 'grand staircase', Kott imagined Shakespeare's kings and would-be kings perpetually shuffling up and down the steps, knocking each other over on their way to the top. No reason to think that the accession of Henry VII would change matters, since the 1960s inclined to the same inhuman, brutal, absurdist politics: It Was Ever Thus. As Brook in *Lear* (and in his production of Peter Weiss's *Marat/Sade* of 1964), Hall found Kott's It Was Ever Thus philosophy more intellectually apposite than Brecht's marxist conviction that We Can Change the World. Needless to say, in a Western capitalist environment IWETers are more congenial than WeCaners. Even the overall title, *The Wars of the Roses*, emphasized the continuing nature of unhappy history.

So one of the major outcomes of Hall's cycle was a foregrounding of the histories as contemporary Cold War plays.[6] Serial performance of the histories then became a major way to honour Shakespeare's 400th birthday, usually under the same influences. Various signs of those two rationales for revivals were apparent in a politically and textually conservative serial production by Leopold Lindtberg in Vienna (which actually began before Hall, in 1961), a more radical one by Giorgio Strehler in Milan (*Il gioco dei potenti*, 'The game of the mighty', 1965) and in *Der Krieg der Rosen* by Peter Palitzsch in Stuttgart (1967). A wide European re-evaluation of Shakespeare followed in Kott's wake, and he and Brecht continued to affect Shakespeare production in general well into the 1980s. They could even be seen to lurk under the surface in Michael Bogdanov's *The Wars of the Roses* for the touring English Shakespeare Company in 1986, though that cycle was definitely more WeCaner than IWETer.

When I put *Foreign Shakespeare* together in 1991 and 1992, the book as a whole was greatly affected by the political changes in Europe and the Soviet Union that had just occurred. The violence which followed in the former Soviet empire highlighted the ways Shakespeare had been employed for nationalist causes during the Cold War on both sides of the Iron Curtain. The end of that period also clarified the movements away from the political uses of the plays that started to appear in the late 1970s. While the histories always remain political at some level, a postmodern turn appeared in production, most notably in Ariane Mnouchkine's *Richard II* and *1 Henry IV* in Paris (1981, 1984), part of an aborted six-play Shakespeare cycle that was to include the full *Richard II* tetralogy. Mnouchkine consciously denied Kott's approach – 'Shakespeare is not our contemporary,' she said, 'and must not be treated as such'[7] – and drew instead on Asian performance methods, nô and kabuki in particular, a thorough-going aestheticizing of the historical material.

Seen at the Olympic Arts Festival in Los Angeles in 1984, Mnouchkine's orientalist work also prefigured another change, the globalized or festivalized performance of marathon productions for an international audience. The RSC in Stratford has always relied on tourist spectators, and the histories appear with some regularity there, most recently in quasi-serial form in 2000. Even the heavily touristic new Globe in London offered *Henry V* as its official opening production in 1997, which local audiences insistently made into a chauvinist statement by hissing the French at their every entrance. In England, at least, a nationalist interpretation of the chronicle plays appears to be part of the game. But the number of intercultural and non-anglophone productions of the histories seen at international festivals, and a growing attention to these plays in Asia (including a politically aggravating *Richard III* in Beijing in 2001, directed in an international style by Lin Zhaohua), suggest that there is large room for future studies of global Shakespeare performance.

The great paradox of our time is the intense exercise of a residual form of nationalism amid a globalized economy and transnational politics. The low cost of air travel, the ease of touring, the universal acceptance of credit cards, the introduction of the euro as currency, the rise of the Internet, the prevalence of English as the language of trade, the opening of the bazaars of the second-world and third-world economies to the powerful forces of Western capital – all of these suggest a 'one-world' planet where cultural difference is tolerated for its marketability, or where the 'glocal' operates as a simulated but efficient substitute for the indigenous. Yet at the same time we witness daily examples of fervent nationalism or of cultural and religious tribalism that seek to close borders, both physical and psychological ones, often through violent means that deny humanity to the other.

At the level of surrogation, the ritualized combat of sport may provide the best example of the national in the midst of the global, as so many games on the world stage rely upon the creation of national squads or permit nationalist identification with the participants. We can see on television, that prime agent of the global, regular international competitions in rugby, soccer, cricket, lawn tennis, prize fighting, horse racing (on the flat and over fences), show jumping, polo, squash, even snooker and billiards. Other sports can be added, of course, but I choose that list because all of those games are English in foundation. Some of them have maintained overtones of the colonial, especially cricket and polo, but most of them long ago lost any connection to the land of their birth. Soccer, the world's most popular spectator sport, played almost everywhere, may have originally spread through informal colonialist patterns, but few people today identify it principally with England and even fewer know the origin of its name (Association Football is its formal title in English, soccer a nickname derived from the abbreviation 'Assoc.').

And with the necessary changes for its different cultural field, a similar pattern can be applied to Shakespeare's history plays. They came from England, they are about England and they can be made to speak for England, but they have been discharged from their uniquely nationalist obligations. Their reception and performance in the other Six Nations, and in wider nations as well, the topic of this book, show that when the history plays are spoken in foreign climes and foreign tongues they often speak of matters foreign to England. In international rugby matches England frequently wins these days, but has long been thoroughly used to being beaten in soccer, cricket and tennis. When the Empire (and the nations of rest of the world) write back about sport, it's often to say we play differently from you but are just as good if not better. Why shouldn't that be true of Shakespeare as well, England's most famous export?

NOTES

1 The first Four Nations Tournament took place in 1882. France joined in 1910 and Italy only in 1998, though rugby has been played there competitively since 1909. My thanks to Edward Braun for help on the history of English sports.

2 Quoted from the cover of the original box set of Tom Lanoye and Luk Perceval, *Ten Oorlog*, 3 vols. (Amsterdam: Prometheus, 1997).

3 Russ McDonald, *The Bedford Companion to Shakespeare: An Introduction with Documents*, 2nd edn (Boston: Bedford/St Martin's, 2001), 90.

4 Nicholas Grene, *Shakespeare's Serial History Plays* (Cambridge: Cambridge University Press, 2002).

5 See Simon Williams, *Shakespeare on the German Stage, 1586–1914* (Cambridge: Cambridge University Press, 1990), 153–4.

6 I take up this argument in another context in 'Shakespeare and the Cold War', in *Four Hundred Years of Shakespeare in Europe*, edited by A. Luis Pujante and Ton Hoenselaars, with a Foreword by Stanley Wells (Newark, NJ: University of Delaware Press, 2003), 163–79.

7 Quoted in David Bradley and David Williams, *Director's Theatre* (New York: Macmillan, 1988), 100, 98.

Introduction: Shakespeare's history plays in Britain and abroad

Ton Hoenselaars

The essays collected in this volume address the different attitudes to Shakespeare's English history plays in Britain and abroad, from the early modern period to the present day. One of the aims is to study the various national responses to the plays with an eye to the process whereby different political and cultural contexts have tended to accommodate the plays' implicit 'Englishness', that is, the notion which led Heminges and Condell in 1623 to present these ten plays as 'Histories', plays which subsequently became known also as the 'history plays', but also, in more specifically national terms, as the 'English chronicles', and as the 'English history plays'.[1]

This volume explores the histories within the context of several major recent developments in Shakespeare Studies. One of these developments is the increasing attention devoted to the 'nation', be it as this is represented or defined in Shakespeare's plays, or as various nations, including England, have over the centuries interpreted and appropriated these plays to meet certain ideological ends.[2] Another major development of recent decades acknowledged here is the unprecedented expansion of the field of Shakespeare Studies, as the traditionally Anglo-centred Shakespeare industry has come to recognize the cultural validity of manifestations and appropriations of the playwright beyond the British Isles, in different national contexts, and, nearly as a matter of course, in languages other than Shakespeare's own. An approach like this, it is hoped, will simultaneously enhance our appreciation of the British, more or less self-reflexive preoccupation with the histories, and at the same time our insight into the processes of international appropriation.

Recognizing the predominant concern with notions like 'nationhood' and 'the nation' in either tradition, this volume signals a curious phenomenon: whereas the 'native' tradition in the theatre as well as academe (with ample support from their counterparts in North America, Australia, and New Zealand) has in recent years only broadened its interest in the histories, the academic representatives of the second Shakespeare tradition have largely ignored them. However, this current discrepancy of academic attention to the genre stands in no relation to the fact that these plays have had a formidable stage history, across the world as in Britain, from the earliest times to the present day. It is, therefore, high time to redress the balance.

This introduction provides a broad historical survey of the reception of the histories, devoting special attention to the less familiar foreign traditions. Thus it provides a framework for the essays in this volume which address the various manifestations, British and foreign, in detail, and likewise concentrate on the relatively less accessible non-English-speaking traditions in particular.[3] By presenting the British and foreign traditions side by side, it becomes possible to identify not only traditions of 'foreign' histories beyond the English Channel, but also within the 'native' preoccupation with the genre, in post-devolution Britain.

The introduction concludes with a brief exploration of the apparent divide between the two academic traditions central to this volume. Although there is a significant measure of overlap, interaction and exchange between the native and the foreign Shakespeare industries, geographical as well as linguistic and cultural barriers between them remain. Given the obviously shared concerns and interests on either side, thematic enterprises like the present one might be the most creative way of investigating the cross-cultural and cross-national reception and appropriation of the plays, and promote a more finely integrated world Shakespeare.

The final decades of the twentieth century witnessed a radical reorientation of the traditionally Anglo-centred Shakespeare industry.[4] As the once firm belief in an essentialist Shakespeare embodying universal truths was effectively discarded, and the playwright's status came to be recognized as a complex political construct, it was not long before the process was also exposed, notably by Michael Dobson and Jonathan Bate, by which English Shakespeare had in the course of history been promoted as the 'symbol and exemplar of British national identity'.[5] The assumed cultural identity of 'Britain' that Shakespeare, among others, was made to uphold had tended to obscure internal power relations, as it glossed over differences of race, religion and also region.

As new ways were developed during the late twentieth century to recount the 'English', 'Irish', 'Scottish' and 'Welsh' histories, homogenous British Shakespeare devolved into multiple regional Shakespeares. Following the independent pioneering work of Philip Edwards in the 1970s, the research field of Ireland was effectively opened up by Andrew Hadfield, Brendan

Bradshaw, Willy Maley, Andrew Murphy and others.[6] In their wake, Mark Thornton Burnett and Ramona Wray's *Shakespeare and Ireland* (1997) further extended the scope from the status of Ireland in the early modern period to the subsequent historical relations between England and the Irish nation.[7] Critics including Terence Hawkes and Lisa Hopkins, as well as a notable number of North American scholars, including Ronald Boling, Jodi Mikalachki and Garrett Sullivan, have contributed to a new appreciation of the Welsh angle.[8]

This radical interrogation of a powerful, homogenized British Shakespeare during the 1980s and 1990s, as well as the subsequent modes of devolution that attended on the new interest in the various regional Shakespearean identities, were concurrent with the emergence of distinctly new national perspectives on 'Shakespeare' beyond the British Isles. There, among other things, the decline of the former British supremacy – whether colonialist in the traditional sense, or otherwise – together with a need to recognize and define varying modes of national and cultural diversity, stimulated the recognition of a broad range of independent and often geographically as well as linguistically 'foreign' Shakespeares, all deserving equal attention in their respective historical and politico-cultural contexts.

As part of this parallel tendency, there were the responses from other English-speaking areas. Michael Bristol's *Shakespeare's America/America's Shakespeare* presented a challenging critical analysis of the institutional status of Shakespeare in the US.[9] His initiative is on a par with such studies as Thomas Cartelli's *Repositioning Shakespeare*, with impressive chapters including 'Shakespeare, 1916' (about the tercentenary celebrations of Shakespeare's death in the US), but also with Terence Hawkes's presentist 'Aberdaugleddyf', which re-establishes the connection between the mythic status of Milford Haven and the foundation of the Folger Shakespeare Library in Washington.[10]

There has also been an unprecedented outpouring of studies devoted to Shakespeare and Shakespearean practice abroad in non-English-speaking areas. Beginning in Europe, the final decades of the second millennium witnessed the publication of Simon Williams and Wilhelm Hortmann's invaluable two-part history of Shakespeare on the German stage, as well as the monograph studies devoted to Shakespeare in Hungary by Péter Dávidházi, and Alexander Shurbanov and Boika Sokolova's record of Shakespeare in communist Bulgaria, *Painting Shakespeare Red*.[11] Focusing on narrower themes, but no less relevant to the debate were Marta Gibińska's *Polish Poets Read Shakespeare*, Manfred Pfister's 'Hamlet und der deutsche Geist', Brigitte Schulze's 'Shakespeare's Way into the West Slavic Literatures and

Cultures', as well as Lawrence Guntner and Andrew McClean's collection
of essays on Shakespeare in the German Democratic Republic.[12]

With such an impressive listing of monographs and articles, one should
not ignore the theatre reviews that have captured the appeal of Shakespearean practice in Britain as in other countries. Unfortunately, not all of
these have yet been catalogued or been presented in as neat a digested format
as Samuel Leiter's prescient *Shakespeare Around the Globe*, which, despite
its emphasis on North American and British productions since 1945, may
nevertheless lay claim to a geographical range 'from Adelaide to Zurich'.[13]

It is easy to underestimate a theatre review project like Leiter's, whose
impact on the critical branch of academe is unmistakable. This may be illustrated with an example from the American response to the histories. Frank
Rich's *New York Times* review of Kenneth Branagh's *Henry V* suggested
an intriguing national application of the English play when it famously
described the eponymous character as 'a boyish, idealistic Henry who may
rouse American theatregoers' ambivalent feelings about John F. Kennedy'
(Leiter, *Shakespeare Around the Globe*, 228). Few have noted that this review,
in turn, creatively inspired Harold Bloom, the self-confessed incarnation of
Falstaff, to state that 'power keeps its habit through the ages', and, with sly
reference also to *Henry V*'s deprecatory reference to Alexander the Great,
to add that 'Our nation's Henry V (some might say) was John Fitzgerald
Kennedy, who gave us the Bay of Pigs and the enhancement of our Vietnam
adventure.'[14] Academic discourse, as Leiter's manual here helps us recognize,
may entertain closer relations with stage practice and the theatre reviewing
tradition than we tend to take for granted.

Naturally, in disseminating international experiences of Shakespeare on
stage, the language barrier continues to play a decisive role. Whereas the
English-language *Shakespeare Bulletin*, after taking over the burgeoning
theatre review section from *Shakespeare Quarterly*, has for many years been
the worthy platform for productions from across the United States and
Canada (three issues annually), and for productions in other parts of
the world (to which it devotes its Winter issue), journals like *Shakespeare
Jahrbuch* or *Cahiers Élisabéthains* continue to present a considerable number of their theatre reviews in German and French respectively, particularly when these concern productions in the country or language area
that the journals were originally designed to represent. Given the language barrier that is likely to prevail as long as the idea of the nation
continues to pursue linguistic self-identity as one of its main pillars (a tendency captured also in Shakespeare's histories themselves), one naturally
welcomes the recent initiative to resuscitate the English-language journal

Shakespeare Worldwide – long one of the main platforms for the exchange of views on the translation, adaptation and production of Shakespeare in non-English-speaking countries – as *Multicultural Shakespeare: Translation, Appropriation, and Performance.*[15]

Some of the excitement of this international exchange of views across languages was communicated by Lois Potter's 1990 review of *2 Henry IV* in Czechoslovakia, which appeared in *Shakespeare Worldwide.* Here, Potter describes how just after the Czech revolution of May 1990, she saw Alois Hajda's production of *2 Henry IV,* whose presentation of the House of Lancaster as 'stifling all political dissent and all individualism' indicated only too clearly that its artistic conception dated from before the revolution.[16] However, although the production seemed to have outlived its time, it also gained new relevance, as contemporary politics, including the rise to power of the nation's foremost playwright Vaclav Havel, fused with Shakespearean history:

> In the new context of spring 1990, the new king, coming to power after long years of a very different life, could be seen as having inhabited, not the modern political Bohemia, but Bohemia in its nineteenth-century meaning: the fringe world of the arts to which Vaclav Havel, until recently, belonged. In that case, the end of the play becomes an oblique comment on events far more recent than the ongoing political corruption originally targetted by the production. How could 'this new and gorgeous garment, majesty' actually affect the new ruler? Would he retain a sense of what he had learned from Falstaff and the others, or would he eventually be compelled to reject them in favour of the political lessons taught by his father? (Potter, '*2 Henry IV*', 254)

As the political questions formulated here have themselves been relegated to the realm of history, and as the combined mood of apprehension and hope has been transformed into one of greater national confidence in the Czech republic, we continue to recognize the remarkable ability of the histories – in the 1950s still defined as 'the living epic of England' – sharply to interrogate the political situation in foreign countries in often unexpected ways.[17]

With the growing tendency to chart the Shakespearean practice, past or present, of individual nations, the focus has also been increasingly directed at a broader 'regional' or transnational Shakespeare. One prominent example revolved around the notion of Shakespeare and 'Europe', although in the annals tracing the development of this concept, Britain is, more often than not, conspicuously absent. This was also noted by Dirk Delabastita and Lieven D'hulst in the introduction to *European Shakespeares,* the outcome of their landmark conference of 1990 devoted to the translation of Shakespeare in Europe during the Romantic period. Acknowledging the

apparent lack of interest on the part of British academe in the European
tradition of Shakespeare translation, they boldly stated that *European
Shakespeares* was itself to be seen 'not just as a supplement to recent
Shakespeare Studies, but in a way as a critical comment on its British
insularity'.[18] The European interest saw a remarkable spread during the
1990s, following the collapse of the communist system, and during the
process by which the western part of the continent was politically and eco-
nomically restructured from its Brussels and Strasbourg headquarters.[19] As
the decade advanced, the Antwerp conference of Delabastita and D'hulst
gradually turned into a useful frame of reference. It slowly became the
model for a series of subsequent conferences, even though, in terms of
scope, these later conferences moved beyond the original focus on cultures
of translation, to include performance, critical traditions, education and
Shakespearean appropriations in a broader sense. Moreover, participation
from Britain increased, on the rostrum and in the proceedings. 1993, for
example, saw the conference in Bankya (Sofia, Bulgaria), which produced
the much-lauded *Shakespeare in the New Europe,* with contributions from
Jonathan Bate, Terence Hawkes and Richard Burt among others.[20] Comparable European conference ventures later took place at Murcia (Spain), Basle
(Switzerland) and at Utrecht (The Netherlands).[21] And with *Shakespeare
and Eastern Europe*, which appeared at the turn of the millennium, Zdeněk
Stříbrný produced a cultural history of Shakespeare in a region of Europe
that had – both due to a complex language barrier and to the more obvious political barriers – for too long been a closed book to international
Shakespeare Studies.[22]

Much of the theoretical underpinning for this remarkable upsurge in
Shakespeare beyond the English Channel in the course of the 1990s came
from Dennis Kennedy's innovative volume of essays, *Foreign Shakespeare.*[23]
Focusing on 'Shakespeare without his language', and the Shakespearean
creativity in languages other than the playwright's antiquated, early modern tongue, Kennedy effectively challenged the prevailing English-language
hegemony in Shakespeare Studies, broadening the area of study to the
world at large. Interestingly, as he charted a series of influential foreign
(meaning, in his definition, non-English-speaking) Shakespeare productions from after 1945, Kennedy felt called upon to acknowledge that
'foreign' Shakespeare was in danger of coming to look very much like
'European' Shakespeare. In the preface, Kennedy admitted that '[i]n object-
ing to Anglo-centric approaches to Shakespeare, the volume . . . runs the
risk of merely substituting European ones' (*Foreign Shakespeare*, xvii). In
his defence, he argued that to a certain extent this was inevitable: 'most

Shakespeare productions outside of English still occur in Europe, and European theatres have led the way in redefining performance models' (xvii–xviii).

However, the scope of *Foreign Shakespeare* – though defining 'foreign' Shakespeare as non-English-speaking Shakespeare – was emphatically not limited to Europe, and included contributions also from and about Canada, Israel and Japan. In his Afterword, Kennedy deftly drew attention to the broader Asian context and its inherent complexities. The appropriation of Shakespeare as a representative of the Christian West is perhaps nowhere more intriguing than it is in the Far East, and it is a study of this area that may well yield the most challenging insights for a future study of Shakespearean appropriation in other cultures. This is, among other things, suggested by Toshiro Date in *Shakespeare East and West* (1996). In a rare reference to the histories, Date observes how the emblematic sequence in *3 Henry VI* with the father who has killed his son and the son who has killed his father, which, from a Western perspective, is likely to be read as a biblical analogue and as an implicit plea for peace, could well, from a Japanese or Buddhist perspective, be interpreted as an appeal to the samurai code of stoicism.[24] Since the appearance of *Foreign Shakespeare* and *Shakespeare East and West*, the Orient has been well served by *Shakespeare and the Japanese Stage* (1998), as well as John Russell Brown's *New Sites for Shakespeare: Theatre, the Audience, and Asia* (1999).[25] Also, Kennedy himself has continued to promote the study of Asian appropriations of Shakespeare.

From our present vantage point, the native English Shakespeare industry and the foreign Shakespeare initiative have their developing national focus in common, but major differences are apparent. The native and 'foreign' fields of theatrical as well as academic practice reveal a marked discrepancy of interest in the histories whose complex reflection on the notions of nation and nationhood has never been in doubt.

In the process of Britain's growing self-reflection and self-scrutiny, Shakespeare's English histories have served, and continue to serve as a vital touchstone. With the pursuit of the distinction between history and historiography, the Shakespearean history play has come to be identified as a genre in English and proto-British history mobilized to boost a unitarian, right-wing myth of Britain. As Shakespeare Studies became ever more politicized from within, and as the defining battles between the Cultural Materialists and the New Historicists got under way, the histories were increasingly mobilized for this radical encounter. Partly as a consequence, there has been no period in the history of Shakespeare Studies that witnessed

a greater academic output devoted to the histories, not only the traditionally popular second tetralogy, but also the long neglected first tetralogy,
King John and *Henry VIII*.

Recognizing the veritable fascination of the English Shakespeare industry with the histories, it may come as a surprise that this genre should only
enjoy such a marginal status in the practice or the discussion of 'foreign'
Shakespeare. A case in point is *Shakespeare in the New Europe*, whose two
valuable essays on the histories both derive from the English-speaking quar-
ters of Shakespeare Studies (Michael Hattaway and Thomas Healy).[26] Also,
both concentrate on the British reception process, although it must be
acknowledged that Healy, addressing the new national reconfigurations in
eastern Europe after the fall of communism, argues a convincing case for
abandoning the doubtful idea of the nation as developed in *Henry V* while
building up a new Europe. Dennis Kennedy's *Foreign Shakespeare*, too,
devotes little attention to the histories, and concentrates on the comedies
and tragedies instead. If, as Kennedy acknowledges, *Foreign Shakespeare*
had briefly seemed in danger of becoming 'European Shakespeare', a no
less natural tendency of the foreign Shakespeare industry, which is to view
Shakespeare primarily as a tragedian and a comedian, has definitely led
to the neglect of Shakespeare's histories abroad.[27] In this light, it is ironic
that the original dust jacket of *Foreign Shakespeare* should have carried the
impressive photograph of Wilfried Minks's set design for Peter Palitzsch's
German production of *Henry VI* (1967).[28]

Given this state of affairs in the current academic discussion, the observer
could easily gain the false impression that the histories have been many times
more popular in Britain than abroad. It is true, of course, that by comparison with the reception of the histories in Britain, the range of foreign
productions may have been less extensive, thus paradoxically suggesting,
not without a degree of truth, that the playwright's unchallenged universal
appeal is determined more by the sonnets, the comedies or the tragedies,
than by material relating more directly to his own country of origin, to
the history of that country, or, rather, to Shakespeare's representation of
its history in a dramatic genre about which Larry Danson has said that
'it would only be a small exaggeration to say that [it] is the only genre he
actually invented'.[29] Such a view might be supported with reference to the
test case of nineteenth-century opera: as a musical genre, it absorbed a considerable amount of Shakespeare, but mainly his tragedies and comedies.
This did not mean that the operatic genre was incompatible with history,
or with English history for that matter. The early nineteenth century produced countless operas on Anne Boleyn, Katherine Howard, Mary Tudor

and Elizabeth I. It suggests that the operatic genre was ready to exploit the potential of history, and the attractions of English history, but hardly ever Shakespeare's choice of English history or his manner of representing it.[30]

If, however, Shakespeare's histories have been more popular in Britain, this is not to say that the foreign reception has been poor in any sense, nor would it seem entirely correct to detect in this apparent imbalance a 'dialectic between Shakespeare as a "national" playwright ideologically implicated (for better or worse) in a nation-building project inextricably linked to the ambitions of (British) empire, and Shakespeare as a writer who belongs to the world and has been appropriated by nations such as Russia, Japan and especially Germany as uniquely their own'.[31] There are countless traces and traditions of foreign cultural and ideological encounters with the histories and of the way in which they mediate in non-English processes of nation formation and preservation. Studying these will shed new light on Anglo-foreign relations and signal new national departures in this genre of English origin. One is fully justified, on many occasions, in speaking of 'foreign' Shakespeare in terms of 'Shakespeare without his language', but it would never be correct to suggest that 'foreign' Shakespeare might be equivalent to 'Shakespeare without his histories'. Theatre practitioners beyond the Channel have always recognized the rich potential of the histories, in terms of staging and political pertinence, but the academy, comprising not so much the British but the international community of Shakespeareans, has so far failed to acknowledge the relevance of the 'foreign' histories to their individual nations.

The reception of *Henry V* in France is a case in point, as we witness how, over the centuries, the play in its new context across the Channel has developed from a painful reminder of the nation's military defeat towards a finely tuned and translated instrument of political analysis and comment. With France as the enemy nation par excellence in the histories, the French have long tried to ignore the last play of the second tetralogy, resisting attempts by others, such as Dr Johnson, to revive the painful memories of Agincourt. As Hester Piozzi records about the Englishman's visit to Versailles:

At Versailles the people showed us the theatre. As we stood on the stage looking at some machinery for play-house purposes:
'Now we are here, what shall we act, Mr Johnson, The Englishman at Paris?'
'No, no,' replied he, 'we will try to act Harry the Fifth.'[32]

With its extreme polarization of the French and the English, the play was bound to remain a source of international friction. Even Laurence Olivier's wartime film version of the play ran into difficulties. Though ostensibly designed as a propaganda movie to further 'Anglo-British relations' (as Olivier himself put it), the film could nevertheless still drive a party of disgruntled Free French sailors out of a cinema in Newcastle upon Tyne during the last year of the war, and even give rise to diplomatic tension between Paris and London in 1947.[33] And as almost 400 years after its London premiere plans were under way to mount the first French production of *Henry V* in France, and centuries of unease over the play seemed to be coming to an end, the artificially encouraged anti-French behaviour of audiences at the London Globe in the summer of 1997 seemed to spoil it all. As Gisèle Venet put it:

Trop souvent l'histoire scénique d'*Henry V* recoupe en effet des moments d'un patriotisme insulaire quelque peu agressif malgré le 'fair play' légendaire. On l'a retrouvé certains soirs de juin 1997 où le brouhaha qui suivait les propos les plus méprisants tenus en scène sur l'arrogance et l'impréparation des Français rejoignait un militantisme anti-européen presque palpable dans l'air mouillé. La critique anglaise, capable de recul, s'en alarme et le regrette. *Le choix de la pièce pour l'ouverture du nouveau Globe ne s'était-elle pas voulue exclusivement commémorative de celle de 1599?*[34]

Indeed the stage history of *Henry V* too often ties up with moments of a somewhat aggressive insular patriotism in spite of the legendary *fair play*. This feeling could be sensed in the course of some evening performances in June 1997 when the uproar following the most contemptuous cues about the arrogance and the lack of preparation of the French army met with an anti-European spirit of militancy which was almost palpable in the damp evening air. The English reviewers who were able to stand back and ponder, were deeply worried and regretted it. *But was not the choice of this play for the opening of the New Globe exclusively meant as a commemoration of the 1599 staging?*

These events only make up the tip of the iceberg, and hence call for a detailed cultural history of the play in France over the centuries. In this respect, the French contributions on the play's translation by Jean-Michel Déprats and on its production by Dominique Goy-Blanquet serve as a first stepping stone.

The situation in France is only one of the more complex examples among many of the 'foreign' careers of the histories, from Shakespeare's own time to the present day. The earliest recorded instance of the English history play abroad dates from 1591, when Philip Waimer's stage version of the history of King Edward III was performed at the Polish city of Gdansk, and several decades later, as Albert Cohn reminds us, Waimer's play was followed by Jacob Ayer's *Comedy of King Edward the Third*.[35] Soon after, in the young Dutch Republic, too, Shakespeare's medieval history first found acceptance. In 1651, playwright and translator Lambert van den Bosch collated a number of historical accounts – including Shakespeare's *Richard III* – to produce *The Red and the White Rose*. A close reading of the Dutch play reveals how van den Bosch used the English nation's past to reflect on contemporary domestic politics not only in the Low Countries, but also on Anglo-Dutch relations.[36] On the domestic level, Richard III's abuse of power as the protector of Edward V captured the anxiety of the Dutch Republic in 1651 when the fatherless, one-year-old heir of Orange – the future William III of England – required a regent, this at a time when the anti-monarchic forces that dominated city councils throughout the republic sought to contain the dynastic ambitions of the Orange family. On an international level, van den Bosch's monarchist play, by suggesting that the assassination of Richard II was typical of the English habit vis-à-vis those monarchs with whom the nation disagreed, also expressed clear misgivings about the Dutch Republic's English neighbours, two years after the death of Charles I, and two years into the reign of Oliver Cromwell.[37]

In Spain, too, Shakespearean history, if not his own history plays, held an early interest. Pedro Calderón de la Barca's first play, *Love, Honour, and Power* (1623), staged Edward III's courtship of the Countess of Salisbury and the king's lesson in self-control. In 1626, English history was again central on the Spanish stage when Calderón presented his *Schism in England*, a play about Henry VIII's break with Rome. Unlike Shakespeare's play on the subject, Calderón's version ended with Mary Tudor forcefully asserting that Catholicism would be re-established in England.[38] In the case of each of these plays, the immediate cultural context sheds light on the apparent interests at stake. *Love, Honour, and Power* was especially performed for Prince Charles Stuart and the Duke of Buckingham during their stay at the Prado during their marriage negotiations for the Spanish Infanta; in this case, the crown prince would have been appropriately confronted with one of his famous forebears who negotiated personal love and state leadership. In the case of Calderón's *Schism in England*, the curious twist at the end of the play, with Mary remarking, full of confidence, that the Reformation would soon be undone, becomes more intelligible in the light of the fact that Spain in 1626 was optimistically preparing for a renewed attempt to invade England.

Before anything, the earliest Dutch and the Spanish examples teach us that, certainly during the seventeenth century, the drama based on English as well as Shakespearean history engaged directly in the contemporary political debate between England and the foreign nations involved. Although the plays, like van den Bosch's *Red and the White Rose*, or Calderón's *Love, Honour, and Power*, or his *Schism in England*, reflected on current issues of native concern, they preserved a direct, one-to-one relationship with the nation whose history the play purported to represent. As British productions of the histories continued to gear their interpretations towards the nation's relations with other European friends or enemies – like Aaron Hill's 1709 rendering of *Henry V* at the time of the Anglo-French War, or Laurence Olivier's screen adaptation of the same play in 1944 – foreign productions of the histories seem increasingly to have become divorced from such interests, even though England, its political status, or its national playwright were never entirely forgotten. Instead, the histories came to serve as a litmus test for new national self-definition, or as a model for new works of literature.[39] As early as the 1770s, the Swedish playwright-king Gustav III (1771–92), together with the poet Johan Henrik Kellgren, who was also his librarian and secretary, wrote a historic opera entitled *Gustavus Vasa*, on a topic from the Swedish national past. Despite the king's obvious affinities with the French Enlightenment, the opera's distinct similarities with *Richard III* betray the formative influence of the Shakespearean genre, several decades before Sir Walter Scott fashioned himself as 'the Shakespeare of novelists' with his novels on Scottish history.[40]

The appropriation of the histories in a foreign context really took on the form of 'renting a past' (to borrow the phrase introduced by Mariangela Tempera in this volume), when August Wilhelm Schlegel advertised the histories in his famous lectures *Über dramatische Kunst und Literatur* [*A Course of Lectures on Dramatic Art and Poetry*] (1809–11). Schlegel ranked Shakespeare's history plays as some of 'the most valuable of Shakespeare's works'.[41] In his eyes, their importance transcended any national or temporal limitations: 'this series of dramas is intended as the vehicle of a much higher and much more general introduction; it furnishes examples of the political course of the world, applicable to all times' (*A Course of Lectures*, 419–20). Recognizing the histories as a timeless and universal model, Schlegel conceived of the plays as a major focus of imitation.

For Schlegel, the histories served not only as a 'mirror of kings' and as 'the manual of young princes' (420), but were also to be accepted in more specific terms as a model for German writers, certainly at a time when interest in Germany's allegedly grand history was at a low ebb, and no fully fledged body of nation-building literature like Shakespeare's epic histories was as yet in existence. In the spirit of Samuel Taylor Coleridge, who, in connection with the historical genre in literature, said that '[i]n order that a drama may be properly historical, it is necessary that it should be the history of the people to whom it is addressed', Shakespeare's proto-British history soon became a model for proto-German history.[42] This becomes particularly apparent in the short chapter on German literature where Schlegel argued that the recent revival of interest in the remains of Germany's 'old national poetry' should afford the poet a foundation for historical drama. Here the history plays of Shakespeare – 'as profound a historian as a poet' (439) – were to be his model: 'What a field for a poet, who, like Shakespeare, could discern the poetic aspect of the great events of the world! But, alas, so little interest do we Germans take in events truly important to our nation, that its greatest achievements still lack even a fitting historical record' (529). The influence of Schlegel should not be underestimated, and a measure of his impact is certainly that the renowned historian Leopold von Ranke should, in his *Englische Geschichte* (or, History of England, 1859–1868) have noted that what Shakespeare depicts in the histories 'are great elements in the history of states . . . not only important for England, but . . . symbolic for all people and their sovereigns'.[43] Also, partly in response to the literary historian Georg Gottfried Gervinus – who around the middle of the nineteenth century helped to promote the view that the histories could function as the model for a new sense of militant nationhood[44] – Franz von Dingelstedt organized the first ever stage production of the two tetralogies of histories together (though with the exclusion of *1 Henry VI*) when the German Shakespeare Society was founded in 1864.[45]

It is well known that, in producing the histories as 'cycles', Dingelstedt realized a wish that Schiller had expressed in a letter to Goethe in 1797:

Ich las in diesen Tagen die Shakespeare'schen Stücke, die den Krieg der zwei Rosen abhandeln, die mich nun, nach Beendigung Richards III, mit einem wahren Staunen erfüllen . . . Der Mühe wäre es wahrhaftig wert, diese Suite von acht Stücken, mit aller Besonnenheit, deren man jetzt fähig ist, für die Bühne zu behandeln. Eine Epoche könnte dadurch eingeleitet werden.

Lately, I have been reading Shakespeare's plays dealing with the Wars of the Roses, and having now finished *Richard III*, I am filled with genuine amazement . . . It would truly be worth the effort to prepare the entire sequence of eight plays for the stage, with all the circumspection we can muster. It would mean the beginning of a new era.[46]

However, Dingelstedt, who was to look back on the cyclical staging of the English history plays as his life's work, did not mean just to realize Schiller's theatrical ambitions as his own (Lehnert, 'Hundert Jahre', 11). The official

minutes of the general meeting at which the German Shakespeare Society
was founded ('Protokoll der konstituierenden Generalversammlung der
Shakespearegesellschaft in Weimar am 26en April 1864') report that
Dingelstedt, one of the founding members, came to the session with a
request to the new society officially to take into its special protection
Shakespeare's history plays. After the meeting had decided not to include in
the first article of its statutes a statement to the effect that its activities were
primarily to benefit contemporary dramatic practice, Dingelstedt decided
to withdraw his request:

Herr Generalintendant von Dingelstedt zieht seinen aus Opportunitätsgründen
gemachten Vermittlungsvorschlag, daß die Shakespearegesellschaft das historische
Drama in ihren besonderen Schutz nehmen wolle, hierauf zurück. (Lehnert,
'Hundert Jahre', 12)

Artistic director von Dingelstedt hereupon withdraws the proposal, made for pragmatic reasons, that the German Shakespeare Society take the histories under its
special protection.

It is remarkable that the Society, despite its rejection of the proposal, should
nevertheless have continued to rely so heavily on the perceived ideology
of the histories in later years. The German Shakespeare Society's 1868 call
for new members hardly makes a secret of its deeper political motives.
First, the *Aufruf* emphatically drives home to the German monarchs and
the nation as a whole ('die deutschen Fürsten wie die deutsche Nation')
the importance of education, which should enable the people to make up
their own minds about the extremely difficult social and political issues
of the day ('in den so schwierigen politischen und socialen [sic] Fragen').
With obvious reference to Dingelstedt's favourite history plays, it continues to stress that for an understanding of the laws of history ('in der
Geschichte waltenden Gesetze'), for the development of political insight
('die Förderung politischer Einsicht'), and for the 'elevation of patriotic sentiment' ('die Hebung patriotischer Gesinnung'), there is no better educator
of the people ('Volkslehrer') than Shakespeare (Lehnert, 'Hundert Jahre',
15). Shakespeare, the society felt, ought to be mobilized much in the spirit
that Schlegel had described, only the history plays were no longer merely
seen as 'the manual of young princes', but also as the *Bildungs*-paradigm
for the new national German *Bürgertum*.[47]

   This also explains the situation that prevailed in the household of Richard
and Cosima Wagner shortly after the outbreak of Germany's war on France
in 1870. As Cosima noted in her diary on 9 August 1870, with undisguised
anti-French sentiment:

Letter from Prof. Nietzsche, who has resolved to join the army. I reply to him, saying the time is not yet ripe. We are having trouble with [Hans] Richter, for he, too, would like to join up. Our one consolation yesterday we found in scenes from *Henry V* by Shakespeare.[48]

If, under the circumstances, Wagner's preference here was for the most rabidly anti-French play in the entire Shakespeare canon, this should not blind one to the fact that the composer's appreciation of the histories as a group bordered on the religious. Certainly, a religious note was also struck by Samuel Taylor Coleridge when he remarked about Shakespeare's history plays that '[i]t would be a fine national custom to act such a series of dramatic histories in orderly succession every Christmas holiday'.[49] However, such devotion is at a far remove from the vision of Wagner, to whom the Shakespeare histories served as a model in shaping the stage festival opera tetralogy of *The Ring of the Nibelung* (1876). As Cosima Wagner recorded in her diary at the time, Wagner was finishing *Parsifal* (1882), the ultimate fusion of his ideals of art and religion:

[Wagner] brings up Shakespeare and says people ought to perform one of his plays and then, having thus been brought into very close contact with the horrors of life, go to Holy Communion. And especially the historical plays – they ought to be seen every year . . . [I]n Shakespeare there is neither mood nor purpose, a veil is torn aside, and we see things as they are. Particularly in the histories.[50]

These developments, though not necessarily nationwide at the time, were certainly not limited to Germany.[51] When Franz von Dingelstedt moved to Vienna Burgtheater, Austria, too, was to develop a lively tradition of the tetralogies, some four decades before such thinking in terms of cycles was to be introduced in Britain. In the footsteps of Dingelstedt, we find Franz Herterich as well as the legendary Leopold Lindtberg, who staged the two complete cycles on the occasion of the quatercentenary of Shakespeare's birth in 1964.[52] Notably, directing Shakespeare's medieval histories at Vienna during the early 1960s, he was acutely aware of the way in which the plays still interreflected with the memories (on a universal scale) of more recent political events, particularly where *Richard III* was concerned. Yet, in his production of the play, Lindtberg sought to avoid exploiting any unnecessarily 'crude' equations, possibly also because he realized, with the reviewers that Manfred Draudt has studied, that his representation of the hunchbacked Yorkist king could allude to Adolf Hitler, but just as easily to the then artistic director of the State Opera, or to the Archbishop of Vienna. As Draudt writes in his contribution based on new research at the Burgtheater archives, this awareness explains Lindtberg's bold and ironic emphasis on the play's universal rather than its national relevance: 'Any similarity between the play's characters and persons alive or recently deceased is not intentional but purely coincidental.' Clearly, during the early post-war years, certainly in areas as politically sensitive as Germany or Austria, it had become opportune to defuse Schlegel's nineteenth-century emphasis on the nation and to stress the histories' universal pertinence.

Although for the sake of the argument it has been considered useful to draw a distinction between English and non-English-speaking Shakespeare, or between British and 'foreign' Shakespeare, it must be emphasized that these distinctions should not be taken to suggest too broad a divide between the two traditions. In fact, Britain itself has always contributed to the production of 'foreign' Shakespeare: from the first movements of the strolling players performing *Edward III*, or the contested 1607 performance of *Richard II* (together with *Hamlet*) on shipboard off Sierra Leone, via the 1939 Old Vic-cum-British Council's mystifying performance of Tyrone Guthrie's *Henry V* in Fascist Italy, to the world tour of Bogdanov and Pennington's *Wars of the Roses*.[53] Occasionally, foreign tours and performances of the histories in new, foreign contexts yielded unexpected insights into contemporary British society. Thus, during his third tour with the English Shakespeare Company in 1988, Bogdanov wondered:

Why is it that one had to go to Australia, Canada, provincial America, to get some coherent views (good or bad) of what we were attempting? The reputation that these countries – the Mid West, the far flung remnants of the Empire – have for conservatism is completely belied by the quality of the writing and the minds at work in journals such as the *Toronto Globe*, the *Sun Times*, and the *Chicago Tribune*, to name but three. It merely confirms one's impression that London is the real provincial, bourgeois capital of the world . . . In a way, it is lucky for London that America exists.[54]

Altogether different, but no less insightful, is Ian McKellen's experience of performing *Richard II* in Bratislava, Czechoslovakia, in 1969, during the Russian occupation. As McKellen describes it, Richard's return from Ireland and his touching of the home nation's soil produced unease in the audience:

I have never heard it since; an audience crying. They were grieving, I understood, fool that I had been, because Richard's words could have been their own, when their land was invaded recently, when sticks and stones had been pelted at armoured cars and tanks, when the earth was their only symbol of a future freedom, of a continuing past.[55]

Twenty years later, playing *Richard III* in Romania, McKellen was again to be touched by the audience, though for different reasons: 'when Richard was slain, the Romanians stopped the show with heartfelt cheers, in memory of their recent freedom from Ceaucescu's regime'.[56]

There is also another way in which the two traditions distinguished here – that of native, 'English' Shakespeare and 'foreign' Shakespeare – do not really represent a rift or divide.[57] *Foreign Shakespeare* by Dennis Kennedy may have shed light on a creative tradition of non-English-speaking Shakespeares, but the venture itself also establishes beyond doubt that the academic branch of the 'foreign' Shakespeare industry, as well as academe's supporting institutions, including the publishing world, continue fully to respect 'English' as the lingua franca.

Kennedy's *Foreign Shakespeare* was published by Cambridge University Press, the institution that also commissioned the *Shakespeare on the German Stage* project. Surely, one of the ironies, in the case of the volume by Wilhelm Hortmann, is that its German author produced his typescript in English, and that only after it had appeared with Cambridge University Press, was it translated into his native language for publication in German-speaking countries. Further examples of English-language publications providing a platform to express the national and regional diversity of Shakespeare's afterlives include the University of Delaware Press series devoted to International Studies in Shakespeare and His Contemporaries, coordinated by Jay L. Halio; the *Shakespeare Yearbook* (general-edited by Holger Klein until 2003, and after that date by Douglas Brooks), with volumes devoted to France, Hungary, Italy, Eastern Europe and Japan; and a major journal like *Shakespeare Bulletin* whose annual winter issue, under the editorship of Jim Lusardi and June Schlueter, was traditionally devoted to international theatre productions, a policy which the new editors, Andrew Hartley and Jeremy Lopez, have decided to continue.[58] The present volume, comprising contributions by a host of international scholars, is once again no exception to this rule.

There is a general consensus about the relevance of native as well as foreign productions of Shakespeare. This is, among other things, revealed by a potent tendency to share and exchange production data and other information. However, a number of barriers still remain. As Manchester University Press's 'Shakespeare and Performance' series (currently under the editorship of J. R. Mulryne and J. C. Bulman), or Cambridge University Press's 'Shakespeare in Production' series (edited by J. S. Bratton and Julie Hankey) are continually expanding the scope of productions and films discussed by their authors and editors, and try to include as many 'foreign' materials as possible, there is a continuing tendency in reviews to ask for more foreign Shakespeare in order to avoid a politically incorrect, meaning Anglo-centred, bias.

The editors of these performance series are in an unenviable situation indeed, and it is as difficult to identify the problem as it is to remedy the situation. On the face of it, judging by the reviews, the problem would primarily seem to be one of selecting the relevant international materials, and, perhaps even one of observing a more accurate degree of proportional representation. But it is clear that any selection is likely always to come under fire, and that proportional representation of the various national histories in the performance series concerned is bound, eventually, to meet with new criticism, since it would eventually marginalize British Shakespeare beyond recognition, and undermine the series' commercial viability for the English-language publisher as well.

The real problem that outward-looking editors as well as scholars and readers are facing is that 'foreign' Shakespeare documentation and evidence are seriously lacking both in Britain and on the international market, in English and in other, more or less internationally accessible languages. And if it exists, it is often simply too difficult to obtain. If we define 'foreign' Shakespeare in linguistic terms, like Kennedy, as Shakespeare without his language, there is an obvious language barrier. Defining 'foreign' Shakespeare, as in this volume, also in geographical terms, another perennial barrier looms up which, even in our age of travel, it is extremely difficult to raze.

From whichever perspective one approaches the issue, one arrives at the conclusion that English-speaking publishers are prepared to assume a responsibility which is nearly impossible to meet. Its inherent hazards would seem also to explain why English scholars and publishers, though still promoting a full exchange with the 'foreign' Shakespeare industry, are now, gradually, also beginning to manifest a need to re-entrench themselves. This may be in a survey as relevant as *English Shakespeares*, in a series with a regional focus like Arden's 'Shakespeare at Stratford', in the publication of the 2003 Blackwell Companion to Shakespeare's histories (with an exclusive British and North American authorship and with little or no attention to the international issues raised in this introduction) or the foundation of a British Shakespeare Association.[59]

To resolve part of the problem, it might (prompted somewhat by the current British tendency of entrenchment in native materials), seem attractive to propose that every nation beyond the British Isles has its own responsibility to produce those materials that will further the international dialogue in which English-language performance or reception series have been trying to engage. But is it really possible to hold each country responsible for its own Shakespeare in this manner? Under the present circumstances, a policy of this kind could only count on limited success. 'Shakespeare' may be popular worldwide, but he is not likely to generate the necessary research funds in those countries where he remains a 'foreign' playwright, and where native writers, like Molière, Cervantes or Vondel, will be granted institutional priority. Clearly, the 'foreign' Shakespeare industry, and with it the Shakespeare industry as a whole, discloses a set of limitations, which, curiously perhaps, has its roots in the same politico-linguistic soil that engendered the histories in England, and produced their fascination for the proto-British lobby, as well as their popularity in the newly emergent nations of Europe and the rest of the world.

Given a situation of such complexity, this volume has tried, among other things, to create a platform for scholars representing countries where Shakespeare is an 'outsider', often forced, among other things, to compete with other, local celebrities, thus losing out on the academic attention he deserves. This step towards the emancipation of multiple regional manifestations of Shakespeare's histories bears a close resemblance to the devolutionary process of British Shakespeare via the histories, of which the 'insider' essays in this volume are an integral part. One hopes that the various national experiences presented here will stimulate further research into this area. It is true that the international cultural history of Shakespeare's histories still needs to be written, but the collection presented here may convince colleagues worldwide of the pertinence of such an endeavour.

NOTES

1 The title of E. M. W. Tillyard's famous study, *Shakespeare's History Plays* (London: Chatto & Windus, 1944), refers to the English histories, and, like this collection of essays, excludes the Roman histories that might have qualified under the title heading. In the subtitle to her *Stages of History* (Ithaca, NY: Cornell University Press, 1990), Phyllis Rackin refers to the histories as the 'chronicle plays', but in the subtitle of her *Engendering a Nation* (co-authored with Jean Howard, [London and New York: Routledge, 1997]), the same plays are termed 'Shakespeare's English histories'.

2 See Richard Helgerson, *Forms of Nationhood: The Elizabethan Writing of England* (Chicago and London: University of Chicago Press, 1992); Claire McEachern, *Poetics of Nationhood, 1590–1612* (Cambridge: Cambridge University Press, 1996); and Gary Taylor, *Reinventing Shakespeare: A Cultural History from the Restoration to the Present* (London: The Hogarth Press, 1990).

3 The definition of the term 'foreign' in this volume is in the first instance of a geographical nature. It includes all Shakespeare traditions beyond the British Isles. In terms of the traditions discussed, this volume concentrates on non-English-speaking traditions. This corresponds with its aim of making available in our century's lingua franca the materials relevant for a multinational appreciation of the histories.

4 *Alternative Shakespeares*, edited by John Drakakis (London: Methuen, 1985); Jonathan Dollimore and Alan Sinfield's *Political Shakespeare: New Essays in Cultural Materialism* (Manchester: Manchester University Press, 1985); as well as *The Shakespeare Myth*, edited by Graham Holderness (Manchester: Manchester University Press, 1988).

5 For Michael Dobson's historical exploration of the way in which Shakespeare was fundamental to a sense of British national identity, see *The Making of the National Poet: Shakespeare, Adaptation, and Authorship, 1660–1769* (Oxford: Clarendon Press, 1992). Some of Dobson's later work has fine-tuned his views expressed in *The Making of the National Poet*, and militantly brought the use of Shakespeare to define Englishness and Britishness closer to present-day practice and concerns. See especially his 'Falstaff after John Bull: Shakespearean History, Britishness, and the Former United Kingdom', *Shakespeare Jahrbuch* 136 (2000), 40–55. See also Jonathan Bate, *Shakespearean Constitutions: Politics, Theatre, Criticism, 1730–1830* (Oxford: Clarendon Press, 1989), and Taylor, *Reinventing Shakespeare*.

6 Philip Edwards, *Threshold of a Nation: A Study in English and Irish Drama* (Cambridge: Cambridge University Press, 1979); *Representing Ireland: Literature and the Origins of Conflict, 1534–1660*, edited by Brendan Bradshaw, Andrew Hadfield and Willy Maley (Cambridge: Cambridge University Press, 1993); Andrew Murphy, *But the Irish Sea Betwixt Us: Ireland, Colonialism, and Renaissance Literature* (Lexington: The University Press of Kentucky, 1999). See also Michael Neill, 'Broken English and Broken Irish: Nation, Language, and the Optic of Power in Shakespeare's Histories', *Shakespeare Quarterly* 45:1 (1994), 1–32 (reprinted in his *Putting History to the Question: Power, Politics, and Society in English Renaissance Drama* [New York: Columbia University Press, 2000], 339–72).

7 *Shakespeare and Ireland: History, Politics, Culture*, edited by Mark Thornton Burnett and Ramona Wray (Houndmills: Macmillan, 1997).

8 See Ronald J. Boling, 'Anglo-Welsh Relations in *Cymbeline*', in *Shakespeare Quarterly* 51:1 (2000), 33–66; and Terence Hawkes, 'Bryn Glas', in *Post-colonial Shakespeares*, edited by Ania Loomba and Martin Orkin (London: Routledge, 1998), 117–40 (reprinted in his *Shakespeare in the Present* [London and New York: Routledge, 2002], 23–45). See also Lisa Hopkins, 'Neighbourhood in *Henry V* ', in *Shakespeare and Ireland,* edited by Mark Thornton Burnett and Ramona Wray, 9–26; Jodi Mikalachki, 'The Masculine Romance of Roman Britain: *Cymbeline* and Early Modern English Nationalism', *Shakespeare Quarterly* 46:3 (1995), 301–22; Garrett A. Sullivan, Jr., *The Drama of Landscape: Land, Property, and Social Relations on the Early Modern Stage* (Stanford, CA: Stanford University Press, 1998), especially 'Civilizing Wales: *Cymbeline*, Roads, and the Landscapes of

Early Modern Britain', 127–58; and David J. Baker, 'Imagining Britain: William Shakespeare's *Henry V*', in his *Between Nations: Shakespeare, Spenser, Marvell, and the Question of Britain* (Stanford, CA: Stanford University Press, 1997), 17–65.

9 See Michael D. Bristol, *Shakespeare's America/America's Shakespeare* (London and New York: Routledge, 1990).

10 See Thomas Cartelli, *Repositioning Shakespeare: National Formations, Postcolonial Appropriations* (London and New York: Routledge, 1999), especially 'Shakespeare, 1916: *Caliban by the Yellow Sands* and the New Dramas of Democracy', 63–83; and Terence Hawkes, 'Aberdaugleddyf', *Shakespeare Jahrbuch* 136 (2000), 56–73. 'Aberdaugleddyf' is also included in Terence Hawkes, *Shakespeare in the Present* (New York and London: Routledge, 2002).

11 Simon Williams, *Shakespeare on the German Stage. Vol. 1: 1586–1914* (Cambridge: Cambridge University Press, 1989); Wilhelm Hortmann, *Shakespeare on the German Stage: The Twentieth Century* (Cambridge: Cambridge University Press, 1998); Péter Dávidházi, *The Romantic Cult of Shakespeare: Literary Reception in an Anthropological Perspective* (London: Macmillan, 1998); and Alexander Shurbanov and Boika Sokolova's *Painting Shakespeare Red* (Newark, NJ: University of Delaware Press, 2001).

12 Marta Gibińska, *Polish Poets Read Shakespeare: Refashioning of the Tradition* (Kraków: Towarzystwo Naukowe 'Societas Vistulana', 1999); Manfred Pfister, 'Hamlet und der deutsche Geist: Die Geschichte einer politischen Interpretation', *Shakespeare Jahrbuch* (1992), 13–38; Brigitte Schulze, 'Shakespeare's Way into the West Slavic Literatures and Cultures', in *European Shakespeares: Translating Shakespeare in the Romantic Age*, edited by Dirk Delabastita and Lieven D'hulst (Amsterdam and Philadelphia, PA: John Benjamins, 1993), 55–74; and *Redefining Shakespeare: Literary Theory and Theater Practice in the German Democratic Republic*, edited by J. Lawrence Guntner and Andrew M. McClean (Newark, NJ: University of Delaware Press, 1998). See also Werner Habicht, *Shakespeare and the German Imagination* (Hertford: Stephen Austin and Sons, 1994).

13 Samuel L. Leiter, *Shakespeare Around the Globe: A Guide to Notable Postwar Revivals* (Westport, CT: Greenwood Press, 1986), ix.

14 Harold Bloom, *Shakespeare: The Invention of the Human* (New York: Riverhead Books, 1998), 320. The Vietnam war was also problematized, of course, in Michael Kahn's controversial 1969 production of *Henry V* for the American Shakespeare Festival at Stratford, Connecticut (Leiter, *Shakespeare Around the Globe*, 225–6).

15 The initiative to launch *Shakespeare Translation* is recorded in *Shakespeare 1971. Proceedings of the World Shakespeare Congress, Vancouver, August 1971*, edited by Clifford Leech and J. M. R. Margeson (Toronto: University of Toronto Press, 1972), 279. The original title of the journal, *Shakespeare Translation*, was changed into *Shakespeare Worldwide: Translation and Adaptation* at the third meeting of the World Shakespeare Congress in (what was at the time still) West Berlin (1986).

16 Lois Potter, '*2 Henry IV* and the Czech Political Context', *Shakespeare Worldwide* 14–15 (1995), 252–5 (p. 254).

17 Nicholas Grene, *Shakespeare's Serial History Plays* (Cambridge: Cambridge University Press, 2002), 41 (quoting the program notes for the Festival of Britain production of the second tetralogy in 1951).

18 *European Shakespeares*, ed. Delabastita and D'hulst, 21. The Antwerp conference took place two years after the publication of *Das Shakespeare-Bild in Europa zwischen Aufklärung und Romantik*, edited by Roger Bauer (Bern: Peter Lang, 1988), and in the same year that saw the publication of Jonathan Bate's essay on 'The Politics of Romantic Shakespeare Criticism: Germany, England, France', *European Romantic Review* 1:1 (1990), 1–26.

19 On other occasions, editorial policy may reflect the view that British means non-European. Exemplary is *Shakespeare in Europe*, edited by Oswald LeWinter (1963. Rpt. Harmondsworth: Penguin Books, 1970).

20 *Shakespeare in the New Europe,* edited by Michael Hattaway, Boika Sokolova and Derek Roper (Sheffield: Sheffield Academic Press, 1994). For a review see Peter Holland, 'Shakespeare in the New Europe', *The European English Messenger* 6:2 (1997), 75–7. Holland's review implicitly acknowledges the reservations of Delabastita and D'hulst:

> Analysis of Shakespeare production is too often Anglophone-centred and, within that, dominated by the work of the Royal Shakespeare Company. *Shakespeare in the New Europe* is a brilliant and powerful collection attesting to the world elsewhere, the rich cultures in which Shakespeare speaks, in which, indeed, he is the uniquely necessary voice, often speaking with many times the eloquence he currently attains in English. (77)

21 The proceedings of the 1999 conference at Murcia (Spain) has been published as *Four Hundred Years of Shakespeare in Europe*, edited by A. Luis Pujante and Ton Hoenselaars. With a foreword by Stanley Wells (Newark, NJ: University of Delaware Press, 2003).

22 Zdeněk Stříbrný, *Shakespeare and Eastern Europe* (Oxford and New York: Oxford University Press, 2000). Also testifying to a European interest, though with a focus primarily on the variety of responses, are *Shakespeare and His Contemporaries: Eastern and Central European Studies*, edited by Jerzy Limon and Jay L. Halio (Newark, NJ: University of Delaware Press, 1993); and *Hamlet East–West*, edited by Marta Gibińska and Jerzy Limon (Gdansk: Theatrum Gedanense Foundation, 1998).

23 *Foreign Shakespeare: Contemporary Performance*, edited by Dennis Kennedy (Cambridge: Cambridge University Press, 1993).

24 Toshiro Date, 'A Bridge between Shakespeare and the Traditional Theatre of Japan', in *Shakespeare East and West*, edited by Minoru Fujita and Leonard Pronko (New York: St Martin's Press, 1996), 77–101 (p. 84).

25 See *Shakespeare East and West*, ed. Fujita and Pronko; Xiao Yang Zhang, *Shakespeare in China* (Newark, NJ: University of Delaware Press, 1996);

Shakespeare and the Japanese Stage, edited by Takashi Sasayama, J. R. Mulryne and Margaret Shewring (Cambridge: Cambridge University Press, 1998); *Japanese Studies in Shakespeare and His Contemporaries*, edited by Yoshiko Kawachi (Newark, NJ: University of Delaware Press, 1998); John Russell Brown, *New Sites for Shakespeare: Theatre, the Audience, and Asia* (London and New York: Routledge, 1999); and *Shakespeare in Japan*, edited by Tetsuo Anzai, Soji Iwasaki, Holger Klein and Peter Milward (Lewiston, Queenston, and Lampeter: The Edwin Mellen Press, 1999).

26 Michael Hattaway, 'Shakespeare's Histories: The Politics of Recent British Productions', in *Shakespeare in the New Europe*, ed. Hattaway, Sokolova and Roper, 351–69; and Thomas Healy, 'Remembering with Advantages: Nation and Ideology in *Henry V* ', in *Shakespeare in the New Europe*, 174–93.

27 This situation is also visually captured by Richard Westall's allegorical painting of *William Shakespeare between Tragedy and Comedy* (1825).

28 The photograph is reproduced as part of James N. Loehlin's contribution to this collection on 'Brecht and the rediscovery of *Henry VI* '. One hastens to add that Dennis Kennedy devotes much detailed attention to the histories in *Looking at Shakespeare: A Visual History of Twentieth-Century Performance*, 2nd edition (Cambridge: Cambridge University Press, 2001).

29 Lawrence Danson, *Shakespeare's Dramatic Genres*, Oxford Shakespeare Topics (Oxford: Oxford University Press, 2000), 87.

30 The operatic canon of the early nineteenth century reveals that English history was considered a valuable plot source indeed. The nineteenth century produced operas about Anne Boleyn (Gaitano Donizetti, *Anna Bolena*, 1830; and Camille Saint-Saëns, *Henry VIII*, 1883); Catherine Howard (Giuseppe Lillo, *Catarina Howard*, 1849); Mary Stuart (François-Joseph Fétis, *Marie Stuart en Écosse*, 1823; and Donizetti, *Maria Stuarda*, 1834); Mary Tudor (approximately ten operas, including Giacomo Ferrari, *Maria d'Inghilterra*, 1840; Giovanni Pacini, *Maria, regina d'Inghilterra*, 1843; and Carlos Gomes, *Maria Tudor*, 1879); Robert Devereux, Earl of Essex (Donizetti, *Roberto Devereux, ossia il conte d'Essex*, 1837); Robert Dudley, Earl of Leicester (D.-F.-E. Auber, *Leicester* [1823]; Isodore de Lara, *Amy Robsart*, 1893); and Queen Elizabeth I (nine operas to date, by composers including Stefano Pavesi (1810) and Michele Carafa (1818), and including Giacomo Rossini's *Elisabetta, regina d'Inghilterra* (1814), and Donizetti's *Elisabetta al castello di Kenilworth*, 1829).

31 Anthony B. Dawson, 'International Shakespeare', in *The Cambridge Companion to Shakespeare on Stage*, edited by Stanley Wells and Sarah Stanton (Cambridge: Cambridge University Press, 2002), 174–93 (p. 176).

32 Quoted in *Dr Johnson on Shakespeare*, edited by W. K. Wimsatt (1960. Rpt. Harmondsworth: Penguin Books, 1969), 121.

33 For Olivier's statement, see Harry M. Geduld, *Filmguide to 'Henry V'* (Bloomington and London: Indiana University Press, 1973), 17. The anecdote of the Free French sailors is told by D. K. C. Todd in *Shakespeare's Agincourt* (Durham: The New Century Press, 1985), 7. On the diplomatic friction see Neil

Taylor, 'National and Racial Stereotypes in Shakespeare Films', in *The Cambridge Companion to Shakespeare on Film*, edited by Russell Jackson (Cambridge: Cambridge University Press, 2000), 261–73 (esp. 265–6).

34 *La Vie du roi Henry V*, translated by Jean-Michel Déprats, introduced and annotated by Gisèle Venet (Paris: Éditions Gallimard, 1999), 397–8 (italics added). See also Paul Franssen, 'The Wrong Globe: Zooming in on Shakespeare's Theatre', *Folio* 7:1 (2000), 26–32.

35 Jerzy Limon, *Gentlemen of a Company: English Players in Central and Eastern Europe, 1590–1660* (Cambridge: Cambridge University Press, 1985), 160n1. In writing his play entitled *Elisa*, also known as *Edward III*, Waimer is likely to have been acquainted with a version of the play staged during a foreign tour of English strolling players in 1587. See also Albert Cohn, *Shakespeare in Germany in the Sixteenth and Seventeenth Centuries: An Account of English Actors in Germany and The Netherlands and of the Plays Performed by Them during the Same Period* (1865. Rpt. New York: Haskell House Publishers, 1971), lxvii. Limon informs us that during the 1620s, also such plays as *The King of England and the King of Scotland*, as well as *King Lear* were performed (*Gentlemen of a Company*, 22).

36 Oscar James Campbell, *The Position of the 'Roode en Witte Roos' in the Saga of King Richard III* (1919. Rpt. New York: AMS, 1971).

37 In a lengthy monologue, Lord Stanley speaks of the chaos that wrecks the nation. Curiously, recounting the assassination of Richard II, the Dutch text refers to the murder of kings in general, thus inviting an application to Charles I as well: 'Everyone considers it a disgrace to England, that she so easily lays hands upon her legitimate *Lords*' (Campbell, *The Position of the 'Roode'*, 103–04; italics added). This quotation is a corrected version of Campbell's translation, which renders the Dutch plural 'Heeren' as 'Lord'. For a more detailed discussion of the play and its political contexts, see my 'Shakespeare and the Early Modern History Play', in *The Cambridge Companion to Shakespeare's History Plays*, edited by Michael Hattaway (Cambridge: Cambridge University Press, 2002), 25–40.

38 See Pedro Calderón de la Barca, *The Schism in England (La cisma da Inglaterra)*, translated by Kenneth Muir and Ann L. Mackenzie, and edited by Ann L. Mackenzie (Warminster: Aris & Phillips, 1990). See also John Loftis, *Renaissance Drama in England and Spain: Topical Allusion and History Plays* (Princeton, NJ: Princeton University Press, 1987).

39 These developments add force to E. J. Hobsbawm's argument that it would be pedantic to refuse the label of 'proto-nationalism . . . to Shakespeare's propagandist plays about English history'. See *Nations and Nationalism since 1780: Programme, Myth, Reality*, second edition (Cambridge: Cambridge University Press, 1992), 75.

40 Kristian Smidt, 'The Discovery of Shakespeare in Scandinavia', in *European Shakespeares*, ed. Delabastita and D'hulst, 91–103. On Shakespeare and the English historical novel in context, see Nicola J. Watson, 'Kemble, Scott, and the Mantle of the Bard', in *The Appropriation of Shakespeare: Post-Renaissance*

Reconstructions of the Works and the Myth, edited by Jean I. Marsden (New York: Harvester Wheatsheaf, 1991), 73–92.

41 August Wilhelm Schlegel, *A Course of Lectures on Dramatic Art and Literature*, translated by John Black. Revised according to the last German edition by A. J. W. Robertson (London: Henry G. Bohn, 1846), 419.

42 Samuel Taylor Coleridge, *Literary Remains*, edited by H. N. Coleridge, 4 vols. (London, 1836–9), II, 160–1.

43 Quoted in *Shakespeare in Europe*, edited by LeWinter, 138. See also Adam Müller, who refers to Schlegel in his 'Fragments Concerning William Shakespeare' (1806). See *The Romantics on Shakespeare*, edited by Jonathan Bate (Harmondsworth: Penguin Books, 1992), 83–7 ('British history has the peculiar characteristic that it offers a concentrated account of the history of the rest of Europe', p. 85).

44 See also Arthur M. Eastman, *A Short History of Shakespearean Criticism* (1968. Rpt. New York: W. W. Norton, 1974), 116–30.

45 Williams, *Shakespeare on the German Stage*. See also Robert K. Sarlos, 'Dingelstedt's Celebration of the Tercentenary: Shakespeare's Histories as a Cycle', *Theatre Survey* 5 (1964), 117–31. As Manfred Draudt remarks in his contribution to this collection, though, the first ever stage production of the histories in cycles postdated Karl von Holtei's public reading of them in Austria by two decades.

46 Martin Lehnert, 'Hundert Jahre deutsche Shakespeare-Gesellschaft', *Shakespeare Jubiläum 1964. Festschrift zu Ehren des 400. Geburtstages William Shakespeares und des 100jährigen Bestehens der deutschen Shakespeare-Gesellschaft*, edited by Anselm Schlösser (Weimar: Hermann Böhlaus Nachfolger, 1964), 1–40 (p. 3).

47 Curiously, in 1875, the German scholar Alexander Teetgen climbed on to the academic barricades especially to protect Shakespeare's *Edward III*, whose authorship English scholars were still not prepared to assign to Shakespeare. For a taste of his militant argument, see Alexander Teetgen, *Shakespeare's 'King Edward the Third', Absurdly Called, and Scandalously Treated as, a 'Doubtful Play': An Indignation Pamphlet* (London: Williams and Norgate, 1875).

48 *Cosima Wagner's Diaries*, edited and annotated by Martin Gregor-Dellin and Dietrich Mack. Translated with an Introduction by Geoffrey Skelton, 2 vols. (New York and London: Harcourt Brace Jovanovich, 1978), I, 9 August 1870.

49 Samuel Taylor Coleridge, *Coleridge's Shakespeare Criticism*, edited by Thomas Middleton Raysor, 2 vols. (London: Constable, 1960), I, 126.

50 *Cosima Wagner's Diaries*, II, 14 September 1880.

51 See H. Freih. von Friesen, 'Ein Wort über Shakespeares Historien', *Shakespeare Jahrbuch* 8 (1873), 1–27. Von Friesen is sceptical about the German audience's readiness to be captivated by the patriotic events of *Henry V*.

52 Christian Jauslin, 'Leopold Lindtberg (1902–1984) zum 100. Geburtstag', *Shakespeare Jahrbuch* 138 (2002), 287–9.

53 See Ania Loomba, 'Shakespearean Transformation', in *Shakespeare and National Culture*, edited by John J. Joughin (Manchester: Manchester University Press, 1997), 109–41 (pp. 109–14). But see also Frederick S. Boas, '*Hamlet* and *Richard II*

34 TON HOENSELAARS

on the High Seas', in his *Shakespeare and the Universities, and Other Studies in Elizabethan Drama* (Oxford: Basil Blackwell, 1923), 84–95.

54 Michael Bogdanov and Michael Pennington, *The English Shakespeare Company: The Story of 'The Wars of the Roses', 1986–1989* (London: Nick Hern Books, 1992), 181.

55 Ian McKellen, 'The Czech Significance', in *A Night at the Theatre*, edited by Ronald Harwood (London: Methuen, 1982), 103–8 (p. 108). See also Margaret Shewring, *King Richard II*, Shakespeare in Performance (Manchester: Manchester University Press, 1996), 29; and Ian McKellen, 'Tears in Bratislava' (from the *Telegraph Sunday Magazine*, 1982), at http://www.mckellen.com.

56 Quoted in Peter Holland, *English Shakespeares: Shakespeare on the English Stage in the 1990s* (Cambridge: Cambridge University Press, 1997), 273 n14.

57 One has the feeling, though, that more than just the title of Peter Holland's *English Shakespeares* plays off against Delabastita and D'hulst's *European Shakespeares* and Kennedy's *Foreign Shakespeare*.

58 *Shakespeare and France*, edited by Holger Klein and Jean-Marie Maguin (Lewiston, NY: The Edwin Mellen Press, 1994); *Shakespeare and Hungary. Special Theme Section: The Law and Shakespeare*, edited by Holger Klein, Péter Dávidházi and B. J. Sokol. Shakespeare Yearbook, 7 (Lewiston, NY: The Edwin Mellen Press, 1996). See also *French Essays on Shakespeare and His Contemporaries: 'What Would France With Us?'*, edited by Jean-Marie Maguin and Michèle Willems (Newark, NJ: University of Delaware Press, 1995); *Russian Essays: on Shakespeare and His Contemporaries*, edited by A. T. Parfenov and Joseph G. Price (Newark, NJ: University of Delaware Press, 1998); *Strands Afar Remote: Israeli Perspectives on Shakespeare*, edited by Avraham Oz (Newark, NJ: University of Delaware Press, 1998); *Italian Studies in Shakespeare and His Contemporaries*, edited by Michele Marrapodi and Giorgio Melchiori (Newark, NJ: University of Delaware Press, 1999).

59 *A Companion to Shakespeare's Works: Volume II – The Histories*, edited by Richard Dutton and Jean E. Howard (Oxford: Blackwell, 2003).

PART I

Introduction: alienating histories

Ton Hoenselaars

In his introduction to *Shakespeare in the Present*, Terence Hawkes notes how, following the major constitutional changes of the late 1990s, 'the "Great Britain" project, chronicled and championed repeatedly in the Shakespeare canon, must henceforth be seen, not just as the opening of a new and apparently permanent world order, but as the beginning of an enterprise that, after four hundred years, has now reached its conclusion'.[1] This new situation, with repercussions that are both national and worldwide, has created new challenges for Shakespeare. It has given rise to a great effort on behalf of the regions of Britain to reclaim and retell their part in Shakespeare's 'English' histories.

Andrew Murphy's chapter in this section addresses the interrelation between England and Ireland in the histories. Concentrating on the Duke of York and Jack Cade in the second part of *Henry VI*, the 'Irish wars' in *Richard II*, the Welsh campaign in the first part of *Henry IV* and the troubled issues of nationhood and union in *Henry V*, Murphy reconstructs the anxiety captured in Shakespeare's histories that was occasioned by the Nine Years' War and the remarkable career of Hugh O'Neill during the 1590s. Queen Elizabeth's ongoing war with the Irish and O'Neill's part in it problematized the colonial factor inherent in Anglo-Irish relations, and subverted the Englishman's facile, stereotypical construction of a sense of self-identity predicated on a definition of the Irish other as a 'wild' nation.[2]

Lisa Hopkins writes about England and Wales, and illustrates how in the histories these two regions tend to be played off against one another, with the Welsh perspective serving as a persistent challenge to any monolithic sense of Englishness. Unlike Murphy, Hopkins focuses not primarily on the plays' early modern historical contexts, but reads the depiction of the relationship between matters English and matters Welsh along the lines of genre, illustrating how England tends to be associated with 'history' and Wales with 'comedy'. In this way, she also manages to bring into focus the plays' gender concerns by analysing the various representations of the domineering female from Wales and the English male who is effeminized on entering this foreign territory.

None of the histories better illustrates the imperial ambitions of England, within both the British and the broader European context, than *Henry V*. Significantly, as Willy Maley has argued, the two enterprises are closely connected: the focus on the conquest of France in *Henry V* may be interpreted as a strategy to obfuscate the play's true colonialist concerns with regard to Wales and Ireland.[3] The deconstruction of this binary cultural strategy comes at a time when also 'foreign', non-British countries that once came under English rule, have learned to speak Shakespeare, albeit without his language. Landmark events in this respect were Jean-Michel Déprats's two French translations of *Henry V*, one to dub the Kenneth Branagh film adaptation of 1989 (which, like Al Pacino's *Looking for Richard*, did much to enhance the popularity of Shakespeare's histories in France), and another translation for the French premiere of the play at the Avignon Festival in 1999, directed by Jean-Louis Benoit. The double effort of Déprats was certainly at a far remove from the gesture in 1746 of Pierre-Antoine de la Place (1707–83), who, in his translation of Shakespeare's work, reduced the war play to a five-page summary.[4] Déprats's is certainly a heroic achievement in a linguistic sense. One can hardly imagine conditions more difficult for the empire to speak back than for a French translator with a heavily accented *Henry V*: the English military conquest at Agincourt is closely joined to a linguistic conquest on the part of Shakespeare because, as also Derrida argues, multilingual, babylonian texts like *Henry V* are by their very nature untranslatable.[5]

In his account of translating *Henry V*, Déprats describes how he developed linguistic ways around the many problems that lie in wait for the French translator, but also how, in order to complement the verbal translation, he relied on intersemiotic, scenic translation, moving from a set of spoken to one of acted signs in order to raze the play's daunting language barrier.[6] Déprats's achievement is perhaps best measured by the fact that it defies, in style, Thomas Healy's surprisingly narrow-minded and insular assumption that *Henry V* in translation could only look like a 'perverse beast'.[7]

Beyond linguistic and political difference, the histories that travel abroad also have to negotiate complex forms of cultural difference. This explains the irony, noted by Daniel Gallimore in his chapter, of the Japanese playwright and translator Kinoshita Junji, who remarked that for his 'Wars of the Roses' (*Bara sensō*) – a free rendering of what was really John Barton and Peter Hall's *Wars of the Roses* – he had to study the historical period and the geography of the histories so thoroughly that he probably knew them better now than Shakespeare had ever done. However, the gap between the two cultures remains enormous, and as a result the histories can only appeal in a very general sense. As Gallimore puts it: 'If the cultural frameworks – the Thomist natural order against Buddhist mutability – are fatally dissimilar, then where the two cultures may begin to meet is through that handful of characters in the history plays who are large enough to step outside their historical context and be accepted in a new one.' Against this background one may begin to appreciate the creativity and the success of some forms of appropriation discussed by Gallimore. Among other things, he illustrates how, through the manipulation of the phrase 'This England' in his translation of the 'Scept'red isle' speech by John of Gaunt, Odashima Yūshi managed to allude to 'The English disease'. By stressing England's then current economic malaise, thus capitalizing on difference, the Japanese translator transformed the famous monologue into a potent and dismissive comment on the rivalry between England and Japan on the world economic stage in the early 1980s.

As Shakespeare's histories are appropriated, they come to mediate between medieval past and contemporary politics in a way the other genres are less likely to do, thus writing modern history both in Britain and abroad. In England, it has become a tendency, in the criticism and on the stage, to question and subvert the unitarian myth of England which is demonstrably at odds with the political and geographical realities of Great Britain. Alternatively, in countries like Australia that have shed the yoke of empire in more recent years, the histories are seen as an occasion to celebrate Shakespeare at England's expense, and, as Rosemary Gaby argues, prominent Australian directors like John Bell find it hard to represent the England of *Henry IV* and *Henry V* as other than 'a place of cracked roadways, dirty tenements, and seedy music halls', or not to 'thumb their nose at notions of empire'.[8] Surely, against this background, France's attempt to use the histories to achieve greater mutual understanding must be recognized as rare, certainly if we also care to remember the curious manifestations of xenophobia during the performances of *Henry V* at the London Globe in 1997.[9] Shakespeare's plays about 'This England' have deterred neither the British, nor the other Europeans, nor the extra-Europeans from reading into them a political relevance for their own present-day and often diverse realities. All would subscribe to Robert Shaughnessy's assertion that the histories 'have (or can be made to have) a recurrent topicality that is perhaps unique among Shakespeare's plays'.[10]

NOTES

1 Terence Hawkes, *Shakespeare in the Present* (New York and London: Routledge, 2002), 4.
2 Willy Maley describes the Irish connections in the histories in terms of a type of friction between 'text' and 'subtext', in 'The Irish Text and Subtext of Shakespeare's English Histories', in *A Companion to Shakespeare's Works: Volume II – The Histories*, edited by Richard Dutton and Jean E. Howard (Oxford: Blackwell, 2003), 94–124.
3 Willy Maley, '"This Sceptred Isle": Shakespeare and the British Problem', in *Shakespeare and National Culture*, edited by John J. Joughin (Manchester: Manchester University Press, 1997), 83–108.
4 Pierre-Antoine de la Place only included ten Shakespeare plays in *Le Théâtre Anglois*; the first five out of the total eight volumes were devoted to Shakespeare. Yet, de la Place's choice to translate only the third part of *Henry VI* (vol. I) and *Richard III* (vol. II), thus underrepresenting the histories, strongly suggests that Shakespeare's plays on Anglo-French rivalry were no favourites in his view. As he says in his commentary about *Henry V*: 'On juge bien que tout doit y être outré; & que, pour faire sa cour à la populace Angloise, l'Auteur a crû ne pouvoir mieux décorer son Héros, qu'en exagérant autant la gloire du Vainqueur que la disgrâce des Vaincus' ('It is rightly considered that everything had to be overdone, and that, in order to court the English rabble, the author thought that there was no better way of embellishing his hero than by exaggerating the glory of the victor as much as the disgrace of the vanquished.') See *Le Théâtre Angloise*, translated by Pierre-Antoine de la Place, 8 vols. (London, 1746–9), III, 492.
5 See Jacques Derrida, *The Ear of the Other: Otobiography, Transference, Translation*, edited by Christie V. McDonald and translated by Peggy Kamuf (New York: Schocken Books, 1985), 99.
6 With its linguistic complexity, *Henry V* has also been a potent means to address the friction between the English-speaking majority in Canada and the French-Canadians in Quebec. On Michael Langham's productions of the play, giving it local political importance at Stratford, Ontario, in 1956 and 1966, see Samuel L. Leiter, *Shakespeare around the Globe: A Guide to Notable Postwar Revivals* (Westport, CT: Greenwood Press, 1986), 221–2; and James N. Loehlin, *Henry V* (Manchester: Manchester University Press, 1996), 152–5.
7 Thomas Healy, 'Remembering with Advantages: Nation and Ideology in *Henry V*', in *Shakespeare in the New Europe*, edited by Michael Hattaway, Boika Sokolova and Derek Roper (Sheffield: Sheffield Academic Press, 1994), 174–93 (p. 177).
8 Rosemary Gaby, '"What ish my nation?": Reconstructing Shakespeare's Henriad for the Australian Stage', *Shakespeare Bulletin* 18:1 (Winter 2000), 43–6 (p. 45). See also Lucy Hamilton, '*Henry IV*', Shakespeare *Bulletin* 17:1 (Winter 1999), 31–2.

9 The xenophobia at the new Globe cannot be interpreted as a mark of English sentiment vis-à-vis the French, but ought to be seen as a serious side effect of a complex globalizing tendency. The 1997 production of *Henry V* was 'certainly post-British, but it was about as English as peanut butter', with its battle scenes 'reduced to factitious confrontations between an American Dauphin and those members of the multinational audience who felt licensed or obliged to boo him when he kicked straw into their faces'. See Michael Dobson, "Falstaff after John Bull: Shakespearean History, Britishness, and the Former United Kingdom,' *Shakespeare Jahrbuch* 136 (2000), 40–55 (p. 54).

10 Robert Shaughnessy, *Representing Shakespeare: England, History and the RSC* (New York: Harvester Wheatsheaf, 1994), xi.

CHAPTER I

Ireland as foreign and familiar in Shakespeare's histories

Andrew Murphy

Ireland is somewhat oddly placed in relation to the notion of an international context for Shakespeare's history plays. Ireland is indeed a foreign country from an English perspective and the plays themselves on occasion envision a venturing into that foreign territory, or an impinging of that territory and its history upon the English 'homeland'. This chapter will argue, however, that, owing to the complex historical interconnectedness of the two islands, Ireland never wholly serves as a truly foreign location for the literature of the period, but that it rather functions as a kind of liminal space – at one and the same time foreign and familiar. The chapter will read a selection of the history plays against the background of the crisis in Ireland in the closing decades of the sixteenth century, suggesting that the plays in question are significantly informed by the context of the Nine Years War (1594–1603). In this war the Irish were led by Hugh O'Neill, a complex and mercurial figure who began his career as, essentially, an agent of the British colonial project in Ireland, but who ultimately fought to secure a severing of the link between the two islands.[1]

I would like to begin my analysis of the cycle of history plays with a text which, while it does not include the greatest amount of material explicitly connected with Ireland (it does not, for instance, like *Henry the Fift*, include an Irish character), nevertheless, does contain the greatest number of actual references to 'Ireland' and the 'Irish' of any Shakespeare play. This is the second play of the first Henriad, known in its First Folio version as *The Second Part of Henry the Sixt*.[2]

The exact year of composition of this play is uncertain, but it seems likely that it was written sometime around 1591.[3] The play thus predates the Nine Years War, being located within an Anglo-Irish decade during which, as David Quinn has noted, 'a kind of peace was attained . . . as Munster settled into a plantation and Connacht achieved an apparent equilibrium under a rationalized form of military taxation . . . and while, too, Hugh O'Neill, before and after he attained the title of Earl of Tyrone in 1587, maintained a pacific policy behind which his effective strength grew'.[4] The relative stability of the English position in Ireland in this period is reflected in the manner in which Ireland figures in the text of Shakespeare's play. It is the Duke of Yorke who is most associated with Ireland in the text. He has seen service there, and, in the play's opening scene, Salisbury, in praising him, comments:

> . . . Brother Yorke, thy Acts in Ireland,
> In bringing them to ciuill Discipline:
> Thy late exploits done in the heart of France,
> When thou wert Regent for our Soueraigne,
> Haue made thee fear'd and honor'd of the people.
> (TLN 202–6)

Yorke himself claims in the same scene:

> Methinkes the Realmes of England, France, & Ireland,
> Beare that proportion to my flesh and blood,
> As did the fatall brand *Althæa* burnt,
> Vnto the Princes heart of *Calidon*.   (TLN 244–7)

Later in the play, we learn of an Irish uprising and Yorke takes advantage of this turn of events to plot his attempt on the English throne. His Irish strategy is twofold: he will go there himself and use the occasion as an excuse to raise an army, but in his absence, he will employ Jack Cade 'To make Commotion' in England (TLN 1664). Though 'a headstrong Kentishman' (TLN 1662), Cade also has strong Irish connections, having served Yorke there. Cade is a multiply transgressive character in the play: a commoner who pretends to aristocratic parentage, but also an Englishman who is able to transform himself into a native Irishman. Yorke says of him:

> Full often, like a shaghayr'd craftie Kerne,
> Hath he conuersed with the Enemie,
> And vndiscouer'd, come to me againe,
> And giuen me notice of their Villanies.
> (TLN 1673–6)

The composite presentation of Cade appears here much like the figure that Captain Thomas Lee (who was also much given to disguise) presents in his 1594 portrait by Marcus Gheeraedts the Younger.[5] As James P. Myers has noted of the portrait, Lee's 'pointed beard, his red military cape and white-and-delft-blue floral undergarment distinguish him readily as an Elizabethan; his high-peake morion, long spear, round shield strapped to his back, and his shoeless feet and hoseless legs mark him as an Irish chieftain'.[6]

What is striking about Shakespeare's Cade (and indeed about Lee also) is that not only is he presented as being able to assume, convincingly, an Irish appearance, adopting the 'shag-hayr' of the Irish 'glib' (a forward-combed hairstyle), but in the act of thus transforming himself, he deploys a strategy that English writers traditionally associated with the Irish themselves: the ability to shift into a different identity. This is one of the aspects of Irishness to which Spenser most vigorously objects in *A View of the Present State of Ireland* and which he delineates in Book v of the *Faerie Queene* in the figure of Malengin.[7] In the *View*, Spenser specifically links such mutability to the traditional Irish hairstyle, observing that when a thief 'hathe rune himself in to that perill of lawe that he will not be knowen he either Cuttethe of his glibbe quite by which he becommethe nothinge like himselfe, or pulleth it so lowe downe over his eyes that it is verye harde to discerne his thevishe Countenaunce'.[8] Cade's power, therefore, is presented as the power to forge (in every sense) an Irish strategy as a weapon against the Irish themselves. In the greater narrative of the play, Yorke also performs something like a version of this manoeuvre, in that he uses the realm of Ireland as a launching point for his own campaign in England. Thus the messenger registers his return from Ireland, at the head of a mixed army:

> The Duke of Yorke is newly come from Ireland,
> And with a puissant and a mighty power
> Of Gallow-glasses and stout Kernes,
> Is marching hitherward in proud array.
> (TLN 2877–80)

Yorke himself proclaims, on entering with his army:

> From Ireland thus comes York to claim his right,
> And plucke the Crowne from feeble *Henries* head.
> (TLN 2991–2)

What is striking about this text, then, is the confidence which it projects in an English ability to penetrate, master, marshal and control the Irish forces and the power which they represent. Indeed, we might say that this is a play in which Otherness of every kind is seen to be available to be recruited and subverted to serve the ends of a particular aristocratic class faction: the text presents Yorke as commanding and deploying both the lower orders within English society and the native Irish to serve his military and political ambition.

Just prior to his departure for Ireland in *The Second Part of Henry the Sixt*, Yorke observes:

> Well, Nobles, well; 'tis politikely done,
> To send me packing with an Hoast of men:
> I feare me, you but warme the starued Snake,
> Who cherisht in your breasts, will sting your hearts,
> 'Twas men I lackt, and you will giue them me.
>
> (TLN 1647–51)

This same proverb of the frozen snake revived is also deployed by Spenser in his *View*, which was likely written in the mid-1590s. Spenser writes of Hugh O'Neill's early years:

He was I assure youe the moste outcaste of all the Oneals then, and lifted vp by her maiestie out of the duste to that he nowe hathe wraughte himselfe vnto, And now he playeth like the frozen Snake whoe beinge for Compassion releived by the husbandman sone after he was warme, begane to hisse and threaten daunger even to him and his. (*View of the Present State of Ireland*, 168)

We notice a shift between these two deployments of the parable. In the play, Yorke sees *himself* as the snake, and the image is indicative of a certain English capacity for covert and measured action. Spenser's Irenius, by contrast, sees the Irish O'Neill as the snake, and, in a reversal of the image of the disguised Cade, he cautions that O'Neill has duplicitously penetrated the English realm and thus 'threaten[s] daunger'. The shift in perspective registered by these different deployments of the proverb is perhaps indicative of the shift which occurred in Ireland in the years between the writing of Shakespeare's play and Spenser's tract. In the likely year of composition of the second Henry VI play Hugh O'Neill was still more or less willing to act as agent for the crown. We might say that as an Irish ally he was available to be deployed by the English in much the same way as Irish power is available to be harnessed and directed by Yorke. By 1595, however, O'Neill was in open rebellion and was proclaimed a traitor by the queen. In February of that year his brother, Art, attacked and burned the strategically important Blackwater Fort; Enniskillen was taken in mid-May; and the Irish inflicted a heavy defeat on the English at Clontibret in June. As O'Neill's novelist biographer, Seán Ó Faoláin, rather melodramatically puts it in describing the ongoing campaign: 'Cavan was burned flat. Louth was ravaged as far south as Drogheda. The colonists fled to their towns, and every gate and door was barred. After that there could be no retraction.'[9] It was most likely in this same year of 1595 that Shakespeare wrote *The life and death of Richard the second* (to adopt again the First Folio title). In an odd way, the relationship between this play and its Henry VI predecessor is much the same as the relationship between the two versions of the parable of the frozen snake.

Each play has its Irish dimension and the basic trajectory of the Irish material is much the same in each case. Ireland lies in the background of both
plays as 'a world elsewhere' and it serves as a convenient peripheral vehicle
for manoeuverings within the realm of England itself – in Yorke's case, the
raising of an army to support his attempt on the throne; in Richard's case,
the appropriation of Gaunt's resources. As Richard comments, on hearing
of Gaunt's death:

> Now for our Irish warres,
> We must supplant those rough rug-headed Kernes,
> Which liue like venom, where no venom else
> But onely they, haue priuiledge to liue.
> And for these great affayres do aske some charge
> Towards our assistance, we do seize to vs
> The plate, coine, reuennewes, and moueables,
> Whereof our Vncle *Gaunt* did stand possest.
>   (TLN 802–9)

Both Yorke and Richard are absented from part of their respective plays
as they conduct their Irish campaigns, and both finally return to Britain
to face conflict there. However, again as in the case of the parable of the
snake, when the story is told a second time, it has a different force and
outcome. Where Yorke returns triumphant, at the head of an army which
has incorporated elements of the Irish, Richard's return is, by contrast,
signalled by a progressive depletion of his followers. As Salisbury informs
Richard on his arrival on the shores of Britain:

> One day too late, I feare (my Noble Lord)
> Hath clouded all thy happie dayes on Earth:
> Oh call backe Yesterday, bid Time returne,
> And thou shalt haue twelue thousand fighting men.
>   (TLN 1423–6)

Richard loses his army before he even arrives back in Britain and then loses
his crown in his Welsh confrontation with Henry. Between the 1591 play
and its 1595 successor, then, we get a shift in the way in which Ireland
is presented on the Shakespearean stage. In the first instance, Ireland is a
territory to be deployed as an English source of strength; in the second, it
is associated with a catastrophic draining away of that strength, leading to
Richard's loss of power, and ultimately to his death.

Moving on to the Henry IV plays, we see that, here, divisions within the
island of Britain itself are foregrounded, as the stability of the national unit
is threatened by a shifting alliance forged among the Welsh, the Scots and
certain elements of the English themselves. What we find in these plays is a

profound engagement with the issue of the uncertainties and fragmentation of national identities. It is as if the failure to secure a stable positive English identity contradistinguished from a negative Irish identity has prompted a re-examination of the relationships among the populations of Britain itself, giving rise to a realization that these relationships also cannot be securely distinguished and sustained. In the first of the Henry IV plays, the source of the disruption within Britain is initially identified as being Wales and, specifically, the Welsh leader, Owen Glendower. Westmerland, briefing Henry on the Crusade preparations, informs him that the discussions were interrupted when

> all athwart there came
> A Post from Wales, loaden with heauy Newes;
> Whose worst was, That the Noble *Mortimer*,
> Leading the men of Herefordshire to fight
> Against the irregular and wilde *Glendower*,
> Was by the rude hands of that Welshman taken,
> And a thousand of his people butchered.
>
> (TLN 40–6)

Glendower and his Welsh allies appear here as alien forces stationed on the borders of the English state, threatening its integrity. The actions of the Welsh women in the wake of the battle serve to emphasize the barbaric Otherness of this people. As Westmerland's report continues, taking up the fate of the 'thousand . . . people butchered', we learn that:

> Vpon [their] dead corpses there was such misuse,
> Such beastly, shamelesse transformation,
> By those Welshwomen done, as may not be
> (Without much shame) be told or spoken of.
>
> (TLN 47–50)

The implied sexual brutality of the Welsh women, transgressing codes of martial and gender roles and of bodily as well as national integrity, empha-sizes a multiple lack of civility on the part of the Welsh. And yet, as the play proceeds, these easy distinctions and dichotomies begin to fragment. In the first instance, Mortimer, having been despatched against Glendower and defeated by him, ultimately becomes Glendower's ally and his son-in-law. In this sense, the division between the civilized Self and the barbarian Other fails to be sustained in the text, as their forces and objectives combine, within the broader framework of a northern English/Welsh/Scottish coali-tion. Mortimer might, of course, be seen simply as an early instance of the phenomenon of the colonist 'going native', seduced by Glendower's daugh-ter, that 'faire Queene in a Summers Bowre' (TLN 1748). And, indeed, we might find here echoes of a certain 'fair[i]e Queene' and of another 'Summers Bowre'. In the play, Glendower, translating for Mortimer's wife, informs Mortimer that

> She bids you,
> On the wanton Rushes lay you downe,
> And rest your gentle Head vpon her Lappe
> And she will sing the Song that pleaseth you.
>
> (TLN 1753–6)

In a similar moment, in Book II of Spenser's poem, we find that 'the whiles some one did chaunt [a] louely lay',[10] Guyon and the Palmer seek and finally encounter Acrasia in the Bower of Bliss, keeping their way

> Through many couert groues, and thickets close,
> In which they creeping did at last display
> That wanton Ladie, with her louer lose,
> Whose sleepie head she in her lap did soft dispose.
>
> (II.xii.76.6–9)

Shakespeare's play, however, presents a rather more complex picture than Spenser's poem. The Welsh bower does not simply evoke a decadent alien formation which proves attractive to the defecting Mortimer. In fact, even as, on the one hand, the scene registers a sharp division between the worlds of English and Welsh – literally, in its inclusion of both the Welsh and English languages in the script (or rather, on the stage, since the Welsh material is not included in the printed text of the play) – at the same time, these divisions are put into question in the scene, most notably in the figure of Glendower, who contrives to straddle both worlds. Glendower is presented as moving fluently between the registers of English and Welsh. At a purely linguistic level, we see him act as interpreter, mediating between his daughter and her English husband. But Glendower himself also draws attention to the greater significance of his medial position and of his own cross-cultural history. When challenged by Percy during the dispute over the division of the kingdom, he proclaims

> I can speake English, Lord as well as you:
> For I was trayn'd vp in the English Court;
> Where, being but young, I framed to the Harpe
> Many an English Dittie, louely well,
> And gaue the Tongue a helpefull Ornament;
> A Vertue that was neuer seene in you.
>
> (TLN 1650–5)

Christopher Highley, in an article on 'Wales, Ireland, and *Henry IV*', has astutely noted how remarkably resonant this portrait of the early fifteenth-century Glendower is with the contemporary image of the late sixteenth-century Hugh O'Neill. As Highley observes, hearing this speech of Glendower's 'the play's first audiences could have recalled Tyrone's similar upbringing' and he goes on to note that

Both Glendower and Tyrone had experienced the 'civilizing' effect of English culture and both had served English authority: Glendower as a follower of Henry Bolingbroke, Tyrone as an ally of Elizabeth. With both men, though, familiarity with English ways had only bred a latent resentment, and upon returning to their respective homes they had rebelled against their former English benefactors and masters.[11]

Highley further draws our attention to the various ways in which the connection between O'Neill and Glendower was indeed made by many of Shakespeare's contemporaries. He directs us, for instance, to a text included among the Irish state papers for 1598, entitled a 'Report by divers Welshmen concerning the Earl of Tyrone', which includes the following observation:

That he was proclaimed King of Ireland, and that he was called 'Earl Terowyne, which is a word of Welsh, which is in English, the Earl of Owen's land', also, that 'he descended of Owyne Clyne Dore, who had interest both in Ireland and Wales', and 'that there was a prophecy the Earl of Tyrone should prevail against the Engllish nation'. Further, that he was proclaimed Prince of Wales, and that he had friends in Wales that looked for him, as he was both favourable and bountiful to Welshmen.[12]

On the basis of the connections established by Christopher Highley, then, we might say that Ireland, though it does not figure explicitly in the text of the Henry IV plays, nevertheless, has an odd kind of dual presence in the narrative.

On the one hand, I have been suggesting that the contemporary situation in Ireland, which disrupts the process of establishing any stable sense of an easy binary relationship between England and Ireland, prompts a reconsideration of the broader issue of how national identity is constituted within the island of Britain itself. On the other hand, we might say that we can see adumbrated within the figure of Glendower the image of Hugh O'Neill, emerging again, we might say, as a figure of liminal disruption, serving to interrogate the easy tropes of national self-imagining. We find these issues focused with particular clarity in the final play of the second Henriad, *Henry the fift*.

The second of the Henry IV plays was most likely written in 1598. In August of that year, the northern Irish forces secured their greatest victory over the English, at the battle of the Yellow Ford. Before the year was out, they had swept southward, destroying the Munster plantation, and driving the colonists (including Spenser and his family) from the land.[13] Fynes Moryson, in his memoir of the Nine Years War, wrote that the year 1598, together with 'the next following, became so disasterous to the English, and successfull in action to the Irish, as they shaked the English gouernement in this kingdome, till it tottered, and wanted little of fatall ruine'.[14] In 1599, despite some opposition in the Privy Council, Robert Devereux, the second Earl of Essex, won the commission for Ireland and set off, declaring, 'I have beaten Knollys and Montjoye in the councele, and by G–d I will beat Tyr-Owen in the feilde' (Moryson, *An Itinerary*, II, 21). For the purpose of the campaign, 'he had,' Moryson informs us, 'an Army assigned him, as great as himselfe required, and such for number and strength, as *Ireland* had neuer yet seene' (II, 27). Essex's departure was much heralded and his triumphant return much anticipated.[15] We find this anticipation registered, of course, in the text of the Folio version of *Henry the Fift*.[16] It occurs when the chorus to Act v, imagining Henry's triumphant return to London, proclaims: 'But now behold,'

> How London doth powre out her Citizens . . .
> As by a lower, but by louing likelyhood,
> Were now the Generall of our gracious Empresse,
> As in good time he may, from Ireland comming,
> Bringing Rebellion broached on his Sword;
> How many would the peacefull Citie quit,
> To welcome him?   (TLN 2872–84)

The text of *Henry the Fift* extends the engagement with the issue of national identities and of the relations among the various communities within the British Isles initiated in the Henry IV plays. The second scene of the play touches on the adversarial relationship that exists between England and its northern neighbour, as Henry warns his council

> We must not onely arme t'inuade the French,
> But lay downe our proportions, to defend
> Against the Scot, who will make roade vpon vs,
> With all aduantages.   (TLN 283–6)

Canterbury and Exeter seek to reassure Henry that the Scots present no real threat to the integrity of England, that his northern English loyalists

Shall be a Wall sufficient to defend
Our in-land from the pilfering Borderers.
(TLN 288–9)

We get a sense here of England's being drawn in behind its northern borders, which are marked now not by what Gaunt in *Richard the Second*
characterized as a

triumphant sea,
Whose rocky shore beates backe the enuious siedge
Of watery Neptune   (TLN 702–4)

but rather by a Hadrianesque defensive wall which serves to keep the alien
element at bay (as if Gaunt's English island has now shrunk to Canterbury's
'in-land' England). Canterbury concludes with a piece of confident advice:

Diuide your happy England into foure,
Whereof, take you one quarter into France,
And you withall shall make all Gallia shake.
If we with thrice such powers left at home,
Cannot defend our Owne doores from the dogge,
Let vs be worried, and our Nation lose
The name of hardiness and policie.   (TLN 361–7)

The play is finally, however, unwilling to settle for such ceding of territory
as this and such retrenchment upon firmer ground. Where Canterbury calls
on Henry to 'divide [his] happy England into foure', the play as a whole
shows a willingness to explore the fact that the monarch's realm is *already*
divided into four distinct units and the play struggles to make sense of the
relationship that exists among the four elements. These issues are brought
sharply into focus in the 'four captains' scene of the play, where we are
presented with an English army that is, as David Cairns and Shaun Richards
have noted, paradigmatic of the nation as a whole, as its membership is
shown to include English, Welsh, Scots and Irish representatives.[17] Cairns
and Richards conceive of this scene as ultimately figuring a bogus vision
of unity within the British realm, with the playwright taking great care
to include markers of *exclusion* in his characterization of the three Celtic
captains, even as they are incorporated into the larger institution of the
English army. They argue that while the three Celts 'are united in their
service to the English Crown', their

use of the English language . . . reveals that 'service' is the operative word, for
in rank, in dramatic importance, and in linguistic competence, they are comical
second-order citizens. They are, moreover, disputatious, and the argument between

Fluellen and Macmorris, which is resolved by Gower's admonition, is further dramatic evidence of the harmony which England has brought to the fractious occupants of the Celtic fringe.[18]

Cairns's and Richards's point is well made, but it fails to attend, I would argue, to the complexities of the Irish situation as they are written through this scene.

Discussions of the Irish dimension of the scene have tended to centre on the figure of the Irish captain Mackmorrice, specifically on his explosive outburst when his Welsh counterpart, Fluellen, begins to talk about the Irishman's 'nation':

WELCH. Captaine *Mackmorrice*, I thinke, looke you, vnder your correction, there is not many of your Nation.
IRISH. Of my Nation? What ish my Nation? Ish a Villaine, and a Basterd, and a Knaue, and a Rascall. What ish my Nation? Who talkes of my Nation?

(TLN 1237–42)

Mackmorrice's response is obscure and has given rise to a number of different interpretations. In an influential commentary on the passage, Philip Edwards has suggested that

[t]he paraphrase should run something like this. 'What is this separate race you're implying by using the phrase "your nation"? Who are you, a Welshman, to talk of the Irish as though they were a separate nation from you? I belong in this family as much as you do.' This is the essence of it – indignation that a Welshman should think of Ireland as a separate nation from the great (British) nation to which the Welshman apparently thought he belonged.[19]

Most subsequent critics have adopted Edwards's interpretation of the exchange, with Gary Taylor, for instance, quoting Edwards's proffered paraphrase as his gloss on the line 'What ish my nation' in his Oxford edition of the play. One of the problems with Edwards's interpretation is that it seeks to produce a single meaning from what is, in fact, a profoundly ambiguous passage. In the process, Edwards misses the deeper resonances of Mackmorrice's response. In addition we should note that Edwards essentially treats the Irish captain's interrogative not as a question but as a statement – 'a furious repudiation of difference', as he calls it (*Threshold of a Nation*, 76). But in so doing, he disregards the possibility that Mackmorrice's question may be just that – a genuine question: 'What ish my nation?' Taken as a question, Mackmorrice's interrogative opens up a variety of issues pertinent to the play in the context of the particular historical moment in which it was written. In the first instance, we note that Mackmorrice's remark can be seen as resonating with a general English anxiety regarding the project of establishing a coherent sense of Irish identity. In this sense, his question appears in the text as a challenge, throwing into doubt the issue of how the Irish can properly be classified and identified. 'What ish my nation' is a blunt expression of this uncertainty, an interrogation of what *constitutes* the Irish nation. We can see the extent to which this challenge to the construction of stable identities is encoded in the text if we recall the particularities of Mackmorrice's positioning in the play. Like Hugh O'Neill, Mackmorrice is himself an oddly ambiguous figure. Although this stage Irishman's speech betokens a stereotypical Irish identity, he nevertheless takes his place within the English army, fighting for the English imperial cause.[20] And like O'Neill's own soldiers, he appears, we presume, as an Irishman garbed in the redcoated uniform of an English soldier. To the extent, then, that Mackmorrice is, like O'Neill himself, ambiguously and mercurially aligned with both an Irish and an English identity, the question 'What ish my nation?' may emerge as being directed both at and from that very condition of liminal uncertainty itself. In this sense we might say that Edwards's assessment of the passage as 'a furious repudiation of difference' is exactly right, at least in the sense that what Mackmorrice's questioning serves to effect is an interrogation of difference itself – of the bases on which difference is erected and achieved. As David Baker has astutely observed of this exchange in general: 'MacMorris' questions have the effect of preventing any final meaning – any discursive end 'point' – from emerging at all. Here, the voicing of imperial power gives way to a discursive heterogeneity, interrogates itself, and finds itself unable to sustain the distinctions on which it rests.'[21] We find this failure to sustain distinctions at play later in the text also, as the play draws on toward its conclusion in Frye's 'happy rustle of bridal gowns and banknotes'.[22] In the final scene, the conflict between England and France has been resolved and the royal parties of French and English come together in an effort to secure the peace. The scene is the occasion for what Gary Taylor has termed a 'Freudian slip' in the F1 text of the play.[23] As the scene opens, Henry extends a welcome to the French party and his courtesy is returned by the French king, Charles:

> Right ioyous are we to behold your face,
> Most worthy brother England, fairely met.
> So are you, Princes (English) euery one.
>
> (TLN 2996–8)

Queen Isabel then moves to second her husband's sentiment, but, addressing Henry, she makes a revealing substitution. 'So happy be the Issue Brother *Ireland*' (TLN 2999), she greets him, rather than, as we might expect, 'So happy be the issue brother *England*.'[24] This error in the text could be recruited in support of the view of the ending of *Henry the Fift* put forward by Alan Sinfield and Jonathan Dollimore. Taking their cue from Edwards they 'see the attempt to conquer France and the union in peace at the end of the play as a re-presentation of the attempt to conquer Ireland and the hoped-for unity of Britain . . . The play offers a displaced, imaginary resolution of one of the state's most intractable problems' ('History and Ideology', 225). It should be noted, however, that it is not the conquered France that gets confused with Ireland but rather the conquering England. Again, this overlapping seems to point less to what Sinfield and Dollimore have traced in the play as 'the ideal subservience' of Ireland to England, than to the deep interconnectedness of the two national groups and to the intense difficulty of the task of distinguishing discrete, coherent (and hierarchically organized) separate national identities from among them.

Henry the Fift appears to end in a grand gesture of unity, as Henry, in wooing Katherine, tells her that 'England is thine, Ireland is thine, France is thine, and *Henry Plantaginet* is thine' (TLN 3226–8), holding out the possibility of a great union of thrones, nations and bodies. Seen in this light, Cairns and Richards may well be right when they see the play as presenting 'a piece of dramatic wish-fulfilment: that a contemporary cause of discord, namely Ireland, should come to [a] satisfactory conclusion' (*Writing Ireland*, 9). For all that, however, we must also say that the play finally fails to effect its ambitious project of maintaining a certain Gauntean sense of a coherent England, while somehow simultaneously (through the attempted incorporation/subordination/unification of the diverse national elements within the realm) accommodating to that sense of England the very boundaries and differences that Gaunt ignored. Ireland is crucially at the centre of that failure, as it raises issues of equivalence, proximity and identity which the play is finally unable to assimilate to its grand unifying ambition.

Essex did not succeed in his grand ambition of 'beat[ing] Tyr-Owen in the feilde'. He proved unequal to the task of managing O'Neill's transgressive liminality. In a half-hour meeting with the Lord Lieutenant, O'Neill succeeded in wresting from him a truce that was greatly to the advantage of the Irish, leading to Essex's disgrace and, ultimately, to his execution.[25] Essex was succeeded in Ireland by Charles Blount, Lord Mountjoy. The style of Mountjoy's departure from England was in marked contrast to that of his predecessor: 'without any publique ostentation, or great attendancy, in the month of February 1600. [H]e tooke his iourney toward *Ireland*'

(Gainsford, *True and Exemplary History*, 28). Mountjoy inflicted a decisive defeat on O'Neill at Kinsale in 1601 and finally accepted his surrender at Mellifont on 30 March 1603. The date of O'Neill's surrender is, of course, significant, as it came just six days after the death of Elizabeth (a fact which Mountjoy concealed from O'Neill until after he had made his surrender). With the accession of James VI as king of Scotland, England, Wales and an Ireland that had, for the first time ever, been brought into complete submission, the way seemed open for a new imagining of the national unit and the relations between its constituent parts. James certainly pushed for such a reimagining, as he sought to enact a grand project that would unite his territories into a single realm.

With the exception of *Henry VIII*, the Shakespeare canon after *Henry the Fift* confines itself to the mythical historiographic tradition where Britain is concerned. As Leah Marcus has shown in *Puzzling Shakespeare*, however, this mythic history is also deeply enmeshed in contemporary history and politics, with the Lear plays and *Cymbeline* taking up issues of union and disunity.[26] In *Cymbeline*, we encounter a series of disjunctions, both domestic and political, which the play resolves in its conclusion, as lovers are reunited, lost children are restored to their inheritance and the nation is connected with its imperial destiny. We might say of the play that it seeks to return us to the world of *The Second Part of Henry the Sixt*, which sees a variety of different communities as being readily available for the service of a particular aristocratic fraction within the state. The confidence of the play's vision of union resonates with the confidence expressed just a couple of years later in John Davies's *Discouerie of the Trve Cavses why Ireland was neuer Entirely Subdued* (1612), in which Davies charts the success of his colonial project of integrating Ireland into the British legal realm. What both *Cymbeline* and the *Discouerie* neglect in their respective accounts of union, however, is the fact that the grand union scheme of the early seventeenth century was entirely notional: James failed to secure the necessary backing for the proposals in the English parliament and, in addition, Ireland's place within the scheme was never exactly clear.[27] In Britain, differences between England and Scotland would contribute to the eruption of the Civil War; in Ireland, Davies's imperial legal policy would play a part not just in the Irish uprising of 1641 (sensationally chronicled in John Temple's *The Irish Rebellion* of 1646), but would also serve to intensify the Anglo-Irish conflict by introducing an entrenched group of Scottish Protestant settlers into Ulster. Despite the apparent confidence of *Cymbeline*'s mythic pastoralism, then, and the triumph of Mountjoy's having succeeded (where Essex failed) in 'Bringing Rebellion broached on his Sword', what persisted in the Irish situation, long after the deaths of both Shakespeare and O'Neill in 1616, is the confusion and anxiety registered in the plays written during the course of the Nine Years War. Ireland thus serves as an ideal location for both debating and defining some of the issues which lie at the heart of this collection. The Brittano-Hibernic dimension of Shakespeare's histories leads us to question just exactly how history is constructed – both in drama and in other contexts. It also prompts us to ask ourselves what exactly constitutes the 'foreign' and to consider the question of where exactly the boundaries between the 'domestic' and the 'foreign' can be drawn.[28]

NOTES

1 This chapter is based in part on my 'Shakespeare's Irish History', published in *Literature and History* 5:1 (Spring 1996), 38–59. I kindly acknowledge the permission of Manchester University Press to discuss and reconsider some of the materials analysed in *Literature and History*. I have set out my arguments for the importance of the relationship of geographic, cultural and religious proximity of Britain and Ireland in greater detail in my *But the Irish Sea Betwixt Us: Ireland, Colonialism, and Renaissance Literature* (Lexington: The University Press of Kentucky, 1999).

2 All titles, names and quotations are taken from the First Folio, using the Charlton Hinman (and Peter Blayney) facsimile (New York: Norton, 1996). All references to this edition will be marked TLN (through line numbering).

3 For the dating of the plays, I rely on Stanley Wells and Gary Taylor, with John Jowett and William Montgomery, *William Shakespeare: A Textual Companion* (Oxford: Oxford University Press, 1987). For *The Second Part of Henry the Sixt*, see 111–12, under the play's quarto title, *The First Part of the Contention*.

4 David Beers Quinn, *The Elizabethans and the Irish* (Ithaca, NY: Cornell University Press, 1966), 133.

5 Both Cade and Lee eventually suffered the same fate, in that involvement with aristocratic conspiracies brought them finally to their deaths: Cade is killed when the rebellion which he is prompted to by Yorke fails and Lee is executed as a traitor at Tyburn, following his involvement with the abortive Essex rebellion.

6 James P. Myers, 'Early English Colonial Experiences in Ireland: Captain Thomas Lee and Sir John Davies', *Eire-Ireland* 23:1 (Spring 1988), 11. See also Brian de Breffny, 'An Elizabethan Political Painting', *Irish Arts Review* 1.1 (Spring 1984); and Hiram Morgan, 'Tom Lee: The Posing Peacemaker', in *Representing Ireland: Literature and the Origins of Conflict, 1534–1660*, edited by Brendan Bradshaw, Andrew Hadfield and Willy Maley (Cambridge: Cambridge University Press, 1993).

7 See *Faerie Queene*, Book V, canto ix. It is no coincidence that the final fragment of the poem – the 'Two Cantos of Mvtabilitie' – should be set in Ireland.

8 *A View of the Present State of Ireland*, in *The Works of Edmund Spenser: A Variorum Edition*, edited by Rudolf Gottfried (Baltimore, MD: Johns Hopkins University

Press, 1949), 102. There has been some discussion of whether Spenser was indeed the author of the *View*. See Jean Brink, 'Constructing the *View of the Present State of Ireland*', *Spenser Studies* 11 (1990), 203–28.

9 Seán Ó Faoláin, *The Great O'Neill* (London: Longmans, 1942), 195. In fact, Ó Faoláin overstates the case here: the defining characteristic of O'Neill's career was his ability to temporize with the English authorities – strategic retraction and submission came as easily to him as rebellion and he contrived to secure a pardon from the queen more than once during the course of the Nine Years War.

10 Edmund Spenser, *The Faerie Queene*, edited by Thomas P. Roche and C. Patrick O'Donnell (New Haven: Yale University Press, 1991), II.xii.74.1.

11 Christopher Highley, 'Wales, Ireland, and *Henry IV* ', *Renaissance Drama* n.s. 21 (1990), 94. See also Christopher Highley, *Shakespeare, Spenser and the Crisis in Ireland* (Cambridge: Cambridge University Press, 1997).

12 See Chris Highley, *Shakespeare, Spenser, and the Crisis in Ireland* (Cambridge: Cambridge University Press, 1997), 87.

13 A contemporary account of the Munster campaign, possibly written by Spenser himself, describes the overwhelming of the settlements:

> There came vpp latelie of the Rebells not past 2000. being sent by the said Traitour E: of Tyreone vpon whose ariveall all the Irish rose vpp in Armes against the english which were lately planted theire . . . And going straight vppon the English as they dwelt disparsed before they could assemble themselues spoiled them all, their howses sacked and them selues forced to flie away for safetye . . . (included in *The Works of Edmund Spenser*, 238)

14 Fynes Moryson, *An Itinerary*, 3 parts (London, 1617), II, 24.

15 From William Camden we learn that he departed 'out of London accompanied with a gallant traine of the flower of the Nobility, and saluted by the people with ioyfull acclamations.' Camden's *Annales* was published in an English translation by R. Norton in 1630, under the title *The Historie of the Most Renowned and Victorious Princesse Elizabeth*. This quotation is from IV, 139.

16 Almost all of the Irish references are lacking from the Quarto version of the play, published in 1600. See Annabel Patterson's reading of the differences between the two texts in *Shakespeare and the Popular Voice* (Oxford: Blackwell, 1989). For a facsimile of the Quarto text, see *Shakespeare's Plays in Quarto*, edited by Michael Allen and Kenneth Muir (Berkeley: University of California Press, 1981).

17 David Cairns and Shaun Richards, *Writing Ireland: Colonialism, Nationalism and Culture* (Manchester: Manchester University Press, 1988), 12.

18 *Ibid.*, 10. See also Jonathan Dollimore and Alan Sinfield's analysis of the play in 'History and Ideology: The Instances of *Henry V* ', in *Alternative Shakespeares*, edited by John Drakakis (London: Methuen, 1985), 206–27. Of this scene Dollimore and Sinfield observe: 'the Irish, Welsh and Scottish soldiers manifest not their countries' centrifugal relationship to England but an ideal subservience of margin to centre' (217).

19 Philip Edwards, *Threshold of a Nation: A Study in English and Irish Drama* (Cambridge: Cambridge University Press, 1979), 75–6.

20 For a useful 'historical study of the earliest Irish, Welsh and Scottish characters in English plays', see J. O. Bartley, *Teague, Shenkin and Sawney* (Cork: Cork University Press, 1954). Bartley discusses 'Shakespeare's Irish Soldier' at 16–17.

21 David J. Baker, '"Wildehirissheman": Colonialist Representation in Shakespeare's *Henry V*', *English Literary Renaissance* 22 (1992), 46. See also David J. Baker, *Between Nations: Shakespeare, Spenser, Marvell, and the Question of Britain* (Stanford, CA: Stanford University Press, 1997).

22 Northrop Frye, *Anatomy of Criticism: Four Essays* (1957. Rpt. Princeton, NJ: Princeton University Press, 1971), 44.

23 *Henry V*, edited by Gary Taylor, The Oxford Shakespeare (Oxford: Oxford University Press, 1982), 18.

24 In common with most other editors, Taylor emends 'Ireland' to 'England'. By contrast, Barbara Mowatt and Paul Werstine's edition of the play in the Folger Shakespeare series (New York: Washington Square Press, 1995), retains 'Ireland' here. The Mowatt and Werstine edition includes an astute essay by Michael Neill, '*Henry V*: A Modern Perspective', 253–78.

25 Thomas Gainsford in his *True and Exemplary and Remarkable History of the Earle of Tirone* (London, 1619), in a single paragraph-long sentence, details item by item Essex's progress from his 'priuate parley with Tyrone' to 'how his fortunes and Life ended' (24). On Essex's encounter with O'Neill, see the 'Journall of the L. Lieutenants procedinges from the xxviiith Aug. tyll the viiith of Sept. 1599' included with John Harington's various writings in Harington *Nugae Antiquae, being a collection of original papers in prose and verse* (London: Vernor and Hood, 1804); and John Dymmock, *A Treatise of Ireland*, included *Tracts Relating to Ireland*, edited by Richard Butler (Dublin, 1843). Both accounts present O'Neill as offering Essex virtually a parody of English courtly behaviour in the encounter. Dymmock writes: 'before the Lord Lieutenant was fully aryved . . . Tyrone tooke of his hatt and enclyninge his body did his duty unto his Lordship with very humble ceremony, contynewynge the same observancy the whole tyme of the parlye' (501).

26 Leah Marcus, *Puzzling Shakespeare: Local Reading and Its Discontents* (Berkeley: University of California Press, 1988), 116–48.

27 Most of the texts produced in support of the union cause – for example, the pamphlets written by Francis Bacon, John Hayward, John Thornborough, John Skynner, William Cornwallys and John Gordon, or the literary texts produced by, among others, Samuel Daniel, John Ford and Ben Jonson – focused on the union of the island of Britain, to the exclusion of the realm of Ireland. James himself, in his first speech to the English parliament, imagined the union in terms of a marriage between himself and Britain: 'What God hath conioyned then, let no man separate. I am the Husband, and all the whole Isle is my lawfull Wife.' He goes on to hope that 'no man will be so vnreasonable as to thinke that I that am a Christian King vnder the Gospel, should be a Polygamist and husband to two wiues'. See *The Political Works of James I*, edited by Charles

Howard McIlwain (Cambridge, MA: Harvard University Press, 1918), 272. On Ireland and the Union, see also my *But the Irish Sea Betwixt Us*, chapter 5.

28 Historians and literary critics alike have turned their attention to the complex interaction of multiple political communities in the 'British' Isles (or the 'Atlantic Archipelago', to use a less charged, if more cumbersome, alternative). This work represents a revival of interest in a historiographical model first proposed by J. G. A. Pocock in such studies as 'British History: A Plea for a New Subject', *Journal of Modern History* 47 (1975), 601–28; and 'Limits and Divisions in British History: In Search of the Unknown Subject', *American Historical Review* 87 (1982), 311–36. For a representative collection of essays which deploys this approach in the context of literary analysis, see *British Identities and English Renaissance Literature*, edited by David J. Baker and Willy Maley (Cambridge: Cambridge University Press, 2002).

CHAPTER 2

Welshness in Shakespeare's English histories

Lisa Hopkins

Much recent work on Renaissance senses of history, geography and chorography has stressed the anomalous position of Wales, more foreign than England and less foreign than Ireland, and seen in some sense as the home and locus of a Britishness which is not quite Englishness. As Garrett Sullivan has noted, 'Wales figures for early modern England as that which is both familiar and strange', not least because it is allegedly the Welsh who have transmitted descent from Brut, great-grandson of Aeneas, after whom the island of Britain is allegedly named, and who is thus at once the encapsulation of Britishness and, by reason of his birth in Rome and Trojan ancestry, the extreme case of its alienation from identification with the actual geographical boundaries of Britain.[1] In Shakespeare's histories, Englishness is repeatedly offset and counterpointed by images of Welshness, which often further serve to cushion and deflect a more threatening and problematic association with Irishness. Henry V, confiding in Fluellen, identifies himself as Welsh; Mortimer, sometime heir to the throne of England, marries into a Welsh family, an act which he apparently envisages as strengthening his cause and claim. The Welsh associations of both Henry VII and the powerful Buckingham family are of crucial importance in *Richard III*, and, as is less often noticed, Wales also features in *Henry VIII*, where Anne Boleyn's first step to the crown is her creation as Marchioness of Pembroke, something which is emphasized by that play's chronological closeness to *Cymbeline*, with the open nostalgia of its excursus to Milford Haven, home of the Tudor dynasty, and its praise of early British valour. Finally, Richard II meets his downfall in Wales, which for him serves as a literal halfway stage between England and Ireland.

Images of Welshness serve a number of crucial purposes in Shakespeare's stagings of English history. They enable him to lighten the tone by the introduction of elements of comedy, as with the counterpoint afforded by the Glendower and Fluellen scenes, or to deepen it by incorporating mythical allusions and appealing to a legendary British past. The analogy I will suggest is that in the history plays, Welshness is to Englishness as genre-mixing is in tragedies and comedies, functioning much as the gravedigger does in *Hamlet*, or the death of Olivia's brother in *Twelfth Night*. Critical debate about the histories has often centred on the question of whether Shakespeare celebrates or critiques the past that he stages, and whether *Henry V* in particular is, in Norman Rabkin's celebrated phrase, laudatory 'rabbit' or cynical 'duck'; I would suggest that it is in the double-edgedness and ambiguity of Welshness, which offers an English audience a dual position of simultaneous similarity and estrangement, that the roots of this duality of construction are to be found.[2] If Shakespeare's audience (and later critics) bring to these plays any expectation that what they are being offered is a glorification of their own past from their own perspective, they are rapidly forced to reassess their position as it becomes increasingly apparent that Welshness, and awareness of Welsh perspectives, always inflects unitary and monolithic ideas of Englishness, just as the generic certainties of comedy and tragedy are interrogated within the plays by the persistent allusions to elements of other genres. Beyond even genre, however, is the question of the ultimate mode of the play. History, certainly in Sir Philip Sidney's formulation, appears to be the ultimate realist mode, but the presence of Wales, I shall argue, allows Shakespeare's English histories to transcend realism and aspire to the imaginative breadth of poetry in their narrative strategies as well as in their language.

The Wales of which Shakespeare writes was uneasily poised between enmity – the King of England in *Henry IV, Part One* calls the Prince of Wales 'my nearest and dearest enemy' – and friendship.[3] As Sullivan reminds us, 'even early in Elizabeth's reign Humfrey Lhuyd noted that "you shall finde but few noble men in England, but that the greater parte of their retinew (wherin Englishmen exceed all other nations) are welsh men borne"' ('Civilizing Wales', 9), but in the period of history which Shakespeare stages, as opposed to that at which he wrote (our awareness of this distinction of course setting up a further imaginative gap through which to probe apparent certainties and ideologies), Wales was by no means so successfully absorbed. Although the theory of Lancastrian warfare is expounded at the beginning of *Henry V* as being 'If you would France win, you must with Scotland first begin', it is in fact the Welsh on whom Henry and his brothers first see fit to practise, something of which we are perhaps made particularly aware by the insistent use of the term 'neighbour' to designate England's enemies ('Now, neighbour confines, purge you of your scum!' moans the dying King Henry IV, and the word resonates ominously throughout *Henry V*).[4] Henry IV himself at the beginning of *Henry IV,*

Part One is anxious for any further fighting 'To be commenced in strands afar remote' (*1 Henry IV*, 1.1.4). Therefore, he hopes that his subjects 'Shall now, in mutual well-beseeming ranks, / March all one way' (*1 Henry IV*, 1.1.14–15), but his very choice of words undoes his speech because the March is also the title of the English border with Wales: King Henry's realm is not, as John of Gaunt suggests in *Richard II* and as Rambures in *Henry V* will misname it, '[t]hat island of England', but a more complex, less easily definable territory.[5]

The often-emphasized liminal status of Wales is further inflected by a distinct difference in gender representation. While Welshmen are bluff and valiant (though prone to superstition and to cheese-eating), Welshwomen are threatening, alien presences who typically cannot speak English and who perform acts of depravity and emasculating mutilation on corpses. Elizabeth I herself was referred to by Philip of Spain as 'that Welsh harridan', and her Welsh ancestry was generally much commented on: Ralph A. Griffiths and Roger S. Thomas point in particular to the sudden resurgence of interest in Henry VII during and just before the accession of James, including *The First Booke of the Preservation of King Henry VII* (published in 1599 though unfinished), dedicated to Elizabeth.[6] Attention to the origins of Elizabeth's dynasty, as this suggests, inevitably entailed an accompanying awareness that it would end with her, and a corresponding focus on the queen's problematic virginity, and thus on her gender role as a whole. Jean Howard and Phyllis Rackin suggestively comment that '[t]he presence of a woman on the English throne, like the matter of Wales, haunts the borders of Shakespeare's Lancastrian histories', and the link between these two seemingly very different ideas may in fact be causal rather than accidental; indeed, '[t]he double association of Wales with savagery and with female power had a precedent as ancient as Geoffrey of Monmouth's *Historia Regum Britanniae*, which records that the name *Welsh* derives 'either from their leader Gualo, or from their Queen *Galaes*, or else from their being so barbarous'.[7] The suggestive gender indeterminacy of Gualo/Galaes affects the representation of the principality as a whole. Wales is thus often feminized, as Terence Hawkes observes when he remarks of the singing of Glendower's daughter,

To stress as 'feminine' the narcotic aspect of Welsh, its capacity to create a 'bower of bliss' whose modes dissolve and transcend the male, order-giving boundaries of an English-speaking world, is to draw attention to the culture's larger, subversive, and in a complex sense 'effeminate' role in early modern Britain. Hotspur's 'manly' rejection of such charms – 'I had rather hear Lady my brach howl in Irish'

(III.i.230) – not only reinforces the contrast, it neatly reminds the audience of that larger Celtic world which its own commitment to English and Englishness had long been trying to suppress.[8]

Hawkes goes even further when he speaks of 'a submerged "Welshness" which, perhaps surprisingly, turns out to link Falstaff and Glendower' because 'an element of "effeminacy" characterizes Falstaff . . . set against the project of the creation of a "manly" unity which will form the basis of the emerging British state' ('Bryn Glas', 128): Falstaff not only mutilates the corpse of Hotspur in the thigh, echoing the unspeakable actions of the Welshwomen of which we are so obliquely informed at the outset of the play, but his ultimate destination, according to Mistress Quickly, is the distinctively Welsh bosom of Arthur rather than the biblical one of Abraham, and he is also described by Hal as 'gross as a mountain' (*1 Henry IV*, 2.4.221), echoing the mountainous nature of Wales on which the play so often insists.

Falstaff, however, is not the only figure encoding both feminization and Welshness, for the insistence on the northern affiliations of Hal's father, a former Duke of Lancaster who made his bid for the crown from Ravenspurgh, makes it abundantly obvious that it must be from his *mother* that he is able to claim Welshness (in fact she gave birth to him in a gatehouse tower in Monmouth), and I have argued elsewhere that Fluellen is a figure of particular consolation to Henry V because his lack of a patronymic, something highly unusual in Welsh nomenclature, offers at least a temporary respite from the conflicted paternal relations found elsewhere in the plays.[9] Both parts of *Henry IV* are remarkable for the paucity of actual women, and those who do appear or are mentioned tend – like Wales itself, as I will discuss below – to be the subject of fantasy, like Poins's sister Nell, or of uncertain report (Nell again, and Mistress Quickly), so that the suggestion of a psychological equivalence between the territory of women and the territory of Wales is quite strongly developed.

This would seem to suggest that the gendering of Wales as feminine grants its presence in the history plays an effect loosely equivalent to that of actual women elsewhere in the Shakespearean canon. It is a critical commonplace that men predominate in Shakespeare's tragedies and women in his comedies; feminized Wales, like feminized Falstaff, seems similarly to lighten the tone. If, for instance, there is any truth in the much-repeated story that the *Merry Wives of Windsor* was written at the specific request of Elizabeth I, then it must surely have been supposed that its cheese-eating

Welshman would be received by the part-Welsh queen as a genuinely funny joke, while for my money the funniest riposte in Shakespeare is Hotspur's to Glendower's 'I can call spirits from the vasty deep': 'Why, so can I, or so can any man: / But will they come when you do call for them?' (*1 Henry IV*, 3.1.50–2), which seems to me to be actually structured like a piece of straight man/funny man dialogue. Similarly, Fluellen, who must surely have been played by the same Welsh-accented actor as Glendower and is thus, in the double-haunted world of these plays, his symbolic replacement, is also obviously conceived of as a comic character, even if the joke has worn rather thin over time.

Philip Schwyzer alerts us to a further blurring of geography and gender when he observes that in *Henry IV, Part One* '[t]he Severn attains a symbolic status early on in the play when the blood of the English Mortimer mingles in its waters with that of the Welsh rebel, as it will shortly be mingled again through Mortimer's marriage to Glyndwr's daughter'.[10] The Severn was particularly important because it, along with the Wye, formed one of the few natural and indissoluble markers to show where Wales actually was. In fact, at 3.1.61–6, Shakespeare couples them in precisely this way, as the borders from which Glendower has repelled King Henry: the country, as Garrett Sullivan observes, had not been fully mapped, and Schwyzer points out that '[a]s Shakespeare reminded his audience in *1 Henry IV*, Owain Glyndwr had claimed the entire west bank for his enlarged and independent Cambria'.[11] Wales, it seems, is thus not only itself geographically marginal, but can also stand as a signal or synecdoche for other things which are marginal in other ways, and I want to suggest that it does so not only in the question of gender but also in that fundamentally interwoven one of genre.

This troubled realm with its dual nature is of course the perfect principality for the most double-edged of all the characters in Shakespeare's histories, Hal. At the end of *Henry IV, Part Two*, as Hal finally (after several false starts) prepares to succeed his father, the dying Henry IV advises him to consolidate the unity of his realm by giving it a firmly externalized enemy, France. In a sense, though, the advice is redundant, and acts more as a final ironic testimony to Henry IV's failure ever to understand his son than as a genuine political testament, for it is what Hal has been doing all along. His mode of establishing his selfhood has from the outset been by alternately incorporating and rejecting selected others: poised between Hotspur and Falstaff like a character in a medieval psychomachia, and sharing with at least one of them a relationship explicitly structured by reference to the language and conventions of the morality play – 'that reverend Vice, that grey Iniquity, that Father Ruffian, that Vanity in years' (*1 Henry IV*, 2.4.441–2) – he has fundamentally departed from those traditions by definitively siding with neither but rather by proceeding by the revolutionary method of analysis, dissection and highly selective internalization of aspects of both. This, of course, is closely analogous to the mechanisms by which the embryonic British Empire was attempting to establish itself: England did not want to cast off Wales and Ireland, but to assimilate them, while at the same time purging them of unpalatable qualities. Not only are we told in *Henry V* that 'wholesome berries thrive and ripen best / Neighboured by fruit of baser quality' (1.1.61–2), but the very status of the British crown as imperial rather than merely kingly, on which the plays repeatedly insist (*1 Henry IV*, 4.5.42, *Henry V* 1.2.35, 5.2.233 and Epilogue 8), depended on there being more than one kingdom in the king of England's realms – otherwise the king can never be so good a gentleman as the emperor (*Henry V*, 4.1.42–3). This method of assimilation is much how Hal will try to win round the Earl of Douglas after the battle of Shrewsbury (*1 Henry IV*, 5.5.29–31), a parallel between individuals and countries to which Andrew Murphy draws implicit attention when he observes: '[t]he construction of the image of the nation is . . . in the first instance intimately bound up with the construction of Henry himself as a unified subject. Out of the dissonance and dissidence of Prince Hal arises the appearance of unitary coherence of the King.'[12] Thus while Falstaff is effectively a human waste disposal unit, and Hotspur travesties food consumption by his killing 'some six or seven dozen of Scots at a breakfast' (*1 Henry IV*, 2.4.101–2), Hal, bucking the system of contrasts between Carnival and Lent which may appear to have been set up, imitates neither. Similarly, he deviates significantly from the fixture of identity emblematized by these two extremes by being Welsh only when he wants to be and, in a move which seems to me perfectly to capture and indeed arguably to inaugurate modern conceptions of national identity, slipping effortlessly into other identities when they suit him better. As Willy Maley points out: '[i]t pleases his majesty to "preserve" his "Welsh plood" no longer than is politically expedient. His earlier battle cry: "God for Harry! England and Saint George!" made no mention of Wales or Saint David.'[13]

Towards the beginning of *Henry IV, Part One*, Hal occupies that distinctively Welsh identity of a Trojan, when Gadshill tells the Chamberlain, 'Tut, there are other Troyans that thou dreamest not of, the which for sport sake are content to do the profession some grace, that would, if matters should be looked into, for their own credit sake make all whole' (*1 Henry IV*, 2.2.70–4). In Part Two, however, it is the rebel Northumberland who identifies himself with the Trojans when he compares Morton to the one who 'Drew

Priam's curtain in the dead of night / And would have told him half his
Troy was burnt' (*2 Henry IV*, 1.1.72–3), while Hal has already been forcefully
identified with the traditional enemies of the Trojans, the Greeks, first as a
'Corinthian' (*1 Henry IV*, 2.4.11) and then when Vernon tells Hotspur that
Hal mounted his horse, 'As if an angel dropped down from the clouds /
To turn and wind a fiery Pegasus' (*1 Henry IV*, 4.1.109–10). And yet no
sooner has Vernon uttered this praise than he adds to it another line which
may not sit entirely harmoniously with it: 'And witch the world with noble
horsemanship' (*1 Henry IV*, 4.1.110). 'Witch' may not only be an obviously
effeminizing word which also sets up a sharp clash with the 'angel' of two
lines earlier; it may, too, remind us that echoes of magical Wales are perhaps not to be shaken off at will, just as even in his transition from Prince
of Wales to King of England Hal finds dangerous difficulty in casting off
playfulness as he once again falls into the habit of playing to a line only to
catch himself just in time:

> know the grave doth gape
> For thee thrice wider than for other men.
> Reply not to me with a fool-born jest.
> (*2 Henry IV*, 5.5.56–8)

In these protean shifts Hal's role as Prince of Wales, and his subsequent move
from that to King of England, are crucial. It has often been remarked that
in *Henry V*, there is considerable slippage between France and Ireland.[14]
It is less often noticed that Wales has already functioned as the practice
ground on which some of those dangerous equivalences and tensions have
already been played out, with 'the French and Welsh' coupled as the enemy
(*2 Henry IV*, 1.3.79), both having mountains (*Henry V*, 4.2.28), members
of both nations notable for boasting, and Henry V's French wife speaking
only marginally more English than Mortimer's Welsh one (Katherine and
Lady Mortimer might even have been played by the same boy actor). I use
the word 'played' for this process advisedly because although I think a fully-
blown Turnerian anthropological analysis of the liminal configuration of
England and Wales is only partially relevant to early modern understandings
of the relationship between the two countries, I do think that Shakespeare's
representation of Wales and of its role in the life of the English kings he
depicts is structured by a sense of it as offering a different form of psychological space from that of the rational agendas of everyday life. For Shakespeare,
I would suggest, and perhaps for wider sections of his culture as a whole,
Wales's status as physically marginal makes it prone to being treated as
psychologically marginal too, a place where rationality is prone to sudden,
violent, almost Gothic encounters with its Others. In France, English boys

will be killed in the bloody hinterland of Agincourt; in Wales, English men will be hideously mutilated, but only after they are dead – almost as though what happens to them is in some sense understood as something incompatible with full consciousness, a haunting emblem of the periphery of the mind. It is violence so horrible that it literally cannot be spoken of, rather as the speech and song of Mortimer's Welsh wife also cannot be scripted and remains for ever opaque (*1 Henry IV*, 3.1.185ff.); Shakespeare never actually and explicitly tells his audience what happened to the bodies, since it 'may not be / Without much shame retold or spoken of' (*1 Henry IV*, 1.1.45–6), but seems to rely on them to know this, as part of a common cultural framework, something which further suggests the almost fairy-tale affiliations of Wales. (Similarly in *Henry V* the story behind the wearing of leeks is referred to without ever being elaborated upon.) The closest that Westmorland can come to describing it, 'beastly shameless transformation' (*1 Henry IV*, 1.1.44), is even more suggestive in this sense, since the word 'transformation', particularly in conjunction with 'beastly', gestures so strongly in the direction of an Ovidian metamorphosis.

Indeed at one point in *Henry IV, Part One* Shakespeare may well appear to be deliberately equating Wales with a land of mythology when Falstaff calls Glendower 'he of Wales that gave Amamon the bastinado, and made Lucifer cuckold, and swore the devil his own liegeman upon the cross of a Welsh hook' (2.4.229–31), because there may just possibly be an allusion here to one of the Welsh legends recorded in *The Mabinogion*. Of course it is impossible to be sure of the status or even the existence of the various component parts of *The Mabinogion* before their collation by Lady Charlotte Guest in the nineteenth century, but there are some possible similarities between Falstaff's rather unusual insult and the story of Pwyll, Prince of Dyfed. Pwyll is induced by Arawn, ruler of the underworld, to change places with him for a year. Each takes the other's shape, and no one suspects the deception; however, Arawn's wife is surprised to find that the false Arawn refrains from sleeping with her for the whole year. When the true Arawn discovers Pwyll's self-restraint in this, he is very impressed (since Pwyll is, at this point of the story, unmarried, the issue of reciprocity does not arise here). Pwyll's celibacy bulks quite large in the narrative, and the story as a whole seems to provide the closest mythological analogue for the image of cuckolding the devil, although, since Pwyll did *not* – at least in the version which has come down to us – cuckold Arawn, it is by no means a close fit.

There is, however, at least one certain association of the Welsh with the world of sleep and the unconscious to which Falstaff, squire of the night, has such easy access, and which remains so stubbornly closed to Henry IV.[15] Glendower translates Lady Mortimer's words to her husband as,

> She bids you on the wanton rushes lay you down,
> And rest your gentle head upon her lap,
> And she will sing the song that pleaseth you,
> And on your eyelids crown the god of sleep,
> Charming your blood with pleasing heaviness.
>
> (*1 Henry IV*, 3.1.207–11)

Again Wales is envisioned here as offering access to the realm of dreams, just as the appearance of the ghosts to Richard III at Bosworth makes his subsequent defeat by a Welsh-led army look uncannily like the return of the repressed, with soldiers advancing on him from the place of his dreams. In keeping with this emphasis on Wales as a territory of the fantastic is the remarkable fact that although we hear so much about it during the course of *Henry IV, Part One*, events there never actually threaten the security of England at all, and later even Fluellen, apparently so steeped in military theory, makes a really startling misjudgement of war-related matters when he praises so extravagantly the braggardly Pistol.

Since the second play in the series actually opens with the figure of Rumour, who explicitly informs us that many of the things we hear are likely to be false, it is perhaps unsurprising that many of the things we hear about Wales in Part One turn out to be false, or, at best, misleading – something which is appropriate given that Rumour descends fairly clearly from the Virgilian figure of Fama, and it is Virgil who sings of the Aeneas whose great-grandson Brut (according, ironically enough, to fame) founds that British community of which traces survived mainly in Wales. It is, therefore, unsurprising that the Wales of the play is imaged as an inaccessible, romantic-sounding place of 'barren mountains' (*1 Henry IV*, 1.3.88) apparently inhabited only by goats (*1 Henry IV*, 3.1.36) and of a Severn as personified as any river of classical mythology, who 'hid his crisp head in the hollow bank' (*1 Henry IV*, 1.3.105), rather than any of the perfectly populous towns of which Shakespeare must surely have heard (and if he had not the obviously Welsh-speaking actor who is required to play Lady Mortimer could have informed him).

There is also another thing worthy of note about Hotspur's evocative description of the Severn: he is unique in gendering the river masculine. Said to have been named after the drowned British princess Sabrina, it is consistently feminine in Renaissance writing. Hotspur's departure from this strongly marked tradition might be due to a number of factors. In the first place, he is not noted for his sensitivity either to learning, of which he shows no evidence at all, or to rivers, since he will later want to move the river Trent in order to ensure what he feels is a more equitable division of land (*1 Henry IV*, 3.1.97–9), something which appals Glendower, in the demarcation of whose territories rivers have played so important a part (*1 Henry IV*, 3.1.102). More subtly, we may be being deliberately invited to register Hotspur as making an error here, because the king is about to challenge the veracity of everything else he says. No sooner has Hotspur finished his blow-by-blow account of the fierce hand-to-hand combat between his brother-in-law Mortimer and the latter's future father-in-law Glendower than Henry IV says flatly,

> Thou dost belie him, Percy, thou dost belie him;
> He never did encounter with Glendower.
> I tell thee, he durst as well have met the devil alone
> As Owen Glendower for an enemy.
>
> (*1 Henry IV*, 1.3.112–15)

This is an unusual moment in Shakespeare, because we do not know whom to believe. In one way, this could be seen as prefiguring that later non-existent fight between Falstaff and Hotspur which lasts a long hour by Shrewsbury clock (especially since both are measured in terms of an hour – Glendower's and Mortimer's, according to Hotspur, lasting 'the best part of an hour' [*1 Henry IV*, 1.3.99]), or the eleven men in buckram; but in both those later cases there can be no doubt of which version of events is actually true. Here there is no such epistemological security, and the matter is never clarified. We are left simply with a long and rather charming account of a fight, without actually knowing whether it ever occurred or not – not a bad analogue for the entire Matter of Britain material, indeed.

This unreliability of information about Wales is signalled from the outset of the *Henriad*. In the opening scene of Part One, Henry IV informs the audience (not his court because, as he himself remarks, they already know) that he would like to go on pilgrimage to Jerusalem. He then asks Westmorland:

> What yesternight our Council did decree
> In forwarding this dear expedience,

to which Westmorland replies:

> My liege, this haste was hot in question,
> And many limits of the charge set down
> But yesternight, when all athwart there came
> A post from Wales, loaden with heavy news.
>
> (*1 Henry IV*, 1.1.32–7)

Some of the news is so 'heavy' that Westmorland is, as we have just seen, forced to censor it, but it seems to be quite clearly implied that whatever it is, it sabotaged the discussion of the king's plan to go abroad. Westmorland then reveals that he has some more news, this time from Scotland, but that he does not know the full story:

> For he that brought them, in the very heat
> And pride of their contention, did take horse,
> Uncertain of the issue any way.
>
> (*1 Henry IV*, 1.1.59–61)

Rather surprisingly, however, King Henry turns out to know all about this already, and is indeed able to inform Westmorland on the subject, because Sir Walter Blunt has outstripped the messenger, even though he had waited for the end of the fight before setting out. The impression created is thus that 'news from Scotland' seems to travel much faster, more reliably and by a greater variety of routes than that from Wales. Even more surprisingly, though, it turns out to be this later news, rather than that from Wales, which will mean that King Henry's plans for a pilgrimage will have to be postponed, for Harry Percy 'sends me word' (1.1.93) – whether by Blunt or by still a third messenger is not clear – that he refuses his prisoners, and Henry says,

> But I have sent for him to answer this,
> And for this cause awhile we must neglect
> Our holy purpose to Jerusalem.
>
> (*1 Henry IV*, 1.1.99–101)

Wales, it turns out, has nothing to do with it; the real threat is Hotspur, just as later all the build-up to Glendower being a wizard will instantly evaporate. Henry introduces him to us as 'that great magician, damned Glendower' (*1 Henry IV*, 1.3.82), but Glendower's impressive 'at my birth / The frame and huge foundation of the earth / Shaked like a coward', is comprehensively debunked by Hotspur's immediate, disbelieving riposte:

> Why, so it would have done
> At the same season if your mother's cat
> Had but kittened, though yourself had never been born.
>
> (*1 Henry IV*, 3.1.15–17)

Again, what is reported from Wales is not believed by at least one of its hearers, just as when Hotspur complains of Glendower that

> Sometime he angers me
> With telling me of the moldwarp and the ant,
> Of the dreamer Merlin and his prophecies,
> And of a dragon and a finless fish,
> A clip-winged griffin and a moulten raven,
> A couching lion and a ramping cat,
> And such a deal of skimble-skamble stuff
> As puts me from my faith.
>
> (*1 Henry IV*, 3.1.142–9)

In a nice parallel touch, the first time that we hear Hal mentioned in the play is when his father says,

> O that it could be proved
> That some night-tripping fairy had exchanged
> In cradle-clothes our children where they lay.
>
> (*1 Henry IV*, 1.1.85–7)

For both Wales and its prince, the idea of magic is thus evoked only to be immediately dismissed. Finally, even the reasons for Glendower's failure to appear at the final battle are obscured: Vernon says, 'I learned in Worcester as I rode along / He cannot draw his power this fourteen days' (*1 Henry IV*, 4.1.125–6), but the Archbishop of York's version is that Glendower 'comes not in, o'er ruled by prophecies' (*1 Henry IV*, 4.4.16). As so often with matters Welsh in the play, we never learn the truth of the matter, but either way Glendower's absence, coupled with the similar – and similarly unexplained – failure of Mortimer to appear either (*1 Henry IV*, 4.4.23), means that once again Wales poses only an illusory rather than an actual threat. And when Warwick in Part Two assures the king that 'I have received / A certain instance that Glendower is dead' (3.1.99–100), at least some members of the audience would presumably have known that what had become of Glendower had in fact remained a mystery which has still never been solved.

This repeated pattern of threat and withdrawal of danger thus makes the violence associated with Wales come to seem symbolic rather than actual, something which one might compare with the disappearing Welsh army in *Richard II* and also with the obviously emblematic figure of the Mower who in Marlowe's *Edward II* betrays the king in Neath. Coupled with the references to the morality tradition in *Henry IV, Part One* and with that play and its sequel's unusually high number of references to religion, particularly those which insist on the ways in which characters are beset by things that can 'divide / The action of their bodies from their souls', the overall impression becomes definitively one of a psychomachia (*2 Henry IV*, 1.1.183–4; see also the fragmented bodies of *Henry V*, 4.1.131–2 and 4.3.85–9). It is therefore suggestive that the final battle, complete with its significant absences, is insistently imaged in terms so redolent of psychological rather than actual conflict: on a field where Hal and his father will at least temporarily redefine their relationship, the king has numerous substitutes impersonating him, and the dying Hotspur eerily morphs into his ostensible opposite Glendower as he contradicts all he has previously maintained by saying 'O, I could prophesy' (*1 Henry IV*, 5.4.82). When Falstaff says 'I am not a double-man' after Hal has wondered 'is it fantasy that plays upon our eyesight' (*1 Henry IV*, 5.4.133 and 136), we might well believe that we are firmly in the realm of the Gothic (an effect hardly lessened by reference in Part Two to a character actually called Double (*2 Henry IV*, 3.2.39), the presence there of two characters called Bardolph, the Lord Chief Justice's mention of 'a second body' for the king (*2 Henry IV*, 5.2.90), and the new king's suggestion that he and his father have changed places (*2 Henry IV*, 5.2.123–4), and when King Henry announces at the end of the battle 'Myself and you, son Harry, will towards Wales' (*1 Henry IV*, 5.5.41), ostensibly to fight a battle which nothing has previously suggested actually needs to be fought, we are surely in no doubt about the psychologized status of warfare in Wales.

There is, moreover, one final effect of Shakespeare's insistence on tempering his presentation of English history by a stress on Welshness which is further reinforced by what I have been suggesting is this status of Wales as a place of collective cultural fantasy. Wales is above all a point of origins: it is the home of the Tudor dynasty, location of the Arthurian legends and of the myth of British descent from the great-grandson of Trojan Aeneas. It is, therefore, unsurprising that the Welsh characters in the plays are so often identified with the past: the 'out of fashion' Fluellen (*Henry V*, 4.1.82) harks back to classical wars and to Alexander the Great, and Glendower exhibits a superstitiousness which even Hotspur, hardly noted for his adherence to the modern, seems to consider outmoded. But while Welshness is thus constituted as nostalgia, the plays' allegiance to change and their faith in the future must always be rendered provisional, as indeed is clearly signalled when the glories of the marriage between Henry V and Katherine of France are immediately shadowed by the Chorus's foretelling of the disastrous reign of their son (not to mention the audience's knowledge that it will be the child of Katherine's second marriage, to a Welshman, who will ultimately found the Tudor dynasty). A return to the past is in fact encoded into Shakespeare's history plays by the very sequence of their composition, which not only disregards but actually inverts the procession of chronological time: *Henry V* is written after *Henry VI*, and many critics would argue that even the three parts of *Henry VI* were composed out of their apparent order, with Part One postdating Parts Two and Three. This may well seem to be yet another manifestation of the Backward Glance which is so fundamental a feature of a distinctively late-sixteenth and early-seventeenth mentality. A history play is of course by definition a piece of sustained engagement with the past, but to stress Welshness, with its associated nostalgia, suggests the strength of the grip of that past on our present and its imaginative attraction for us at the same time as it makes it strange. To emphasize the Welshness of the past is to make it, literally, another country, and to emphasize the importance of that other country in the collective imagination of contemporary England is perhaps one of Shakespeare's most powerful revelations of the otherness at the heart of all selfhood: as Hawkes notes, Fluellen's 'Welsh "accent" unexpectedly homes in on and ignites explosive material at the heart of some of the English words', and he wonders specifically '[d]oes Fluellen's Welsh accent effectively turn on those who have been laughing at it here? Does it unveil, in "Alexander the Pig", a glimpse of a potential "beastly transformation" dormant yet potent at the heart of the new Britain as corrosively as it was at the old? Does a sow-like Falstaff stalk even this field?'[16] Can England, in short, ever escape from its Welshness – or would to do so actually make it less than England?

NOTES

1 Garrett Sullivan, 'Civilizing Wales: *Cymbeline*, Roads and the Landscape of Early Modern Britain', *Early Modern Literary Studies* 4:2. The Internet address of this issue of the journal is http://purl.oclc.org/emls/04-2/sullshak.html.

2 Norman Rabkin, 'Rabbits, Ducks and *Henry V* ', *Shakespeare Quarterly* 28 (1977), 279–96.

3 *Henry IV, Part One*, edited by P. H. Davison (Harmondsworth: Penguin, 1968), 3.2.123. Further references to the play in the text will be to this edition.

4 *Henry IV, Part Two*, edited by P. H. Davison (Harmondsworth: Penguin, 1977), 4.5.124. Further references to the play in the text will be to this edition.

5 William Shakespeare, *Henry V*, edited by A. R. Humphreys (Harmondsworth: Penguin, 1968), 3.7.137–8, 4.5.124. Further references to the play in the text will be to this edition.

6 Ralph A. Griffiths and Roger S. Thomas, *The Making of the Tudor Dynasty* (1985. Rpt. Gloucester: Alan Sutton, 1987), 2.

7 Jean E. Howard and Phyllis Rackin, *Engendering a Nation: A Feminist Account of Shakespeare's English Histories* (London and New York: Routledge, 1997), 168 and 169.

8 Terence Hawkes, 'Bryn Glas', in *Post-Colonial Shakespeares*, edited by Ania Loomba and Martin Orkin (London: Routledge, 1998), 117–40 (pp. 124–25). The essay is also included in Terence Hawkes, *Shakespeare in the Present*, Accents on Shakespeare (New York and London: Routledge, 2002), 23–45.

9 See Lisa Hopkins, 'Fluellen's Name', *Shakespeare Studies* 24 (1996), 148–55.

10 Philip Schwyzer, 'A Map of Greater Cambria', *Early Modern Literary Studies* 4:2 http://purl.oclc.org/emls/04-2/schwamap.html.

11 *Ibid.*

12 Andrew Murphy, *But the Irish Sea Betwixt Us: Ireland, Colonialism, and Renaissance Literature* (Lexington: The University Press of Kentucky, 1999), 114.

13 Willy Maley, '"This sceptred isle": Shakespeare and the British Problem', in *Shakespeare and National Culture*, edited by John J. Joughin (Manchester: Manchester University Press, 1997), 83–108 (p. 103).

14 See for instance Joel Altman, '"Vile Participation": The Amplification of Violence in The Theater of *Henry V*', *Shakespeare Quarterly* 42 (1991), 13; Michael Neill, 'Broken English and Broken Irish: Nation, Language, and the Optic of Power in Shakespeare's Histories', *Shakespeare Quarterly* 45:1 (1994), 22; William Shakespeare, *Henry V*, edited by Gary Taylor (Oxford: Clarendon Press, 1994), 7; and Andrew Murphy, '"'Tish ill done": *Henry the Fift* and the Politics of Editing', and my own 'Neighbourhood in *Henry V*', both in *Shakespeare and Ireland: History, Politics, Culture*, edited by Mark Thornton Burnett and Ramona Wray (Basingstoke: Macmillan, 1997), respectively 213–34 and 9–26.

15 This inaccessibility is described to us in a passage which explicitly genders sleep feminine. See *2 Henry IV*, 3.1.6.

16 Hawkes, 'Bryn Glas', 134 and 135.

CHAPTER 3

A French history of Henry V

Jean-Michel Déprats

On 9 July 1999, the first French production of *Henry V*, directed by Jean-Louis Benoit, and featuring Philippe Torreton in the title role, was premiered at the Cour d'Honneur du Palais des Papes in Avignon, almost exactly four centuries after it was written by Shakespeare and performed on the Elizabethan stage.[1] This date will remain as a landmark in the history of Shakespeare's reception in France, as until 1999, *Henry V* was the only history play that had never before been performed in French. The celebrated 1975 production by the RSC (directed by Terry Hands and starring Alan Howard as King Henry) did come on tour for a few performances at the Théâtre de l'Odéon, but these were obviously in what the French call 'la langue de Shakespeare'. To the best of my knowledge, before the Avignon production, no French professional, or even amateur, theatre company had ever planned to present Shakespeare's epic on the French stage.

Is it because the British 'National Anthem in five acts', as Trevor Nunn calls it, celebrates a military defeat over the French, displays anti-French feelings and assaults Gallic national pride?[2] Indeed, one cannot ignore the element of xenophobia – notably anti-French xenophobia – in Shakespeare's plays, yet, nowadays, broad-minded aloofness on this point prevails, together with allowance made for old-time mentalities. My hypothesis is rather that French directors shirk from staging *Henry V* because of its dominant heroic note and jingoistic politics. *Henry V* does not square with their Jan Kott-inspired notion of Shakespeare's exposure of power politics stripped of all kind of mythology. The idea of Shakespeare's disillusioned outlook on the violence of history is indeed questioned in his most idealized and patriotic play, one which can be judged as less dialectic and ambiguous than the eight history plays that preceded it.

For modern audiences, before Kenneth Branagh's film of 1989 explored the darker, rawer elements of the piece, the abiding image of *Henry V* was provided by Laurence Olivier's famous film version (1944), which, it must be remembered, was financed by the British government as a piece of wartime propaganda. In it, the most unpleasant references to Henry were cut, and the chief concern was with the English military success. But despite the powerful Elizabethan pageantry and chivalric splendour of this extraordinary film, its apparent nationalistic and militaristic emphasis created a great deal of suspicion and doubt about the value, relevance and topicality of the play for a late twentieth-century audience. By emphasizing significant scenes that the Olivier film had chosen to downplay (the conspirators scene at Southampton, and the savage threat to the Governor of Harfleur, where the king talks of possible rape and infanticide), and by turning the play into an uncompromising debate about war and the nature of leadership, Branagh alerted his audience to the complexity and ambiguity contained in the play.

My first in-depth involvement with the play goes back to 1990, when Gérard Depardieu, wildly enthusiastic about Branagh's film, asked me to translate the text for the French dubbed version (he lent his voice to Henry in that version). Branagh's screen adaptation reduces the play by more than one third. In particular, it cuts out the not very funny leek scene, most of the Fluellen–Pistol antagonism, the exchange between Henry and Burgundy in Act 5, Elizabethan linguistic obscurities in the Boar's Head scenes, as well as plot repetitions. Yet, whereas most Shakespeare films resort to a great deal of reshuffling, Branagh's screenplay does keep Shakespeare's text in a strictly chronological order. Before adapting my translation to the constraints of dubbing, I worked according to my usual method.[3] I aimed for a French version that would be both accurate and theatrically dynamic.[4] But, over and above the more common difficulties of Shakespearean translation, *Henry V* confronts one with specific linguistic problems and oddities that baffle the French translator, leaving him at many points with little choice but to adapt, transpose, recreate, 'undertranslating' in some instances (dealing with dialectical accents), or leaving it to the actors to translate the untranslatable.[5]

Some passages of *Henry V* defy not only translation but even comprehension, seemingly suffering from the Babylonian curse. One such instance is Pistol's macaronic line: 'Qualtitie calmie custure me' (Folio), responding to the French prisoner, Monsieur Le Fer's 'Je pense que vous estes le Gentilhomme de bon qualitee' (Folio spelling). Publishers, commentators and translators still wonder what this word pudding is supposed to mean. According to Warburton (1747), Pistol actually says 'Qualtitie call you me, construe me!' or perhaps even 'Qualtitie, cullion, construe me!' Some later commentators have suggested the odd statement may be in Irish. As Sylvère Monod states, 'Pistol begins by repeating a twisted version of the last word he has heard, then, so as not to be wanting in jargon, he cites the first words of an Irish song, as it appears in printed form around 1565 (in Clement Robinson's *Handeful of Pleasant Delites*). The exact text, identified in 1939 by Pr. Gérard Murphy, is "Caílín ó tSiúre mé" (I am a maid from the river Suir).'[6] Both J. H. Walter, in the 1954 Arden edition, and T. W. Craik, in the 1995 Arden edition, point to an Irish origin too, but they trace Pistol's 'calmie custure me' to a deformation of 'Cailin ôg a' stor' (young maid, my treasure).

The following play on the words 'moi' and 'moy' poses the same type of questions:

FRENCH SOLDIER O prenez miséricorde! Ayez pitié de moi!
PISTOL Moy shall not serve, I will have forty moys.

(4.4.10–11)

According to Andrew Gurr, 'Pistol hears the French "moi" (pronounced as "moy" in Middle French) as a half, a moiety.'[7] But for J. H. Walter and Gary Taylor, 'moy' refers to a unit of measure roughly equivalent to a bushel.[8] Other commentators argue that, Pistol having talked about a ransom, he believes it is a currency.[9] Probably, though, it is not the Portuguese *moidore*, since this was not introduced into England until the eighteenth century.[10]

In fact, the whole scene is interspersed with instances of bilingual word-play, more or less subtle, but all based on Pistol's miscomprehension. One instance plays on the French word 'bras' and the English word 'brass'[11] Another case turns on the prisoner's name, Monsieur Le Fer, to which Pistol responds with a series of homophonic terms: 'Master Fer? I'll fer him, and firk him, and ferret him.'[12] In this scene, all the comic effects stem from the communication problems due to the linguistic barrier. The French soldier speaks French, the Boy speaks to Pistol in English and to the prisoner in French, and of course, Pistol speaks English, even if he begins one of his lines with 'Owy, cuppele gorge permafoy', which he does seem to understand. Even then, to say that the French soldier and the Boy speak French is to simplify matters a lot. They speak an odd lingua franca, half sixteenth-century French, half gobbledegook, made up by Shakespeare with the main aim to entertain a British audience.

Four scenes or sequences pose particular translation problems. They are, in chronological order:

The dialectal scene (3.3) between three officers: one is Welsh (Fluellen), one is Irish (Macmorris), and the third is Scottish (Jamy); and all speak in regional-specific ways.

The scene of the English lesson between Katharine and Alice (3.5),
in which the drive to find obscenities in the foreign language runs
throughout (as we all know, language learning begins with the 'dirty
words').

The scene we have already discussed (4.4), between Pistol, Monsieur Le
Fer and the Boy, often cut in performance, the actors regarding it as
the result of Shakespeare's all-too complacent punning.

The wooing scene (5.2), in which Shakespeare intertwines Katharine's
and Alice's broken English and odd French, together with Henry's
poorly mastered French, into a more standard, 'Shakespearean'
English.

The three French scenes are characterized by the presence of an interpreter
or translator: Alice in 3.5 and 5.2, and the Boy in 4.4. The metalinguistic
aspect of these scenes is especially marked since they involve language-
learning, translation exercises and bilingual puns, all of which combine to
raise questions and puzzlement on the borders of languages. The linguistic exchanges, taking the form of negotiations and mediations, symbolize
instances of political power play. This is, perhaps, never more clearly visible than in Katharine's line: 'I cannot speak your England' (5.2.102–3). The
mastery, or lack of mastery, of foreign languages situates the characters in
an interplay of political forces led by the British desire for domination.

In the tragic scenes, the French language only appears briefly, and,
one could say, decoratively. Besides a citation from the Bible – when the
Dauphin states that 'Le chien est retourné à son propre vomissement et la
truie lavée au bourbier'[13] – it mostly takes the form of exclamations: the
Dauphin: 'O Dieu vivant!' (3.6.5); Bourbon: 'Mort de ma vie' (3.6.11);
Constable: 'Dieu des batailles' (3.6.15); Constable: 'O diable!' (4.5.1);
Orléans: 'O Seigneur! Le jour est perdu, tout est perdu!' (4.5.2.); the
Dauphin: 'Mort de ma vie! . . . O méchante fortune' (4.5.3–6); and the
Dauphin: 'Ch' ha! . . . Le cheval volant, *the Pegasus*, qui a des narines
de feu' (3.8). The comic scenes use instances of wordplay which only an
audience with a knowledge of both languages can fully understand. As
Jean-Claude Sallé writes:

The use of the French language in several scenes reveals the same critical awareness,
the same questioning of theatrical conventions [as does the presence of a Chorus].
Indeed, the bilingualism may seem required by the subject: eighteen of the twenty-
three scenes in the play take place in France. But in the first part of *Henry IV*,
the characters who speak in Welsh do so on the side (3.1), during an interlude
which remains outside of the English dialogue, as the Welsh text is not given.
Henry V is thus exceptional in taking a double stand: the decision to follow the
tacit convention according to which the audience will not be surprised if one party

speaks the enemy's language, and at the same time, the position of realism, which allows for comic effects due to the problems of communication across the language barrier.[14]

While the French king speaks in English, Shakespeare has the three other French characters, Alice, Katharine and Monsieur Le Fer, speak a half-authentic, half-fanciful French. But it is not irrelevant that these three characters are two women and a prisoner: the defeated speak French, the conquerors speak English. And thus, the telling scene in which Henry tries to conquer the heart of the French princess Katharine, turns into a linguistic battle meant to reaffirm the supremacy of the English language.

Faced with this complexity, the French translator has to decide between two perhaps equally failing alternatives. On the one hand, the decision to retain the original French – which is, after all, full of fancy and charm, even if at the cost of a certain chaos – will result in only three characters speaking a bizarre French: the princess of France, her attendant lady and a captured officer, while all of the British characters speak a fully understandable modern French! On the other hand, to 'translate' Shakespeare's French into twentieth-century French loses most of that exotic and exquisite lingo's sweetness and old-fashioned colouration. For the dubbing of Branagh's film, I had opted for the first alternative, because it was a British film with British actors. For Jean-Louis Benoit's staging, I decided to go with the second alternative: to translate Shakespeare's French into modern French.

Another option would be to translate the whole play into sixteenth-century French, but this proves more theoretical than actually practical, as the resulting literary curiosity would not lend itself to a viable performance for today. What's more, this would only manage to disguise the fundamental untranslatability of the effect of a foreign language inserted within a given text. Whichever alternative is resorted to, any translation of *Henry V* into French erases the bilingualism of the play. As Ton Hoenselaars forcefully states: 'With a macaronic, Babylonian text, it is impossible to provide a fully convincing and satisfying translation.'[15]

Most translators acknowledge this impossibility, and give as is, if sometimes in italics (which lose all meaning in performance), the parts in 'Shakespearean French', correcting the more glaring errors without rewriting the text. Geneviève and Daniel Bournet, two translators from Marseilles, are the only ones to have translated Shakespeare's peculiar French into medieval French. In a note, they explain their choice:

In a French translation, the distance between Katharine's language and the words she is learning obviously runs the risk of vanishing. The idea of a theatre performance in French demands that this distance be kept. Given that theatrical

Figure 1. Philippe Torreton as Henry V. Dir. Jean-Louis Benoit. Festival d'Avignon 1999.

convention allows Shakespeare's English to be turned into French for the French stage, and given that the princess and her attendant are medieval French characters, we shall transcribe the few English words into modern French, and Katharine and Alice's lines into old French, which, one can surmise, will have for a French audience, the exotic character of French words for an English audience.[16]

Accordingly, Katharine's English lesson becomes a lesson in modern French – this is how it begins:

Kath. Alice, tu fus chieux les Anglois, et tu ben paroles li langaige.
Al. Alques, madame.
Kath. Jo toi prie m'enseigniez, me faust apenre à paroler . . . Coument est appeled le paulme, en anglois?
Al. Le paulme? Il est appeled 'main'.
Kath. 'Main'? Et li deies?
Al. Li deies? Meie feid, jo m'oblie li deies, mes me sovenira. Li deies? Jo crei que sont appeled 'doives'. Oïl, 'doives'.
Kath. Le paulme, 'main'. Li deies, 'doives'. Jo crei que jo suis li buen escoulier. J'ai gaigned dous moz anglois vistement. Coument est appeled les grifz?
Al. Les grifz? Nos les appelons 'oncles'.
Kath. 'Oncles'. Oyez, diste-mei se jo parole ben: 'main', 'doives', 'oncles'.
Al. Cel est ben dist, madame; forz buen anglois![17]

At the very least, it is a 'forz buen françois' that was to be expected here. But given how far into crazy inventiveness the translators have got, common sense is hardly de rigueur anymore. No doubt, this medieval version of *Henry V* is rather delightful, but its paradoxical result is that Katharine and Alice's French is a lot less understandable than even the original was. What's more, this translation option greatly accentuates the contrast between on the one hand the French princess and her attendant, and, on the other, the rest of the characters who speak in a twentieth-century French. One cannot uphold both linguistic truthfulness and theatrical convention.

But, to just what extent is Shakespeare's French historically accurate? Sometimes a little too taken to the cult of the Bard, many British editors are very willing to excuse Shakespeare's mistakes and fanciful statements, often in fact praising his French. Thus, in the New Cambridge edition, Andrew Gurr writes:

Shakespeare may have acquired his French from the Mountjoy family, with whom he is known to have lodged in 1604 and probably for some time before that. His French contacts probably began early with the Huguenot wife of Richard Field, the Stratford-born man who printed *Venus and Adonis* and *The Rape of Lucrece* in 1593 and 1594. His command of the language was evidently quite good. But in French as in English, sixteenth-century pronunciation differed in several ways from modern

French. Henry's response to Pistol's question about his name at 4.1.48, for instance, where he turns 'Harry the king' into 'Harry le Roy', which Pistol hears as Cornish 'Leroy', and Pistol's mishearing of M. Le Fer's '*moi*' as 'moys' at 4.4.17 both reflect the old French pronunciation of 'oi', now changed.

Yet, further on, he admits that:

The use of 4.4.44 'j'ai tombé' for 'je suis tombé' and 5.2.109 'à les anges' for 'aux anges' are common enough mistakes in English translation today, and are more likely to have been made in the original manuscript than misprinted by the F compositor. The same may be true of 4.4.13 and 42, where 'le' appears when it should agree with its noun as 'la'. The F compositors, however, did struggle with the French, some of which they set nearly as phonetically as the Q version.[18]

In the Bouquins edition, Jean-Claude Sallé sides with the hypothesis of faulty typescripts, arguing that the errors seem to be due to English compositors who did not know French and did not read the manuscripts correctly. What he says about sixteenth-century form, vocabulary and syntax is very relevant to our discussion:

The French spelling had not been fixed yet; the letters *s* and *z* were often interchangeable, so that one could write 'ilz' just as well as 'ils'. Many forms were equivalent: 'disent' and 'dient', 'aille' and 'voise', etc. The fancies in Shakespeare's French spelling go much beyond this diversity, however, such that one finds 'sae palla' (Q1) for 's'appelle', 'souermeray' (F) for 'souviendrai', 'e' for 'et', '&' for 'est', 'en' for 'un', etc. However, some of the spelling oddities in the Folio are also found, for instance, in French manuals edited in England. *The French Schoolmaster*, by the Huguenot Claude Desainliens (1573), prints 'asses' (1582 edition) for 'assez' (as does F: 3.4.52). And in another manual by the same author (*The French Littleton*, 1593 edition), one can even find phonetic spellings meant to help the pronunciation of French words, for example, 'tans' (for 'temps'), which is not very far from the 'tanes' found in the quarto. Finally, what may seem incorrect to the reader of modern French was sometimes correct then. The Shakespearean text contains archaic vocabulary ('vitement', 'varlet', etc.), but even more so, old-fashioned constructions: one could say 'Je vous prie de faire cela' (Cotgrave) like today, but also 'L'autheur prye les lecteurs differer leur jugement jusques à la fin du liure' (J. Du Bellay). When Alice tells Kate 'Vous parle fort bon Angloys' (Q1), one has no trouble modernizing it into 'Vous parlez fort bon Anglais', even if the temptation may be to add 'un' or 'du', but the form without article was idiomatic at the time, such that Desainliens proposes 'Parlez vous bon Anglois' and 'Jehan scauez vous parler bon Français.'[19]

I asked my Nanterre colleague André Eskénazi, a specialist in old French, to comment on the text of the French scenes. Here are some excerpts from his letter along with his careful and nuanced conclusion:

Four centuries ago in France, nobody but the unlearned would have said: 'Je te prie m'enſeigniez, il faut que je apprend à parler. Comment appelle-vous le main en Anglois?' The form would have been 'Je te prie (de) m'enseigner; il faut que j'apprenne; comment appelez-vous la main?', and so on. The conjugated form 'je me ſouvenierai' was not used, and 'tout le monde' was used (rather than 'toute le monde') . . . In short, Shakespeare seems to have attributed to the French the approximative language he heard the English speak . . . But the Oxford edition sometimes overcorrects the text (for instance, 'tout asture' in 'Le soldat ici est disposé tout asture de couper votre gorge'[20] was very common then, more than 'à cette heure').

Some quick remarks. About 3.5.[21] 'Et tu bien parles le langage': the insertion of an adverb between the subject and the verb was common in old French, but I can't find any instances of it in the 16th century. 'Je te prie m'enseigniez' or 'Je te prie, m'enseigniez' – no (line 4). 'Le bon écolier' – of course not; but 'vitement' – yes (line 12). 'Il est fort bon anglais' (line 17), and 'Il est trop difficile' (line 24) are both possible formulations. 'Je m'en fais la répétition de tous les mots que vous m'avez appris' (lines 22, 23) – additions of this type are found with 'dont' as well as 'duquel'. 'Comme je pense' may be an Anglicism, as the old French had 'si com je pens' (line 24). 'Je m'en oublié d'elbow' – 's'oublier de' exists along with 'oublier', even if it is not mentioned by all grammarians (line 28). 'Droit' can be used as an adverb, as it is in 'vous prononcez les mots aussi droit que les natifs d'Angleterre' (line 35). 'Je reciterai à vous' – yes, since 'à' can mean in front of (line 39). 'De foot et de count? O seigneur Dieu! Ils sont des mots de son mauvais et non pour les dames d'honneur d'user': this is jargon (lines 47–9). The phrase 'allons nous à dîner' is impossible (line 55).

About 4.4.[22] 'Prenez miséricorde' seems to be a confusion with 'prenez pitié' (line 9). 'Il me commande à vous dire' exists, together with 'il me commande de vous dire' (line 26). There is little doubt that 'Ce soldat ici' to mean 'ce soldat-ci' is French (line 27). 'Je vous supplie me pardonner' – yes (line 32). 'Il est content à vous donner' – no (line 42). 'Heureux' with the indicative, as in 'je m'estime heureux que j'ai tombé entre les mains', can be found (lines 44–5).

About 5.2.[23] 'Semblable à des anges' – no (line 108). 'L'anglais lequel je parle' is possible, if barely so (line 173). 'Mon très cher et divin déesse' – clearly not (line 196). 'Serviteur' in 'je ne veux point que vous abaissez votre grandeur en baisant le main notre seigneur indigne serviteur' (to mean 'd'une indigne servante de votre seigneurerie') – no (lines 225–7). 'Les dames et demoiselles pour être baisées devant leurs noces, il n'est pas la coutume de France' is an English form (line 230).

André Eskénazi's conclusion is a cautious one:

Sometimes, the form is attested; more often, it seems a possible one. When an attested form is found in Shakespeare's French, I have the feeling it is due to chance, that the author, aware of widely known, incontestable schemes, patterned similar phrases after them, and it is a matter of chance whether these are actually correct there. In the case they are not, it often results in solecisms which the plasticity of late-sixteenth-century or early-seventeenth-century French renders more or less acceptable, but which cannot be actually identified since they cannot be verified. Of necessity, this language is not fully known: not all authentic forms are found in grammar books or dictionaries – nor indeed could they be. There may be more fancifulness in Shakespeare's French than I make it sound, but if so, this fancifulness is a plausible one.[24]

According to this detailed discussion, then, one cannot conclude that the French scenes are in an altogether, or even essentially, authentic sixteenth-century French. At any rate, the question of the relative authenticity of Shakespeare's French, along with the problems it poses to the translator, both become less acute when it comes to the actual staging, where scenic translation can take over where linguistic translation left off. In Jean-Louis Benoit's stage adaptation, the English lesson scene turned into a little marvel of theatrical and linguistic humour. The actress who plays Katharine, Marie Vialle, invented a series of comic gestures to sum up the English words she learns, gestures that veer toward the explicit to better make her point. A closed fist with raised middle finger, illustrating the word 'fingres', summons an obscene imagery which runs the course of the scene, culminating in the titillating discovery that the English words 'foot' and 'gown' sound dangerously like the French 'foutre' and 'con' ('cum' and 'cunt').

The scene during which Henry courts Katharine (5.2) poses more complex linguistic questions, as it is not simply a matter of alternating between English and French, but also of a string of intermediary steps, of more or less monstrous intermixings between the two languages. Sylvère Monod opted to warn the reader about the original form with directions in italics after the speech heading. He distinguishes six different modes of enunciation:

1. *Statements in English.* These comprise most of Henry's lines.
2. *Statements in bad English.* These include Katharine's 'Your majesty shall mock me, I cannot speak your England' (which, for the Avignon production, I left in the original, whereas Sylvère Monod translated it as 'Votre Majesté va se rire de moi, je ne peux pas parler votre langue Angleterre').
3. *Statements mixing French and bad English.* An example is Katharine's 'Pardonnez-moi. I cannot tell vat is "like me".'
4. *Statements in French.* See Katharine's 'O bon Dieu, les langues des hommes sont pleines de tromperies.'
5. *Statements alternating between English and bad French.* Typical is Henry's 'No Kate, I will tell thee in French . . . Je quand sur le possession de Fraunce, & quand vous aves le possession de moy' (Folio spelling).

6. *Statements mixing English and French.* For instance, Katharine's 'Your
   majesty ave fausse french enough to deceive de most sage demoiselle dat
   is en France.'[25]

In this scene, no more than in the other one discussed, does it seem to
me appropriate to have Katharine and Alice speak in dog French when,
following theatrical convention, Henry speaks in perfect French (except
when, in the more 'realistic' moments, he tries a few 'beginner's French'
words).[26] In order to maintain this bilingualism, I kept some English lines
in Henry's part, a few simple phrases that any French audience can follow,
and I left in English – in bad English as it is transcribed – the lines in
which Katharine and Alice try to speak the language of the conqueror.
This solution was taken up by the actors, and worked all the better since
the staging emphasized the comic effect of the interlocutors' imperfect
comprehension. As is often done in front of foreigners, the character made
up for miscomprehension by miming the simplest phrases: to die, to speak,
to kiss . . . In fact, Henry makes as much of a touching effort to speak
French and be understood, as Katharine, already conquered but playing
hard to get, does to speak the language of the victor.

The most acute translation problems stem from the scenes in dialects.
The short sequence which brings together the Welshman Fluellen (or,
as Andrew Gurr calls him, Llewellyn[27]), the Irishman Macmorris and the
Scotsman Jamy, is of great political import as it portrays both the diversity –
linguistically represented – and the unity of the kingdom, gathered in
the patriotism of the war effort. The presence, however unsystematic, of
local accents underscores the linguistic differences and stresses the normative value of the king's English. The more developed of the three officers,
Fluellen, displays comic traits to emphasize the king's role, as Falstaff did
with respect to Prince Hal in *Henry IV*. Fluellen's lines contain stylistic
and morpho-syntactic idiosyncrasies that are perfectly translatable (strings
of synonyms, circumvoluted run-on sentences, erroneous agreements, like
'The mines is not according to the disciplines of the war'). But they also
contain phonetic distortions (for example, 'digt' for 'digged', 'aunchient'
for 'ancient') which prove much more difficult to translate or transpose.
Fluellen uses unvoiced plosives for voiced ones (*b* is pronounced *p*, *v* is
pronounced *f*, *j* is pronounced *ch*), and as a result says 'Cheshu' for 'Jesus',
'athversary' for 'adversary', and so on. But these distortions are neither
constant nor systematic. And, as a matter of fact, they do not sound particularly Welsh to a modern English-speaking audience. Indeed, it is likely
that, since the sixteenth century, Welsh, Irish and Scottish have changed as
much as 'standard' French or English.

Figure 2. Marie Vialle as Princess Katharine, and Philippe Torreton as Henry V. Dir.
Jean-Louis Benoit. Festival d'Avignon 1999.

In general, it is agreed that the English spoken in Wales and in Ireland is characterized by a so-called 'rhotic' *r* (pronounced in postocalic position), as well as by long rather than diphthongized vowels. In southern Wales, the intonation tends to be musical. The English spoken in Ireland varies according to region, but has an overall ascending intonation and uses a 'retroflexive' *t*. Scottish English rolls the *r* and pronounces the *l* as a velar.[28] But none of these characteristics are found in Shakespeare's dialects, even if, as Gurr writes, Fluellen's 'lengthy sentences full of syntactical inversions as well as the insistent "look you" (which occurs even more frequently in Q), probably indicate something not entirely different from the modern use of English in southern Wales'.[29] But neither Macmorris's use of palato-alveolar fricatives for sibilants ('Be Chrish' for 'By Christ'), nor Jamy's specific vocalizations ('gud' for 'good', 'baith' for 'both', 'wad' for 'would'), seem to be attested in the few historical documents available (including, for instance, a letter of the king of Scotland to Henry IV concerning his son James's captivity).[30] One can thus surmise that Shakespeare's are stylized dialects, theatrical Welsh, Irish or Scottish, meant to *present* a linguistic difference rather than *characterize* it in any precise fashion.

Most of the time, French translators try to transpose these English local ways of speaking into French or French-speaking equivalents. Thus, François-Victor Hugo gives Jamy a Creole accent, supposed to account for the Scottish rolled *r*.[31]

Jamy: Ce seha pafait, su ma paole, mes baves capitaines . . . Par la messe, avant que ces yeux là se livrent au sommeil, ze fehai de la besogne ou je sehai poté en terre: oui-dah! ou je sahai mort; paiehah de ma personne aussi vaillamment que ze pouhai, ze m'y engaze, en un mot comme en mille. Mobleu! ze sehais bien aise d'ouïr une discussion entre vous deux.[32]

This rather strange option seems to us neither politically correct, nor, more decisively, linguistically or intellectually convincing. Nevertheless, the drive to find French-speaking equivalents to these dialects is found in later translations too. If M. J. Lavelle transcribes the officers' lines into standard French,[33] Marcel Sallé gives Jamy a lisp and Fluellen something of an Alsatian accent: 'Che vous en brie . . . Foyez-fous . . . la discibline.'[34] Jean-Claude Sallé has Macmorris speak with an Auvergne accent: 'Che n'est pas le moment de discourir . . . Que le Chricht me garde.'[35] When translated by Sylvère Monod, the same Macmorris now speaks a North-African French straight out of the Casbah: 'Té, par le Chrisse, c'est un beau gâchis.' He explains his choice in a note:

Our translation attenuates, without being overly systematic, the irregularities in the written pronunciations (sometimes turning grammatical oddities into particularities in the spoken form). Moreover, in order to give French readers a sense more or less equivalent to what happens in the original text, we have taken Fluellen's phonetic and psychological particularities to be like those of an Eastern Frenchman, those of Macmorris, to a Southern Frenchman, and those of Jamy, to a Normandy Frenchman.[36]

I, for one, am totally opposed to these transpositions into French local manners of speaking. All vernacular languages are specific and cannot be transported or transposed.[37] To have Fluellen, Macmorris or Jamy speak like a Frenchman from Alsace, Brittany, Picardy, or a Belgian or a Swiss, makes no sense anyway. Never will this evoke a Welshman, Irishman or Scotsman to a French reader or theatregoer. Even supposing Welsh, Irish or Scottish people have a particular accent when they speak French, nothing indicates that this accent is the same when they speak English. So to transcribe faithfully distortions in consonants can only lead to altogether contrived and ridiculous sounding ways of speaking. It is part of the actor's role to find the pronunciation specificities which will particularize his character. I wholly agree with Monod's suggestion that the many erroneous, heavy, or fanciful forms 'are interspersed in an irregular fashion through Fluellen's lines because Shakespeare probably deemed it enough to indicate only now and then the type of pronunciation which the actors should adopt'.[38] Accordingly, in my translation, I only reproduced Shakespeare's transcribed distortions where they happened and when they took place on the same consonants in French, thus resisting the temptation of necessarily artificial manners of speaking. For the solution is not a written, but an oral one.

In Jean-Louis Benoit's stage performance, the problem of the Welsh, Irish and Scottish accents disappeared, as the whole scene was cut out (so as to lighten and shorten the play as a whole).[39] But it remained, transposed into the French-speaking sphere, since the director had asked several actors playing French characters to put on regional accents. Indeed, fifteenth-century France was a mosaic of languages and dialects. As a result, for the premiere in Avignon, the Governor of Harfleur spoke with a vaguely eastern French accent, and one of the French nobles had a southern accent.[40]

Although, as we have seen, some translators desperately try to invent homogenized parlances and distinct mannerisms in French, my absolute conviction is that there can be no valid purely *linguistic* translation of regional accents – genuine or artificial – into another language, only a temporary, individualized and always to be reinvented, *scenic* translation.

To put it in Roman Jakobson's terms, intersemiotic translation (from word to gesture, from speech to acting) takes up where interlinguistic translation leaves off.[41] This could be the conclusion to a discussion of the failings and limits in translating a bilingual text. When the text at stake is meant for the theatre, a purely verbal translation can never be complete in and of itself. It is to be completed by a scenic translation which fills in the gaps, and, above all, actualizes the potential effects – on the condition that the translator think in terms of transposition and adaptation, rather than simply interlinguistic translation.

NOTES

1 *Henry V* was almost certainly written in the spring or summer of 1599, between 27 March, when Essex left London, and 28 September, when he returned after failing in his task (see the reference to the Earl of Essex's expedition into Ireland to crush Tyrone's rebellion, in Act 5, Chorus, 30–2). The play was most likely performed before 15 October 1599. See *King Henry V*, edited by J. H. Walter (London and New York: Methuen, 1954), xi.
2 See Ralph Berry, *On Directing Shakespeare: Interviews with Contemporary Directors* (London: Croom Helm/New York: Barnes & Noble, 1977), 57.
3 This is a different topic, which deserves attention in its own right. These constraints and technicalities mainly involve questions of duration, phonological coincidences regarding certain consonants (mainly labials) and temporal coincidences of motions of the mouth.
4 For the specific requirements of translation for the stage, see my 'Translating Shakespeare for the Theatre', in *Shakespeare and France*, edited by Holger Klein and Jean-Marie Maguin (Lewiston, NY: The Edwin Mellen Press, 1995), 345–58.
5 On the notions of 'undertranslation' and 'overtranslation', see Antoine Vitez, *Le devoir de traduire* (Montpellier: Editions Climats et Maison Antoine Vitez, 1996), 45–7.
6 *Henry V*, translated by Sylvère Monod, in Shakespeare, *Œuvres Complètes*, 12 vols. (Paris: Collection Formes et Reflets, Le Club Français du Livre, 1957), VI, 238–9.
7 *King Henry V*, edited by Andrew Gurr (Cambridge: Cambridge University Press, 1984), 171 (note to line 11).
8 *Henry V*, edited by Gary Taylor (Oxford: Oxford University Press, 1982), 235n.
9 *King Henry V*, edited by T. W. Craik (London and New York: Routledge, 1995), 298.
10 This was Dr Johnson's hypothesis in *Shakespeare's Plays*, edited by Samuel Johnson, 8 vols. (1765).
11 *King Henry V*, ed. Craik, 299. I rendered this as the monolingual pun 'Que je t'embrasse, roquet? Sacré bouc lubrique des montagnes, tu veux que je t'embrasse?' ('That I should Kiss you, cur? Damned lustful ram from the mountains, do you want me to kiss you?') See *Henry V*, translated into French

by Jean-Michel Déprats and edited by Gisèle Venet (Paris: Gallimard, 1999), 273.

12 I translated this freely as 'Je vais me le faire, le ferrer et le faire taire.' ('I am going to get him, fetter him, and make him stop talking.') See *Henry V*, trans. Déprats, ed. Venet, 275.

13 The Folio gives 'La leuye' (*la laie*).

14 William Shakespeare, *Œuvres Complètes*, bilingual edition, 2 vols. (Paris: Laffont, Paris, 1997), vol. 1 (Histories), 760.

15 See Ton Hoenselaars's article on François-Victor Hugo as translator of *Henry V*: 'Shakespeare for "the People": François-Victor Hugo Translates *Henry V*', *Documenta* (Ghent), 13:4 (1995), 243–52.

16 *William Shakespeare, Théâtre Complet*, 4 vols., translated by Daniel and Geneviève Bournet, vol. IV (Lausanne: L'Age d'Homme, 1992), 371n.

17 *Ibid.*, 372.

18 *King Henry V*, edited by Gurr, 61.

19 *Henri V*, translated by Jean-Claude Sallé, in William Shakespeare, *Œuvres Complètes: Histoires*, 2 vols. (Paris: Bouquins/Robert Laffout, 1997), I, 934.

20 *Henry V*, ed. Venet, 274 (*Henry V*, 4.4).

21 In *ibid.*, 3.5 (164–72).

22 In *ibid.*, 4.4 (270–9).

23 In *ibid.*, 5.2 (342–57).

24 Private correspondence between André Eskénazi and Jean-Michel Déprats.

25 *Henry V*, trans. Monod, 5.2 (215–27).

26 The audience accepts without problems the rules of this game and the passage from a conventional language to an 'actually spoken' language. If the actors speak a few phrases with an English accent and cite some 'English' Latin, they can further help the passage from one register to the other.

27 *King Henry V*, ed. Gurr, 63.

28 For a more detailed and scientific description of regional accents, along with a very complete overview of linguistic variations in the English-speaking world, see J. C. Welles, *Accents of English* (Cambridge: Cambridge University Press, 1982).

29 *King Henry V*, ed. Gurr, 62.

30 *Ibid.*

31 He is perhaps hinting at a similarity in their colonial situations.

32 Shakespeare, *Œuvres Complètes*, Bibliothèque de la Pléiade, 2 vols. (Paris: Gallimard, 1959), 1:782–3. See also *Henry V*, ed. Venet, 3.3 (154–7).

33 *Henri V*, translated with an introduction by M. J. Lavelle, Collection Bilingue des Classiques Etrangers (Paris: Aubier, Editions Montaigne, 1947).

34 *Henri V*, translated by Marcel Sallé (Paris: Les Belles Lettres, 1961). To French ears, the result sounds more like the caricatures of German soldiers in comedies about World War II. See also *Henry V*, ed. Venet, 3.3 (158–9).

35 *Henri V*, trans. Jean-Claude Sallé.

36 *Henry V*, trans. Monod, 237.

37 Cf. *14ᵉ Assises de la traduction littéraire en Arles* (Arles: Actes Sud, 1998), 95–128 (round-table discussion on the translation of dialects and regional or popular manners of speaking in the theatre, chaired by Jean-Michel Déprats).

38 *Henry V*, trans. Monod, 237.

39 Which was performed again in Paris, at the Théâtre de l'Aquarium, from 12 December 1999 to 5 March 2000.

40 Paradoxically, this southerner plays the role of 'Britain' (Bretagne) in the original – which only proves again that everything is a matter of stylization in theatre, and that accuracy has little relevance to artistic invention.

41 See Roman Jakobson, 'On Linguistic Aspects of Translation', in *On Translation*, edited by R. A. Brower (New York: Oxford University Press, 1966), 232–9.

CHAPTER 4

Shakespeare's history plays in Japan

Daniel Gallimore

Shakespeare's history plays remain the least known of the three main genres in Japan. Although they were first translated for a reading public between 1919 and 1928, it was not until 1962 that a complete and unadapted version of one of the plays (*Richard III*) appeared on the Japanese stage. By comparison, the first such production of a comedy (*The Merchant of Venice*) was in 1910 and of a tragedy (*Hamlet*) in 1911. All the histories have now been staged in Japanese but – with the exception of *Richard III* – new productions and revivals are rare.[1] In 1990, for example, when Shakespearean production was enjoying a minor boom in Japan, there were no fewer than ten new productions of *Hamlet*, whereas the only histories to be staged during that year were an adaptation entitled *Falstaff* and a touring production of *Richard III* by the Royal National Theatre. Of course, also in Britain the histories are performed less often than the major comedies and tragedies, but their peripheral position in Japan is explained as much by culturally specific factors as by an adherence to foreign trends.

It is probable that the first copy of one or more of the histories to have passed into Japanese hands did so soon after the Meiji Restoration of 1868, when Japan was finally made accessible to the outside world after 250 years of isolation; there is no evidence of any of the histories being known in Japan before that time.[2] In 1873 the Englishman James Summers was appointed first Professor of English Literature and Logic at the newly created Kaisei Gakkō (later the Imperial University of Tokyo).[3] It is recorded that in 1875 he examined his class on *Hamlet* and *Henry VIII*, requiring them to paraphrase and write from memory excerpts from the speeches of Hamlet and Cardinal Wolsey. By the end of the Meiji Era (1868–1912), *Hamlet* had become well known through a series of adaptations, translations and stage productions, but *Henry VIII* was not staged at all until 1980. It is ironic perhaps that the historical events dramatized in the latter play were only twenty or so years old by the time that European missionaries and traders arrived on Japanese shores in the 1550s, whereas it was the procrastinating prince who caught the imagination of modernizing Japan. To paraphrase Kawatake and Takahashi, Hamlet's plight reflected the plight both of a country seeking to reinvent itself against the threat of Western imperialism and of the numerous young men of the educated elite for whom there was no longer a role in life predetermined by the old feudal hierarchy. These young men needed ideas not history, still less scheming politicians like Wolsey.[4]

1893 – TSUBOUCHI SHŌYŌ AND HISTORICAL DRAMA

One of the young 'Hamlets' of Meiji was Tsubouchi Shōyō (1859–1935), who first encountered Shakespeare under a successor of Summers and who was more than anyone else the pioneer of Shakespeare studies and translation in Japan. It was Shōyō who first translated the histories between 1919 and 1928, but in an essay published in 1892, he suggested that the history plays could 'only be of interest to those with a particular interest in English history'.[5] Influenced by contemporary Western critics such as Edward Dowden, the interest of Shōyō and other Meiji scholars was not in English history as such but in Shakespeare's characters and the life of Shakespeare himself.[6] His remark came in his 'Preface to a Commentary on *Macbeth*', one of the first critical studies of Shakespeare by a Japanese scholar. As an emerging authority in the field, it was no doubt prudent for him to concentrate his attentions and the attentions of his public on a limited selection of the plays. Yet his remark is contradicted to some extent by his previous and lifelong interest in *jidaimono* (*kabuki* period plays), which are the closest Japanese equivalent to the Shakespearean genre of historical drama.

In *Shōsetsu shinzui* ('The Essence of the Novel') of 1885, his first critical work and still regarded as his most important, Shōyō castigated the Japanese novel for its imbalance of stylistic and moralistic elements: for veering between crass didacticism and superfluous sensuality.[7] This was iconoclastic enough but in 1893 he extended his criticism to the greatest of the *kabuki* playwrights, Chikamatsu Monzaemon (1653–1725):

Some of Chikamatsu's historical plays, if considered as dream-fantasies of a kind, spectacles that appeal exclusively to the eyes, are remarkably skilful, but the incidents are too implausible, the characters too uncomplicated for them to be called historical plays in the strict sense, and it is difficult for a contemporary spectator to experience an illusion of historical reality. In general, one may say of Chikamatsu's *jidaimono* that they are tales of a dream-fantasy land, which borrow from reality hardly more than the names of places and people.[8]

To continue with Keene's translation of the excerpt, Shōyō defines Chikamatsu's 'dream-fantasies' as lying in 'their absurd plots, their incidents which have not the least bases in fact, their unnatural characters, their illogical construction, their diffuse relationships or, again their plethora of metamorphoses and inconsistencies, their lack of unity of interest, their unexpected complications and their exaggeration of the materials – in every respect they are fantasies within a dream'.[9] One may wish to question the seriousness with which Shōyō criticizes Chikamatsu quite out of cultural context and also the depth of his knowledge of Shakespeare's histories, which can be equally guilty of 'dream-fantasy'. Moreover, a skilled *kabuki* actor has the capacity to improve on 'uncomplicated' characterization. Yet the differing roles of characterization between Shakespeare's history plays and Japanese *jidaimono*, together with the differing treatments of historical materials, cannot be ignored, and so in this sense, Shōyō made an essential connection between drama, history and character that is reasserted by later Japanese scholars.

1997 – KINOSHITA JUNJI AND THE RESONANCE OF HISTORY

The twentieth-century historian E. H. Carr described 'the two heresies' of historiography as being 'scissors-and-paste history without meaning or significance' and 'propaganda or historical fiction' which merely uses 'facts of the past to embroider a kind of writing which has nothing to do with history'.[10] The corollary might be true of historical fiction and drama as well: that it may consist either of a random series of literary effects or simply be history in disguise. Above all, the writer may continue to read history simply as history and ignore its literary potential. E. M. W. Tillyard (1889– 1962), who was Carr's near contemporary at Cambridge, understood this point well in his study of Shakespeare's treatment of medieval English history, *Shakespeare's History Plays*, first published in 1944 and still 'influential' in both Britain and Japan.[11] In particular, Tillyard's account of medieval kingship as both mythic and political in dimension is analogous not only to how Shakespeare treats it but it also pinpoints that tension between fact and fantasy which must be relevant to any literary genre.

Shōyō's advocacy of historical realism can be read as a modernist redress of the balance away from literary fantasy but there is another important context to be considered. *Fin-de-siècle* Japan saw a developing controversy between two schools of historiography, the nationalists who interpreted Japanese history within a hierarchical, Confucianist framework, and a liberal school which espoused a critical, objectivist methodology. In the 1920s a third, marxian school emerged, attacking the nationalists for their suppression of proletarian aspirations and the liberals for their claims to be apart from history. Shōyō's own ideology is an ambiguous mix of subjective and objective that makes him eminently suited to the task of translating Shakespeare, and which foresees the synthesis achieved by the marxists who gained increasing influence in the modern Japanese theatre (*shingeki*) from the 1920s onwards.

One translator of Shakespeare who has undoubtedly been influenced by marxist ideology is Kinoshita Junji (b. 1914). Kinoshita is better known as an original playwright and has translated only a handful of Shakespeare's plays. What is significant about his contribution to the variegated field of Shakespeare translation in Japan is his seriousness about history and language, which is a quality surely influenced by his encounter with marxism as a student at Tokyo University in the 1930s. He suggests that any kind of historical writing, whether fact or fiction, should steer a way between propaganda and writing that is so objective as to become sentimental, and has had a long-term interest in the histories and other plays with a strong historical content like *Macbeth*.[12] Of the translations, his most impressive achievement to date is his *Bara sensō* ('Wars of the Roses'), a serial translation of the first tetralogy (*Henry VI* and *Richard III*), published in 1997. Kinoshita used the script prepared by John Barton and Peter Hall for their Royal Shakespeare Company production of the *Wars of the Roses*, but his work is remarkable for being the first Japanese translation in this format and for the care with which Kinoshita handles those historical events so distant in space and time from his own experience.[13] He is not being wholly ironic when he suggests that his knowledge of the period, derived as it was from extensive documentary material, from visits to Bosworth Field and so on, was greater than Shakespeare's ever was.[14]

In his attempts to experience the pathos of that tragic period in English history, Kinoshita draws an analogy between the *Wars of the Roses* tetralogy and one of the masterpieces of Japanese literature, *Heike monogatari*.[15] 'The Tale of the Heike' was originally a thirteenth-century oral narrative recounting the feud between the Heike and the Genji – the two great clans of medieval Japan – which lead to the routing of the Heike in 1185. As with the Houses of York and Lancaster in fifteenth-century England, the clans were represented by the colours white and red respectively – although in the Japanese case it was the whites who won – and in both cases also, the victories overcame inalienable historical tensions. Yet as a translator of historical drama and connoisseur of Japanese literature, Kinoshita is actually more interested in the question 'What was it like to have been there?' This question partly explains his interest in sources and the genealogy of oral narrative, but it also leads to the admission that he can never truly know what it was like; he can only feel the aftermath of events.

The actual emptiness of the historical scene is stated to memorable effect in the opening lines of 'The Tale of the Heike':

The sound of the Gion Shōja bells echoes the impermanence of all things; the colour of the *śāla* flowers reveals the truth that the prosperous must decline. The proud do not endure, they are like a dream on a spring night; the mighty fall at last, they are as dust before the wind.[16]

Yoshio Arai is reminded of this passage by Warwick's farewell speech in *Henry VI:*

> My parks, my walks, my manors that I had,
> Even now forsake me; and of all my lands
> Is nothing left me but my body's length.
> Why, what is pomp, rule, reign, but earth and dust?
> And live we how we can, yet die we must.[17]

For Kinoshita, the lines may carry a dual significance beyond the historical analogy. The tolling of the bell can be understood as a representation of the continuum between thought and sound that constitutes the spoken act, but its sound may also echo the cries of the wounded and dying on the battlefield and the vocalized grief of the bereaved. The analogy with *Heike*, therefore, is an analogy about language.

Since the 1950s, Kinoshita has shown an active interest in Japanese phonology and prosody, with the general concern that spoken sounds should be a sincere representation of speakers' thoughts. By way of illustration, he fears that Shakespeare translation in an arcane, metrical style may sound like parody to modern ears, and he has therefore avoided the temptation of using the rhythms and archaic idioms of *Heike monogatari* in *Bara sensō*, opting for colloquial, unrhythmical language.[18] This avoidance of overt prosody and concentration instead on narrative technique (*katari*) is typical also of Kinoshita's contemporary Fukuda Tsuneari (1912–94), who translated and directed the 1962 *Richard III*, but in Kinoshita's case he relates what he is doing to a theory expounded in works such as *Gekiteki to wa* ('What is Drama?', 1995): that writing a play (and, presumably, translating one) is not unlike riding a horse.[19] Successful playwrighting involves a mutual dependence of master and animal, and the horse, as we know, is the other key player in medieval history, English and Japanese. It is only when Richard loses his horse at Bosworth Field that we can be sure he has lost the crown, since without a horse he is unable to flee the field and persuade another army to follow him: 'A horse! A horse! My kingdom for a horse!'[20] Matsuoka Kazuko (b. 1942), the most recent translator of that play (1999), opens her afterword to the translation with the exclamation 'Uma ni kodawatta', which can be literally translated as 'I stayed on my horse', but more freely as 'I stuck to my guns', or 'The bastard didn't get me down!'[21] Perhaps it is the translator who knows Richard's evil better than anyone, since the translator is more intimately involved with the individual words of the text than even the director but (like the director) must coordinate Richard's character against the other dramatic elements. The challenge is to prevent the force of Richard's rhetoric from taking over the translation as a whole.

RICHARD'S BAD *KARMA* AND THE SENSE OF HISTORY

One of the central difficulties faced by the Japanese interpreter of *Richard III* and the other history plays may be that Shakespeare's philosophy of the evil ruler can come perilously close to a fatalistic strain inherent in Japanese thought: that evil actions are justified, or at least explicated, by the Buddhist doctrine of *karma*, whose most general definition is the theory of 'inevitable consequence'. According to Tudor historians, Richard's evil was the necessary vehicle of a greater good, but in Buddhist philosophy Richard's physical deformity would be regarded as a punishment for sins committed in a former life for which the only possible atonement is good deeds in the present life to be rewarded by a more perfect body in the next. As he acts in the play, Richard can only be preparing himself for an inferior destiny although this behaviour may itself be ascribed to bad *karma* rather than a conscious choice between good and evil. This reluctance to distinguish between good and evil is present within the dramatic tradition as well. It is no wonder that the *jidaimono* criticized by Shōyō were seen by him to lack moral purpose when playwrights such as Chikamatsu were themselves steeped in Buddhist tradition. The main interest of the feudal authorities to which Chikamatsu was accountable was simply to preserve the peace and maintain the hierarchy, not to side with semi-legendary heroes; the literary interest of medieval Japanese history was in its wealth of pathos. Shōyō was correct to leave Shakespeare's histories to the historians. For while comparisons between the tragedies and Japanese culture – whether as critical studies or stage interpretations – have been commonplace, interpretations of the history plays have been mainly on their own terms.[22]

If the cultural frameworks – the Thomist natural order against Buddhist mutability – are fatally dissimilar, then where the two cultures may begin to meet is through that handful of characters in the history plays who are large enough to step outside their historical context and be accepted in a new one. These would include Richard III (as opposed to Edward IV), Falstaff (as opposed to the Bastard) and Henry V (as opposed to his father). As has been mentioned, Shōyō recognized the importance of strong characterization to reforming (and indeed creating) Japan's modern drama. Although the emergence of Richard and Falstaff on the Japanese stage in the 1960s had long been preceded by Macbeth and Hamlet, the two characters were at least fresh blood and have remained the object of critical interest and attention. The actor Nakadai Tatsuya's creation of both these roles for the Japanese stage in the 1962 and 1967 productions by Fukuda Tsuneari respectively is still remembered.

The character of Falstaff had been known since 1937 when Mikami Isao and Nishikawa Masami translated *The Merry Wives of Windsor* for Senda Koreya (1904–94), a production which was revived twice in the 1950s. For Senda, who pioneered Brechtian theatre in Japan, Falstaff became an archetypal figure, frustrated by bourgeois conventionalism, rather than someone who might once have belonged to English history. It is said of Japanese directors that they have 'a total lack of awe' with regard to Shakespeare, of which Senda's Falstaff might be one such example.[23] Until recently, Shakespeare production in Japan meant little to scholars and audiences in the English-speaking world, and now that it does mean something, thoughts of plagiarism are dulled by the realizations of post-colonialism. Japanese directors are returning a product of Anglophone culture, with a difference. Yet Fukuda Tsuneari was one director who not only had first-hand experience of the English theatre but also a belief in Western individualism.[24] It was therefore appropriate for him to be the first to demonstrate to Japanese audiences the basic significance of Falstaff in his historical context: that 'into this world of intrigue, rebellion and conflict that constitutes Shakespeare's history plays the perennial Falstaff breathes a spirit of comic freedom' (Arai, 'Reciting the Works of Shakespeare', 175).

Fukuda's productions can be said to have appropriated English history to the Japanese stage but in fact the characters of Richard III and Henry V were already known to Japanese audiences through the release of the Laurence Olivier films during the Occupation years (1945–52). Olivier's film of *Henry V* was voted top foreign film in 1948 by the Tokyo magazine *Kinema*. For the generation of Japanese Shakespeareans now in their sixties or seventies, the two films were indeed their first significant exposure to the plays. Yet the bold cinematography and Plantagenet costumes, while certainly memorable, offered only distant models of human behaviour that meant little on Japanese soil. The character of Falstaff, however – also known to Japanese filmgoers thanks to the portrayals by Orson Welles (1966) and Anthony Quayle (1979) – differs from Richard and Henry in being 'not wholly sympathetic to Japanese people' (Arai, 'Reciting the Works of Shakespeare', 162).

Odashima Yūshi (b. 1930), who is the second person to have translated the complete works of Shakespeare into Japanese, describes Falstaff as 'a huge meat dumpling of a man, concocted of realism and humour'.[25] What Japanese audiences may dislike about him is that the realism (the acceptance of life as it is) and the humour (the determination to get on with life) are balanced in a way that is at odds with the realities of modern Japanese life. This is to say that the 'workaholic' salary-man may become an 'alcoholic' at night – and each role be considered socially acceptable – but the two attitudes (the loyal *samurai* and 'floating world' of popular Japanese culture) cannot exist simultaneously. Falstaff cannot and does not 'get on'. Professor Arai goes on to write of Falstaff's eventual rejection by Hal at the end of *Henry IV, Part Two*, that 'the drama is controlled with such skill that we end up hating Shakespeare' (Arai, 'Reciting the Works of Shakespeare', 175). In his relationship with Hal, Falstaff presents a personality that is only partly attractive to Japanese people but in his rejection evokes a pathos that may be considered typical of traditional Japanese drama.

Tillyard concluded his classic study of Shakespeare's history plays with a four-page chapter on *Macbeth*, which he described as 'the epilogue of the Histories'.[26] Although the play was beyond the remit of Tillyard's book to merit full analysis he clearly regarded it as the ideal history play: '*Macbeth* not only is a great tragedy, not only includes the high political theme with the personal and the cosmic, but it represents its age in showing how all these things should be blended and proportioned' (Tillyard, *Shakespeare's History Plays*, 322). Not only does the play locate kingship within the natural order in the same way that the earlier histories had done, but its plot is derived from comparable historical sources. Early Japanese Shakespeareans – such as Mori Ōgai (1860–1922), an army surgeon with literary accomplishments – were fascinated by the psychopathology of Macbeth and Lady Macbeth and sought a rational understanding of Shakespeare's use of the supernatural in that play. The interest, as with *Hamlet*, was in problems of characterization rather than in history per se, and in the theatre at least, Japanese audiences were alienated by realistic costuming and scenery that presented a touristic image of Scotland but little to make the Scottish play relevant to their own cultural context.

The first serious challenge to this style of production was Akira Kurosawa's 1957 film adaptation 'Throne of Blood' (orig. *Kumonosujō*) which was always more faithful to the details of its setting in medieval Japan than it ever was to Shakespeare's text. Kurosawa's medium gave him a flexibility that the realist *shingeki* theatre could never have, and in doing so usurped two of its traditional advantages: it concentrated the eyes of the audience into a single lens and so exploited a more rigorous exploration of character than the *shingeki* actors could have hoped to effect. Kurosawa's film, together with the emergence of the underground theatre (*angura*) in the 1960s, can be said therefore to have paved the way towards the experimental, Japanized Shakespeare of the last three decades of the twentieth century.

Representative of the new style, at least to non-Japanese audiences, was the production by Ninagawa Yukio (b. 1935) which won international acclaim at the Edinburgh Festival in 1985. Ninagawa borrowed from Kurosawa the historic setting and costuming but supplemented it with the huge facade of a Buddhist temple which served to frame the action and its chief protagonist in a postmodern representation of the cinematographic eye. The director still had the authority to shape the action but it was an authority matched by the audience's interpretation of what it was seeing. The interpretation of historical drama had been democratized in another sense as well, as increasing numbers of Japanese people in the 1980s had the time and money to travel to Britain and visit Cawdor Castle and other sites associated with the histories. Analogous sites preserved to the same degree are much rarer in Japan, which is due partly to the urbanization of the country's plains and valleys (the remaining four-fifths of the land mass being mountainous) and partly to the traditional preference for perishable wood over stone as the main building material. History in Japan, if it is felt at all, is felt in the influence of intangible traditions and survival of domestic objets d'art such as calligraphies and tea bowls. Bashō's *haiku* from the seventeenth century refers to a medieval battlefield which is unusual in still being preserved:

> Summer grasses
> where stalwart soldiers
> once dreamed a dream.[27]

Bosworth Field is also still grassland (used for annual re-enactments of the famous battle) and yet while only a page of Shakespeare's handwriting has survived for posterity, whole manuscripts are preserved from the hand of the founding dramaturg of *nō* drama, Zeami (1363–1443).

ODASHIMA YŪSHI AND 'THE ENGLISH DISEASE'

In Meiji Japan, with 250 years of feudal isolation behind them, the educated elite were either confident or hopeful enough of their identity to preclude the extensive investigation of other national histories. In Heisei Japan that confidence has evaporated to give way to a more intense and anxious historiography that seeks answers to the Japanese present as much from the foreign past as from Japanese history. Despite their continuing peripheral position in relation to the production of other Shakespeare plays in Japan, the histories are nevertheless relevant to the ongoing discourse. The medium (as always) is language and so it should be instructive to see what a contemporary translator like Odashima makes of Gaunt's speech 'this scept'red isle' in his 1983 translation of the play. If it is true that literary translation is interpretation then it should be possible even from a brief excerpt to discern the translator's approach to such key themes of the play as England and kingship.

The dramatic significance of the speech is as a highly rhetorical representation of 'England' that eventually serves to pull the role of chief mythmaker (= king) away from Richard II to Gaunt's son, Henry Bolingbroke. Richard signally fails to act out the myth of kingship, either in his deeds or (until his dethronement by Henry) his rhetoric. Gaunt's speech is given a deeper poignancy by his death soon after, which Richard disregards although his behaviour and deposition conclude with his martyrdom at the end of the play. Part of the speech (the excerpt quoted below) had been anthologized by the time of Shakespeare's death, and even today it is one of those speeches widely known and quoted by English people (who do not necessarily know the source); it speaks for itself:

> This royal throne of kings, this scept'red isle,
> This earth of majesty, this seat of Mars,
> This other Eden, demi-paradise,
> This fortress built by Nature for herself
> Against infection and the hand of war,
> This happy breed of men, this little world,
> This precious stone set in a silver sea,
> Which serves it in the office of a wall,
> Or as a moat defensive to a house,
> Against the envy of less happier lands;

This blessed plot, this earth, this realm, this England,
This nurse, this teeming womb of royal kings,
Fear'd by their breed, and famous by their birth,
Renowned for their deeds as far from home,
For Christian service and true chivalry,
As is the sepulchre in stubborn Jewry
Of the world's ransom, blessed Mary's son.[28]

One of the reasons for the speech's popularity must – quite apart from its patriotic sentiments – be the logical, uncomplicated quality of the metaphors and that the allusions to Christian and Roman mythology are also readily accessible; it is the speech of a dying man recalling the lessons of his childhood. Odashima has an original way of dealing with the allusions. He gives Mars the epithet *gunshin* ('God of War') but the epithet *seibo* ('Holy Mother') translates Shakespeare's epithet 'blessed' in addition to being the term familiarly used in Japanese for Mary. He is sensitive to the rhetoric, to which end the Japanese language gives him at least two advantages. The free verse format replicates the shape of the original and provides Odashima with a structure in which to engender rhythmic and phonic tensions, both of which are standard to his practice. What is more unusual is his literal treatment of the demonstrative pronoun 'this'. The Japanese equivalent *kono* is used sparingly in Japanese. Its consistent use is considered awkward and unnecessary and, indeed, it is only used when a distinction between 'this' and 'the other' must be made to avoid ambiguity. It is also more emphatically deictic than its English equivalent since it refers strictly to things or people in the speaker's immediate vicinity as opposed to that of the addressee (for which *sono*/'that' is used) or else distant from both speaker and addressee (*ano*/'that other there'). The repetition of *kono* twelve times in Odashima's translation is unusual in Japanese and so becomes the rhetorical device on which the translation hinges:

Kono rekidai no ō no gyokuza, kono ōken ni suberareta shima,
Kono sonkei ni michita ōdo, kono gunshin Marusu no ryōdo,
Kono daini no Eden, chijō ni okeru Paradaisu,
Shizen no megami ga, totsukuni kara no akueki wo fusegi,
Ikusa no te kara mamoran toshite kizuita, kono toride,
Kono kōfukuna shuzoku, kono shōchūtaru bettenchi,
Shiawase usuku shite netami ni toritsukareta gaiteki no
Akui no te no shin'nyū ni sonaete mizukara wo mamoru
Jōheki tomo nari, yakata wo meguru hori tomo naru,
Shirogane no umi ni zōgun sareta kono kichōna hōseki,
Kono shukufuku sareta chi, kono daichi, kono ryōchi, kono Ingurando,

Daidai no ō wo umisodateta kono botai, kono ubo,
Sono shuzoku yue ni osorerare, sono kettō yue ni nadakaku,
Ganrai naru Yudaya no chi ni aru, kono yo no sukuinushi,
Seibo Maria no miko no haka wo torimodosan toshite.[29]

The underlying pattern established by the repetition of *kono* culminates in a series of four *kono*s in line 11, each one linked with the character for *chi* meaning 'land' or 'earth'. A similar repetition occurs in the following lines 12 and 15 of the character for 'mother', *bo*. In the first case, the repetition *kono . . . chi* ('this . . . earth') leads inexorably into the keyword of Odashima's translation, *Ingurando*. 'England' is probably the keyword of the original as well since even if the significance of the word was self-evident to Shakespeare's audience it may still be read as a speech act: Gaunt wants his words to mean something more than mere fantasy. The extra syllable at the end of the line enables him to pause on the phrase, to take stock once more of what England actually means to him, and as a sick man the first word that comes to mind is 'nurse'. In translation, the rhythm is pushed forward by the juxtaposition of the two dental sounds -*do* and *Dai*, which gives the effect of a final rhetorical exertion; Gaunt is sustained by a belief in his own posterity.

The common word for 'England' is *Igirisu*, which is derived from Portuguese and more generally denotes 'the United Kingdom'. *Ingurando* is the phonetic version, used much less frequently than *Igirisu* as it excludes Scotland, Wales and Northern Ireland. It therefore sounds rather unusual to Japanese ears and with the other rhetorical devices deployed by Odashima serves to foreground the medieval state as a place with a definite geographical identity. His translation was first staged by Deguchi Norio's Shakespeare Theatre in Tokyo in December 1979, and published by Hakusui Books in 1983. Deguchi's approach was to assemble a group of inexperienced actors and then educate them in a way of 'doing Shakespeare' through a routine of improvisation, short rehearsal periods, short runs and frequent revivals; sets and costuming were minimal and contemporary. During this period (*c.* 1975–85) Odashima was translating and the group rehearsing a new play at the rate of one every three months. It was also the period when the Japanese economy was gearing itself toward the boom years of the late 1980s and when articles started to appear in the Japanese press about the poor state of the British economy, the frequent strikes and high rate of inflation, in short the condition known as *Igirisu byō* ('the English disease'). 'The English disease' was surely one of the resonances felt by Tokyo audiences when Odashima's translation of *Richard II* was first staged in 1979.

Odashima's *Ingurando* offers a palpable 'sense of English history' which may otherwise elude Japanese audiences. *Richard II* is a play that confounds one myth of Englishness still popular in Japan – of England as the land of 'gentlemen' (*shinshi*) – given the behaviour of both king and usurper. In a book on Shakespeare and Japanese identity, Miyoshi Hiroshi notes that by the end of the play Richard has lost all semblance of kingship and has become 'no more than some woebegone philosopher'.[30] Murai Kazuhiko discusses the contrariness of language, the way that in *Richard II* (of all the history plays) rhetoric subverts meaning in the pursuit of power.[31] Insincerity and superfluity of speech are frequently admonished in Japanese Buddhist discourse; Richard III is obviously in that sense 'a wicked person'. The tight rhetorical structures of Shakespearean drama are also foreign to traditional Japanese drama, for whom structure is created through the cumulative resonances of loosely connected happenings. For Japanese audiences, Shakespeare's history plays may appear to be a rather predictable series of battle scenes in which a myth of English greatness always manages to assert itself both as theatre and language. It goes without saying that Japan enjoyed neither imperial success in the twentieth century nor its language global acceptance. The fate of the second Richard is to lose linguistic sovereignty, which for Japanese audiences who have sat through the play (and however long of their own modern history) may offer one opening into Shakespeare's interpretation of English history. Shakespeare's histories are made meaningful in Japan by their dramatic victims.

NOTES

All Japanese personal names cited in this article and of authors in the list of references are given in the Japanese order, surname first. Long vowels in Japanese words are marked with macrons (except in the case of Tokyo).

1 Professional productions of unadapted Japanese translations of the histories up to 1994 are listed as follows in chronological order with debut productions marked by an asterisk: *Richard III** (1962); *Richard III* (1964); *Henry IV, Pt.1** (1967); *Richard III* (1974); *Richard III* (twice) (1976); *Richard III* (twice) (1977); *Henry IV, Pt.1, Henry IV, Pt.2*, Henry V*, Richard II** (1979); *King John*, Richard III* (three times), *Henry VIII*, Henry VI, Pt.1*, Henry VI, Pt.2*, Henry VI, Pt.3** (1980); *Henry VIII, Richard III, Henry VI* trilogy (1981); *Henry VI* trilogy, *Henry IV, Pts.1* and *2* (1982); *King John* (1983); *Richard III* (1985); *Richard III* (1987); *Richard III* (1989); *Richard III* (1992); *Richard III* (three times), *King John, Henry VIII* (1993); *Richard III, Richard II* (1994). The first production in English was of *Richard II* by the Miln Company at the Yokohama Public Hall in May 1891. In January 1931 the Chikyū-za theatre company performed scenes from Tsubouchi Shōyō's translation of *Henry IV, Pt.1* and in February 1951 Wada Shōichi directed his

adaptation of Act 2, scene 4 of the same play; these were the first times that part of a history play or an adaptation were performed in Japanese. Other productions of note are Abe Ryō's adaptation of the *Henry VI/Richard III* tetralogy, 'The Wars of the Roses or Blood' (November 1971), Wada Yutaka's production of the old Shōyō translation of *Richard III* with the *kabuki* actor Onoe Tatsunosuke in the title role (September 1980), Michael Bogdanov's touring production with the English Shakespeare Company of all seven of the Wars of the Roses plays (April 1988) and a production by Sam Mendes of *Richard III* with the Royal Shakespeare Company (February 1993). With the exception of *Richard III* and *Henry IV, Pt.1* (directed and translated by Fukuda Tsuneari), all the debut productions of an unadapted translation were of the translation by Odashima Yūshi, directed by Deguchi Norio for the Shakespeare Theatre. For further details, see Minami Ryūta, 'Chronological Table of Shakespeare Productions in Japan 1866–1994', in *Shakespeare and the Japanese Stage*, edited by Sasayama Takashi, J. R. Mulryne and Margaret Shewring (Cambridge: Cambridge University Press, 1998), 257–331.

2 In 1868, the last of the Tokugawa Shōguns was overthrown and replaced with the Meiji Emperor as constitutional head of state. Modern Japanese history is often divided according to the names of the Imperial eras: Meiji (1868–1912), Taishō (1912–25), Shōwa (1925–89) and Heisei (since 1989).

3 Sumimoto Noriko, 'Early Shakespeare Scholarship in Japan: the Formative Years', in *Shakespeare in Japan*, edited by Anzai Tetsuo, Sōji Iwasaki, Holger Klein and Peter Milward (Lewiston, NY: The Edwin Mellen Press, 1999), 13–29 (pp. 13–14).

4 See Kawatake Toshio, *Nihon no Hamuretto* ('Hamlet in Japan'), (Tokyo: Nansōsha, 1972); and Takahashi Yasunari, '*Hamlet* and the Anxiety of Modern Japan', *Shakespeare Survey* 48 (1995), 99–111.

5 *Tsubouchi Shōyō shū* ('Selected Works of Tsubouchi Shōyō'), (Tokyo: Chikuma Shobō, 1969), 162. My translation.

6 Edward Dowden's *Shakspere: A Critical Study of His Mind and Art* (1875) and *A Shakspere Primer* (1877) were both published in Japanese during the 1890s.

7 Tsubouchi Shōyō (1885–6), *The Essence of the Novel*, edited and translated by Nanette Twine, *Occasional Papers* (Department of Japanese, University of Queensland), 11 (1981), ii.

8 *Tsubouchi Shōyō shū* ('Selected Works of Tsubouchi Shōyō'), 287. Quoted in Donald Keene, *Dawn to the West: Japanese Literature of the Modern Era – Poetry, Drama, Criticism* (New York: Columbia University Press, 1999), 411. Keene's translation.

9 *Tsubouchi Shōyō shū*, 307 (quoted in Keene, *Dawn to the West*, 411. Keene's translation).

10 E. H. Carr, *What is History?* (Harmondsworth: Penguin Books, 1964), 29.

11 Saitō Mamoru, 'Tiriyādo saidoku' ('Tillyard Revisited'), in *Sheikusupia no rekishigeki* ('Shakespeare's History Plays'), edited by Nihon Sheikusupia Kyōkai (Tokyo: Kenkyūsha, 1994), 167–92 (p. 167).

12 In his own historical dramas Kinoshita is apparently quite free with his sources (Keene, *Dawn to the West*, 483) but justifies this approach in comparison with Shakespeare's use of history. See Junji Kinoshita, *Sheikusupia: 'Bara sensō'* ('Shakespeare's "Wars of the Roses" tetralogy'), (Tokyo: Kōdansha, 1997), 7–8. He is interested in archetypal events and characters of universal significance.

13 This does not imply textual fidelity since Kinoshita cut the original text by two-fifths in translation in order to preserve the narrative impetus.

14 Junji Kinoshita, *Sheikusupia: 'Bara sensō'*, 7–8.

15 *Ibid.*, 23.

16 *The Tale of the Heike*, translated by Helen Craig McCullough (Stanford, CA: Stanford University Press, 1988), 23. The Gion Shōja is 'said to have been the first Buddhist monastery', built for Buddha by a rich merchant. 'At the four corners of its Hall of Impermanence (Mujōdō), an infirmary, there were four glass bells, shaped like hand drums, which rang when a monk patient was about to die' (McCullough, *The Tale of the Heike*, 479). 'The śāla, a native of India, is a tall evergreen bearing small, pale yellow flowers. According to legend, as the Buddha lay dying in a grove of these trees, their flowers turned white and fell' (484).

17 *Henry VI , Part 3*, edited by Andrew S. Cairncross (London: Methuen, 1969), 5.2.24–8. See also Yoshio Arai, *Rōdoku Sheikusupia zenshū no sekai* ('Reciting the Works of Shakespeare in Japanese: A Personal Account'), (Tokyo: Shinjusha, 1993), 191.

18 Junji Kinoshita, *Sheikusupia*, 23.

19 Junji Kinoshita, *Gekiteki to wa* ('What is Drama?'), (Tokyo: Iwanami Shoten, 1995). The essay is translated in Junji Kinoshita, *'Requiem on the Great Meridian and Selected Essays'*, translated by Brian Powell and Jason Daniel (Tokyo: Nan'un-do, 2000), 303–31.

20 *Richard III*, edited by Antony Hammond (London: Methuen, 1981), 5.5.13.

21 Matsuoka Kazuko, *'Richādo san-sei'* ('Richard III'), (Tokyo: Chikuma Shobō, 1999).

22 For example, see Nihon Sheikusupia Kyōkai (1994). None of this collection of essays by members of the Shakespeare Society of Japan makes explicit reference to comparative questions.

23 Suematsu Michiko, 'The Remarkable License: Shakespeare on the Recent Japanese Stage', in *Shakespeare in Japan*, edited by Anzai Tetsuo *et al.*, 92–104 (p. 98).

24 Fukuda visited England in 1953 to collect ideas for producing Shakespeare. He was a friend of the English director David Benthall, who visited Japan in the 1960s to train Fukuda's actors.

25 Odashima Yūshi, *Sheikusupia no ningenzō* ('Shakespeare and Humanity'), (Tokyo: Nihon Hōsō Shuppan Kyōkai, 1982), 44.

26 E. M. W. Tillyard, *Shakespeare's History Plays* (1944. Rpt. Harmondsworth: Penguin Books, 1944), 319.

27 Ueda Makoto, *Bashō and His Interpreters* (Stanford, CA: Stanford University Press, 1992), 242. The battlefield is in Hiraizumi, in north-east Japan. Bashō visited it 'in search of history', and reported that he was moved to tears.

28 *Richard II*, edited by Peter Ure (London: Methuen, 1966), 2.1.40–56.

29 *'Richādo ni-sei'* ('Richard II'), translated by Odashima Yūshi (Tokyo: Hakusui Books, 1983), 55–6.

30 Miyoshi Hiroshi, *Sheikusupia to Nihonjin no kokoro* ('Shakespeare and the Japanese Soul'), (Tokyo: Kōronsha, 1983), 259.

31 Murai Kazuhiko, 'Sakurau kotoba' ('Contrary Words'), in *Sheikusupia no rekishigeki* ('Shakespeare's History Plays'), edited by Nihon Sheikusupia Kyōkai (Tokyo: Kenkyūsha, 1994), 57–74.

PART II

Introduction: the appropriated past

Ton Hoenselaars

Both in England and abroad, the histories represent the least popular of the three major genres. This is always a relative matter, of course. Given Shakespeare's reputation worldwide, any post-Renaissance playwright is still likely to envy their increasing success. Of the individual histories, the most popular is *Richard III*. It is often assumed that the play's popularity is due to its complex and versatile main character, but also the medieval history of which Richard is part has managed to rally foreign audiences, in Italy for example. As Mariangela Tempera writes, after 1848 it was Richmond's successful invasion of England rather than any intimations of universal evil or the tragedy of the individual that made *Richard III* meaningful, as it evoked associations with the exiled Italian patriots. But just as Giorgio Strehler used his 1950 production of *Riccardo III* to address the monstrous years of Italian fascism, countless productions since the 1930s in Britain and abroad have, inadvertently or self-consciously, alluded to the Nazi dictatorship as personified by the person of the would-be rhetorician Adolf Hitler, but also by his club-footed Minister of Propaganda, Joseph Goebbels. Wartime productions of the play in Britain – like Donald Wolfit's at the Strand (1942) or Laurence Olivier's at the New Theatre (1944) – inevitably commented on the specific horrors of the time, but so did Bertolt Brecht's adaptation of *Richard III* as *The Resistible Rise of Arturo Ui* (1941).[1] It was not until the end of the 1980s, however, that a director like Richard Eyre could relativize this rather facile British way of projecting Ricardian evil on to the foreign other. As his production of *Richard III* with Ian McKellen in the title role (as well as the successful 1996 film that Richard Loncraine directed after the production) suggested, the German monstrosities could be imagined to have occurred just as well under the charismatic leadership of Sir Oswald Mosley in Britain.[2]

The most popular histories after *Richard III* have been the two plays on *Henry IV*. Like *Richard III*, these plays, as Alexander Shurbanov and Boika Sokolova put it in their discussion of the histories in Bulgaria, would appear to 'transcend the perceived "deficiencies" of the genre'. Just as *Richard III* manages to hold its own also as a tragedy and even as a comedy, *Henry IV* holds the stage – particularly where its history is perceived as foreign – due to the comic spirit that persists nearly throughout the plays. Among other things, this explains the Italian example discussed by Mariangela Tempera, of Hal's exploits with Falstaff in the two parts of *Henry IV* serving as the basis for Felice Romani's libretto of Saverio Mercadante's now almost totally forgotten comic opera, *La gioventù di Enrico V* (1834). Drawing on the comic moments from the *Henry IV* diptych, Romani took a markedly different approach from composers like Antonio Salieri or Otto Nicolai, who both relied on *The Merry Wives of Windsor*. These two traditions neatly serve to set off the uniqueness of Arrigo Boito, who, by a reverse motion, introduced material from the two histories into the *Merry Wives* libretto for Giuseppe Verdi. It is as a consequence of his complex genre bending and blending that Italians today are likely to be more familiar with the 'Honour' speech (*1 Henry IV*) as well as the 'Sherry' speech (*2 Henry IV*) via Verdi's *Falstaff* (1893).

Easily the least popular of the histories, in Britain and abroad, have been the three plays devoted to the reign of Henry VI. When they are successful, this is often due to a series of shifting conditions that attend on the individual cases of appropriation. This is also what George Bernard Shaw suggested in 'The Theatre of the Future' (1905), an absurdist tale which recounts how the *Henry VI* trilogy could become a box office success due to the introduction of a cash-for-admission system in London theatres.[3] However, as James Loehlin writes in his chapter on the trilogy, it was really Bertolt Brecht and the impact of his theory of drama that gave *Henry VI* a new lease of life during the twentieth century. The German playwright, who wrote his own stage histories, provided a theatrical language and advanced a method of social analysis which together proved capable of turning Shakespeare's representation of politics in action into compelling drama. This occurred in Britain, Europe and further afield. The impact of Brecht's view of the early histories as representations of the now historically distant decline and fall of medieval feudalism and the rise of the bourgeoisie, was obvious in Peter Hall and John Barton's landmark production of *The Wars of the Roses* at the RSC (1963), Giorgio Strehler's internationally renowned *Il gioco dei potenti* (1964) and Peter Palitzsch's equally distinguished *Krieg der Rosen* (1967). One of the major reasons why Brecht could trigger a truly international revival of interest in the neglected *Henry VI* plays was that by the 1960s specific national interests were subordinated to supranational class concerns.

Since then, numerous productions of the once so problematic plays have been staged with different agendas in England and across the world. Particularly the advent of the new millennium and the apparent desire to reflect on this historical moment has boosted the trilogy as well as the two tetralogies, alone or together, with Leon Rubin presenting the *Henry VI* plays in two parts at Stratford, Ontario (as *Henry VI: Revenge in France* and *Henry VI: Revolt in England*); with the Royal Shakespeare Company's 'This England'; and with Edward Hall's Propeller production of the plays as *Rose Rage*.[4]

It is on the occasion of these last two productions that Edward Burns comments on the tendency to string the histories together as tetralogies and cycles.[5] Burns argues that the Folio editors opted for homogeneity, associating the group of plays listed under histories with 'a sense of history which was relatively new and postdated the writing of the plays'. Burns implies that this notion of English history was really the creation of the Folio editors, working under the assumption that the plays dealt not with the matter of 'myth', like *King Lear*, but with recorded facts that were more or less verifiable. Recognizing the assemblage mode of the histories in the Folio as a fiction, Burns argues, facilitates a challenging reappraisal of *King John*, a play whose political stance interrogates and demystifies rather than supports a unitary notion of 'This England'.

Edward Burns's enticing theory about the way in which the retroactive construction of the two 'cycles' of histories as we know them today has tended to obscure the political relevance of *King John*, presents an intriguing counterpart to the account of the histories in Bulgaria as narrated by Alexander Shurbanov and Boika Sokolova. It is remarkable that in a country with a tradition of performing some of the individual, canonical histories but without a custom of presenting Shakespeare's histories in cycles, it was *King John* (as adapted by Friedrich Dürrenmatt) which should have held the stage at a vital juncture in its recent national history. Dürrenmatt's version of *King John* – a political reform play which had transported German audiences 'with the sheer force of its debunking political philosophy' during the volatile 1960s – proved immensely successful also on the stage of Sofia's Youth Theatre, and was played during two consecutive seasons, well into 1989, as in the political arena communist rule experienced its final collapse.[6] After the many years of socialism, during which the anti-tyrant chronicle of *Richard III* had increasingly come to adopt the identity of a 'foreign' history with a vengeance, the nation's political sentiments were now best expressed by means of uncanonical Shakespeare in a foreign, Swiss adaptation. Few canonical histories are likely to have negotiated a more complex field of international, political tension than *King John* on this occasion.

NOTES

1 For a concise discussion see *Richard III*, edited by John Jowett, The Oxford Shakespeare (Oxford: Oxford University Press, 2000), 96–100. On Brecht, see *Adaptations of Shakespeare: A Critical Anthology of Plays from the Seventeenth Century to the Present*, edited by Daniel Fischlin and Mark Fortier (London and New York: Routledge, 2000), 125–62.
2 Peter Holland, *English Shakespeares: Shakespeare on the English Stage in the 1990s* (Cambridge: Cambridge University Press, 1997), 49–54. On the way in which in recent years Richard III has tended be contrasted with Henry V, see Lois Potter, 'Bad and Good Authority Figures: *Richard III* and *Henry V* since 1945', *Shakespeare Jahrbuch* (1992), 39–54.
3 Bernard Shaw, 'The Theatre of the Future', in *'The Black Girl in Search of God' and Other Tales* (Harmondsworth: Penguin Books, 1946), 121–51. Also Shaw's own *Saint Joan* (1923) may be read as a thinly veiled comment on the artistic merits of the first part of *Henry VI*.
4 For the individual productions see William T. Liston's review of *Henry VI: Revenge in France* and *Henry VI: Revolt in England* in *Cahiers Elisabéthains* 62 (2002): 111–14; Patricia Lennox, '1, 2, and 3 *Henry VI*' (RSC), *Shakespeare Bulletin* 20:1 (Winter 2002), 8–10; Michael Dobson, 'Shakespeare Performances in England', *Shakespeare Survey* 54 (2001), 246–82 (pp. 274–82) and *Shakespeare Survey* 55 (2002), 285–321 (pp. 286–92); and Patricia Tatspaugh, 'Rose Rage', *Shakespeare Bulletin* 21:1 (Winter 2003), 25–6.
5 For other recent views of the cycles see Nicholas Grene, *Shakespeare's Serial History Plays* (Cambridge: Cambridge University Press, 2002), who counters the argument of recent years that the histories were not conceived of as cycles; and Stuart Hampton-Reeves, 'Theatrical After Lives', in *The Cambridge Companion to Shakespeare's History Plays*, edited by Michael Hattaway (Cambridge: Cambridge University Press, 2002), 229–44.
6 Wilhelm Hortmann, *Shakespeare on the German Stage: The Twentieth Century* (Cambridge: Cambridge University Press, 1998), 232. With great accuracy and insight, Hortmann describes the 'revolutionary' climate of the late 1960s in Germany where the prevailing feeling resulted in the premiere of two *King John* adaptations in 1968: the famous version by Friedrich Dürrenmatt, and the now rather neglected rendering by Hartmut Lange (235).

CHAPTER 5

Rent-a-past: Italian responses to Shakespeare's histories (1800–1950)

Mariangela Tempera

AN UNUSUAL EVENING

Milan, 9 February 1939: a few days after their successful *Hamlet*, the actors of the Old Vic performed *Henry V* in front of an Italian audience.[1] The hostile reaction of English public opinion to the company's presence in a fascist country had already forced the Old Vic Governors to issue a nervously worded statement about their belief 'that art has no frontiers'.[2] As for problems at the other end, the actors sent back to London anodyne reports of complete success, but the irony of the situation was not wasted on all of them. Anthony Quayle, who, in the title role, had to spur a bunch of uncomprehending foreign extras to fight for England and St George, had already remarked on the oddity of such a set-up in Lisbon, where he addressed Portuguese extras 'whose chain mail hung down beyond their fingertips, and whose helmets rested on their shoulders like coal scuttles'.[3] He must have found the scene even stranger in Milan, where the same production rules obtained and where his Italian 'band of brothers' was even more likely than the Portuguese to be soon at war with England. He was also sensitive to a strained atmosphere: throughout the Italian tour 'the intelligentsia cooed at us like doves, but from the background came the ever-growing strains of *Giovinezza*'.[4]

If the spectators had doubts about the suitability of the play for an Italian audience at that particular time in history, they knew better than to voice them. In reviewing the evening for the leading Milan newspaper, Renato Simoni carefully avoided any reference to the politics of the play in favour of uncontroversial comments on the choice to downplay the comic parts to enhance the poetry and the 'lofty patriotic rhetoric that make of *Henry V* almost an epic poem'.[5] Like the fascist censors who had (overhastily?) approved the programme, Simoni could count only on a reading knowledge of the play that, though readily available in translation, had not been previously performed in Milan. According to both Italian and English sources, *Henry V* was quite successful, and yet the next day the Governors of the Old Vic were informed that '*Hamlet* in modern dress had proved so popular in Milan that performances of other plays had been cancelled, and *Hamlet* substituted'.[6] Very likely, somebody had come to the belated conclusion that it would have been unwise to allow performances of *Henry V* in Rome, and had quietly solved the potential problem.

How could fascist censorship have failed to see from the beginning that the exaltation of British military prowess against overwhelming enemy forces was hardly the right fare for an Italian audience that was on the verge of taking arms against 'perfidious Albion'? The answer may lie in the sketchy tradition of Italian response to the histories, one that tends to drop the 'English' and to see them as a reservoir of stories that anybody can appropriate. As such, they have been anthologized as bravura pieces, set to music for the opera house or selected as star vehicles for famous actors. Occasionally, they have been pressed into service when Italian intellectuals have felt the need to make their political statements more palatable by 'renting a past', by projecting their interpretations of Italian history on to some other people's. It is a response more evident from the beginning of the nineteenth century to the 1950s than in more recent productions.

A SKETCHY KNOWLEDGE

In the early nineteenth century, the Italians' knowledge of Shakespeare's plays was limited to a handful of major tragedies and to the Italian comedies. It was mediated through the French translation of Pierre Letourneur (aka Le Tourneur) at best and through the classicist rewritings of Jean-François Ducis at worst. Some curious explorers, however, ventured into the undiscovered country of the histories. As early as 1811, for example, the anonymous author of a slim anthology of excerpts from Shakespeare offered to the attention of his readers and drawing-room actors his own translations (from the French) of a fairly unusual selection of passages. Seven excerpts out of twenty-two are from the histories. From the wealth of materials offered by Shakespeare's cycle, the choice of 'Anonymous' was idiosyncratic to say the least: it ranged from the fairly predictable 'How many thousand of my poorest subjects' (*2 Henry IV*) as an illustration of 'Sleep' to such gems as Warwick's 'See how the blood is settled in his face' (*2 Henry VI*) as the poetic rendering of 'Indizi di soffocamento in un uomo assassinato' ('Clues of death by smothering in a murdered man').[7]

A few histories were among the plays translated by Michele Leoni, while the entire cycle was included in the translations of the complete works by Carlo Rusconi (in prose) and by Giulio Carcano (in verse).[8] The problem of making the names of the characters less alien to Italian readers was brilliantly solved by Leoni, who chose as his model the list of British warriors in Ludovico Ariosto's *Orlando Furioso* (Canto x).[9] The list included Ritmonda (Richmond), Bocchingamia (Buckingham), Norfozia (Norfolk), Dorsezia (Dorset), and so on; thus altered, the protagonists of English history were ready to be woven into Italian verse and eventually to move from the world of Shakespeare's *Opere* to that of the operatic librettos. While never so popular as the great tragedies, the histories did find a select number of estimators among those readers whose interest in English history had been whetted by Sir Walter Scott's novels.

Whatever response Shakespeare's plays elicited, however, was confined to readers because no theatre company saw them as fit for performance. On the Italian scene, strictly classicist when it came to tragedies and dominated by operas, his works appeared totally unacceptable. Paradoxically, it was an elite of highly educated readers, which included the authors of truly unstageable (and unstaged) tragedies, who found fault with Shakespeare's works on the ground that his disregard for the so-called Aristotelian unities would have outraged any self-respecting theatregoer. Voltaire had found the infinite variety of his dramatic world objectionable and the Italians followed suit. Shakespeare was the product of an 'energetic, questioning, ferocious nation'.[10] Therefore, nineteenth-century Englishmen should know better than applaud his works: 'Without any rule of ideal beauty . . . their Shakespeare paints Nature in its primitive savagery. Uncouth, ferocious, cruel customs, silly servants, brutal masters, poisons, murders, shadows, rude jokes, characters galore; now one cries, now one laughs . . .'[11] The Romantics would soon challenge the imitators of Voltaire's anti-Shakespearean stance, and bring his plays to the attention of all intellectuals.

Alessandro Manzoni, the leading man of letters of nineteenth-century Italy, was very critical of the unities. He read Shakespeare's plays in Letourneur's translation, wrote extensively about them, and drew inspiration from them when writing his own tragedies. In his *Lettre à Mr Chauvet* (published in 1823) he produced a reading of *Richard II* which was heavily influenced by August Wilhelm Schlegel's theories and launched into a spirited defence of Shakespeare's handling of his topic. In his opinion, Shakespeare's reply to a critic reminding him of the twenty-four-hour law

would have been: 'Twenty-four hours? . . . Why? The reading of Holinshed's chronicles has offered my spirit the idea for a simple and great action,
single and varied, full of interest and of teachings, and I should have ruined
it, cut it short on a pure whim?'[12]

A patriot who was well aware of the dangers of openly dealing with
contemporary history in his works, Manzoni selected as the topic for his
most famous tragedy, *Adelchi* (1822), the struggle between Longobards and
Franks for control over Italy. The protagonist, a Longobard prince, bore
a strong resemblance to Hamlet, but it was to *Henry VIII* that the author
turned for his portrayal of Ermengarda, Adelchi's sister who dies after
being rejected by Charlemagne. There are unmistakable textual parallels
between her death and Queen Catherine's.[13] Both queens are models of
Christian resignation to death, but Ermengarda is fairly one-dimensional
in her helpless innocence; she lacks Catherine's political edge. Familiarity
with Manzoni's heroine coloured the subsequent readings of this passage
from *Henry VIII*, which was greatly appreciated in nineteenth-century Italy.

In the preface to his translation of the play (1855), Giulio Carcano made
it clear that he was well aware of the connection between Catherine and
Ermengarda. Manzoni's heroine influenced his own version of the passage;
in it, he toned down Catherine's bitterness and played up her otherworldli-
ness. There were other reasons for offering as favourable as possible a portrait
of the rejected queens, and they were again suggested in the preface, where
Carcano maintained that 'the vision of the dying queen [was] a thoroughly
Catholic dream'.[14] It was a way of offering, though very tentatively, a key
to *Henry VIII* that his Catholic readers, well versed in interpreting texts
written under censorship, would have found particularly appealing: in a
play written for Elizabeth I (so he believed), Shakespeare, a closet Catholic,
had managed to extol the Old Religion in front of Anne Boleyn's daughter. Carcano went on to state that 'one could hardly find a simpler, more
pathetic, truer scene than the dying queen's parting words'.[15] The next year,
he took the further step of isolating this scene, that had such power to move
readers to tears, in view of a potential staging. He offered Adelaide Ristori
Queen Catherine's death – 'a portrait of the most profound pathetic' – as
one of three possible choices for a recital that would showcase her acting
talent, the other two being Ophelia's madness and Lady Macbeth's sleep-
walking scene.[16] The 'pathetic' quality of the scene, Carcano implies, could
easily be appreciated even by that vast majority of spectators who were
totally ignorant of its context.

Ristori eventually opted for Lady Macbeth, but Carcano's selection confirmed that popular episodes could be culled not only from the best-known

tragedies but also from the history plays. While stagings of the complete plays were still unthinkable, they could be offered to the appreciation of the theatre audiences as sort of *romanze* without music. In their hunger for new plots, two librettists went even further and concocted entire operas around Shakespeare's portraits of Henry V and Richard III.

SHAKESPEAREAN LIBRETTOS: THE LOVE INTRIGUE

Along with a number of masterpieces, the history of nineteenth-century Italian opera records hundreds of completely forgotten works that were quickly put together to satisfy public demand. Very often, only the librettos survive, with their hackneyed verses and tangled plots. They testify to a taste for sensationalism which was well served by British history. Together with the several operas devoted to Elizabeth, Anne Boleyn and Mary Stuart, we find examples of works more closely related to Shakespeare's plays, histories included.[17] Inevitably, they were processed through the same ruthlessly efficient machinery that went to work on the dramatist's great tragedies: cut down the number of characters, insert a love intrigue and a mislaid letter, aim for a happy ending. Above all, beware Austrian censorship, which in Milan demanded that a librettist get approval first for a summary of the plot and then for each completed act.

In 1834, Felice Romani, possibly the most accomplished librettist of his day, wrote *La gioventù di Enrico V* for Saverio Mercadante.[18] From the two parts of *Henry IV* he lifted Falstaff, the prince's tavern pranks, the brewing of a rebellion, Henry's redemption. From Alexandre Duval's *La Jeunesse de Henry V* (1806), he took the love intrigue.[19] Arturo di Northumberland, disguised as a coachman, recognizes Elisa, his beloved, in a mysterious damsel who is staying at an inn patronized by Falstaff and by the prince. Enrico arrives with his redoubtable friends, and expounds his philosophy:

> Il regno è nella bettola,
> Lo scettro è la bottiglia.
> (Romani, *La gioventù di
> Enrico V*, 15)

My kingdom is the tavern, my sceptre is the bottle.

On hearing that Enrico plans to kidnap the damsel, Arcourt, one of the prince's friends, offers to try and persuade her to accept his courtship. From his dialogue with Elisa, we learn that she is his sister and is outraged by a letter he sent to her explaining that he wants her to attract the attention of the prince and make him marry her. But she loves Arturo who, she insists, is not a traitor:

> Artur difende
> Sacri diritti. Una corona ci chiede,
> Che ai padri suoi fu dai Lancastri tolta.
>   (18)

Arthur defends his sacred rights. He claims a crown that the Lancasters took from his fathers.

Enter Falstaff (who tries to paw her and is told off by Arcourt), followed by Enrico, who disregards the lady's protests and commands a coach to carry her to London. Arturo comes forward, recognized only by Elisa and her brother, and carries her away to safety.

The next day, Enrico tries to convince Falstaff to return the money they stole from the taxman during the night. He worries about meeting his disgruntled father. Falstaff suggests a rehearsal and plays the role of the king. He tells his 'son' that he should heed the advice of his excellent tutor. Enrico suggests that they exchange roles and as 'king' heaps abuse on Falstaff:

> Che ha sopito nel tuo cuore
> Il dover, la fe, l'onore.   (29)

Who suppressed in your heart duty, faith, and honour.

Not so, replies 'Enrico', the old rascal is better than someone he could name who uses his own sister to seduce a prince. And Falstaff produces Arcourt's incriminating letter, which Elisa lost at the moment of her hasty departure. Enrico bans Arcourt from court.

Elisa attends, masked, the court ball that precedes the departure of the loyalist army to quell Mortimer's rebellion. Enrico confesses to the mysterious stranger his anger at the despicable behaviour of Arcourt's sister. Elisa removes her mask and defends her honour. Enrico is transfixed by love:

> Io mi diedi a vita abbietta,
> Ma il mio cor, oh! il core è buono . . .
> Per voi sola in un istante
> A virtù si risvegliò . . .   (34)

I chose to lead a despicable life, but my heart, oh my heart is good . . . for you alone, in a moment it awoke to virtue . . .

Falstaff rushes in pursued by the sheriff, who wants to arrest him and Enrico for their robbery. Enrico's brother vouchsafes for him, and the prince is further spurred to virtue:

> Vieni al mio sen, fratello,
> Del mio cor grato in segno.

Come to my bosom, brother, as a token of my gratitude.

The next morning, the master of arms reminds the knights that only those who can show a pledge received from a lady can leave for the battlefield. Enrico despairs because he has got nothing to show. Elisa throws him her bracelet and he happily goes to war.

After Mortimer's defeat, Arturo is introduced by Arcourt to a group of lords who, he thinks, are gathering troops to fight Enrico in the field. To his horror, he learns that they are getting ready to ambush the prince that very evening. He manages to pass Elisa a note denouncing the plot. Although convinced that her brother is part of the conspiracy, she warns Enrico and, on hearing the sound of approaching steps, prepares to die with the prince. Arcourt arrives and reassures them: he has alerted Chiarenza (Clarence) and all the conspirators have been arrested. Falstaff rushes in with the news of Mortimer's arrest and the king's death. He hugs Enrico, but is cold-shouldered by him. The new king proposes to Elisa, who feels obliged to accept. At the coronation Falstaff promises advancement to all his creditors and looks forward to meeting the king:

> Fra la calca, fra la pressa
> Già mi cerca, già mi trova . . .
> Lo vedrete a sè chiamarmi,
> Abbracciarmi, accarezzarmi
> (50)

In the surging crowd he looks for me, he finds me . . . you'll see him call me, hug me, caress me.

But the king disowns him:

> Chi sei, vecchio?
> (50)

Who are you, old man?

On realizing that Elisa is still in love with Arturo, he sets her free, and is hailed by all his subjects.

Romani grafted into the inevitable love intrigue an adaptation of a Shakespearean plot which was, for the 1830s, remarkably faithful. He kept the contrast between a reprobate prince and a virtuous nobleman, and endeared Arturo to his audience by touching (very lightly!) upon the theme of dispossessed rights which was foremost in the minds of his Austrian dominated audience. He made the rebel lose in politics but win in love. Above all, he lifted from Shakespeare the relationship between Falstaff and the young prince, all the way up to the rejection of the old knight.

As any professional writer working to a deadline, Romani was appalled to hear that his libretto had been rejected by the censor's office shortly before the opening night:

> I did not consider the topic politically inappropriate because it is about the age-old feud between Lancaster and York which has provided material for innumerable stories, novels, and tragedies in all countries and in all times. As for morality, everybody knows how unruly Henry V's youth was. I show it changed for the better and take the prince up to the beginning of his virtuous reign. It is not true that Lord Harcourt wants to prostitute his sister, he merely wants the king to fall in love with her and then marry her, so that he can advance his own career . . . This intention, perfectly clear to me because I know the subject so well, may very well be unclear to others.[20]

The problem appeared to be with Romani's Harcourt plot rather than with what he had included of Shakespeare's *Henry IV* plays. After the necessary changes were made, and brotherly honour was restored, the opera was allowed to premiere at La Scala – and promptly fell into oblivion.

The House of York's answer to Falstaff, the fat Lancastrian knight that everybody loves, is Richard III, the arch-villain everybody loves to hate. He, too, could boast of at least one libretto on the crowded nineteenth-century musical scene. In 1859, the king had the title role in an opera created by two mediocre craftsmen. Andrea Codebò, the librettist, was an aristocrat from Modena who had served in the Piedmontese army during the Risorgimento wars, while Giambattista Meiners was a fairly competent composer of church music, posted in Vercelli, who would later emigrate to England, where he taught composition at the Guildhall School of Music. On its opening night at La Scala, this opera was not any more successful than Mercadante's *La gioventù di Enrico V*.

Influenced by the French school, Andrea Codebò took greater liberties than Romani with the Shakespearean plot. Over the tomb of the wife he has murdered, Riccardo hears from Rutland, his partner in crime, that Richemont (Richmond) is in arms at Milfort. The king rages against his enemy:

Sciagurato trema, trema,
Già ti colse l'anatema,
Vo' punirti, vo' svenarti
Sotto il piede mio schiacciarti.²¹

Tremble, tremble, you wretch, my curse is on you. I want to punish you, to cut
your veins, to squash you under my foot.

The king then informs Ugo, another of his accomplices, that he intends to
marry Isabella, queen of Normandy; the old man will have to sacrifice his
own daughter if he does not persuade the queen to consent. But Isabella is
in love with Richemont, who comes to see her and swears to save her from
Riccardo. Richemont's partisans at court feel the time has come for open
revolt:

Dunque codardi e taciti
Sempre tremar dovremo? . . .
E i nostri offesi tumuli
Mai vendicar sapremo?
(Codebò, *Riccardo III*, 14)

So in cowardly silence we'll tremble forever? And we will never avenge our defiled
tombs?

Riccardo muses on Isabella's refusal:

Io son deforme! . . . ecco la piaga orrenda
Che mi lacera il cor eternamente!   (15)

I am deformed! . . . Here lies the horrid wound that constantly eats at my heart!

He is tricked by Ugo into accepting a disguised Richemont among his
courtiers and into believing that Isabella will marry him. But the queen
cannot hide her love for Richemont and her revulsion for the king:

Va, fuggi; inulte gemono – Ancor ne' freddi avelli,
L' ombre de' miei fratelli . . .
E me tu ardisci amar! . . .   (23)

Go, leave me; My brothers' shadows still cry out from their unavenged tombs . . .
And you dare love me!

When Riccardo berates her in front of the court, Richemont jumps to her
defence, to be first seized by the king's partisans, then freed thanks to the
start of a general uprising. In the last scene, defeated and wounded to death,
Riccardo tries to stab Isabella, who is rescued by the victorious Richemont.

The tyrant dies: 'Tutti trarvi potessi nel sepolcro' (31) (If only I could drag you all in the grave with me). Everybody rejoices.

Once again, the conventions of the genre demanded that the subject matter be reorganized around a love plot. The rivalry between Richard and Richmond was therefore presented as sentimental rather than political. In the simplistic world of nineteenth-century librettos, which allowed little room for in-depth characterization, the king's deformity became the main cause of his wicked behaviour, thus turning the evil king into a Rigoletto-like figure. The adaptation of the plot to the concerns of an Italian audience went even further. By portraying the English people as humbled and con-fused at first but willing to take arms against the tyrant by the end of the opera, Codebò drew a subtextual parallel between Richard's subjects and his own countrymen on the eve of the 1860 uprisings which would bring about Italy's independence. In doing so, he was following in the footsteps of Giuseppe Verdi, who, in his *Macbeth* (1847), had transformed Ross's description of Scotland into the deeply moving and highly topical chorus, 'Patria oppressa' ('Oppressed homeland').

Outside the opera house, the larger-than-life protagonist and the ever-popular motif of civil strife contributed to single out *Richard III* as the history play that would more frequently attract the attention of Italian playwrights, actors and directors both in the nineteenth and in the twentieth century.

RICHARD III AND THE POLITICS OF EVIL

As early as 1819, *Richard III* was appropriated by an Italian dramatist whose handling of the plot was 'the best proof of his disapproval of Shakespeare's methods'.[22] A strict classicist, Francesco Benedetti set out to mould Shakespeare's chaotic plot into a regular tragedy.

His *Riccardo III* encompasses the day of the final battle, cuts down the characters to eight, and takes a few liberties with the original. Tormented by the shadows of his victims, the king lives in constant terror:

> Torbido sempre e spalancato il guardo
> Vibra qua e là; le orecchie ad ogni moto
> Tende; s' arretra, e colla man s' avventa
> All' elsa in atto di ferir.

He darts his troubled and wide-opened eyes here and there; he cocks his ears at every sound; he falls back and with his hand grabs the sword, ready to strike.[23]

He wants to repudiate Anna, who would be only too pleased to see the last of her murderous husband if only he would grant her custody of their young daughter. But Riccardo refuses. At the same time, he informs Queen Isabella that he intends to marry her daughter Isabella. The queen is outraged: not only did Riccardo poison her husband, but he ordered the murder of her two sons. She herself was a witness to the deed, which she recounts to her daughter in great detail:

> Eran sangue le chiome, i petti sangue,
> Sangue i volti riversi. Eppur con gli occhi
> Nella morte nuotanti, a forza il giorno
> Cercando, m'inviaro il guardo estremo.
> (Benedetti, *Riccardo III*, 53)

Blood on their hair, blood on their bosoms, blood on their upturned faces. And yet with their eyes, clouded by death, straining to seek the light, they looked at me one last time.

Isabella is in love with Arrigo (Richmond), and eagerly awaits the battle that could mark the end of Riccardo's reign.

The Londoners too are beginning to hope for freedom:

> . . . gente vedresti . . .
> Ferocemente stringersi la destra,
> E con sorriso ove la speme pinta,
> Dileguarsi.   (69)

. . . you would see people . . . who fiercely shake hands and then disappear with smiles on which hope is painted.

Riccardo despises them:

> [il popolo britanno] degli altrui ceppi è lieto,
> Né i suoi conosce . . .
> E sa l'oro trattar meglio che il brando . . .
> Altri frattanto dell'oprar suo stolto
> Raccoglie il frutto, e il credulo ne resta
> Deriso e nudo . . .   (70)

[the Britons] gloat over other peoples' shackles and do not see their own . . . They handle gold better than the sword . . . Meanwhile, others profit from their foolish actions, and they remain laughed at and empty-handed.

He doubts his courtiers' loyalty and demands hostages of them. When Isabella rejects him, he grudgingly admits that she has touched his heart, and yet leaves with Norfolck (*sic*) the order to kill her if he is defeated in battle. In the last act the three women anxiously hear news of a battle whose outcome hangs in the balance. Convinced that Riccardo has lost, Norfolck rushes forward to kill Isabella but is stopped by Urswich who, in order to save her, pretends that the tyrant has been defeated. While contradictory reports bring joy and woe, Anna realizes that she has been poisoned by her husband. A defeated Riccardo is dragged on to the stage. He rages because Isabella will live to become Arrigo's wife but takes some comfort in watching Anna die:

> Arda la reggia, e l' empio re con lei.
> Anglia tutta immergete in mar di sangue. Peran tutti, che niun mi sopravviva!
>
> (96)

Let the palace burn, and its evil king with it. Drown the whole of England in a sea of blood. Kill them all, so that nobody should survive me.

Benedetti's *Riccardo III* is a typical example of 'Shakespeare improved'. Not only does its author formally reshape the play, he inserts allusions to contemporary Italy and substantially alters the personality of the protagonist. The negative view of the English expressed by Richard is just as well suited to Benedetti's countrymen and will become a literary commonplace in the following years. As for the protagonist, gone is the undignified deformity of the original. The cause of this Richard's depravity is wholly psychological. It stems from a natural inability to feel:

> Son pur io la strana cosa!
> Intesi dir che dei mortali in seno
> Avvi un affetto, la pietade; io mai
> Non la conobbi . . .   (71–2)

I am a strange thing indeed! I was told that all mortals share one feeling, pity; I never experienced it . . .

Whatever natural feeling he might have had was smothered by ambition:

> Ma da quel dì che balenommi in mente
> La lusinga del trono, in mio cor tacque
> Natura istupidita . . .   (81)

But ever since I was enticed by the vision of kingship, stunned nature went silent in my heart . . .

If Jean-François Ducis had included a version of *Richard III* among his reworkings of Shakespeare's plays, the result would have been along these lines.

Another playwright, Giulio Carcano, undertook the daunting task of a complete translation of Shakespeare's plays in the hope that such a close scrutiny of a master's work would contribute to refining his own tragic skills. Unfortunately, his original plays remained highly forgettable, and Carcano's claim to a modest place in the history of Italian literature rests only on his Shakespearean translations.[24] Although his ambition to make the plays as relevant as possible to contemporary Italian readers was severely curtailed by the need to remain faithful to the original, he managed to make his political beliefs clear through his choice of words and introductory remarks. Actively involved in the Milan uprising of 1848, Carcano was forced into exile when the Austrians re-entered the city. In Switzerland, he continued his work on Shakespeare's plays by translating *Richard III*. His passionate introduction shows why he considered this play especially suited for the times. 'But a powerful and mysterious idea dominates this great tragedy. Heaven's justice descends over the head of the oppressor at the very time when he dares defy it and, in thus doing, he unwittingly fulfils the secret designs of divine Providence.'[25] Within the play, his sympathy goes openly to Richmond's party:

> If you do fight against your country's foes,
> Your country's fat shall pay your pains the hire,[26]

becomes:

> Or della patria . . .
> Combattete i nemici; a voi fra poco
> La patria stessa a larga man compenso
> Recherà d'ogni stento.
> (Carcano, *Teatro di Shakspeare*, 297)

The emphasis is on 'patria', an emotionally charged word at the time that was bound to encourage connections between Richmond's forces and the exiled Italian patriots.

Neither the availability of translations nor the changes in intellectual climate brought about by the Romantics were sufficient to ensure a theatre audience for Shakespeare's history plays. Only in 1877, at the peak of his successful career and long after his Hamlet and Othello had fascinated audiences in Italy and abroad, did Ernesto Rossi tackle the character of

Richard III. He prepared himself thoroughly for the role by attending the performances of English actors and by studying the details of Richard's extant portrait in London. In his autobiography, the artist included a glowing report on his performance from his Russian tour of 1878. The reporter was struck 'not only by the artist's perfect elocution, by his facial mimic and his body language, but also by his artistic way of deforming his face and perfectly rendering the odd and unpleasant aspect that nature had given by chance to the prince of the house of York'.[27]

After Rossi, very few actors dared take up the role of Richard. Mario Fumagalli's attempt in 1907 was booed by critics: 'One does not become a great actor by wearing the clothes of a great character.'[28] Uncut for the first time, the play was staged in 1950 when, once again, political events made it topical for an Italian audience. In post-war Milan, on a stage too small to allow for mass scenes, Giorgio Strehler faced the daunting task of reinventing Italian theatre after fascism and World War II. In an effort to do away with the tradition of the star actor, he turned to plays that encouraged ensemble work. He also felt very strongly that the theatre should stir the conscience of the spectators and make serious demands on their attention. Shakespeare's history plays seemed very well suited for his purposes. The director who was to produce the highly successful *Il gioco dei potenti* ('The game of the mighty') in 1965, first approached the histories via *Riccardo II* (1948). Inspired by Laurence Olivier's Shakespeare films, he resurrected the Elizabethan two-tiered stage and conveyed through a few symbolic elements the scene changes that were made impossible by the cramped conditions of the Piccolo Teatro. The critics enthused over the production and mused over Shakespeare's handling of Holinshed: 'It is as if today one wrote a tragedy on the basis of the many diaries, memoirs and chronicles written by Ciano, Churchill, or Amicucci, or indeed from newspaper collections.'[29] Two years later, Strehler used a similar setting for a *Riccardo III* that did take recent history into account.

By 1950 any hope that the leftist partisans who had fought against the fascist diehards of the Salò Republic might play a central political role in post-war Italy had been quashed by the results of the general election. The wounds of civil war were so recent that the subject could neither be ignored nor directly staged. Once again, Shakespeare's histories, so distant in time and space, provided a welcome vehicle for exploring contemporary themes. Many years later, Strehler looked back on his 1950 show: 'Of course, *Riccardo III* was then the monster, the monstrosity of history. We then felt the need to investigate a certain presence of the Monstrous within us. We came from a traumatic historical experience for our generation:

behind Shakespeare's monsters, there lurked the "black dog" of Vittorini's men . . .'[30] In Elio Vittorini's *Uomini e no* (1945), a novel dealing with partisan actions and black-shirt retaliation in 1944 Milan, 'Black dog' is the nickname of a fascist chief universally feared for his cruelty. Through Richard III, Strehler investigated the kind of evil men turn to when, incapable of being loved, they settle for being feared. The programme notes read: 'The deformed Plantagenet uses his intelligence to avenge himself of the horror caused by his body. He will not have love, but he will conquer power.'[31] Strehler's Richard borrowed a terrible beauty from the symbolism of death that was favoured by the members of the Salò Republic squads: 'Four men in black advanced at the sound of drums. And Richard created the void around himself . . .'[32] Black dominated the scene and the costumes, a skeleton appeared on stage to challenge the right to the throne of the usurper; at the same time, the leisurely pace of the performance ('The perfidious king dies at two a.m.' was the title of one of the reviews) encouraged the spectators to become fully aware of the monotony of evil and of its timeless quality: 'The negative and destructive potential of mankind is already expressed here in absolute terms. Compared to this, even nuclear bombs do not say anything new.'[33] The production was not a success. The spectators did not share, or even understand, Strehler's preoccupation with the eternal return of 'Black dog'. He had chosen *Riccardo III* as a means of helping his countrymen recognize 'the traits of the monster, the brutality of power, so that they and society at large would not forget them'.[34] In the hands of later directors the deformed king became once more a vehicle for star actors.

NOTES

1 The visit was part of a British Council sponsored tour which had started in Lisbon and was going to include Florence, Rome and Cairo. The play was directed by Tyrone Guthrie, Anthony Quayle played the leading role and Alec Guinness was the Chorus. The tour also included performances of *Hamlet*, *The Rivals*, *Man and Superman* and *Trelawney of the Wells*.

2 *The Old Vic and Sadler's Wells Magazine* 7:1 (Dec. 1938–Jan. 1939), 2.

3 Anthony Quayle, *A Time to Speak* (London: Barrie and Jenkins, 1990), 193.

4 *Ibid.*, 194.

5 Renato Simoni, '*Enrico V* di Shakespeare al Manzoni', *Corriere della Sera*, 10 February 1939. Quoted in Anna Cavallone Anzi, *Shakespeare nei teatri milanesi del Novecento (1904–1978)* (Bari: Adriatica, 1980), 67.

6 From the minutes of the meeting of the Governors, 10 February 1939.

7 *Saggi di eloquenza estratti dal teatro di Shakespeare* (Milan: Giuseppe Destefanis, 1811), 22–3.

8 On Leoni's translation and the intellectual climate that made it possible, see Mario Corona, *La fortuna di Shakespeare a Milano (1800–1825)* (Bari: Adriatica, 1970).

9 See Leoni's 'Nota' attached to the list of characters in his version of *Riccardo III* (Verona: Società Tipografica Editrice, 1821).

10 G. U. Pagani-Cesa, *Sovra il teatro tragico italiano* (Venice: Tipografia di Alvisopoli, 1826), 8 ('una Nazione energica, pensante, e feroce').

11 *Ibid.*, 81 (original: 'Senza norme di alcun bello ideale . . . il loro Shakespear dipinge la Natura nella sua prima selvatichezza. Rozzi costumi, feroci, crudeli, servi sciocchi, padroni brutali, veleni, assassinj, ombre, facezie di volgo, personaggi all'infinito; ora si piange, ora si ride . . .).

12 Alessandro Manzoni, *Lettre à M. C**** (1823) in *Opere varie*, edited by Guido Bezzola (Milan: Rizzoli, 1961), 359–60 (original: 'Vingt-quatre heures! . . . mais pourquoi? La lecture de la chronique de Holingshed [*sic*] a fourni à mon esprit l'idée d'une action simple et grande, une et variée, pleine d'intérêt et de leçons; et cette action, j'aurais été la défigurer, la tronquer de pur caprice!'). For Manzoni's interpretation of Shakespeare and in particular of *Richard II*, see Ezio Raimondi, 'Il dramma, il comico, il tragico', in *Il romanzo senza idillio* (Turin: Einaudi, 1974), 79–123.

13 Examined in Patrizia Beronesi, 'Il prologo storico di Manzoni', in *Il teatro del personaggio*, edited by Laura Caretti (Rome: Bulzoni, 1979), 59–60.

14 *Ibid.* (original: 'essere la visione della regina morente un sogno d'ispirazione tutta cattolica').

15 Giulio Carcano, *Teatro di Shakspeare* (Naples: Domenico de Meo, 1884), 119 (original: 'parmi che difficilmente possa additarsi una scena più semplice, più patetica, più vera di quella dell' infelice regina morente').

16 The episode is analysed in Laura Caretti, 'La regia di Lady Macbeth', in *Il teatro del personaggio*, edited by Laura Caretti, 149–50 (original: 'pittura del patetico più profondo').

17 For a survey of Shakespearean librettos see Fabio Vittorini, *Shakespeare e il melodramma romantico* (Florence: La Nuova Italia, 2000).

18 Felice Romani, *La gioventù di Enrico V* (Milan: Luigi di Giacomo Pirola, 1834).

19 For the scenes that Romani adds to Duval's plot from the first and second parts of *Henry IV*, see Stefano Verdino, 'Come lavorava Felice Romani. Dalle fonti tragiche contemporanee ai melodrammi seri', in *Felici Romani: Melodrammi, poesi, documenti*, edited by Andrea Sommariva (Florence: Olschki, 1996), 179n.

20 Felice Romani, 'Letter to C. Visconti di Modrone' (15 October 1834), reprinted in Alessandro Roccatagliati, *Felice Romani librettista* (Lucca: Libreria Musicale Italiana, 1996), 384–5:

Non ho creduto impolitico il soggetto, poiché trattasi in esso degli antichi dissidii fra la casa di Lancastro e d'Yorck di cui sono piene tutte le storie, tutti i Romanzi, e tutte le tragedie d'ogni tempo, e d'ogni nazione. Quanto alla morale, ognun sa quanto sregolata fosse la gioventù d'Enrico quinto. Io la correggo, e conduco il principe al cominciamento del virtuoso suo regno. Non è vero che Lord Harcourt voglia prostituir la sorella, vuole soltanto che il re se ne innamori e che poscia la sposi, per aver mezzo così d'inoltrarsi alle prime cariche del regno . . . Può darsi che a me padrone del soggetto cotesta intenzione paia chiarissima, ad altri no.

21 Andrea Codebò, *Riccardo III* (Milan: Paolo Ripamonti Carpano, 1859), 7.

22 Lacy Collison-Morley, *Shakespeare in Italy* (Stratford-upon-Avon: Shakespeare Head Press, 1916), 109.

23 Francesco Benedetti, *Riccardo III* (1819), in *Opere*, edited by F.-S. Orlandini, 2 vols. (Florence: Felice Le Monnier, 1858), II, 45.

24 For Carcano's translations and Shakespeare's influence on his plays, see Riccardo Duranti, 'La doppia mediazione di Carcano', in *Il teatro del personaggio*, edited by Laura Caretti, 81–111.

25 *Teatro di Shakspeare*, selected and translated into verse by Giulio Carcano (Naples: Domenico de Deo, 1884), 245 (original: 'Ma una idea possente e arcana domina il gran dramma. La giustizia del cielo discende sul capo dell' oppressore nell'ora istessa ch' egli presume di sfidarla, e compie senza saperlo, gli ascosi disegni della Provvidenza').

26 *The Tragedy of King Richard III*, edited by John Jowett (Oxford: Oxford University Press, 2000), 5.4.236–7.

27 Ernesto Rossi, *Quarant'anni di vita artistica*, 3 vols. (Florence: L. Niccolai, 1887), II, 104 (original: 'non solo dal perfetto modo di dire dell'artista, dalla sua mimica o dai suoi gesti, ma eziandio dall'artistica maniera di contraffare il volto e rendere appuntino l'esteriore originale ed antipatico che aveva sortito dalla natura il principe della casa di Yorck').

28 G. P., 'Riccardo III', in *Corriere della Sera*, 6 April 1907. Quoted in Anzi, *Shakespeare nel teatri milanesi*, 25 (original: 'Non si diventa un grande attore vestendo i panni di un grande personaggio').

29 'E' arrivato Riccardo II dopo tre secoli e mezzo', *Corriere Lombardo*, 24 April 1948 (original: 'Come chi oggi scrivesse una tragedia desumendola dai diari, memoriali e cronache di Ciano, o di Churchill, o di Amicucci, o addirittura dalle collezioni dei giornali').

30 Giorgio Strehler, 'Inscenare Shakespeare', in *Shakespeare e Jonson. Il teatro elisabettiano oggi*, edited by Agostino Lombardo (Rome: Officina Edizioni, 1979), 291 (original: 'Certo, *Riccardo III* era allora il mostro, il mostruoso della storia. C'era allora in noi una certa presenza del Mostruoso da inda-gare. Venivamo da un'esperienza storica traumatica per la nostra generazione: c' era dietro ai mostri di Shakespeare, il "cane nero" degli uomini di Vittorini . . .').

31 From the programme of the play, 1950 (original: 'Il deforme Plantageneto si serve dell'intelligenza per vendicarsi dell'orrore che suscita il suo corpo. Non avrà amore, ma conquisterà la potenza').

32 Ettore Gaipa, *Giorgio Strehler* (Bologna: Cappelli, 1959), 61 (original: 'Quattro uomini neri andavano, al rullo dei tamburi. E Riccardo creava il vuoto intorno a sé . . .').

33 Raul Radice, 'Il re perfido muore alle due di notte', *L'Europeo*, 16 February
   1950 (original: 'Le possibilità negative e distruttive dell'uomo sono già poste in
   termini assoluti. Al loro paragone nemmeno le bombe all'idrogeno non dicono
   niente di nuovo').

34 Agostino Lombardo, *Strehler e Shakespeare* (Rome: Bulzoni, 1992), 28 (original:
   'i lineamenti del mostro, la brutalità e la violenza del potere, sì da non farli
   dimenticare a se stessi e alla società . . .').

CHAPTER 6

Brecht and the rediscovery of Henry VI

James N. Loehlin

In the mid-1960s, after centuries of neglect, Shakespeare's *Henry VI* was given major performances all over Europe. The cycle of early plays recounting the dynastic struggles of the Plantagenets was performed in Britain, Italy and West Germany; a French production followed in the seventies. A number of factors contributed to the resurgence of interest in the three-part *Henry VI* cycle. The Shakespeare quatercentenary in 1964 prompted directors to explore lesser-known plays. A trend in the European theatre away from star-centred commercial production and toward ensemble companies facilitated the staging of such large-scale works. Jan Kott's influential essay 'The Kings', in *Shakespeare our Contemporary*, provided a vivid modern reading of the plays as a study of the cyclical nature of tyranny, relevant to a Europe struggling with the legacy of Hitler and Stalin.[1] But perhaps the single greatest factor in the rediscovery of the *Henry VI* plays was the widening influence of Bertolt Brecht on the European theatre of the 1960s.

Though *Richard III*, the fourth play of the early tetralogy, was a regular part of the European repertory because of its flamboyant leading part, the three parts of *Henry VI* had rarely been performed outside the UK. Even within Britain, the plays' sprawling dramaturgy and seeming obscurity made them 'foreign' histories. Ten or more hours of medieval in-fighting, unrelieved by comedy, romance, or even a dominant central character, would seem unlikely material for any director, particularly one without a national connection to the story. Yet beginning in the 1960s, the combination of historical analysis, dramatic theory and theatrical practice associated with Bertolt Brecht provided the European theatre with the key to unlocking these intractable old plays. Brecht's own play of early modern war and politics, *Mother Courage and her Children*, which made an influential European tour in 1956, served as a model for historical theatre. With its harsh, spare staging, its blend of contemporary immediacy and historical detail, and its representation of war as a mixture of cynical politics at the top and brutal economic realities at the base, *Mother Courage* showed

European directors a way to make Shakespeare's early histories intelligible to audiences in the second half of the twentieth century. Brecht's epic dramaturgy provided a justification for the construction of the plays, which retain the episodic narrative of the chronicles in place of an Aristotelian unity. Brecht's theatrical practice, with its attack on comforting illusions, encouraged a stark design style well suited to the plays' emblematic groupings and gritty details. Finally, Brecht's method of political analysis served as an alternative to the prevailing academic interpretation of the plays as conservative homilies on divine providence and the dangers of rebellion. Michael Hattaway exemplifies this alternative interpretation by citing a line from early in *1 Henry VI*. When a messenger reports the loss of France to the nobles assembled for Henry V's funeral, they automatically interpret this political catastrophe in moral and theological terms, as the sin of treachery. 'No treachery,' the messenger replies, 'but want of men and money.'[2] This emphasis on the harsh economics of war and government is thoroughly Brechtian, and serves as a keynote for the modern productions of the *Henry VI* plays.

The three important productions of the sixties were Peter Hall and John Barton's *The Wars of the Roses*, for the Royal Shakespeare Company in 1963 (incorporating *Richard III* as well as *Henry VI*); Giorgio Strehler's *Il gioco dei potenti*, first staged in Milan in 1965; and Peter Palitzsch's *Der Krieg der Rosen*, performed at Stuttgart in 1967. While each of these productions took a different approach to Shakespeare's early dramas of war and politics, all used Brechtian theories and techniques to give the plays powerful contemporary impact.

Both in England and on the continent, previous productions of Shakespeare's history plays had largely been confined to those which had a star part for the leading actor, with *Richard III* the most popular. When the other history plays were produced, they were generally treated as an opportunity for antiquarian pageantry or, in England at least, patriotic propaganda. Aaron Hill's 1745 adaptation of *Henry V* featured the Genius of England singing to 'Happy Albion' at the Battle of Agincourt; John Philip Kemble ended his production of the same play with a stirring apostrophe to the English forces fighting against Napoleon. The few productions of multiple-play cycles placed great emphasis on medieval costumes, banners and heraldry, rather than on the details of political intrigue. Franz von Dingelstedt staged an ambitious version of both historical tetralogies at Weimar in 1864, inspired 'primarily by the opportunities the plays offered for spectacle'.[3] In Bochum in 1927, Saladin Schmidt staged all ten history plays in a manner 'as historically correct and as lavish as possible', according to Wilhelm Hortmann; the Frankfurt critic found it 'a historical pageant' defined by 'the director's ability to fill half a dozen coronation halls with flags, canopies, emblems'.[4] In England in 1951, the year of the Festival of Britain, both history cycles were undertaken in a spirit of patriotic reflection on glories past. Sir Barry Jackson and Douglas Seale commenced the *Henry VI* plays at Birmingham, eventually transferring the whole cycle to the Old Vic in 1953. In Stratford-upon-Avon, Anthony Quayle staged a version of the second tetralogy (*Richard II–Henry V*) that was unified not only by the splendor of Tanya Moiseiwitch's costumes but by a conservative political message derived from contemporary scholarship. Influenced by the work of E. M. W. Tillyard and John Dover Wilson, Quayle made the tetralogy a national epic in which the curse incurred by the deposition of Richard II is expiated through the heroism of Henry V's conquest of France. Falstaff was rejected as 'a gigantic excrescence on the surface of the plays, the symbol of a genial but finally intolerable anarchy'.[5] Quayle's production typified the influential 'Tudor myth' interpretation of the histories propounded by Tillyard: that the plays represent an essentially conservative message legitimizing Elizabethan state power. For Tillyard and Quayle, the plays expressed a longing for order, and an acceptance of a hierarchical form of cosmic and political organization. According to this view, the conception of history embodied by the plays was conservative and providential, with God's hand guiding England to its eventual triumph under the Tudors. This vision of history was turned on its head by Jan Kott and Bertolt Brecht.

Kott's work had, perhaps, a more immediate and obvious impact on the first tetralogy than did Brecht's. His influence was acknowledged by Hall, Strehler and Palitzsch, and widely cited in journalistic discussions of the plays. *Shakespeare Our Contemporary* only appeared in England in 1964, but its impact on Shakespearean performance had already been felt. Peter Brook's 1962 production of *King Lear* was based directly on Kott's essay '*King Lear* or *Endgame*', which Brook had read in French. Hall had read Kott's essay on the histories in proof before beginning rehearsals for *The Wars of the Roses*; he quoted extensively from it at his first meeting of the company, and copies of the book circulated among the actors during rehearsals.[6] 'The Kings' provides a view of history that is bleak, cyclical and grimly fatalistic. Having lived through the Stalinist terror in Poland, Kott was unable to accept the dialectical progress of marxian history. For him, history was a 'Grand Mechanism' of tyranny and usurpation:

Feudal history is like a grand staircase on which there treads a constant procession of kings. Every step upwards is marked by murder, perfidy, treachery. Every step brings the throne nearer. Another step and the crown will fall . . . From the highest step there is only a leap into the abyss. The monarchs change. But all of them – good and bad, brave and cowardly, vile and noble, naive and cynical – tread on the steps that are always the same.[7]

One of the most striking aspects of Kott's reading of Shakespeare's kings is his refusal to make exceptions for the 'good' ones, such as Henry V and the Earl of Richmond, the future Henry VII. 'The Kings' closes with a striking image of Richmond's coronation, inspired by a Polish production: the new king 'suddenly gives a crowing sound like Richard's, and for a moment, the same sort of grimace twists his face. The bars are being lowered. The face of the new king is radiant again' (Kott, *Shakespeare Our Contemporary*, 55).

While Kott's thesis was striking and influential, it lacked the theoretical complexity of Brecht, as well as the practical nature of Brecht's reflections on staging Shakespeare. Brecht saw Shakespeare, not as his contemporary, but as an insightful observer of history who was himself located in history: 'What really matters is to play these old works historically, which means setting them in powerful contrast to our own time. For it is only against the background of our time that their shape emerges as an old shape, and without this background I doubt if they could have any shape at all.'[8] Brecht saw Shakespeare as documenting a unique historical moment, when the world was in transition between the fall of feudalism and the rise of the bourgeoisie. As the philosopher asks in *The Messingkauf Dialogues*: 'How could there be anything more complex, fascinating and important than the decline of the great ruling classes?' (59).

For Brecht, the historical distance of the plays allows a critical perspective on the death throes of feudalism. Brecht felt that Shakespeare's histories, with their episodic staging of events from the old chronicles, had the character of his own 'epic theatre': 'in the historical plays, where the epic element comes through most strongly, the existing material has been most resistant to assimilation' by the bourgeois theatre.[9] The events are 'estranged' or 'alienated', *verfremdet*, in Brecht's term, so that the audience can see them as historically specific and therefore alterable. Brecht felt these built-in alienation-effects could be highlighted in performance: 'If I want to see *Richard III*, I don't want to feel like Richard III, I want to see this phenomenon in its full strangeness and incomprehensibility' (Zander, *Shakespeare 'bearbeitet'*, 80).

Brecht did not himself direct any of Shakespeare's histories, though he adapted *Richard III* into a comic parable about Hitler, *The Resistible Rise of Arturo Ui*. Juxtaposing the techniques of Elizabethan tragedy and the American gangster film, he sought to remove from Hitler the aura of awe and admiration which attends the great villains of drama and of history: 'The great political criminals must be thoroughly stripped bare and exposed to ridicule. Because they are not great political criminals at all, but the perpetrators of great political crimes, which is something very different...'[10] Brecht's detached and critical attitude to history is a bracing alternative to the 'Tudor myth', and provides a shrewd perspective on the power struggles of the Plantagenets. Further, Brecht's interest in the way ordinary people are implicated in the power relations in a given society finds much fertile material in the *Henry VI* plays. In *2 Henry VI*, for instance, the comic episode of Saunder Simpcox and his feigned lameness is given sudden political weight by his wife's cry, 'Alas, sir, we did it for pure need' (2.1.160). The scenes showing the involvement of working people in the machinations of the barons – such as the quarrel between servant and master in *2 Henry VI* – recall Mother Courage's observations that the interests of rulers and ruled rarely coincide during a war. The whole episode of Cade's rebellion shows a range of styles of political manipulation, as the people are led in various ways away from their class interests. Finally, the emblematic battle scenes, notably that of the son who has killed his father and the father who has killed his son, have a stark, anti-illusionistic power in keeping with Brecht's political and theatrical outlook.

Brecht's aesthetic practices proved as germane to the early histories as his dramaturgical ones. Influenced by Erwin Piscator, and working along with designers Teo Otto, Caspar Neher and Karl von Appen, Brecht worked for a theatre free of illusions, one that gave the audience the opportunity to observe events critically and rationally. Harsh white lighting, scene titles, carefully chosen and socially representative properties, emblematic stage pictures, songs – all served, in Brecht's theatre, to disrupt the audience's identification with characters and to reveal the social and historical bases of the events occurring on stage. When the Berliner Ensemble toured Europe in the mid-1950s, these aesthetic choices initially made as much impact as the theory behind the plays, and the design was the most obviously Brechtian aspect of the landmark Hall–Barton *Wars of the Roses* in 1963.

Even before the Hall–Barton production, Brecht's influence was beginning to be felt on the history plays. Roger Planchon staged *Henry IV* for a working class audience at Villeurbanne in 1957, in a production that, according to Dennis Kennedy, 'established the political relevance of the histories for Europe six years prior to Peter Hall's rediscovery of them'.[11] Kennedy cites Kenneth Tynan's description of Planchon's approach:

The plays were boiled down to the bare social bones; each point was made, coolly and pungently, on a rostrum backed by a map of medieval England, and each scene was prefaced by a caption, projected on to a screen, that summed up the import of what we were about to see. Individual characterization was subjected to the larger image of declining feudalism. (*Looking at Shakespeare*, 212)

Planchon repeatedly emphasized the sufferings of the people resulting from the actions of the nobles, and he ended the play with a wholly unsympathetic Hal cruelly rejecting Falstaff.

In the early sixties the Vienna Burgtheater, a bastion of *haute-bourgeois* opulence, staged a complete history cycle as a major cultural event. But the director and designer, Leopold Lindtberg and Teo Otto, had been the team responsible for the world premiere of Brecht's *Mother Courage* in Zurich in 1941. Though the Burgtheater histories had grandeur and epic sweep, they were given a visual sobriety appropriate to the questioning spirit of the period, and in some ways anticipated the work of Hall and Barton. As Dennis Kennedy has observed, 'the Viennese were allowed to have it both ways' (*Looking at Shakespeare*, 215).

There is no doubt, however, that the Hall–Barton cycle was the most influential revaluation of Shakespeare's early histories, nor that Brecht was a significant influence upon it. Hall had formed the RSC in 1961 as an ensemble on the model of the Berliner, and its approach to the material was cool, rational and political. Design was certainly a major factor in the production's impact. John Bury, who had designed the first English production of *Mother Courage* for Theatre Workshop, emulated the principles of Neher and Appen to create a breakthrough in English Shakespeare production. The set was spare and harsh, with an emphasis on real materials, most notably plated steel. The floors and walls of the stage were covered with textured metal, which gave a chilling clang when soldiers marched, fought and fell upon it. Though the walls could be rearranged to suggest specific locales, the effect was minimalist compared to the more heavily pictorial productions at Stratford in the forties and fifties. 'We wanted an image rather than a naturalistic setting,' according to Bury. 'We were trying to make a world, a dangerous world, a terrible world, in which all these happenings fit.'[12] Bury employed the Brechtian device of 'selective realism', choosing a few emblematic properties to convey the social dimensions of the story (Kennedy, *Looking at Shakespeare*, 203). The most important of these was a huge iron council table, which dominated the court scenes. This device provided a concrete visualization of the fluctuations of power, establishing the relations of various factions merely by their position at the table. Other significant properties included carts of war specifically recalling

Mother Courage's wagon and huge ceremonial broadswords too heavy for combat: a vivid metaphor for self-destructive feudalism. The metallic image of the plays extended to Bury's costumes, which were heavy and rough, and took their colours from iron rust, polished steel, gold and copper. Their outlines were medieval, but their weight and texture gave them a gritty immediacy, like those of the soldiers in *Mother Courage* or the Ironshirts in *The Caucasian Chalk Circle*.

Hall acknowledged the importance of both Kott and Brecht in his approach to the material. Kott's influence seems to have been paramount, given Hall's emphasis on the contemporaneity of the plays: 'I realized that the mechanisms of power had not changed in centuries. We also were in the middle of a blood-soaked century. I was convinced that a presentation of one of the bloodiest and most hypocritical periods in history would teach many lessons about the present' (Pearson, *A Band of Heroes*, 9). Alan Sinfield and others have argued that the Kottian influence on the production neutralized it politically.[13] Yet while Hall echoed Kott's ahistoricism, his practical staging choices were often very Brechtian. The workings of politics were foregrounded throughout, as the competing factions used the rhetoric of public welfare to serve naked self-interest. The rebel leader Jack Cade was sometimes comic but never ridiculous and his promise to the people that the realm would be held in common was meant and taken, seriously. The jokes in the Cade sequence were clearly set apart from the genuine political grievances of the commoners. (In the later scenes, Cade became a frightening demagogue, using a Hitlerian style of oratory and engaging in brutal violence against even his own followers.) The Battle of Towton was given a striking, emblematic staging; Henry's emotion was never allowed to overwhelm the simple, powerful images of the son who has killed his father and the father who has killed his son. Their speeches were grave and presentational rather than naturalistic, and Henry's moral and political culpability was laid out all the more starkly.

Character was subordinated to the political narrative throughout *The Wars of the Roses*. The only star performer in the company was Peggy Ashcroft, who played the role of Queen Margaret. Though she was linked to an older stage tradition – she had played Juliet opposite John Gielgud and Laurence Olivier in 1935 – she was also a supporter of the political post-war theatre. She had played Shen Te in *The Good Woman of Setzuan* at the Royal Court, and in preparation for the role she had met with Brecht and Helene Weigel in Berlin. Her Margaret was described by one critic as 'a royal Mother Courage', forging on through decades of war, and losing

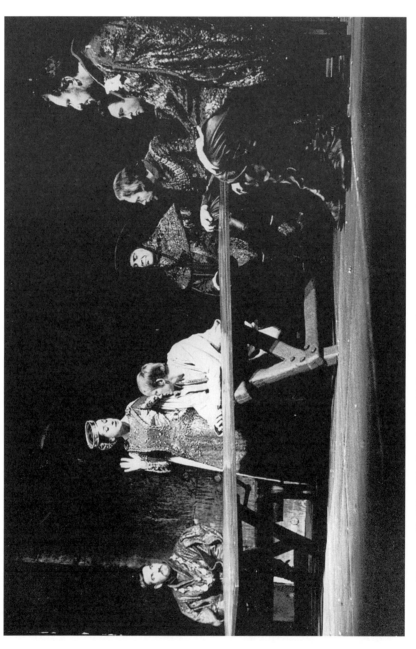

Figure 3. *The Wars of the Roses* (1963) with Peggy Ashcroft as Queen Margaret and David Warner as Henry VI.

her children through her misguided attempt to make that war work for her (Pearson, *A Band of Heroes*, 33). Aside from Ashcroft, the company was relatively young and unknown, and worked together to create an ensemble approach to the plays. Ian Holm made Richard Gloucester not a charismatic demon but merely a perpetrator of political crimes, a representative of his class rather than a fascinating aberration. 'I played Richard very much as a cog in the historical wheel, and not as an individual character,' Holm recalled. 'We tried very hard to get away from the Olivier/Irving image of the great Machiavellian villain' (Pearson, *A Band of Heroes*, 54). The final defeat of Richard therefore did not represent a cleansing of the kingdom. As Hall said, 'I don't think that Shakespeare is saying, when Richmond arrives as a real progressive force at the end, that we are all going to live happily ever after'. Hall's ending was coloured with pessimism: 'Historically the needs of power don't change. Henry VIII kept on murdering. Elizabeth went on murdering . . . The stuff of these plays is still obviously in our lives today' (Pearson, *A Band of Heroes*, 25). The final ideological impact of *The Wars of the Roses* thus owed more to Kott's nihilism than Brecht's marxism. Yet the production nonetheless was one of the most influential attempts to emulate Brecht's stage practice, and thus was a watershed in English Shakespeare production.

John Barton had rewritten and edited *Henry VI* down to two plays, which were presented together with *Richard III*; the following year, in Milan, Giorgio Strehler presented *Henry VI* on its own, over two evenings, under the title *Il gioco dei potenti*. As the title suggests, Strehler treated the civil wars symbolically, as the power games of overgrown children. Strehler cut the scenes of war with France, focusing instead on domestic strife among the English nobility. The central image of the play was a whirling carousel representing the dizzying struggles of the Plantagenet factions. Strehler frequently used emblematic simultaneous staging, sometimes suggesting the three rings of a circus with his multiple playing areas. The opening funeral of Henry V was counterpointed by a children's game ending with the crowning of the boy-king Henry VI. While the funeral proceeded on one side of the stage, a group of children, in silhouette behind a white curtain, playfully dressed themselves in the robes of power. Gradually their shadows grew to monstrous size, and with a sudden light change, they emerged as the new ruling class. The moment invoked the sequence in Brecht's *Galileo* in which the new Pope hardens in his opinions as he is dressed in his robes; it also recalled Pirandello and the Absurd. Throughout the cycle, Strehler portrayed politics as theatre, showing the role-playing and game-playing involved in even the most bitter confrontations. Yet the dominant influence was Brecht, whose work had much occupied Strehler in the preceding years.[14] Accordingly, Strehler had a somewhat more positive, politically engaged approach to the plays than had Hall and Barton. In Strehler's words, the production expressed a 'faith in theatre as something which speaks to lots of people, entertaining but not hypnotising them, faith in the message which comes through by the end of every performance' (Hirst, *Giorgio Strehler*, 72).

Strehler used Brechtian 'selective realism' in his treatment of stage properties. The throne and the crown were central emblems. The former was worn and mildewed, but covered with gold cloth and carried on a plank in processions, so that, in Strehler's words, 'the king is carried around in it like a pope who more clearly resembles a clown' (Hirst, *Giorgio Strehler*, 73). The crown was likewise a symbol of the futility of power, made of tin, with cheap glass jewels, and lopsided.

A celebrated moment from Strehler's production exemplifies his emblematic staging. It is a sort of anti-alienation effect, like the silent scream of Helene Weigel's Mother Courage after she has had to deny knowing her slain son in order to save her own life. In the third part of *Henry VI*, Strehler made much of the scene in which a father discovers he has killed his own son at the Battle of Towton. Strehler had the actor wear a beast's mask, 'which he tore off in discovering the body's identity, to reveal an anguished human face. The audience [was] confronted with the human reality of the Civil Wars.'[15]

Strehler's direction often showed a Brechtian class-consciousness. The battle scenes made a clear distinction between the nobility, menacing masked figures armoured like samurai, and the ordinary soldiers, who fought and died repeatedly in the endless civil wars. 'The image,' wrote Strehler, 'is one of bloodstained puppets which fall down and get up again as soon as the strings are jerked' (Hirst, *Giorgio Strehler*, 74). Strehler did give the people some political legitimacy, especially in the episode of Cade's rebellion, which recalled his similarly leftist interpretation of the plebeian uprising in *Coriolanus* in 1957. Neither the grotesque buffoon suggested by the text nor the charismatic, shifty demagogue of the Hall–Barton version, Strehler's Jack Cade was a populist hero.

Although influenced by Kott's cyclical vision of the histories, Strehler asserted that '[t]he pessimism of Shakespeare's tragic vision is never absolutely negative. He's not a Beckett' (Berry, *On Directing Shakespeare*, 125). Strehler's Brechtian/Marxian viewpoint allowed for the possibility of change through historical dialectic. As he described it:

Perhaps all the plays of Shakespeare are to be seen as a grand allegory of history in which all those with power are kings, who kill each other for power, the power which corrupts. It's a process from which the people are absent . . . The question is whether Shakespeare perceived a point of exit, and that is hard. My view is that Shakespeare had a pessimistic vision of history, but not a pessimistic vision of man . . . The circle is never absolutely closed in itself. (Berry, *On Directing Shakespeare*, 126)

A somewhat bleaker version of the plays was staged by Peter Palitzsch at Stuttgart two years later. Palitzsch had been Brecht's dramaturg and successor at the Berliner Ensemble, but remained in the West when the Berlin Wall was erected. Initially regarded as the inheritor of the classical Brecht style, at least in the West, he soon developed his own artistic identity. For *Der Krieg der Rosen* he worked with the designer Wilfried Minks, best known for his collaborations with the anti-Brechtian iconoclast Peter Zadek. Palitzsch and Minks presented a vision of the Wars of the Roses that was both highly politicized and deeply absurd.[16]

Der Krieg der Rosen was performed over two evenings. It contained all but a few of the nearly eighty scenes of the *Henry VI* trilogy; it ended with the opening monologue of *Richard III*, suggesting further horrors to come. For the most part its outlook was deeply cynical, presenting the feudal conflicts as grotesque, ceaseless and repetitive. The battles were all staged in the same way, so that they took on a ritual character. As Horst Zander observed, 'The impression which results is that the continually recurring events are not limited to feudal society but continue under different social forms – that they constitute a form of 'grand mechanism' with an aura of timelessness' (Zander, *Shakespeare 'bearbeitet'*, 212). This post-marxian attitude obviously follows Jan Kott. Yet many elements of the production and the design indicate Palitzsch's debt to Brecht.

Wilfried Minks's set combined historical specificity with functional modernity, while at the same time solving the practical problem of changing rapidly among many different locales. Just beyond the forestage was a wall of twelve smooth white panels that could be opened up completely or could close off any portion of the stage, allowing great alterations in stage volume. Behind these, at the back of the stage, tapestries or murals were used to suggest the ceremonial aspect of the period. Set pieces were inserted between the panels to represent gates, facades, thrones and the like. The panel arrangement allowed for seamless scene changes as well as the simultaneous presentation of different scenes. The death of Salisbury, for instance, was represented by an artillery gun firing in an opening on the left side of the stage, and, after a brief pause, the ball striking on the opposite side. The grotesquely comic effect was a deliberate part of Palitzsch's approach to the battle scenes; according to *Theater Heute*, 'in the French part of the plot Palitzsch has elevated the scenic joke to a principle'.[17]

There were many specifically Brechtian aspects to the design. The presence of the smooth, modern white panels between the audience and the action was inherently alienating, keeping events at a historical and emotional distance. The scene locations were flashed on a band just below the stage, emphasizing the historical specificity as Brecht had done in *Mother Courage*. The leather and metal costumes conveyed period detail as well as typically Brechtian materiality, and the harsh white lights remained uniform and visible throughout. The lighting instruments were incorporated into the most distinctive feature of the design. The light bridge over the proscenium was filled with the bones of men and horses and broken implements of war. This 'death frieze' embodied a central idea of the production, the idea of life observed by the dead:

I think that came about because we thought, what's important in this Shakespeare, where the figures are involved in fierce power struggles . . . only when they die, that is only when they are out of the direct power struggle do they begin to reflect and ask, 'Why, all of that?' . . . We sought a sensual expression for this and found the frieze.[18]

The frieze was connected with Palitzsch's conception of the 'wheel of power'. For Palitzsch, the moment of death brings some kind of recognition of the absurdity of the cycles of power, and perhaps some hope for change: 'Only when the wheel brings them down do they begin to think historically' (Rouse, 'Bertolt Brecht's Interpretational Model', 418).

Many of Palitzsch's staging choices recalled Brecht's use of irony. The English hero Talbot, a pillar of virtue in Shakespeare, was made a cowardly braggart: his big speeches were undercut by his flights from the enemy and his willingness to stab people in the back. Many of Palitzsch's choices were specifically class-conscious. In Shakespeare's *1 Henry VI*, an English soldier manages to rout the French merely with Talbot's name, crying 'A Talbot, a Talbot!' during the recapture of Orleans (2.1.78–81). In Palitzsch's version, it was a French soldier who used this trick, in order to seize some plunder from the French nobility. As Horst Zander observed, 'The adaptors illustrate that the real front runs not between the nations, as in Shakespeare, but through them, between classes, not nations' (*Shakespeare 'bearbeitet'*, 214). At the beginning of the scene, Palitzsch used his subdivided stage to show both the French generals carousing over their victory and their freezing

Figure 4. Peter Palitzsch's *Der Krieg der Rosen*, Stuttgart, 1967.

sentries keeping watch outside, who speak lines adapted by Paltizsch's dramaturg, Jörg Wehmeier:

> It is not right that we poor souls,
> While others gluttonously eat and drink and whore,
> Must keep our watch here in the dark and cold.[19]

The civil wars in England were likewise represented not in terms of the conflict between noble factions but that between rulers and ruled. At one point, an English sailor responds to Queen Margaret's battle speech with lines that could have been written by Brecht:

> Ruled by a woman and a child
> Harried and stirred up by big speeches
> It's nothing to us, nothing at all
> But how will it turn out for those to whom it is nothing?[20]

One element of Shakespeare's play Palitzsch chose to expand and emphasize was the manipulation of the people by political rhetoric. In this Palitzsch was directly alluding to what he saw as contemporary attempts to distract the masses from their own interests. His Jack Cade, unlike Strehler's, was purely a tool of the York faction, 'just as power-hungry, brutal, and butcherlike as the feudal nobility' (Zander, Shakespeare 'bearbeitet', 270). His cruelty in the murder of Lord Say prevented any audience identification, and his own stabbing by the self-righteous and hypocritical squire Iden was merely an appropriately ironic end.

While most of the heroic or noble figures in Shakespeare's play, like Talbot and Duke Humphrey, were made to appear selfish and cruel, Palitzsch's King Henry remained a gentle and humane figure. His melancholy reflections were given at full length and with great impact. His very powerlessness allowed him to see through the mechanisms of power, so that the production's bitterness was not wholly unleavened by idealism. Henry's humanity signalled at least the possibility of an alternative to the prevailing system, some hope for change. Yet Palitzsch's main focus was on the system itself, a historical order founded on insupportable inequities and bound for self-destruction. Palitzsch's shrewd stagecraft, his use of Brechtian irony and counterpoint, tellingly illustrated the cracks in medieval ideology. As Wilhelm Hortmann describes the production: 'The inherent self-contradictions of feudal society, its moral indifference and stark brutality were thus exposed to the criticism of the audience without resort to overt agitation. It was a highly instructive history lesson in applied dialectical materialism, the first and most successful of many' (*Shakespeare on the German Stage*, 230).

The success of these productions established the *Henry VI* plays as viable texts for performance; the ensuing decades saw numerous productions across Europe and North America. When Terry Hands directed an uncut production of the *Henry VI* trilogy for the RSC in 1977, Homer Swander lauded the event in *Shakespeare Quarterly* as 'The Rediscovery of *Henry VI* '. Yet that process of rediscovery had begun over a decade before, and has continued ever since. As Thomas Pendleton writes in his introduction to *Henry VI: Critical Essays*: '*Henry VI* has been rediscovered by audiences and critics every time a major production has been mounted. It has been reestablished on the stage now for a half century, although productions are still infrequent enough that audiences are usually seeing the plays for the first time.'[21] Subsequent RSC directors of the *Henry VI* plays – Adrian Noble in 1988, Katie Mitchell in 1994 and Michael Boyd in 2000 – have each taken different approaches to the dramaturgical and ideological challenges posed by the plays. As Robert Shaughnessy has observed, regular productions of history cycles have become occasions for the RSC to redefine itself; though that self-definition has often tended away from the Brechtian model with which the company began in the early sixties.[22]

By the late 1980s *Henry VI* was established as a regular part of the European repertoire, sometimes in conjunction with *Richard III* or the second tetralogy, and usually in large-scale productions that gave it the status of an epic theatrical event. The English Shakespeare Company toured internationally in 1987–9 with an influential seven-play cycle that was aggressively leftist, populist and contemporary.[23] In the 1990s there was at least one major European production virtually every year. The plays have been especially popular in Germany, perhaps because of the concern with history and politics that is Brecht's legacy, but they have been staged recently in most European countries.[24]

Two further versions are worth mentioning. The most influential European production of Shakespeare's history plays in the late 1990s was *Ten Oorlog* ('To War', 'Into Battle'), discussed elsewhere in this volume by Ton Hoenselaars. First staged in Ghent (Belgium) in 1998, it was eventually performed at the Salzburg Festival, in Hamburg and at the Berlin Theatertreffen in a German-language version called *Schlachten!* ('wars' or 'slaughter'). Adapted by Tom Lanoye and directed by Luk Perceval, *Schlachten!* cut all eight Plantagenet histories into a twelve-hour marathon of gangersterism, sex and violence.[25] In a sense, the production was antimarxist, in that it reversed the idea of historical dialectic, to show instead a medieval civilization descending into modern barbarity. Similarly, an adaptation of *Henry VI* directed by Edward Hall (Peter Hall's son), entitled *Rose Rage*, reduced the politics of *Henry VI* to a simple vision of brutality: the action was set, literally, in an abattoir. The feuding Plantagenets, represented by a cast of twelve male actors in surgical masks, hacked up pieces of raw meat to represent the bloody outcome of their power struggles. The naked savagery of these versions owes something to Kott's bleak view of Shakespearean history. Yet it has moved some distance from the Brechtian rationalism of Peter Hall's RSC, the guarded optimism of Strehler or the dialectical materialism of Brecht's disciple Palitzsch.

Nonetheless, even if these productions suggest that the quasi-Brechtian interpretation of the *Henry VI* plays is no longer predominant, the very existence of such a range of performances reveals the effectiveness of the original cycle productions of the 1960s. By providing a theatrical language and a social analysis that could make the workings of politics into compelling drama, Brecht helped recover Shakespeare's most neglected histories from centuries of obscurity. The success of all three major cycle productions bore out Brecht's own belief, expressed in his discussions of *Coriolanus*, that audiences could enjoy and profit from 'a slice of illuminated history'.[26]

NOTES

1 Jan Kott, 'The Kings', in his *Shakespeare Our Contemporary*, translated by Bolesław Taborski (London: Methuen, 1964), 3–55.
2 *1 Henry VI*, 1.1.69. All references to the plays are to *The Complete Works of Shakespeare*, edited by David Bevington, updated fourth edition (New York: Longman, 1997). For Hattaway's comment see *The Second Part of King Henry VI*, edited by Michael Hattaway (Cambridge: Cambridge University Press, 1991), 1.
3 Simon Williams, *Shakespeare on the German Stage. Vol. 1: 1586–1914* (Cambridge: Cambridge University Press, 1989), 155.
4 Wilhelm Hortman, *Shakespeare on the German Stage: The Twentieth Century* (Cambridge: Cambridge University Press, 1998), 97.
5 Robert Speaight, *Shakespeare on the Stage: An Illustrated History of Shakespearean Performance* (Boston: Little, Brown, 1973), 248.
6 Richard Pearson, *A Band of Arrogant and United Heroes: The Story of the Royal Shakespeare Company Production of The Wars of the Roses* (London: Adelphi Press, 1990), 26.
7 Kott, *Shakespeare Our Contemporary*, 10–11.
8 Bertolt Brecht, *The Messingkauf Dialogues*, translated by John Willett (London: Methuen 1965), 63–4.
9 Horst Zander, *Shakespeare 'bearbeitet': Eine Untersuchung am Beispiel der Historien: Inszenierungen 1945–75 in der Bundesrepublik Deutschland* (Tübingen: Narr, 1983), 80 (translated by Jennifer Loehlin).

10 Bertolt Brecht, 'Notes on the Resistable Rise of Arturo Ui', trans. Ralph Manheim, in *Collected Plays*, edited by Ralph Manheim and John Willett, 9 vols. (New York: Vintage, 1976), VI, 455–9.

11 Dennis Kennedy, *Looking at Shakespeare: A Visual History of Twentieth-Century Performance* (Cambridge: Cambridge University Press, 1993), 212.

12 Michael Greenwald, '*Henry VI* ', in *Shakespeare Around the Globe: A Guide to Notable Postwar Revivals*, edited by Samuel L. Leiter (New York: Greenwood Press, 1986), 234.

13 Alan Sinfield, 'Royal Shakespeare', in *Political Shakespeare: New Essays in Cultural Materialism*, edited by Jonathan Dollimore and Alan Sinfield (Ithaca, NY: Cornell University Press, 1985), 158–81.

14 Brecht had admired Strehler's 1956 staging of *The Threepenny Opera*, and Helene Weigel offered Strehler the artistic directorship of the Berliner Ensemble after Brecht's death. See David Hirst, *Giorgio Strehler* (Cambridge: Cambridge University Press, 1993), 95–6.

15 Ralph Berry, *On Directing Shakespeare: Interviews with Contemporary Directors* (London: Hamish Hamilton, 1997), 20.

16 See also Richard Riddell, 'Wilfried Minks and the Bremer Stil', unpublished Ph.D dissertation, Stanford University (1978).

17 Ernst Wendt, 'Sind Brecht-Schüler Formalisten?', *Theater Heute* 8:3 (March 1967), 26 (translated by Jennifer Loehlin).

18 John Rouse, 'Bertolt Brecht's Interpretational Model and its Influence on West German Theater Directing', unpublished Ph.D dissertation, Stanford University (1984), 416.

19 Quoted in Zander, *Shakespeare 'bearbeitet'*, 214.

20 Quoted in *ibid.*

21 *Henry VI: Critical Essays*, edited by Thomas A. Pendleton (New York and London: Routledge, 2001), 24.

22 Robert Shaughnessy, *Representing Shakespeare: England, History, and the RSC* (Hemel Hempstead: Harvester Wheatsheaf, 1994), 2.

23 A full and lively record of the production is provided in Michael Bogdanov and Michael Pennington, *The English Shakespeare Company: The Story of 'The Wars of the Roses', 1986–1989* (London: Nick Hern Books, 1992).

24 The following is a representative listing of productions of the *Henry VI* trilogy, drawn from the World Shakespeare Bibliography (edited by J. L. Harner), which is published as part of *Shakespeare Quarterly*:

    Deutsches Theater, Berlin, 1991 (dir. Katja Paryla);

    Folkteatern I Gävleborg, Gävle, Sweden, 1993 (dir. Ulf Fembro);

    Centre Dramatique Régional Poitou-Charentes/Théâtre de Gennevilliers, Paris, 1993 (dir. Stuart Seide), also presented at the Avignon Festival (1994);

    Teatrul National, Timosoara, Romania, 1995 (dir. Joan Jeremia), also presented at Novi Sad, Yugoslavia (1995);

    Tensta Teater, Stockholm, 1995 (dir. Vanda Monaco Westerståhl);

    Bremer Shakespeare Company, Theater am Leibnizplatz, Bremen, 1998 (dir. Rainer Iwerson);

Centro Servizi e Spettacoli at Cantiere, Udine, 1998 (dir. Antonio Sixty);
Volksbühne, Berlin, 1999 (dir. Frank Castorf);
Schauspielhaus, Zurich, 2000 (dir. Rüdiger Burbach);
Royal Dramatic Theatre at Elverket, Stockholm, 2000 (dir. Stein Winge).

25 Maik Hamburger, 'Salzburger Schlachteplatte', *Shakespeare Jahrbuch* 136 (2000), 209–12 (p. 210).
26 Bertolt Brecht, 'Study of the First Scene of Shakespeare's *Coriolanus*', in *Brecht on Theatre: The Development of an Aesthetic*, edited and trans. John Willett (New York: Hill and Wang, 1957), 252–65.

CHAPTER 7

Shakespeare's histories in cycles

Edward Burns

This England was the overall title of the Royal Shakespeare Company's grouping of the Shakespeare 'Histories' in their millennium season, 2000/1. One question immediately arises – but 'what England?' – and not simply because the histories of Wales, France and Burgundy are also theatrically presented, and those of Ireland and Scotland figured implicitly, but because the phrase itself is, in the RSC's citing of it, John of Gaunt's in his great scene in *Richard II*.[1] 'England' may be imaginatively present ('this') to the dying man, but the play, like the others often grouped into the 'cycle' presents us with the untenability of an iconic, emotionally graspable idea of 'England'. As we hear Gaunt articulate it, we know that 'this' is already no longer here, already in the past.

I would argue that the conception behind this kind of presentation of the plays is now, if not yet in the past, still somehow *of* it. This is a twentieth-century performance history with a romantic rationale, and its source in an editorial decision. The decision was that of Heminges and Condell, in their compilation of the Folio in 1623, to group the histories together – overriding the presence of 'tragedy' in the Quarto titles of several of them, and thus making secondary the possibility of reading them as the tragic stories of individuals or groups – and to present them in the order of the chronology of the events they depict.[2] This ordering may seem commonsensical to us, but it stems from a sense of history which was relatively new and postdated the writing of the plays.

The growth of an empirical discipline of history in Britain is often credited to figures like William Camden, and seems to be a shared intellectual interest of the antiquarians of the early seventeenth century. This involves the move towards a history based on evidence, whether of documents or existing monuments, and so a stripping away of accretions of legend, and towards a separation of history and myth.[3] Some difficulties are presented to the Folio compilers by this classification of the plays. *King Lear* is an English history as far as Shakespeare and his audience were concerned, and indeed this is how the Quarto labels it. *Macbeth* is a Scottish history, with sources as, if not more, 'historically' reputable than those of the English 'cycle'. A case could indeed be made for *Troilus and Cressida* as history from Shakespeare's point of view, and *Cymbeline* is so anomalous in this context that it becomes unclassifiable. It ends up in the tragedies, with much less right to be there than *Richard II* or *Richard III*. Shakespeare wrote it as a history, if within a definition of history already becoming outdated ('history', of course, has a history too). He was writing the same kind of history as he worked on in his early career in competition, and arguably collaboration, with playwrights like Robert Greene, George Peele and more shadowy figures, like the author of *Locrine*, a shared version of history where legend and myth are part of the articulation of the meaning of the past, if not as necessarily a matter of investigable 'fact'.

This begs two large questions; can we reconstruct Shakespeare's idea of 'history'? And what is/was 'the history' as a dramatic genre? The word is etymologically continuous with 'story', and that is a primary meaning for Shakespeare, where for us the priority is reversed. Story is only of the past in that any narration moves through the assumption that any event is antecedent or precedent in relation to others. Use of the word 'history' survives later in this context – as far as, for example, H. G. Wells's *The History of Mr Polly* (1910) – but its use, as here, is often arch, drawing attention to the littleness of the individual who is, in conventional terms, 'outside' history. We have to accept that the 'history play' is, unlike comedy, tragedy and tragicomedy, a retrospectively created generic category; it can perhaps be seen to be created in English contexts, if created inadvertently, by Heminges and Condell.

To deduce a generic rule for Shakespeare – who seems in relation to tragedy, tragicomedy and comedy to have taken accepted models and proceeded imaginatively from them, rather than seeking to replace or subvert them – would also have to be done cautiously. We have no way of knowing whether the titles on published versions of the plays were his (or what the published versions used as a source – there are, of course, no surviving manuscripts). We do not know in what form playgoers to public performances would receive information of play titles, or of the identity of the dramatist; or what precisely they would care about, or know, when they made the decision whether to see a particular play or not. All we can say is that the plays we class as the history sequence contain pieces that avoid closure of the kind that other genres might demand, and so tend to establish a habit of constructing the meaning of a moment in such a play in an open-ended reading forward/reading back to events we may already know, or have reason to feel we can predict. And, perhaps as a consequence, a convention of local closure, of episode, allows tragic and comic elements to succeed each other, or to exist in juxtaposition, without the need for reconciliation that predicates the neo-classical genre of tragicomedy. There is one element, however, which while not perhaps clear-cut enough to provide a generic marker, is both common to the plays and a link into our post-empirical sense of what 'history' is. This is an interest in 'truth' – however that is understood – and in how we know what we know – whether through the unreliable, all too falsifiable means of written documentation, through the matter of popular memory, as prompted often by the markers of existing monuments, and a concomitant interest in the hidden places of history – the dungeons and the council chambers opened up to us fiction-ally and so giving us the thrill of an imaginative relation to the hidden. I will return to this later, as it casts some light on the paths and possibilities the plays create for audiences to link and make sense of the plays, in a com-plicity within the process of making meaning – and in that sense, making history.

In presenting the plays together as a reading experience (the 'cycle' was never, in so far as we can tell, a theatre experience, until the nineteenth century) the Folio creates a new massive play from a collection of material performed at different times, to tell a story that takes us from Richard's banishing of Bolingbroke through to the accession of Henry VI. This so impressed Samuel Taylor Coleridge that he proposed, in one of his celebrated lectures on Shakespeare, that someone should fill in the gaps to tell an even longer continuous tale:

it would be desirable that some man of dramatic genius, to which I have no pretensions, should dramatise all those omitted by Shakespeare, as far down as Henry VII. Inclusive . . . It would be a fine national custom to act such a series of dramatic histories in orderly succession every Christmas holiday, and could not but tend to counteract that mock cosmopolitanism, which under a positive term really implies nothing but a negation of, or indifference to, the particular love of our country.[4]

Coleridge's aim in this is an education in patriotism, of a kind which reminds us that its context is the aftermath of the French Revolution, and the beginning of the Napoleonic wars. The 'Christmas' context suggests a family event, a marker also of the turning of the year. Coleridge seems either to ignore or wish to correct, the tradition of saturnalian, of festively

condoned sexually and politically subversive, pantomime at this time of
the British year.

This is an England – a romantic reactionary England – consciously
cutting itself off from Europe. These specific Shakespearean plays – luckily,
perhaps, nobody seems to have tried to write the others – were to become
a national epic, an epic of 'this England', a making visible and 'real' an
England to be defended and to command the loyalty of children perhaps
secretly pining for something more entertaining.

Theatrical realization of this, at least in relation to the three *Henry VI*
plays, waited for Frank Benson's performances of the plays in Stratford-
upon-Avon, 1906, greeted by one of the reviewers as 'what we would now
call a cycle'.[5] 'Now' means after Wagner's *Ring* cycle, as well as after Benson's
touring version of Aeschylus's *Oresteia*, a 'cycle' to which reviewers compared the rediscovery of the Shakespeare, largely to Shakespeare's advantage.
This was a turn-of-the-century event, like the RSC's 'millennium project'
This England, and the two points of comparison reviewers offered remind
us that on the cusp of the nineteenth and twentieth centuries history looked
more like a *Götterdämmerung* or a fall of the house of Agamemnon than
like the confident imperialist nationalism which Coleridge sought to build.
Then again, all three cycles end with disaster redeemed, even if an audience's more powerful theatrical experience is of the 'casual slaughters' of
the preceding action; after all, at this point the meaning of the twentieth
century was still very much a matter of speculative potential.

Benson's 'cycle' was performed at Stratford-upon-Avon (which thus in
the process became a kind of English Bayreuth), and this has been the
venue of a sequence of 'cycle' presentations from John Barton and Peter
Hall's adaptation of the plays as *The Wars of the Roses* of the early sixties
(1964–5) on to the millennium sequence, *This England: The Histories*. The
only other major English language presentation of the 'sequence' was that
directed by Michael Bogdanov, and devised by him and the actor Michael
Pennington for their newly formed 'English Shakespeare Company' as,
again, *The Wars of the Roses* (1986). As this suggests, the company was
formed as a challenge to the perceived hegemony of the older established
enterprise, but the choice of opening repertoire also suggests a perception
of the identity of the 'history cycle' with Stratford, and an aim to liberate
it into a more wide-ranging, more contemporary, more media-conscious
arena.

In returning to this material – and making the interesting choice of *not*
dominating it with a unified directorial vision, in employing a sequence
of different directors and designers – the millennium RSC production has

reaffirmed a sense of it as central to their repertoire, and of their repertoire as somehow of national importance.[6] The main advantage of these plays in building a company is in its requirement of an ensemble – actors can develop characterizations over a large span of time and material, but no one at the end is a star, a factor probably ever more valuable to individual performers as the company relies increasingly on aesthetically unadventurous productions of a handful of the best-known plays. The main disadvantage – and one could argue that the ESC has never recovered from this – is that it builds a male-centred, male-defined company. History apart, the main interest of the plays is in a certain kind of male heterosexual pathology, and though there are showy moments for many of the female performers, there is only – across the whole 'cycle' – one woman with a powerful position in the narrative, Margaret.

The plays, in their (in my argument) *remaking* as a larger epic, have travelled across the second half of the twentieth century, as markers of the politics, not only of their times but of that of the national companies – whatever they might be taken to stand/stand in for – that have been their home. And, largely, that home has been Stratford, an unremarkable market town, where someone happened to be born. At least Salzburg has fine buildings. But the tourist slogan for the area *is* the 'heart of England'.

There is one more Romantic legacy in this construction of a history cycle, and that is the idea of individual genius, a genius that may, even without knowing it, have had a 'vision' of England, and created an organic literary 'masterpiece' to convey it. While even conservative literary critics would feel they had to employ, at the very least, some fancy rhetorical footwork if this kind of idea homed into view in their arguments, it is part of our taken-for-granted as far as Shakespeare goes, that he may well have operated in this way. This is – probably in the light of an awareness of how scholarly arguments would challenge the assumption – the way the RSC publicity presented the millennium 'cycle': 'Conceived by Shakespeare at different times, and written in non-chronological order, they also display the genius of Shakespeare and form an incisive personal vision of what was his own recent history.'[7]

Intelligent publicity people are an ideal route, if not to commonsense, then to received opinion. What makes the notion of a 'personal vision' necessary is the absence of any evidence from the period of consecutive performances of any other than *two*-part plays and the very few published sequences of pieces that consist of three or more installments. The *Henry VI* plays do not, without controversy, fit into this category. The best evidence suggests that what we now know as parts II and III were the two parts of *The True Contention between the houses of York and Lancaster*, a play tracing the catastrophic effects of Henry VI, from, in the first moments of the play, giving away England's territories in France, to his murder by the future Richard III. What we now call *The First Part of King Henry the Sixth* may well, as I have argued elsewhere, been an ironic 'prequel', originally performed as *Harry Six* ('Harey sixt' – more or less, but variously spelled in Henslowe's 'diary').[8] Also, more significantly, given that one can, by definition, never say that evidence of a possible event *never* existed, one can argue that there is no *need* for the plays to have been conceived of in this way.

Henslowe's diary alone gives plentiful evidence of a vast theatrical recycling of the history of reasonably recent times (say, the previous 150 years), as well as of much other material perceived as historical, by a wide range of writers, working, more often than not, in an ill-defined collaboration with each other. A small proportion only has survived of this material. And while the tradition of Shakespeare scholarship has tended to study 'sources' as unitary objects of adaptation and primarily within a recoverable print culture, many of the historical events invoked in the plays were (just about) in living memory. In any case, oral culture and manuscript culture were still immensely vital; a model of dramatization of sources by which a single author took home a printed text assigned to him and 'adapted' it, is a retrospective imposition from modern working practices. The need of a modern audience for this kind of 'cycle' presentation stems, simply, from the fact that we do not know this history, and will not, unless we see it presented before us sequentially, but that would scarcely be the case for the audience for whom the plays were conceived, for whom a network of memories and information existed. The 'cycle' is also, for a modern audience, made plausible, and more attractive, by an attachment to Shakespeare as 'genius' (or, 'brand-name'?), in a way that would not have been available to an audience of the period. While the plays move from the nineteenth century to the twentieth trailing clouds of Wagner and Aeschylus, their dramatist moved from the sixteenth to the seventeenth, with little, as far as we can tell, to mark out his name from that of his fellow Henslowe employees. Plays were not marketed on writers' names; I suspect that our contemporary equivalent would be the scripting of films; it is a specialized activity, looking out for the writing credits on all but the more highly publicized 'art-movies', but one often does find out – largely by other means – that a set of movies one liked were scripted by the same person. From this point of view, Shakespeare's 'project' is not so much Romantic as quixotic – who was to know, who was to care?

To say, as I wish to argue, that what twentieth-century theatrical practice has presented to us as 'the Shakespeare Histories' is an assemblage, a compelling new fiction with no relation whatever to the original author's local aims or context, is not to say that the theatrical events that have stemmed from it have no value. Quite the contrary.

My history of 'the Shakespeare Histories' so far has taken us to a kind of paradox: the establishment of an epic 'this England' in a situation where any certainty of the value of such an enterprise is called into question by the nature and tendency of the dramatic material from which the epic is built. It seems to me that the 'history' plays question what history is, and show us 'history in the making' in that they derive so much of their dynamic from the clash between rival characters or rival groups who seek to make 'history' – in both our sense and in the Shakespearean sense, of memorable narrative, narrative extorting, to some extent, for some time, imaginative assent – in their own competing terms. The battle is over what is digested, remembered, understood. The internal dramas of the plays are in themselves a challenge to the idea of an overarching 'historical' structure on which the 'cycles' are predicated. While it is an intriguing and important part of attention to the plays to try to work back to the intellectual context that formed them, it is a fact that the theatrical life of the plays has in the recent past depended on their reshaping into something unimaginable by their instigators. But we should still ask what has been lost, and seek to turn our attention back to it. Ways of reading – ways of reading other than the cause-and-effect acceptance of what history is that the 'cycle' presentation is predicated on – have disappeared to the effect that the plays have lost, if not a dimension, at least significant resonance. And so have whole plays.

The chronological hiatus between it and the plays of the cycle have cost *King John* dear in terms of performance history and critical attention. In terms, that is, of twentieth-century performance history. For earlier audiences it was, with *Richard III*, one of the most often performed of Shakespeare's plays. To consider the reason for its disappearance from theatrical currency is to come up against the reinstatement of the *Henry VI* plays, not simply because there is only room in any one season for so many rarities – though it is undoubtedly tough at the bottom of the Shakespearean canon – but because of significant difference in the way it dramatizes history from that of the 'cycle' plays – once, that is, that they have become part of a cycle. Two interrelated questions present themselves here – what is the subliminal inclusion or exclusion strategy when it comes to things 'English'? And how do family relations, patterns of kinship operate across it? Perhaps we can find things in a closer attention to this play that take us back to the other histories, and enable us to see them differently.

The idea of the 'epic of England' is dependent on its opposite, on that sense of 'the other', expressible through the idea of 'the foreign'. The millennium RSC enterprise was coloured by debates in the British media about Englishness, in the light of the establishment of Welsh and Scottish parliaments, of increasing involvement in the European Union, even of the 'foreign' perception of English football fans. A heavily defeated Conservative party went out with a vision, derived, oddly perhaps, from George Orwell, of a semi-rural 'little England', dowdy and inconsequential, but still of value, and a then popular 'new Labour' government was formed and linked to a formula of 'Cool Britannia', a newly fashionable and highly metropolitan England, centred on the arts and on finance.[9] Running the cycle through this cultural uncertainty was certainly intriguing, but there was little or no sense of that resonance with an immediate politics which triggered debate around the Hall–Barton cycle of the sixties – a growing public disrespect for corrupt 'establishment' power-broking, an awareness of the effects of the loss of empire – or of an effect like that of the closeness in the modern dress ESC cycle to the look of contemporary 'news', which rendered the plays grotesquely satirical, especially when the audience was invited to match a belligerent and increasingly batty Margaret to a Margaret of their own times.[10]

The one RSC production of a history which has, in relatively recent times, invoked the same kind of comment on the topicality of the play as those earlier twentieth-century stagings was Katie Mitchell's of *The Third Part of Henry the Sixth* (1998), at 'The Other Place' (a not insignificant name for a self-consciously 'fringe' venue, given the context of this argument). The link made there was to the war in Bosnia, intentionally so on the part of the director, who has had extensive experience of working in Eastern Europe, so the play functioned as a bridge between the 'heart of England' and contemporary experience all too easy to dismiss as 'foreign'. Significantly, this may well be a unique instance of the play performed outside the context of a 'cycle', and so independent both of that convention, and of the investment in 'Englishness' that it has come to imply.[11]

King John may seem an odd place to begin, but we need to remind ourselves of its former popularity. John's death scene, in Beerbohm-Tree's performance, was the first Shakespeare to be filmed – rather touchingly, as this must have been just at the time that the play was passing, it would seem irrevocably, out of the repertoire.[12] Its previous place there was due to an investment in precisely those things which become marginal in a 'cycle' production of the other plays. That is, a darkly comic confusion of the matter of national identity, a sense of the provisional, the non-linear unstructured movement of events that we have the impulse to shape into a 'history' – in either the modern or the Shakespearean sense of the word – and, most importantly for the play's popular success – its insistence that history is written by and on women and children, as much as by men, and that the family is its primal locus.

We can see much of this in the opening of the play;

> KING JOHN Now say, Châtillon, what would France with us?
> CHÂTILLON Thus, after greeting, speaks the King of France,
>   In my behaviour, to the majesty –
>   The borrowed majesty – of England here.
> QUEEN ELEANOR A strange beginning: 'borrowed majesty'?
> KING JOHN Silence, good mother, hear the embassy.
>
> (*King John*, 1.1.1–6)

'France' and 'England' are not nations, or territories, or even geographical expressions here, but individual men, whose title to that appellation, in John's case at least, is disputed. The title of 'France' is not, but the dry, unceremoniously ironic self-presentation of Chatillon, his ambassador, undercuts that too, as he demonstrates how authority can, under licence be transferred and assumed – 'in my behaviour' means something like 'in my performance'. This feeds into the play from its very beginning the question as to what titles of national identity inhere in. It is a premise of the English epic/cycle presentations that we already know this, that our experience of the play(s) is included in a sense of England and Englishness, however hard put we might be to define it; more likely than not, to have had such a theatrical experience we have travelled to either London, or to the 'heart of England'. But in *King John* we see the matter in play, to be resolved temporarily at different points in its progress: an England – 'this England', indeed – emerges in the very last lines of the play, but its provenance has been tortuous and darkly comic. So, having started at the beginning, let us proceed immediately to the end.

> This England never did, nor never shall,
> Lie at the proud foot of a conqueror
> But when it first did help to wound itself.
> Now these her princes are come home again,
> Come the three corners of the world in arms
> And we shall shock them. Naught shall make us rue
> If England to itself do rest but true.
>
> (*King John*, 5.7.112–18)

The speaker of the last speech is referred to throughout the play as 'The Bastard', and the perfunctory business of setting out on (another) French/English war is sidelined by the comic dispute over his patrimony. 'Philip', as he starts the play, becomes Sir Richard Plantagenet, as John and Eleanor discover in him physical traits of Richard Coeur-de-Lion, John's dead brother. His new identity is born, or made, out of a crisis of legitimacy, identity and a controversial title to territory, the family lands. He is the audience's clue through the action of the play, beginning as a kind of 'vice' figure – cheering the audience up with asides through protracted and decisive scenes of political negotiation – ending . . . where? That he speaks those last 'patriotic' lines does not necessarily undercut them, but it does remind us of a journey he, we and the play, have had to make to reach 'this England'.

The end of the play instates 'this England' as the ground beneath our feet (definitely *not* at the 'foot' of a 'conqueror'), and so not just as the identity of a man who may not be entirely sure himself of his claim to the title. However, within the context of the stage performance, it is the stage/scaffold to which attention is drawn, and so attention is also drawn to the process of construction, the construction of a fiction aiming to extort our assent. But the halfway point of this journey is more disturbing still.

Like *Richard III*, this is a play that centres on child-murder. This factor – Arthur's murder, and his mother Constance's pre-emptive grief at his capture – was crucial to the height of its British popularity, as focused by the great success in the role of Constance of the actress Sarah Siddons. After being threatened with blinding, Arthur dies in an attempt to escape; his body is found first by some already dissident nobles, then by Philip/Sir Richard/the 'Bastard' and by Hubert, the boy's keeper, who seems, in some sense, to have loved him:

> BASTARD Go bear him in thine arms.
> I am amazed, methinks, and lose my way
> Among the thorns and dangers of this world.
> (*Hubert takes up Arthur in his arms*)
> How easy dost thou take all England up!
> From forth this morsel of dead royalty,
> The life, the right, and truth of all this realm
> Is fled to heaven, and England now is left
> To tug and scramble, and to part by th' teeth
> The unowed interest of proud swelling state.
> . . . Bear away that child.
> (*King John*, 4.3.140–57)

If Arthur is 'all England', then the Bastard is admitting the falseness of John's claim; he also draws attention to the precariousness, pathetically embodied in the littleness, the vulnerability of Arthur, of the identity of England – whatever that is, John can no longer claim a title over it. But then 'England' is invoked again – 'England now is left'. It is as if, once Arthur is dead, and by his death John discredited, 'England' is a rhetorical concept, open to remaking and redefinition.

It is important also that by this point the powerful women who dominated the opening acts of the play – Eleanor and Constance – are both dead, and their deaths casually, almost comically, reported and responded to:

> KING JOHN O, where hath our intelligence been drunk?
> Where hath it slept? Where is my mother's ear,
> That such an army could be drawn in France,
> And she not hear of it?
> MESSENGER   My liege, her ear
> Is stopped with dust. The first of April died
> Your noble mother. And as I hear, my lord,
> The Lady Constance in a frenzy died
> Three days before; but this from rumour's tongue
> I idly heard; if true or false I know not.
>
>   (*King John*, 4.2.116–24)

After this – no woman appears in the play after Constance's last exit, at 3.4.105, no child after Arthur's death at 4.3.10 – England becomes in the rhetoric of the play, a woman, and the male figures her children, but 'she' is a vulnerable imperilled woman, very unlike the actual women all of whom, including the, in narrative terms, apparently passive Blanch, are rhetorically powerful and self-possessed.

Salisbury, one of the dissident nobles, introduces this idea, when joining up with the French against John:

> And is't not pity, O my grievèd friends,
> That we the sons and children of this isle
> Was born to see so sad an hour as this,
> Wherein we step after a stranger, march
> Upon her gentle bosom, and fill up
> Her enemies' ranks? I must withdraw and weep
> Upon the spot of this enforcèd cause –
> To grace the gentry of a land remote,
> And follow unacquainted colours here.
> What, here? O nation, that thou couldst remove;
> That Neptune's arms who clippeth thee about

Would bear thee from the knowledge of thyself
And gripple thee unto a pagan shore,
Where these two Christian armies might combine
The blood of malice in a vein of league,
And not to spend it so unneighbourly.

(*King John*, 5.2.24–39)

In the all (adult) male arena of the last act of *King John*, England becomes open to rhetorical reinvention within the terms of an almost sadistic sense of England, as imaginary woman, available to attack equally from either group of men who claim protection/possession of her/it/this England, thus no longer identified with the male monarch, but with an imaginary woman-as-victim, as Arthur had been both 'England' and victim-as-child. In operating by the identification of – and in determining the metaphorical reading of – the 'other', the validation of adult male power is established more stably than has been possible when one locally inept, possibly disengaged male individual has had such power symbolically invested in him.

At the risk of seeming simplistic, one could sum up the crucial question – raised at the beginning, and developed with daring intelligence as the spine of this play – as 'what is England?' The Bastard proceeds from a questioning, audience-friendly mockery of the various claims more securely heroic characters make in terms of this issue to becoming, in that final speech, an apparent icon of 'this England'. But it is perhaps his characteristic awareness of, and willingness to play explicitly out to, an audience that allows him to realize the transition, and so, if we were to read the play in terms of 'realist' 'character', to remake himself. At the siege of Angiers, the citizens of the town – some of Shakespeare's cleverest, most resiliently witty unnamed characters – dryly draw attention to the basic problems involved in the conflict played out in front them, as it threatens to destroy their town. The two kings – 'England' and 'France' – have entered with their armies, but the citizens seem unimpressed and unintimidated:

KING PHILIP Speak, citizens, for England: who's your king?
[CITIZEN] The King of England, when we know the King.
KING PHILIP Know him in us, that here hold up his right.
KING JOHN In us, that are our own great deputy
    And bear possession of our person here,
    Lord of our presence, Angers, and of you.

(*King John*, 2.1.362–7)

The Bastard draws on an analogy, one always in the background of Shakespeare's dramaturgy, and one which draws attention to our role, as audience, in the outcome of the crisis of national identity at the dramatic core of the frustratingly static, stop-start action of the play until its crux at Arthur's capture – a comically but also disturbingly perfunctory scene:

> BASTARD By heaven, these scroyles of Angers flout you, Kings,
> And stand securely on their battlements
> As in a theatre, whence they gape and point
> At your industrious scenes and acts of death.
> Your royal presences be ruled by me.
> Do like the mutines of Jerusalem:
> Be friends awhile, and both conjointly bend
> Your sharpest deeds of malice on this town.
> By east and west let France and England mount
> Their battering cannon.
>
> (*King John*, 2.1.373–82)

The Bastard can use the authority he has established not so much *despite* but – within the convention of the vice – *because of* his anomalous situation, his individually asserted legitimacy, to rule over the royal, and he can draw on, and throw back at us, the source of power that comes back to him from us, gaping, pointing and unindustrious spectators. He also, at this point, enjoys the idea that, in pointing their cannons at each other from opposite sides of the town they will destroy not only the town but each other. He is, after all a vice, not just Aaron, Richard or that other bastard, Edmund, but maybe even Puck. But the main point here is his activation of an audience's awareness of itself, to the extent of inviting those present in the tiered enclosure of an Elizabethan theatre to transpose their sense of their presence to an imaginative engagement with the situation of the citizens in their imperilled walled town. And from that we proceed to the realization that it is our decision who and what has legitimacy; like the citizens we decide who is royal, what is England.

Of the later Shakespearean plays, the one that seems to me to be closest to this play is *Troilus and Cressida*. Like that play, it engages us in a quizzical, often but never *simply* comic, exploration of the way history and nationality are constructed as concepts, in rhetoric, through the interplay of individual identities and in the taxonomies of 'fame'. It demystifies, in other words, 'this England'. But we might question whether that mystique existed for Shakespeare and his audience, or whether it has gradually grown, as co-dependent with reading and presenting the plays as a cycle, given that the absence of cycle presentations at that time would characterize this as a somewhat mystical project – Shakespeare as seer, looking back to the medieval mystery plays, forward to nineteenth-century Romantic imperialism.[13] The cycle also implies a linear reading of history, playing to our need to find a pattern, a rationale for such a large-scale narrative shape. But in a play like *King John* we see such patterns as created out of the characters' needs, and those needs stemming, not from political vision, but from intense primal emotions, of grief, anger, territorial instinct. This, especially as channelled through Constance, was the source of the play's late eighteenth- and early nineteenth-century currency. 'This England' may by the end of the play have been formulated and affirmed, but we have seen history as made out of the uncontrolled, often embarrassing, emotions of a dysfunctional multinational family. We are also – as in the Bastard's 'theatre' analogy – made aware of the role of spectatorship, of the notion of partial interpretation in the making of history, as of the precarious validity of the signs – most specifically the crown. 'Doth not the crown of England prove the King?' (2.2.272) asks John, when the citizens of Angiers coolly question his right to call himself 'England', but if this was ever so, he devalues the symbol himself, as the barons are aware, in his second coronation, and then in his humiliatingly having to take it a third time, at the hands of the pope's legate. That same legate – supremely worldly and rational, like so many of Shakespeare's clerics – points out that in a crisis of public confidence after Arthur's disappearance, *anything* will be read as a sign of divinely ordained punishment, and so of an underlying moral/historical order. Again, as this happens, it can be seen to mock the audience's need to pull together, to find a larger frame for the interfamilial squabbles in front of us.[14]

This kind of scepticism seems to me to be a constituent of all the histories, and to be overridden in the 'heroic epic of England' reading of them. I would suggest that pretty soon after the late Elizabethan popularity of the histories, audiences became alienated from them, largely because an open-mindedly questioning attitude to historical 'truth', and a sense that both nationhood and the sense of history as a linear progression were open to question, became, not so much untenable, as unrecognizable, in the shaping of a contrary idea of history, and in the redefinition of nationhood in the union with Scotland, the creation of 'Britain'. So the texts are relocated, into – for all their local horrors – an essentially nostalgic myth.

If – as is the premise of this volume – the histories export less well than the tragedies or the comedies, it may well be the consequence of this perception of them, this entrapping of them in an anachronistic national myth. The French novelist François Mauriac recorded his rediscovery of the plays after the Second World War as follows: 'I had found them tedious before and had never really got inside them, but the drama of war that we have come through has strangely illuminated the beauty of these plays . . . Shakespeare has helped me follow with my mind's eye the leading roles played in our wars . . .'[15] As Katie Mitchell's *Third Part of Henry the Sixth* showed all too clearly, the contemporary power of the plays resides in the fact that 'we', if we think of ourselves as Europeans or world citizens rather than privileged denizens of a never-present jewel in a silver sea, must recognize that we are in continuity, and community, with the same forces and the same seemingly unrealizable demand to know, to understand, to make sense of 'history' as shape the plays. It is, perhaps paradoxically, in moving on from a sense of 'This England' that the histories can become less foreign to us now.

Time chases and catches up on critics of the history plays as inexorably as it does on their protagonists. When the race is between theatre history and the production, however adept, of an academic book, time marks the process with a Shakespearean insistence. Shortly after completing and submitting to this volume the piece that ended with the preceding paragraph, *This England: the Histories* opened in London's Young Vic. More recently still, Michael Boyd, the director of its 'tetralogy' (the *Henry VI* plays plus *Richard III*) was appointed the company's new artistic director. The 'cycle' had been the major artistic and critical success of recent seasons, and so Boyd has actually anticipated the tradition of the artistic director's historical epic. London also saw, in 2002, Edward Hall's all-male Propeller company in a two-part adaptation called *Rose Rage*. The show was set in something between a locker room and an abattoir, and its texture was built of reference to the fustier side of English institutional life; including, in perhaps the least successful aspect of the production, unapologetically camp, marginally misogynistic projection of the female characters. This was a black-comedy exploration of the introvertedly national motivation of England's violent history.[16]

I realize that to raise the question of the international is to dig deeper into the national, and that that is what I have been doing. Paradoxically, though, these RSC history productions have tended to look to Europe for theatrical idiom, and so been less *This England* than most British productions of the 'universal' plays. Barton and Hall were massively influenced by the clarity and materialist approach both to history (and very literally) to stage design, of Brecht's company, only recently seen in the West. Terry Hands in 1977 brought an unembarrassed approach to rhetoric and a large-scale sense of heroic conflict from his work on French tragedy at the Comédie Française. Katie Mitchell worked through the rich, complex, always incipiently tragic, culture of the Balkans. And Michael Boyd, who studied in Moscow, brought both a vividly coloured and hyperactively kinetic style to his staging, and an almost Bulgakov-like sense of the demonic intervention into history at the beginning – if anyone wore red you could be pretty sure that they would turn out to be a demon in league with their other scarlet brothers and sisters – which then drained away, to leave a sense of a bleak and endless human evil. I did not much enjoy his production – it overrode any kind of scepticism or ambiguity, which seem to me to be Shakespeare's hallmarks in dealing with history. But Boyd was clearly the right choice, in sustaining artistic growth, moving the company to some larger, more eclectic stylistic vision, while working from within the historical (in all senses) core of the company's work.

The history plays do seem to reflect a European experience, and not an Asian or American one. And that is a matter of history. It was the experience of many on both sides of the former 'Iron Curtain' that after the rise of Stalin and of Hitler, and of living through, in Europe, the horrors and conflicts of the Second World War, the histories emerged as some of the most engrossing works not only of Shakespeare's, but of all world literature.

My history of the 'Histories' took me to a kind of paradox: the establishment of an epic 'this England' in a situation where any certainty of the value of such an enterprise is called into question by the nature and tendency of the dramatic material from which the epic is built. It seems to me that the Shakespeare 'history' plays question what history is, and show us 'history in the making' in that they derive so much of their dynamic from the clash between rival characters or rival groups who seek to make 'history' – in both our sense and in the Shakespearean sense, of memorable narrative, narrative extorting, to some extent, for some time, imaginative assent – in their own competing terms. The battle is over what is digested, remembered, understood. This – history as debate, even while it 'happens' – is vital and valuable, and why the Shakespeare histories will remain a rich quarry of theatrical material. To continue with 'Shakespeare' we must welcome both the universal, which has its own history, national and international, and the particular – particularly the nitty-gritty of the histories, which become universally valuable in bringing us up against the very limits of cultural identity.

NOTES

1 *Richard II*, 2.1.50. All quotations from the plays in this chapter are taken from *Shakespeare: The Complete Works*, edited by Stanley Wells and Gary Taylor (Oxford: Oxford University Press, 1988).

2 Heminges and Condell seem to have, in most cases, settled on 'the life and death of . . .' as an admittedly neat compromise between 'history' and 'tragedy'.

3 William Camden (1551–1623) is largely credited with shifting history-writing from the relaying of written myth to an empirical investigation of sources and sites; his historiography, published as *Britannia* in 1586, then much revised and reprinted, *Anglica* (1602) and *Remains Concerning Britain* (1605, rev. 1623) established an exploratory antiquarian approach to the study of the past, determined also by a strong sense of place and nationhood.

4 For Coleridge's lecture see *Coleridge's Shakespeare Criticism*, edited by Thomas Middleton Raysor, 2 vols. (London: Constable, 1960), I, 126.

5 I cite an anonymous review from *The Herald*, dated 4 May 1906.

6 Steven Pimlott directed *Richard II* (The Other Place), Michael Attenborough directed the two parts of *Henry IV* (The Swan), and Edward Hall was responsible for *Henry V* (Royal Shakespeare Theatre). Michael Boyd directed all four plays of the 'first' cycle: the three parts of *Henry VI* and *Richard III* (The Swan).

7 I have taken this quotation from a publicity leaflet issued by the RSC and marked as 'printed in January 2001'.

8 See *King Henry VI, part I*, edited by Edward Burns, Arden Third Series (London: Thomson Learning, 2000), 69–73.

9 John Major's speech was to a Conservative party conference, and its echoes of a mid twentieth-century socialist writer's Second World War meditations on 'Englishness' were the source of much satire in the liberal press – a sign, perhaps, of how fraught the idea of 'this England' is.

10 Robert Shaughnessy's *Representing Shakespeare: England, History and the RSC* (New York: Harvester Wheatsheaf, 1994) is a masterful account of the RSC's history productions in their complex social and cultural contexts.

11 On Katie Mitchell's production of *The Third Part of Henry the Sixth* see Peter Holland, *English Shakespeares: Shakespeare on the English Stage in the 1990s* (Cambridge: Cambridge University Press, 1997), 199–202.

12 The fragment is currently available on the British Film Institute's immensely valuable and entertaining Video/DVD compilation, *Silent Shakespeare* (UK, 2000).

13 The traditional rationale of the 'cycle', as the argument of a coherent structure that asserts the move from medieval chaos to Tudor stability, has its *loci classici* in E. M. W. Tillyard's *Shakespeare's History Plays* (London: Chatto & Windus, 1944) and in Lily B. Campbell's *Shakespeare's Histories: Mirrors of Elizabethan Policy* (San Marino, CA: The Huntington Library, 1947). But the idea has survived the politics of its original formulation, and is sometimes reinterpreted as subversive of 'Tudor policy', or, more often, simply taken for granted.

14 Hubert reports public reaction to Arthur's death (4.2.183–203) in exactly the
   terms that Pandolf cynically predicted:

> No natural exhalation in the sky,
>   . . .
> But they will pluck away his natural cause,
> And call them meteors, prodigies, and signs,
>   . . .
> Plainly denouncing vengeance upon John.
>   (*King John*, 4.1.153–9)

15 François Mauriac, *Second Thoughts on Literature and Life*, translated by Adrienne
   Foulk (London: Darwen Finlayson, 1961), 107.
16 For a discussion of the play, see Patricia Tatspaugh's review, 'Rose Rage' in
   Shakespeare Bulletin 21:1 (Winter 2003), 25–6.

CHAPTER 8

Shakespeare's history plays in Bulgaria

Alexander Shurbanov and Boika Sokolova

Due to the long centuries of Ottoman occupation, Bulgaria discovered Shakespeare later than many other European countries, but towards the end of the nineteenth century it had already seen the most popular plays on stage and on the page, and by the middle of the twentieth surpassed its Balkan neighbours in the number of translations and theatre productions. The first to arrive were the 'Tragedies' followed by the 'Comedies' and, some decades later, by a few of the 'Histories'. It was only with the strong ideologization of Shakespeare's reception during the communist period after World War II, that the 'Histories' with their political potential first reached a state of prominence.

In *The Gulag Archipelago*, the most vehement denouncer of Stalinist despotism, Alexander Solzhenitsyn, wrote: 'The imagination and inner strength of Shakespeare's villains stopped short at ten or so cadavers because they had no ideology . . . It is thanks to ideology that it fell to the lot of the twentieth century to experience villainy on the scale of millions.'[1] While this distinction is legitimate, the value of the plays dealing with political villainy for the unmasking of modern tyranny should not be underestimated. In the context of communist ideology, the barbarism pictured in them, however limited in scale, became symbolic of its monstrous sway in real life. Characters like Richard III began to appear in the theatre more and more often with a muted yet unmistakable suggestion of their relevance to the current situation at home. It was in this context that in 1986, towards the end of the totalitarian period, the following text was published in a Bulgarian literary journal:

Before the curtain. At one end appears a ragged woodcutter tugging at a rope. He stops and rolls a cigarette in a piece of newspaper.
WOODCUTTER Well, my horse, see how the sun is scorching – it might rain. And the damn wood is so far away! How long will it take, my horse, to get there the devil only knows . . . Gee, gee up my horse! Let's not tarry, gee up, there's still a long way to go.

KING RICHARD (*Rushes in from the other end.*) A horse, a horse. Give me a horse. A kingdom for a horse!

WOODCUTTER Your Highness, who are you? What's the matter with you?

KING RICHARD I am King Richard. I offer thee my entire kingdom for thy horse.

WOODCUTTER But, Your Highness, I am on my way to chop some wood. If I give up my horse I'll have to carry the wood on my own back. I can't survive without my horse.

KING RICHARD Oh God! Wretch, what art thou talking about? How canst thou think of carrying wood on thy back when a whole kingdom will be chopping wood for thee! Don't miss thy chance, rascal. Come on, give me thy horse. I am exchanging a whole kingdom for this jade.

WOODCUTTER Your Highness, pardon me for asking. Have you been in this swapping business for long?

KING RICHARD I can't remember how long I've been roaming around. I've grown hoarse from offering my kingdom for a horse, yet I can never get a fair deal. They think I'm mad . . . Thou'lt be in luck, poor man, if thou give me thy horse. Thou'lt be in luck: instead of rags thou'lt wear regalia. Come on, give up thy horse. If thou get rid of this bony jade thou shalt be made a man. Canst thou see what wretches you both are?

WOODCUTTER That's right, Your Highness, the very truth. Take my horse if you are so minded. Don't forget to fill his bag with oats and, I promise, he will serve you well. Good luck with your horse! (*Hands him the rope.*)

KING RICHARD (*Taking the rope.*) And good luck to thee, my poor fellow, with the kingly crown! God be wi'you!

WOODCUTTER God be with ye, and fare ye well. (*A horse neighs and the clatter of hooves dies away.*) A kingdom for a horse! Is it possible? Is this not a dream?

The above is not a recovered missing scene of *Richard III* but the opening episode of *In His Own Image*, a play by the renowned Bulgarian dramatist Yordan Radichkov which never made it to the stage.[2] Its protagonist, the poor peasant hoisted on to the throne by a quirk of history, soon manages, by a series of misguided reforms and sheer ineptitude, to bring his accidentally acquired kingdom to destitution. Towards the end, as the realm begins to crumble and threatens to bury him under its debris, he is himself compelled to exchange it for a horse in order to escape from the impending disaster.

On the eve of the communist system's demise, the authorities rightly saw in this appropriation of King Richard a parable of their own predicament. The regime, which had originally come to power as the champion of the lower social strata, had, in the final analysis, only perched at the top of its new rigid hierarchy a peasant king, a role played by Todor Zhivkov, who ruled the country for thirty-six years, parading his simple-mindedness and glorying in the pose of 'a man of the people'.[3] It was he and his retinue who brought the nation to the dire straits of economic bankruptcy, already apparent in the mid-1980s, and who were eager to barter everything for whatever was on offer. But their grip on the country's life was still quite palpable, and *In His Own Image* had no chance of passing through the fine sieve of censorship.

The interest of Radichkov's text for the literary historian lies not only in its dissident theme, but also in its rare quotation from a Shakespearean history play, the dramatic genre that has lagged considerably behind the tragedies and comedies in the overall reception of Shakespeare's legacy but has nonetheless managed to produce at least one household figure comparable to Hamlet or Othello in its unmistakable identity.

Incidentally, the discrimination against the histories is not specifically Bulgarian. Their delayed introduction is a phenomenon characteristic of the whole of Central and Eastern Europe, where, to this day, plays like *Henry V, Henry VI, Henry VIII* and *King John* remain largely confined to the printed page. The only representative of this genre that can boast a stage life comparable to that of the tragedies and comedies is *Richard III* with *Richard II* and *Henry IV* trailing behind it, a situation not very different from what may be observed in other regions outside the English-speaking countries.

A look at the possible reasons for the resulting generic imbalance of Shakespeare's international reception reveals a critical tradition that has regarded the histories as dwelling on specifically English matters and offering little else of more general interest than information about their author's views of exotic politics and personalities, without any inherent dramatic merit.[4] But there have also been other, no less important factors working in the same direction.

Indeed, the quick change of locality and the numerous crowd episodes (more typical of the histories than of the other genres) have not been easy to deal with in the altered conditions of the post-seventeenth-century proscenium-arch stage. Aesthetically too, in the eyes of the new audiences these dramas were becoming more and more puzzling with their lack of focus on a story involving a single exceptional personality. As Michael Hattaway has rightly pointed out, they do not 'invoke the sense of an ending that we associate with the history of heroes'.[5]

There would also seem to be economic as well as cultural reasons for this relative neglect of a section of Shakespeare's dramatic legacy in European theatrical practice. Few companies can commercially afford a

serial presentation of the plays, and although the number of cyclical productions abroad should certainly not be underestimated, there have not
been very many beyond those in Germany, Austria, France or the United
States.[6] More often than not, the plays tend to be performed as independent entities. Sometimes, single normal-sized productions emerge from the
compression and collation of parts.[7] Thus the historical dramatic type is
effectively forced into the mould of other, better established ones.

The tradition in Europe to privilege *Richard III*, *Richard II* and *Henry IV*
over the remaining histories suggests that they transcend the perceived 'deficiencies' of the genre; their more firmly structured plots and impressive protagonists bring them closer to the tragedies and comedies. Both Richard II
and Richard III can be easily placed side by side with Shakespeare's great
tragic heroes on the basis of their passionate natures and their impressive
rhetorical power, while *Henry IV* 's international fame is largely indebted
to the irresistible charm of Falstaff's comic character, which has helped the
fat knight to spread his conquests also through the realms of painting and
musical drama.

This selection of three specific history plays first emerged in Germany
in the course of Shakespeare's Romantic appropriation and gradually grew
into a universal cultural model. Soon naturalized in the Hapsburg Empire,
it penetrated into Russia from where an eddy flowed back into Eastern
Europe. The three histories' prominence can therefore be deemed the product of nineteenth-century international cultural exchange. The ferment of
nationalism in the crumbling empires of the old continent and the subsequent need for modernization of power only added to the relevance of
their subject matter. As a result, in the process of their European contextu-
alization, they lost their moorings in English history to become historical
parables of power relations easily adaptable to different local realities. Relo-
cation and de-naturalization brought out their inherent political potential
more strongly.

Such a shift of focus explains the nervousness of establishments as regards
the appearance of the select histories in print and on the stage. Political regimes, especially in times of crises, have always been suspicious of
texts dealing with the death and deposition of monarchs. The commotion around the staging of *Richard II* on the eve of the Essex rebellion in
London is well known, but even in much later times presenting royalty as
tyrannous, or removable, has been considered politically seditious all over
Europe. Owing to Shakespeare's problematization of issues of royal power,
the histories sat uneasily in the context of the almost uniformly monarchi-
cal European set-up up to World War I. In eighteenth-century England,

Richard II 'lost favour because it portrayed a bad king' and only made a come-back a century later, when 'a poet-king' was constructed 'out of the old story of the tyrant-king'.[8] At the other end of the continent, the interest in the history plays flared up in the midst of the Russian revolutionary aristocrats of the Decembrist movement in the 1820s, whose fellow-traveller, Alexander Pushkin, created his remarkable poetic drama *Boris Godunov* (1825) under the noticeable influence of *Henry IV* and *Richard III* as well as *Macbeth*. As a matter of fact, all these dynastically sensitive plays were banned by the tsarist government, and it was only in the late 1950s, after the Stalinist period, that the awkward histories began to re-emerge in Russia.[9] A list of Shakespearean productions published in a specialized Soviet periodical in 1958 revealed that in the post-war years 1945–57 there had been a single staging of just one of them, unsurprisingly *Richard III*, as against 164 premieres of the tragedies and 138 of the comedies.[10]

    In the nationalist nineteenth-century framework of Eastern Europe, Bulgaria entered the epoch known as the Revival and started developing its modern culture as a largely rural economy with burgeoning small towns closely connected with the countryside. During the five centuries of Ottoman rule, the vigour of communal life had been largely sustained by the traditional serial epic songs, the cycles of legends and the church calendar with its festivals enveloped in ritual and pageantry. Though this might seem like a fertile soil for the appropriation of Shakespeare's historical cycles, the preoccupation of the Bulgarian Revival was with the nation's own history. A flurry of early indigenous dramas glorified heroic moments in the country's past before the invasion. None of the Shakespearean histories was ever shown before the Liberation in 1878. The only representatives of this group that subsequently appeared in print or on the stage were the plays respectively nearest to the tragedies and the comedies, *Richard III* and *Henry IV*.

    In a country striving to recover its long lost cultural context, the theatre focused from the very beginning on the much-coveted Europe. Both repertory and methods were mainly borrowed from the central and eastern parts of the continent. In the process of this transfer, the Bulgarian theatre also imported the established interpretation of Shakespeare with its characteristically Romantic departure from the purely narrative interest of the dramas and its concentration on their individualistically symbolic and poetic aspects. Such privileging of paradigmatic over syntagmatic aesthetic orientation meant that the fates of the heroes acquired the status of a universal pattern transcending their progress through the immediate specifics of the plot. Lear, Othello, Macbeth and the rest were epitomes of the tragic consequences of great passions. The appropriation of the histories was predicated on their compliance with this model and most of them were difficult to adapt to it.

There was perhaps an additional obstacle to the reception of the histories in late nineteenth-century Bulgaria. At such a crucial moment of the country's resurrection for a new independent life, official Britain sided with its arch-enemy, the Ottoman Empire, which meant that links between the two nations were also at a minimum. For the Bulgarians of those days European culture was represented chiefly by France and Germany and often mediated by Russia. Consequently, British influences were indirect and limited. The eventual staging of *1 Henry IV* and the Richard plays in later years was due to the fact that they came to be seen not as plays about English historical figures but as a European legacy dealing with human specimens of the more readily appreciated universalized Schillerian type. Indeed, when in 1893, Acts 1 and 5 of *Richard III* made their way to the Bulgarian stage for the first time, Richard spoke French, because the play was included in a joint Bulgarian–French theatrical event also featuring parts of other classics, such as Racine's *Athalie* (in Bulgarian), *Hamlet* (in Bulgarian), Hugo's *Le Roi s'amuse* (in French) and a pageant dedicated to Hadji Dimitur, a Bulgarian hero who had lost his life in the struggle against the Turks.[11] Alongside classical and Romantic narratives, the Bulgarian and English historical materials were obviously seen as common European heritage.

A glance at the Bulgarian theatre after the communist takeover in 1944 reveals that the national canon of Shakespearean histories on the stage remained largely intact. Although *Richard II* was added to complete the triad in the 1960s, the other histories did not make it to the stage, and have remained unperformed to the present day. Yet the new ideological approach to Shakespeare imported from the Soviet Union gradually brought about an important shift of accent – an increased attention to the histories as political works, revealing their author's 'progressive thinking'.

The histories were first discussed in such terms in critical writings for pedagogical purposes. A textbook for the foundation course on European literature of Sofia University published in 1951 declared Shakespeare a champion of royal absolutism as the appropriate form of government for the new bourgeois social order destined to do away with feudal anarchy. While endorsing the orthodox Tudor doctrine of the divine right of kings, the author Alexander Peshev argued, Shakespeare, who was an exponent of the revolutionary tendencies of his time, was also willing to support regicide in cases when such a radical act could help to destroy a tyrannical regime and further social progress.[12] This theory was promptly illustrated as follows:

The case of Richard III provides ample material revealing Shakespeare's attitude to kings. In principle, he stands for monarchy, which was inevitable in those days. However, he is not an unquestioning champion of royal power. If the ruler is a villain, a bloody murderer, a man of inordinate ambition, if his authority is devoid of moral and political content, the writer denounces it. What is more, Shakespeare accepts its armed overthrow and justifies this act in moral and political terms . . . Any power ought to be based on mutual trust between the rulers and the ruled and it should rest upon a sound moral and political foundation.[13]

In spite of the nauseating repetition of the phrase 'moral and political', its second component quite obviously assumed a dominant position over the first, shaping it according to the laws of expediency. The forward march of history, construed by historical materialism as a series of revolutions, was deemed so important that it could safely dispense with morality in the name of progress. Here is a telling example of this attitude culled from Peshev's *Lectures*: 'Shakespeare grants historical justification to cruel and bloody monarchs like King John and, to a certain extent, Henry V, because their motives and actions are historically meaningful, whereas Richard III is driven exclusively by egoism.'[14] Such interpretation was meant to shape the outlook of the young academic readers in a markedly utilitarian way. As an engine of historical advancement bloodshed was considered acceptable and, therefore, easy to justify when used for the right purpose. To determine what is right and what wrong was wholly entrusted to those in power.

In line with the tenets of historical materialism, the histories were read as allegories of the social and political set-up in Shakespeare's England. The former individualistic paradigm of the Romantic tradition was replaced with a sociological one. Peshev's discussion of *Henry IV* contains the following characteristic observation concerning young Hotspur:

Percy dies as a courageous knight engaged in a single combat with Prince Henry, and through his death the writer seems to depict symbolically the demise of the old aristocracy incapable of understanding the new age, an age when personal courage and the sword cannot solve the great social problems . . . Thus the young knight does not articulate fully the death sentence of his class, but it is clearly implied. In spite of his splendid character, Henry Percy must die, and he does so, because his class is dying in the endless feudal wars. The one who triumphs is Henry V, the representative of the principle of statehood, the personage standing for positive absolute power.[15]

The tendency to discover subtle underlying patterns ran away with its exponents and produced schemes reminiscent of those in the morality plays, a kind of new 'sociomachia'.

Frequently, the educational slant typical of the textbook discourse was ascribed to Shakespeare's own method as a writer: the dramatist was assumed to have been aware of his impact on the minds of the audience and, consequently, to have been cautious about what he imparted. Figures of dubious nature such as Falstaff were to be tackled with great care:

There is in this unique comic character an attraction which can exert an infectious influence on weaker minds. Only Shakespeare's sense of measure and his understanding of the edifying role of the theatre has kept under control the temptation to which a feebler writer would have succumbed in order to create a character with a destructive impact. This Shakespeare has avoided. He creates a vagabond of an aristocrat. Falstaff is outside all classes, outside all morality.[16]

It was precisely the hedonistic attraction which the communist critic feared so much in Falstaff that had been in full swing on the stage in the one and only Bulgarian production of the first part of *Henry IV* at the National Theatre in 1931. The fat knight was played by the legendary Krustyu Sarafov, whose portrait in this role, painted by Dechko Uzunov, is a masterpiece in the genre. Slouching in his great leather boots on a wooden tavern chair, one gloved hand perched over its back, an elbow and his whole bulky body leaning heavily on the edge of the table with the remainder of a mighty feast still heaped up on it, this Bulgarian Falstaff looks contented yet continues to eye shrewdly the surrounding world through lids half closed by too much indulgence in the pleasures of the palate. His impressive bulging belly is the true centre of the composition, belittling the sword and dagger suspended from his belt.

As the contemporary reviews testify, the dynastic problem of *Henry IV* was upstaged by the impressive presence of Falstaff. In the words of Stella Yaneva: 'It is as if all other personages are part of the set and a frame for Shakespeare's most brilliant comic figure. Against a historical background, the poet's imagination has created a character who threatens to overshadow everything else.'[17] The director was Nikolai Massalitinov, one of Stanislavsky's favourite students and assistants, who had played Claudius in his master's and Edward Gordon Craig's celebrated 1911 production of *Hamlet* at MAT. After the bolshevist revolution in Russia Massalitinov had settled in Bulgaria to become the principal director of the National Theatre for many years.

The production was generally criticized for its dramaturgical failings but its most vicious disparagement came from a militant group of marxist journalists around *The Workers' Literary Front* (*WLF*) weekly. They had adopted a particularly aggressive hard line, constantly attacking 'bourgeois

Figure 5. Dechko Uzunov, *Portrait of Actor Krustyu Sarafov as Falstaff* (in Nikolai Massalitinov's 1931 production of *1 Henry IV*, National Theatre, Sofia).

culture' and promoting the tenets of Soviet ideology with its instigation of violence on a massive scale, so pungently diagnosed by Solzhenitsyn. The very language of the paper smacks of military action. In the *WLF*, *Henry IV* was reviewed as an exercise in 'bourgeois demagoguery'. The portrait of Falstaff with his individualistic enjoyment of the pleasures of life as it is was not to the liking of the champions of world revolution. Such productions were meant, according to the *WLF* commentator, to present an idealized picture of 'the good old times' and were written off as a retrograde flight from reality.[18] It took another marxist critic with a less partisan mind to characterize *Henry IV* as 'a profoundly social play', a potential that, according to him, the production failed to realize.[19]

The next appearance of a Shakespeare history play on the Bulgarian stage did not occur until thirty years later, in 1964, when the Khrushchevian period of alternating thaws and freezes, bursts of liberalism and old-style dictatorship, was coming to a close. A new class of immoral philistines had emerged out of the ashes of Stalin's military egalitarianism to perpetuate the oppressive order in its own group interest. Continuing to use the ideology of communism as a smoke-screen for its own selfish pursuits, this coterie deepened the disillusionment among the common people. East European intellectuals voiced the popular sentiment in various acts of defiance, among which the rediscovery by the theatre of *Richard III* and other Shakespearean texts dealing with the mechanism of power loomed large. A theoretical momentum was given to these tendencies by Jan Kott's seminal book on their contemporary political significance.[20] The sociological reading of the plays as a scrutiny of the Shakespearean age, buttressed by official ideology, was transformed into an indictment of the society in which the performances took place. Bulgaria became part of this development with its first complete productions of *Richard II* and *Richard III*.

The former was staged at the Sofia Youth Theatre in 1964 by Vili Tsankov, who had already won himself the reputation of a 'formalist'. From the point of view of official criticism this tendency amounted to an aberration from the norms of socialist realism, the canonized method of all artistic pursuits which in its theatre application was a combination of Stanislavsky's psychological realism and photographic naturalism, confining the plays to their immediate historical context and protecting them from the infusion of modern meaning. Such an approach gave the censors the assurance that old dramatic material would not be used in politically insidious ways – the play would remain a mere illustration of a past period without reference to the present time of the audience or to any generalized human predicament.

Tsankov was not a Stanislavskian and this was made abundantly clear by his work. The young director defined his own artistic style as 'plastic theatre', a method seeking to externalize the inner life of characters through a behaviour that 'follows a different logic, somewhat unrealistic and unrelated to normal conduct'.[21] As a result Tsankov's hallmark became a kind of expressionistic deformation and stylized patterning, translating stage action into 'a higher category of aesthetic or poetic suggestion'.[22] This was the idiosyncratic approach that coloured the belated introduction of *Richard II* to the Bulgarian playgoers. It is certainly ironic that Tsankov had really intended to put on *Richard III*, but, as he was informed, the National Theatre had already invited the eminent Polish actor and director Jacek Woszczerowicz to do that play. Two parallel productions of the same text in the same city would have been against the rules of communist cultural economy. This, for once, was a stroke of luck for Bulgarian public: due to a unique coincidence, they could at last see both *Richard* plays in quick succession.

The director's critical attitude to the current social and political realities of the country was made apparent by the scenography. At the centre of the stage stood an exquisite toy-like palace, the size of a telephone booth, from which the king and queen would issue forth and into which they would again retire. This constrained space of privilege, palace and prison at once, symbolized the precarious nature of power. Richard's court appeared enveloped in Byzantine splendour beneath which ran an undercurrent of coarse interest in financial dealings. The country, which a dying Gaunt from his shabby wheelchair bemoaned for being sold piecemeal to all and sundry, sounded very much like contemporary Bulgaria in the crassly opportunistic mercantile phase of its communist history with the increasingly sybaritic lifestyle of the nomenklatura clique causing muted grumbling among the population and creating a conspicuous rift in the allegedly classless society.[23]

In Tsankov's production the stage around the fragile palace was occupied by a swarm of excited barons, heterogeneous groups whose attitudes to the misrule of the monarch ranged from fearful resignation to amused irony and indignant defiance. Many years later, in his autobiographical sketches, Tsankov revealed his hidden intentions:

I modelled the scene with the lords on the behaviour of Bulgarian intelligentsia. My friends and I would get together and crack jokes about the incredible inanities we were surrounded by. Our laughter implied that we were not dissidents but clever devils jibing at the stupidity of the regime. It didn't go much beyond that but we knew each other's opinions about the problems of the day . . .

And so the lords [on the stage] talk about the scandals in the kingdom and roll with laughter . . . But little by little they advance from groping their way to taking more serious and categorical positions. Three groups are gradually formed: some are frightened and resigned and others waver, while those headed by hotheaded Northumberland are ready to rebel. The lords move in formations of three, each characterized by a behavioural reaction expressive of their emotions and thoughts.

Northumberland's group grows stronger and stronger and begins to prevail with its firm step . . . while the others gravitate towards it in accordance with the degree of their courage. Laughter dies out, the rebellious atmosphere thickens and the militant group strides resolutely towards the audience. The whole scene was underpinned by rhythmic music whose power increased continuously . . .

The logical passage from laughter to seriousness was fathomed by many in the audience but, luckily, not by the censors.[24]

Indeed, one of these, who saw the scene involving the lords in rehearsal, thought that the director was 'barking mad'.[25] Whether censorship read the insidious patterns behind Tsankov's rendition of *Richard II* or not, officialdom was wary of 'plasticity': the freedom of form was an expression of the freedom of spirit, a departure from the predictable safety of socialist realism's antiquarian historicism. At the very same time, at the other end of the European continent, critics were no less surprised by another of the multiple expressions of modernity – Peter Hall and John Barton's Kottian production of *The Wars of the Roses* presented *Richard II* 'arguably for the first time in England, as a genuinely timeless political piece – political in the sense in which Brecht and the Berliner Ensemble would have understood the term'. Politics, timeless or current, was injected in the European life of Shakespeare's histories of the 1960s, both East and West.[26]

Jacek Woszczerowicz, who had recently had a tremendous success with his *Richard III* in Poland and was invited to stage the same play at the National Theatre in Sofia in 1964, had to postpone it until the next year on account of poor health. When his production finally premiered, politicized readings of Shakespeare's plays were already part of local practice. By then, all across Eastern Europe topical messages were being conveyed by classical texts. Jan Kott's book, an eye-opener for the young theatre directors in the West, had in fact drawn on these pervasive developments.[27]

The style in which Woszczerowicz's production was sustained broke away from the tradition of vehemently Romantic tragic Richards. The acting was marked by 'a highly theatrical, idiosyncratic manner deriving, possibly, from *commedia dell' arte* extravagance'.[28] The traditionally hyperbolized figure of the anointed monster had shrunk to a cold-blooded soulless manipulator, a change signalling a departure from the domain of tragedy and a move towards political drama. Kott's discussion of Woszczerowicz's Richard as seen in Poland laid bare the topical significance of such stylistic changes: 'Richard is impersonal like history itself. He is the consciousness and the mastermind of the Grand Mechanism. He puts in motion the steamroller of history and later is crushed by it. Richard is not even cruel. Psychology does not apply to him. He is just history, one of its ever-repeating chapters. He has no face.'[29] In an article mirroring this analysis in an uncannily identical way, one of the officially appointed supervisors of Bulgarian theatre, Dimiter Kanushev, denounced the Sofia production of the play for much the same reasons:

As a director Woszczerowicz has not attained the 'life of human spirit' and appears uninterested in human faces. It is as if he is trying to unveil the mechanism of crime, to show the nature of power struggle and so add to our experience and perspicacity. Maybe in this way he is seeking to emulate the modern touch. But he has not done well to neglect the most potent and truthful tool, that of organic acting. There are no real characters in this performance, for these are all desiccated. And that is precisely the most worrying aspect of the production because it runs counter to a rich and fruitful tradition . . . While watching the play, we feel the need to insist that Shakespeare be *Shakespeareanized*, for what we encounter here are not full, complex, and contradictory characters but mere schematic offshoots of alienation and indifference. And do we have to repeat how foreign this is to the Bulgarian school of acting?[30]

Kanushev had already taken Vili Tsankov to task for lapses in his production of *Richard II* in the previous year, and had again defended the Stanislavsky type of acting as the only true national tradition against the plague of modish deviations.[31] Other indignant voices joined in promptly in the same didactic vein, all in tune with a concerted ideological attack, initiated by Khrushchev himself, on the 'unhealthy Western influences on socialist art'. The new recusant developments on the artistic scene had in fact originated mainly in the provinces of the Soviet empire, though it is also true that some traffic of ideas across the Iron Curtain continued even during the worst periods of the Cold War.

Surely, official criticism was part of the ideological bulwark of the regime and did not approach new developments in an unprejudiced way, yet its objections, based on traditionalist values, are worth taking into account – all the more so because some more conservative critics who cannot be suspected of zealously treading the party line often took a similar position. Curiously enough, in Britain, too, reviewers remarked on the deliberate dwarfing of Richard III in *The Wars of the Roses*, which some labelled 'almost Marxist', while others concluded that 'Kott's ideas, received into the style that in general characterizes our Shakespearean actors, become dry and lifeless'.[32] It is hard to deny that the involvement of Shakespeare's drama into a narrowly political discourse led to the flattening of the plays' complex texture, the reduction of character to a sociological scheme and the erasure of the texts' stylistic subtlety. Heavy cuts and generous modern textual insertions became a directorial norm and performance texts looked often like frank adaptations. An extreme politicization of culture – and of Shakespeare's legacy in particular – was exactly what the revolutionary marxists had preached, and it is ironical that when they came to power in the East they started resenting it as potentially subversive.

If Vili Tsankov was prevented from staging *Richard III* in Sofia in 1964, another talented director, Asen Shopov, proved more fortunate because he worked far from the centre. His production of the same year was mounted in the southern city of Haskovo, offering another modernized version of the play in which the actors wore no make-up and looked very much like people of our own age. The official requirement of 'historical veracity' was openly flouted. The play toured some of the regional centres south of the Balkan Mountains, thus ceasing to be of merely local consequence.

All in all, the 1964–5 season proved more hospitable to Shakespeare's histories than the entire previous or subsequent repertory of the Bulgarian theatre. This sudden outburst may be attributed to the perceived need to explore neglected Shakespearean materials in the year of the quatercentenary of the playwright's birth. Yet it also clearly coincided with a moment when the increasingly dissident theatre behind the Iron Curtain was beginning to make its bitter political statements. The characters of tyrants from the literary classics were openly assuming a topical resonance. Where new plays could not go, the old texts were made to speak with contemporary voices.

In the next decade, *Richard III* rose to prominence everywhere in Eastern Europe as one of Shakespeare's most frequently staged works. Freed from its psychological orientation, the play now addressed burning political issues, exposing the cynical Machiavellian character of a modern society. In Bulgaria, as elsewhere, these new Richards – like top politicians of the contemporary period – were as a rule slick, elegant, even good-looking, uncannily attractive in spite of all their heinous crimes and treasons. In Slavi Shkarov's 1973 production in Rousse, for instance, the protagonist was 'no less majestic for his ignominious thoughts, no less powerful for his despicable treachery, no less charming for his degradation'.[33] He waded through seas of blood without besmearing himself. Conscience and compunction were unknown to this cynic. Like his predecessors of the 1960s, Shkarov's Richard was sombrely farcical rather than tragic, underlining the hopeless absurdity at the heart of his world.

At the end of the decade Vili Tsankov finally realized his dream of the 1960s, and in 1979 his *Richard III* created a definite stir in Sofia. In the intelligent interpretation of Kosta Tsonev, the villainous hero stood out as the only full-blooded human being in a world of senseless automata. The stage was 'cluttered with sumptuous costumes, ribbons, furs, make-up, statue-like majestic poses, false pomposity, ritual gestures'.[34] There was no emotional interaction among the denizens of the corrupt realm. The only substance of these figures was their participation in the ruthless political game of the day. An outsider like Richard had no other option in his drive to the highest reaches of power than to treat his environment as inanimate and use the heads of others as stepping stones without squeamishness. At the end, however, this seemingly undefeatable schemer was stabbed in the back by his own page, a figure that had so far been no more than his own faithful shadow. The Orwellian set-up of the totalitarian suppression of individualism and its consequent aberrations transpired at every step through the thin veil of the old story.

Such treatment was consonant with a number of other contemporaneous Shakespeare productions in Bulgaria, like Nedyalko Yordanov's 1980 *Hamlet* in Burgas, similarly depicting a hollow world of sumptuous appearances, a world which the hero was compelled to join in order to complete his mission. In their endeavour to construct social reality as a realm of evil without hope of deliverance, East European theatres generally resorted to Shakespeare's great tragedies and the darkest of the history plays. Audiences in Western Europe were offered a brilliant illustration of these tendencies, when after 1979 the Georgian Rustaveli Company of Tbilisi went on its famous international tours with a repertory including *Richard III*. The director, Robert Sturua, had steered clear of the tradition of tragedy, highlighting the farcical treatment of the hero that had by then become common to many Eastern European productions, and laying bare the structure of tyranny which the people of the region had come to know so well. With the *Richard III* that Sturua presented to enthusiastic Western European audiences in the late 1970s and early 1980s, he offered a Shakespeare that was neither heroic, nor Romantic, but utterly politicized and horrifying, with an overwhelming sense of absurdity.

In the heady years of Gorbachev's Perestroika after 1985, which preceded the demise of communism, Sofia audiences were treated to a very different Shakespearean history: Friedrich Dürrenmatt's sombre *King John* (orig. *König Johann*). This Swiss adaptation of Shakespeare's *King John* had originally burst on to the Basle stage in 1968, at the peak of the anti-Vietnam-war campaign. In the next two years, Dürrenmatt's *King John* had had five hundred performances in twenty-two theatres in Germany alone, thus profiling itself as a success story which, as Wilhelm Hortmann notes, raised the normal 5 per cent share of the histories in Shakespeare performance to a highly untypical 15–20 per cent.[35]

In reworking the text, Dürrenmatt had encoded the new paradigmatic approach to Shakespeare's material which, in consonance with the trends of the age, was no longer psychological but utterly political. For Dürrenmatt, the reign of King John was a mythical symbol of politics as an eternally recurrent game. This he conveyed with grotesque absurdity and cynicism, making the play speak powerfully of the worthlessness of the ruling classes and of the role of the people in history.

In his own words, Dürrenmatt turned Shakespeare's 'dramatized chronicle' into a 'comedy of politics'. Convinced that the ideological formulae 'John = England and Philip = France' could no longer be upheld, he replaced these by a single new formula: 'John = Philip = feudalism'. As a consequence, his own *King John* captured 'the political struggle for power inside a system' which included the Plantagenets, the Capetians, as well as the church, but which excluded the Bastard. In the course of events, King John became 'a politician of reform' and since Dürrenmatt conveyed a strong sense that reforming a system 'is always a break-neck venture' that nearly as a matter of course implied 'the questioning of the whole system', he produced a political tale of great contemporary relevance, a 'noxious play', as he himself put it, 'confirmed by our time'.[36]

Martin Esslin has argued that Dürrenmatt's drama 'as an exercise in philosophical thought, as a laboratory of ideas, is far from the tastes and traditions of English-speaking theatre', but precisely this attitude (of which Kott is also an exponent) fertilized the efforts of East European and many other directors to analyse their modern world through the prism of old dramatic material.[37] Both Kott's existentialism and Dürrenmatt's Christian humanism were consonant with the anti-establishment Zeitgeist which swept across Europe, east and west. For all the difference in the political systems under which they operated, popular movements and individual dissidence in the two severed halves of the old continent found a common ground for resistance in the revised texts of Shakespeare's history plots, of which Dürrenmatt's adaptation is only one outstanding example. Akin to the interventions of contemporary theatre directors like Peter Hall and John Barton, his play offered, together with tight plotting and intelligent thought, the autonomy of a published text, which made it available for further directorial interpretation. In a sense, Dürrenmatt's adaptation – like Brecht's in a previous generation – gave a long-standing theatre practice an independent status by putting the rewrite in circulation along with the original.[38]

King John was directed by Nikolai Polyakov at the Youth Theatre in 1987. It made use of masks to underline a vision of the world marked by an utter lack of human authenticity. In the course of the performance the original period costumes were replaced with modern dress, suggesting the endless repetition of the power game, while the collusion of political elites was implied by the similarity of outfits worn by the warring parties. As the action was confined to the proscenium, the characters were endowed with a sculpture-like immutability. Behind this facade of political dealings, in the dark recesses of the stage lurked the victimized masses who bore the brunt of the aristocratic feuds. This faceless crowd was crushed by endless suffering and bespattered with blood. In its complete alienation from those in power one could read a verdict on their criminal rule.[39]

Dürrenmatt's understanding of the 'break-neck' effect inherent in any attempt to reform a political order from within was highlighted by a song (now lost) which had been composed especially for the production by Yuri Stupel. It was a topical inset insisting that a system no longer able to function effectively can be replaced but not refurbished. In the days of stunning revelations about the atrocities of communism, made possible by Gorbachev's glasnost campaign, and in the conditions of an actual economic collapse, the impracticability of any ameliorative reform was glaringly conspicuous.[40] Turned into an allegory of a twentieth-century political impasse, the story of a hapless thirteenth-century English monarch unambiguously tolled the knell of a moribund regime. It also, prophetically, envisaged the fall of the reformer who would soon be beaten at his own game. Dürrenmatt's *King John* remained extremely popular in Sofia for two consecutive seasons well into 1989, the year of the final collapse of East European communism.

The Bulgarian story of Shakespeare's histories, as part of a much larger international narrative, started with the plays' loss of their historiographical orientation and with their subjection to a paradigmatic treatment, on a par with the tragedies and the comedies. Their focus shifted to the psychology of exceptional characters regardless of nationality, and three of the histories more susceptible to such interpretation than the others were singled out by critics and theatre directors. Later, this individualistic model was transmuted into a similarly universal sociological one, which became central in the period of twentieth-century totalitarianism. The outlined transformations are probably most striking in the case of *Richard III*, whose once tragically inflated villainous hero mutated to a sign for a political situation, to a voice of ideologized history and, finally, to a mere shadow sliding on the periphery of a radical Bulgarian play. Such changes might be seen as reductive, a deplorable impoverishment of a multi-layered psychological and philosophical suggestiveness. There were some gains, though, for during its travels, the grim English chronicle play had absorbed so much other European history that it acquired a fresh lease of life as the profoundly political drama it had originally been. Stoked up with the ideology of violence through the experience of wars and totalitarian oppression, Shakespeare's histories in their Bulgarian – and East European – guise have become the territory of nullified individuals and of irresponsible criminal cliques disposing of the lives of entire nations. On the stage, the automaton movements of actors depicted the plight of a human race consisting of Gulag inmates. In thus rewriting the histories the twentieth century diagnosed its own painful plight and reinscribed Shakespeare in the body of its post-World War II culture not as the author of unique dramatic creations based on old stories, but as a rich source of old texts to be reshaped for modern use – a legacy whose vigour resides in its endless susceptibility to meaningful revision and adaptation.

NOTES

1 Alexander Solzhenitsyn, *The Gulag Archipelago*, 2 vols. (New York: Harper and Row, 1974), I, 181.
2 *Suvremennik* 2 (1986), 283–329. The excerpt quoted here, as well as all other quotations from Bulgarian, has been translated by the authors.
3 A biographical film entitled *A Man of the People* (scripted and directed by Hristo Kovachev, produced by the Boyana Film Studio) was shown in the Bulgarian cinema in 1981. In a servile manner it exalted the person of the familiar dictator as 'one of us'.
4 Yuri Shvedov, *Istoricheskie hroniki Shekspira* (Moscow: Moscow University Press, 1964), 8.
5 *The First Part of Henry VI*, edited by Michael Hattaway (Cambridge: Cambridge University Press, 1990), Introduction, 1–57 (p. 17).
6 Nicholas Grene reviews the problem of the histories presented as cycles in *Shakespeare's Serial History Plays* (Cambridge: Cambridge University Press, 2002).
7 Such examples are offered by Michael Hattaway in *Henry VI*, Introduction, 45–55.
8 *King Richard II*, edited by Andrew Gurr, New Cambridge Shakespeare (Cambridge: Cambridge University Press, 1984), Introduction, 45.
9 A curious variation of this attitude occurred in mainstream Soviet criticism, which tended to present *Henry V* as a weak play because of its attempt to create an impossible political fiction, the figure of the ideal monarch. See, for instance, Alexander Anikst's very thoughtful and influential popular introduction to Shakespeare's creative work, *Tvorchestvo Shekspira* (Moscow: Izdatelstvo hudozhestvennoy literatury, 1963), 277.
10 Yuri Shvedov, *Istoricheskie hroniki Shekspira* (Moscow: Moscow University Press, 1964), 5 (quoting *Shekspirovskii sbornik*, Moscow: Moscow University Press, 1958).

11 Vassil Mavrodiev, *Shakespeare in Bulgarian and on the Bulgarian Stage* (Sofia: Nauka i izkustvo, 1964), 226. Hadji Dimitur lost his life in an uneven battle with a Turkish detachment in 1868. His heroism became the subject of a poem fundamental to Bulgarian identity, written by Hristo Botev, who also fought to the death against the Turks in 1876.

12 Alexander Peshev, *Lectures on the History of West European Literature* (Sofia: Nauka i izkustvo, 1951), 192–9.

13 *Ibid.*, 198.

14 *Ibid.*, 197.

15 *Ibid.*, 194.

16 *Ibid.*, 193.

17 Stella Yaneva, '*Henrih IV* of Shekspir', *Zlatorog* 4 (1930), 232.

18 Iv. Zaryanov, 'Zakrivane na Sezonite: Teatur' ('The End of the Season: Theatre'), *WLF* 21 (1930), 2.

19 D. B. Mitov, 'Naroden Teatar, Kral Henri IV' ('The National Theatre, King Henry IV'), *Literaturen glas* 71 (1931), 2.

20 *Shakespeare Our Contemporary*, translated by Bolesław Taborski (New York: Norton Library, 1974), 52–5. Kott's book was first published in Polish in 1961, before appearing in French in 1962 and in English in 1964.

21 Vili Tsankov, *Sreburnata payazhina* ('The Silver Web'), (Sofia: Raivill, 1995), 65.

22 *Ibid.*

23 See Alexander Shurbanov and Boika Sokolova, *Painting Shakespeare Red* (Newark and London: University of Delaware Press, 2001), 186.

24 Tsankov, *Sreburnata payazhina*, 65–6.

25 *Ibid.*, 65.

26 Margaret Shewring, *King Richard II*, Shakespeare in Performance (Manchester: Manchester University Press, 1996), 105.

27 See *Richard III*, edited by John Jowett (Oxford: Oxford University Press, 2000), Introduction, 102–4.

28 *Richard III*, edited by Julie Hankey (1981. Rpt. Bristol: Bristol Classical Press, 1988), 73.

29 Kott, *Shakespeare Our Contemporary*, 54.

30 Dimiter Kanushev, '*Richard III*', *Narodna kultura* 20 (1965), 3.

31 Dimiter Kanushev, 'Pretentsiozno i nesuvremenno' ('Pretentious and Anachronistic'), *Narodna kultura* 22 (1964), 4.

32 See Julie Hankey, *Richard III*, Introduction, 71 and 74.

33 Ekaterina Vasileva, 'Protivorechivi vpechatlenia' ('Contradictory Impressions'), *Teatur* 6 (1973), 20–3.

34 Orlin Stefanov, 'Krugovrat na nravite' ('Revolution of Morals'), *Teatur* 9 (1979), 24.

35 Wilhelm Hortmann, *Shakespeare on the German Stage: The Twentieth Century* (Cambridge: Cambridge University Press, 1998), 232. See also 233–4.

36 Friedrich Dürrenmatt, 'Principles of Adaptation', *Writings on Theatre and Drama,* translated with an introduction by H. M. Waidson (London: Jonathan Cape, 1976), 146–9. See also Ruby Cohn, *Modern Shakespeare Offshoots*

(Princeton, NJ: Princeton University Press, 1976), 29–34; and Laurence Lerner, '*King John, König Johann:* War and Peace', *Shakespeare Survey* 54 (2001), 213–22.

37 Friedrich Dürrenmatt, *Plays and Essays,* edited by Volkmar Sander with a foreword by Martin Esslin (New York: Continuum, 1982), xiv.

38 For the adaptation strategies of Hall and Barton in the composition of *The Wars of the Roses* see Cohn, *Modern Shakespeare Offshoots*, 4–7; about Dürrenmatt's and other adaptations of *King John*, see Hortmann, *Shakespeare on the German Stage*, 232–6.

39 An interesting discussion of Polyakov's production is contained in the following reviews: Vesela Grueva, 'Dano poluchim znatsi' ('Hoping for a Sign'), *Narodna kultura* 6 (1988), 6; 'Istinskata zritelska teritoria. "Kral Dzhou" po Durenmat/ Shekspir. Kriticheski dialog mezhdu profesor Lyuobmir Tenev i Nikola Vandov' ('The Spectators' True Perimeter: The Production of *King John* by Dürrenmatt/Shakespeare. A Critical Dialogue between Professor Lyubomir Tenev and Nikola Vandov'), *Narodna kultura* 13 (1988), 8.

40 Unfortunately, the text of the song is not extant, since the composer, Yuri Stupel, never seems to have stored it in his archives. However, both the composer and the play's director (Nikolai Polyakov) clearly remember its tenor.

PART III

Introduction: stage adaptations of the histories

Ton Hoenselaars

There has always been a marked tendency to rewrite the histories for the stage, either to make them fit a specific, new political climate, or to upgrade texts of which parts at least are still considered to be 'not only clumsy, but fairly tedious'.[1] Shakespeare himself revised the histories, as did John Crown in the seventeenth century, and the 'pious heretics' John Barton and Peter Hall in the twentieth.[2] When Terry Hands produced the three *Henry VI* plays in Stratford in the 1970s and explicitly relied on the unadulterated text of Shakespeare's earliest histories ('everything that was there, warts and all'), there was a brief spell during which the 'trust Shakespeare' dictum seemed to prevail, and the notion of new adaptations seemed to belong to the past.[3] But at the turn of the millennium, directors prove to have again taken recourse to the art of rewriting, often also inventing new titles to sharpen the audience focus on their production: *The Battle for the Throne*, *The Rise of Edward IV*, *This England*, *Rose Rage* . . .

This process has not been limited to Britain. Beyond the Channel where, as Tom Lanoye has put it, 'the names of Richmond and Kent mean very little apart from being well-known cigarette brands', translators and adaptors have long sought to achieve both greater intelligibility and a more pleasing aesthetic effect.[4] It is in the very nature of the histories that such often domesticating practices easily tend to acquire new complex cultural and political resonance. Whereas the Italian opera composer working with what one might call Shakespeare's 'foreign' histories was inclined to appeal to his audience's native acquaintance with Ariosto and Italy's own cultural memory in the epic mode, Tom Lanoye and Luk Perceval's *Ten Oorlog* presented Shakespeare's medieval events not as a brand of English history in which Flanders played a role, but as the medieval history of Flanders in which England, too, personified by such dignitaries as John of Gaunt or Lionel of Antwerp, took part.

Especially since the nineteenth century, there have been countless new plays on English history based on Shakespeare's model of nationhood. In

191

Britain, such forms of imitation (if not of emulation) would appear to have been stimulated by Coleridge and his claim about the long line of English kings that 'it would be desirable that some man of dramatic genius . . . should dramatize all those omitted by Shakespeare, as far down as Henry VII'.[5] Less familiar early nineteenth-century attempts include John Keats's *King Stephen* (1819), a fragment 'in the style of Shakespeare', but also William Blake's experiments – with the life of Edward III as a history with a curiously mercantile focus ('Then, my dear lord, / Be England's trade our care; and we, as tradesmen, / Looking to the gain of this our native land'), or with the life of Edward IV, whose prologue betrays a clear debt to *Henry V*:

> Oh, for a voice like thunder, and a tongue
> To drown the throat of war![6]

But these early nineteenth-century examples of native playwrights only represent a fraction of the type of drama that has continued to be written to the present day, including Robert Bolt's *A Man for All Seasons*, Alan Bennett's *The Madness of George III* (changed for the film version to *The Madness of King George*), as well as Rowan Atkinson's revision of the Tudor myth in the *Blackadder* series, where Richard III is made to rouse his troops at Bosworth with the famous words: 'Once more unto the breech, dear friends, once more'.

The infinite number of continental history plays in the Shakespearean vein – including stage epics from Friedrich von Schiller's *Wallenstein* or his *Maid of Orleans*, via Christian Dietrich Grabbe's *Napoleon* epic and Friedrich Hebbel's *Nibelung* trilogy, to Brecht's *Resistible Rise of Arturo Ui*, or his own play devoted to Joan of Arc, and beyond – owe an unmistakable allegiance to Schlegel's famous *Lectures on Dramatic Art and Poetry*, propagating the imitation of Shakespeare's assumed vision of nationhood. It is the perception of Shakespeare's histories thus promoted which led to the first ever stage production of the joint history plays by Franz von Dingelstedt in 1864. As Manfred Draudt writes, though, it is often forgotten that already twenty years before this notable world premiere, in 1844, the Silesian actor and poet Karl von Holtei gave a public recitation of the ten histories (including *King John* and *Henry VIII*) in Vienna. Holtei's public readings were induced, it would seem, by the contemporary view that the traditional stage was not the most appropriate site for appreciating the genius of England's great playwright-cum-poet, and the reading experience the preferable alternative. Nevertheless, the 1864 initiative marked the beginning of a long and powerful stage career of the histories, in Germany, and at the Burgtheater in Vienna.

Also at the Burgtheater, as Draudt notes, *Richard III* was to be the perennial favourite, thus seeming to confirm that its eponymous hero, as R. A. Foakes has put it, is 'the Yorkist monster we *all* love to hate'.[7] On the one hand, the love–hate relationship thus brought into focus enables one to appreciate the language-oriented Lindtberg, who in the 1960s set out to be faithful to the text, and whose writings include *Shakespeares Königsdramen*. On the other, it explains the directorial strategy of Claus Peymann, whose extraordinary 1987 rendering of *Richard III*, with its explicitly Hitlerian overtones and its coarse as well as erroneous translation by Thomas Brasch, would seem to have made the Shakespearean genre of history border rather close on the burlesque.

Interestingly, Tom Lanoye and Luk Perceval's adaptation of the histories as *Ten Oorlog* (aka *Schlachten!*), was undertaken at the moment when it appeared that it would be impossible to stage *Richard III* convincingly without also showing how this particular play developed out of the other seven histories from *Richard II* until *3 Henry VI*. Importantly, though, too much emphasis on this attempt at clarifying the play to foreign audiences in a more or less traditional search for a 'grand narrative' could obscure Lanoye and Perceval's real ambition to imitate and emulate Shakespeare, much in the manner of Blake and Keats. Rewriting the tetralogies as an indictment of Belgian politics in the 1990s, they also attempted to subvert Shakespeare's own supremacy in the field of historical drama. This was a cultural war also on the playwright, an attempt to dethrone the writer whom Thomas Carlyle had in a reactionary vein promoted as the major agent in English history: 'Here, I say, is an English King, whom no time or chance, Parliament or combination of Parliaments, can dethrone! This King Shakespeare, does not he shine, in crowned sovereignty, over us all, as the noblest, gentlest, strongest of rallying-signs; *in*destructible.'[8] Lanoye and Perceval defended their adaptation as a means of making intelligible to foreign audiences the complex history of *Richard III* and to expose the anxiety aroused by Belgian politics in the 1990s, but at the same time theirs was a truly Ricardian desire to undermine the authority of a regnant playwright.

Also in Spain did Shakespeare's *Richard III* enjoy a tyrannical reign on the stage. This lasted until 1998, when, as Keith Gregor writes, Adrián Daumas effectively freed *Richard II* from its grim shadow. Indeed, until the Spanish stage premiere of *Richard II* in 1998, the potentially subversive *Richard II* had been domesticated in Spanish criticism of the play. Under General Franco, for example, it had been defined as 'a marvel of medieval evocation'. Daumas, however, saw the play as an 'implicit critique of

despotism', a model of political systems in flux. In Daumas's version of
the play, it was nearly inevitable that *Richard II* would evoke memories of
Francoist tyranny, invite a traditionally Catholic country to reflect on the
church and the divine legitimation of rule, interrogate the state of the nation
and the virtue of national unity, as well as examine the plight of women in
post-Francoist Spain. A vital key to the analogies between medieval England
and contemporary Spain was the Spanish equivalent that the director chose
for Gaunt's 'This England'. Although the production's original translation
by Angel Luis Pujante had been carefully chosen, Daumas recognized the
phrase 'This England' as the linchpin for the success of this patriotic play's
reception on the Iberian peninsula, and rewrote it as 'This land'.

Together with Germany, France is the country which has been responsible for the most intensive traffic in Shakespeare, including traffic in the
histories that paradoxically capture the past as a sequence of wars between
France itself and that of Shakespeare. Dominique Goy-Blanquet discusses
a number of stage adaptations presented at the Avignon Festival between
the early 1980s and the late 1990s. First, she devotes attention to Ariane
Mnouchkine's early work on the histories (including her *Richard II* with
its evocations of feudal Japan) and argues that Mnouchkine's work on
Shakespeare is to be assessed as part of a consistent artistic and political
development. Goy-Blanquet further analyses French responses to the wars
in the Balkans and Operation 'Desert Storm', such as Matthias Langhoff's
adaptation of *Richard III* (1995), and provides a detailed account of the
politico-cultural contexts that led up to the premiere of the most con-
tentious of the histories in France, *Henry V*. Ironically, this production
of *Henry V* took place during the same Avignon Festival year that saw
the emergence of a new political stage genre, the '*théâtre-document*' with
its unprecedented confrontation between the theatre and the media. As
Goy-Blanquet argues, the juxtaposition of Shakespeare's 'fabled history'
and the 'real politics' of productions such as Olivier Py's *Requiem pour
Srebrenica* (1999) brings into focus a form of schizophrenia about which it
may, as yet, be too early to theorize.

NOTES

1 '*The Plantagenets*': *Adapted by the Royal Shakespeare Company from William
  Shakespeare's 'Henry VI' Parts I, II, III and 'Richard III' as 'Henry VI', 'The Rise of
  Edward IV' and 'Richard III, His Death'*. With an introduction by Adrian Noble
  (London and Boston: Faber and Faber, 1989), xii.
2 On the 'pious heretics' see Ulrich Suerbaum's fine essay, 'Die frommen Häretiker:
  John Barton in Zusammenarbeit mit Peter Hall, *The Wars of the Roses*', in

Anglo-Amerikanische Shakespeare-Bearbeitungen des 20. Jahrhunderts, edited by Horst Priessnitz (Darmstadt: Wissenschaftliche Buchgesellschaft, 1980), 31–43. One of Suerbaum's conclusions in 1980, based on the curiously apologetic approach of Barton and Hall, was that, given the deeply-entrenched Shakespeare tradition in Britain, any 'uninhibited' adapting tendency (of the kind displayed by Nahum Tate) was still lacking ('Was fehlt is die Unbefangenheit eines Nahum Tate', 42).

3 Terry Hands, quoted in Robert Shaughnessy, *Representing Shakespeare: England, History and the RSC* (New York: Harvester Wheatsheaf, 1994), 66. See also the text-oriented praise of the production by Homer D. Swander, 'The Rediscovery of *Henry VI* ', *Shakespeare Quarterly* 29 (1978), 146–63.

4 Jozef de Vos, 'Shakespeare's History Plays in Belgium: Taken Apart and Reconstructed as "Grand Narrative"', in *Four Hundred Years of Shakespeare in Europe*, edited by A. Luis Pujante and Ton Hoenselaars. With a foreword by Stanley Wells (Newark: University of Delaware Press, 2003), 211–22.

5 *Coleridge's Shakespeare Criticism*, edited by Thomas Middleton Raysor, 2 vols. (London: Constable, 1960), i, 126.

6 For Keats see *Adaptations of Shakespeare: A Critical Anthology of Plays from the Seventeenth Century to the Present*, edited by Daniel Fischlin and Mark Fortier (London and New York: Routledge, 2000), 98. For Blake see *The Poems of William Blake*, edited by W. H. Stevenson and David V. Erdman (London: Longman, 1971), 21 (scene 2, lines 33–5); and 37 (lines 1–2).

7 R. A. Foakes, 'Shakespeare's Other Historical Plays', in *The Cambridge Companion to Shakespeare's History Plays*, edited by Michael Hattaway (Cambridge: Cambridge University Press, 2002), 214–28 (p. 214; italics added).

8 Thomas Carlyle, 'The Hero as Poet', in *Shakespeare Criticism: A Selection, 1623–1840*, edited by D. Nichol Smith (1923. Rpt. London: Oxford University Press, 1973), 370.

CHAPTER 9

Shakespeare's English histories at the Vienna Burgtheater

Manfred Draudt

Shakespeare's histories have a long tradition at the Burgtheater, the Austrian national theatre. Under one of its most distinguished artistic directors, Heinrich Laube, *Richard II* and *Richard III* were first performed there in 1852, and 'the most celebrated event' under his successor Franz von Dingelstedt was a Shakespeare week in April 1875, presenting the complete cycle of the histories in his own adaptation.[1] Since *1 Henry VI* was almost totally omitted, the plays could be presented on seven evenings. Dingelstedt's cycle – first mounted in Weimar in order to mark the tercentenary of Shakespeare's birth and the foundation of the Deutsche Shakespeare-Gesellschaft in 1864 – was the first of its kind on the German stage and, in Vienna, the most exciting theatrical happening of its epoch, characterized by splendour, visual effect, powerful movement and impressive battles on a stage filled with people.

Shakespeare's history plays, in fact, first came to Vienna not through theatrical performances but through readings. In 1841, the Silesian writer Karl von Holtei gave a successful reading of *Henry V*; because of the great demand this was repeated both in the same year and again the following year, possibly with another history play added to the bill (which also included a play of Holtei's own). In 1844 he gave his pioneering reading of all ten history plays including *King John* and *Henry VIII* in the old hall of the Musikverein in the Tuchlauben (in use from 1831 to 1869).[2] The three parts of *Henry VI* were severely cut and compressed into a single evening, as was customary in many productions of the time.

At the Burgtheater, particularly *Richard III* was almost continuously in repertoire. Dingelstedt's adaptation was performed until 1904, and it was followed by Baron Berger's adaptation, which played for seven years (from 1910 until 1917). In 1934 the play was produced again by Franz Herterich (artistic director of the Burgtheater from 1923 to 1930), and it achieved no fewer than nineteen performances in a single season.[3]

By far the most ambitious project was that comprising Leopold Lindtberg's production of the complete cycle on the occasion of Shakespeare's
400th anniversary, involving no fewer than eighty-seven actors. Lindtberg's
project began with the two parts of *Henry IV* compressed into a single
evening in 1960, and culminated with the performance of the complete
cycle on successive nights in May 1964.[4] Each year Lindtberg brought out
a new production of a history play: *Henry V* in 1961, *Richard III* in 1962,
Richard II in 1963 and the three parts of *Henry VI* condensed into a single
evening in 1964. Although the whole enterprise won wide critical acclaim,
the most impressive productions, according to contemporary reviews, were
those of *Henry IV* and *Henry V*, and the adaptation of *Henry VI*. *Richard II*
was considered the least successful production, owing to a miscast title
role.

The role of Prince Hal in the original productions of *Henry IV* and
Henry V was played by Oskar Werner, the most distinguished (but also
most difficult) post-war Austrian actor, who later won worldwide acclaim
in a number of memorable films.[5] Unfortunately he left the Burgtheater in
anger in 1961, partly to pursue an international film career. Oskar Werner's
Prince Hal, a role in which he could display his superb rhetorical skill
and extraordinarily wide range of vocal inflections, combined nobility and
superiority with simplicity, irony and humour. In a unique gesture, no
less a person than Herbert von Karajan, then artistic director of the Vienna
State Opera, congratulated him on his outstanding performance.[6] Werner's
successor in the revivals of the two Henry plays, Boy Gobert, never came
up to his standard.

Leopold Lindtberg, the director of the complete cycle, was perfectly
qualified for the job.[7] Born in Vienna in 1902, he had read German and
Art History at Vienna University while training as an actor and director.
Emigrating originally to Paris in 1933, he soon moved to Zurich, Switzerland, where he became principal director at the Schauspielhaus, a position
he held until 1984. A Swiss citizen since 1951, he successfully directed plays
as well as operas for more than forty years not only on all major German
stages, in Berlin, Hamburg, Düsseldorf and Munich, but also in Israel,
Denmark, Japan and in London, where he was responsible for the Covent
Garden *Fledermaus* of 1977. Having directed Shakespeare since 1929 – a
range of twenty different plays in all, in forty-one different productions –
Lindtberg took upon himself the production of the complete cycle at the
Burgtheater, to which he had first returned in 1947.[8] Although he was one
of the many theatrical figures who had been forced into exile in the Nazi

period because of his Jewish origin, he eschewed crudely polemical politi-cal effects, consistently maintaining strictly artistic priorities.[9] In a lecture 'Against Indolence' of 1974 he referred explicitly to 'the boredom of indoc-trination that is alien to art'.[10] Nevertheless, he cannot be accused of being apolitical or of ignoring history, either distant or recent.

In an essay on Shakespeare's histories, he comments on the spontaneous flattery of the people around Richard and on their self-denial, calling *Richard III* a unique piece of political didacticism.[11] Before the Second World War, he argues, the play was regarded as a kind of horror tragedy, as an exaggerated utopia of evil: 'This was sometime a paradox, but now the time gives it proof' (*Hamlet* 3.1.113).[12] Yet he finds it too cheap an effect to mould *Richard III* into a paraphrase of recent historical events. Properly performed, he maintains, *Richard III* can present a model for any dictato-rial regime: under similar conditions men have always reacted in a similar way.[13] After suggesting that 'England' could be replaced by 'Germany', he asks himself whether such crude equations are really necessary. Rather, he proposes ironically, the programme for every production of the play should feature a warning: 'Any similarity between the play's characters and persons alive or recently deceased is not intentional but purely coincidental.'[14]

Although his productions deliberately refrained from using modern dress, with costumes, hairstyle or setting suggestive of Hitler or Nazi Germany (as in Richard Loncraine's 1996 film version of *Richard III*), his subtle implications were clearly understood by many critics and surely also by many members of the audience. In his review of the play in *Neues Österreich* of 10 March 1962, Otto F. Beer called Richard 'a monster of Hitler format', and Edwin Rollet in the *Wiener Zeitung* of the same date was even more explicit:

maybe every period of history has witnessed similarly cruel games with human beings and their fates . . . Yet horrible reminiscences and associations come to the fore, reminiscences of the raging of an amoral, proud, and bloodthirsty usurper and dictator, who rose through deceit and cunning and erected an unparalleled tyranny until he perished in a flood of blood and tears. Do not Richard's words, 'I am determined to prove a villain' bear a resemblance to a phrase that could often be heard: 'So I decided to become a politician'?

Even in other plays of the cycle such associations were conjured up. As Otto Basil put it in his review in *Neues Österreich* (20 May 1964): 'What we see happening in *Henry VI* reminds us of the Third Reich.'[15]

In many respects Lindtberg was the conscious antithesis to then emerg-ing 'Regietheater' (director's theatre), for his main objective was in an unpretentious way to serve the author and his work. This also becomes clear from his essay on *Shakespeares Königsdramen*, which outlines Lindtberg's approach to the histories with reference to the work of seminal Shakespeare scholars of his time, including E. M. W. Tillyard, John Dover Wilson and Wolfgang Clemen. *Shakespeares Königsdramen* constitutes a unique record complementing the prompt books and the numerous reviews, as well as my own memory of the productions; it also allows us to measure the director's ideas against their actual realization on stage. Although he may have failed in details, the reviews confirm that most of his objectives were achieved in performance.[16] It is therefore worth focusing our attention on some key passages of Lindtberg's essay.

The stage, he maintains, must have easily changeable locations, which are to be evoked by suggestive pieces of furniture. Instead of conventional scenery he used high, iron-mounted wooden scaffolds reminiscent of Tudor wooden structures. While these structures remained the same throughout the cycle, the scaffold's decorations, their material and colours, changed from play to play. Heraldic signs, weapons, curtains, animal skins, thick ropes, wooden insets in the shape of a triptych, crumbling walls and straw mats served as such pieces of decoration characterizing the individual locations. They were complemented by just a few realistic pieces of furniture, such as wooden or metal grills, which, according to the reviews, together with the colour red, were most effectively employed in *Richard II* and *Richard III* for symbolizing prisons. Other realistic pieces were door frames and parts of walls. The only piece of furniture that was retained through all the plays was the English throne, serving as a focus for the audience's attention on the struggle for power. On each side of the proscenium arch there was a heavy wooden balcony (sometimes, however, used in a clumsy manner, according to critics). Thus far, the stage was very much inspired by its Elizabethan model. Lindtberg, however, also used low curtains to divide the stage into a front and back stage; and he even believed this to be superior to the Elizabethan stage with regard to its proportions. Furthermore, boards with the locations written on them could be lowered from the loft.

With his emphasis on rich and colourful costumes Lindtberg again came close to the ideas of Shakespeare's theatre. Visually impressive scenes with masses of people were used sparingly: for the coronation of Hal, the crossing of the Channel in *Henry V* and the Te Deum after the battle of Agincourt, as well as for Richard's mighty black army in *Richard III*.

Rather than by masses of supernumeraries, battles were evoked by sound effects, by light and colour and by torn or crossed standards. Generally, only speaking characters would fight on stage. This was in diametrical opposition to Dingelstedt's nineteenth-century production of the cycle.

Antithetical contrasts, according to Lindtberg in *Shakespeares Königs-dramen*, are central to the history plays: they are peopled by kings and beggars, ghosts and drunkards, thieves and heroes, whores and saints, murderers and clowns; he also maintains that kingly dignity and the honour of scoundrels, heroic deaths and corruption, knighthood and gluttony, qualms of conscience and futile atonement are combined in a wild, lewd, grandiose, tragicomic mummery. By common consent, these qualities were convincingly conveyed in his productions. The *Arbeiterzeitung* of 18 March 1964 mentioned the broad comic scenes which provide an ideal counterpart to the high political action in *Henry IV*, and Otto Basil in *Die Presse* of the same date not only spoke of the superb balance between comedy and serious elements (slightly tilted towards comedy) but also referred to the complexity of Falstaff, who combined chivalry with vulgarity, humour and perfidy, gluttony and cowardly emptiness.

One reason why Lindtberg may have been able to capture the subtle humour and the comedy of the histories – which is either missed or coarsened in many continental productions – may be due to the fact that he was also a great director of popular Viennese comedy, in particular of the plays of Johann Nestroy. Commenting on a scene of a Nestroy comedy, he implies that only the theatre can bring alive the contrast of serious intention and highly comic effect – a concept that appears to be equally applicable to the plays of Shakespeare.[17]

Furthermore, a considerable number of the actors involved in the cycle were also accomplished performers in the comic plays of Nestroy. One of them was Josef Meinrad, holder of the Iffland Ring, which is traditionally conferred upon the most distinguished actor in the German tongue. Meinrad was not only a superbly comic Fluellen, who combined boundless enthusiasm with righteous indignation and wild anger, but also a memorable *Henry VI*, who contributed to the exceptional success of this production through his simple and convincing piety and naivety, which appeared totally helpless in the face of political machinations and intrigue.[18]

In addition to emphasizing contrasts, Lindtberg's productions, according to Otto F. Beer's review of *Richard II* in *Neues Österreich* of 29 May 1963, suggestively disclosed interrelations, such as common motifs and echoes, between the individual parts of the cycle. This is supported by Lindtberg's essay on the histories, where he points out parallels between the plays or the characters: 'Thou rag of honour', Margaret's epithet for Richard in *Richard III* (1.3.233), is linked with Falstaff, not only with his 'catechism' on honour in the first part of *Henry IV* (5.1.127–41), but also with his comments on the soldiers he has recruited, who, in Prince Hal's eyes, are 'pitiful rascals' (4.2.63).[19] Falstaff, Lindtberg argues, is also a corrupt scoundrel and a cynic when he contemptuously dismisses them as 'food for powder', who will 'fill a pit as well as better' (*1 Henry IV*, 4.2.65–6). Since both Richard and Falstaff are offsprings of the medieval Vice, this is a perfectly legitimate and convincing reading.

Other links, also spotted by reviewers, were skilfully established between Joan la Pucelle and Margaret, whom Lindtberg presented as counterparts. Shakespeare juxtaposes and frames the scene of Margaret being taken prisoner by Suffolk (*1 Henry VI*, 5.3.44–5) with the episode of the cursing Joan being led to execution, but Lindtberg associated the two figures even more closely by having Margaret emerge from the very crowd around Joan.[20]

Admiring the grandeur, the complexity, the wit and the power of these plays, Lindtberg argued – and general critical opinion confirmed – that a climax of the whole cycle, and indeed one of its most touching scenes, was the episode in the third part of *Henry VI* in which Henry is sitting on a molehill, the emblem of the vanity of kingly power, when the son enters who has killed his father and the father who has killed his son, each with the corpse of the dead man in his arms (2.5). Lindtberg staged the scene as a triptych and associated it with the three wailing women in *Richard III*.

Since historical and genealogical aspects and details are of lesser importance in performances outside England, Lindtberg rightly maintained that the director must establish a meaningful relationship between the plays and the period in which they are performed – without necessarily resorting to modern dress or setting. The title of Elisabeth Pahl's review of *Henry VI* in the *Illustrierte Kronen Zeitung*, 'Shakespeare's World Reaches Powerfully into Our Period', suggests that Lindtberg succeeded in making the plays speak to his own time.[21] The focus, he maintained, must be on man as such, or, as Piero Rismondo put it in his review in *Die Presse* of 19 May 1964, when facing death, aristocratic and kingly characters are reduced to simple human beings. Lindtberg also emphasized that the individual is both the centre of each play and at the same time just a link in a great chain extending over generations.

In order to achieve his aim of distilling unity, clarity and simplicity from an overwhelming complexity of details, he adapted the plays and telescoped two – or even three – plays into a single evening, for which the German theatre tradition offered numerous models: since the first German performance of *Henry IV* in 1778 in Hamburg, the two parts in Friedrich

Ludwig Schröder's translation had been condensed into a single evening, which had also been a tradition at the Burgtheater since the time of Heinrich Laube.

Lindtberg faithfully retained the plays' language in A. W. Schlegel's classic – if now somewhat dated – translation, and stressed the importance of the spoken word.[22] Yet he boldly interfered with the plays' structure, cut rigorously and also reshuffled scenes. When *Richard III* was performed on its own, for example, the play was preceded by a scene (5.5) from *3 Henry VI*, supplying the audience with background information on the characters; on the other hand, the appearance of the ghosts of the dead to Richmond was omitted, because Lindtberg felt that Richard's suppressed conscience should be foregrounded, and that ghosts would be redundant because Richmond explicitly refers to divine support in his oration to his soldiers.[23] However, he also transposed Richmond's speech so that it follows (instead of preceding) Richard's later exchange with Ratcliffe ('Who saw the sun today?'), which ends with his exhortation 'Let us to it pell-mell – / If not to Heaven, then hand in hand to hell!' (5.3.278–314).

Lindtberg's most radical adaptation was of the three parts of *Henry VI*, and his drastic cut of Part One exemplifies his method. Lindtberg omitted most of the battle scenes and the alternating fortunes in the war with France, Joan la Pucelle's rise, the fickleness, cowardice, treachery of the French, including the Countess of Auvergne and the Duke of Burgundy; conversely he cut Talbot's prowess and the figures of Sir John Fastolf and Edmund Mortimer. Yet he kept many of the play's highlights and focused on the English factionalism. This is illustrated by the scenes he retained: the rivalry between Gloucester and Winchester (1.1); the Temple Garden scene (2.4); he also fused the newly flaring up of enmity between Gloucester and Winchester in Parliament (3.1), with Vernon and Basset's quarrel that preceded instead of following Henry's coronation (4.1). The next scene dramatizing the defeat of Talbot telescoped four scenes into a single one: Talbot's speech at the end of 1.5, the exchange between him and Joan in 3.2, his speech at the end of 4.3, and 4.5, his son John's refusal to flee when they are trapped by the French. After Somerset's refusal to come to Talbot's help (4.4), we witness his death and Joan's short-lived triumph (4.7). The change of scene to Gloucester's promotion of Henry's marriage to the daughter of Armagnac (5.1) was followed by Joan's being deserted by her spirits, her capture by York and her curse before being led to execution (5.3 and 5.4). Suffolk's taking Margaret prisoner (5.3) came after Joan's final exit. His triumphant soliloquy, to which were added the play's last two lines (spoken by Suffolk as well), concluded this part.

In spite of radical cuts – even the scenes that Lindtberg retained were frequently reduced to half or even a third of their original length[24] – the essentials of the play were preserved, though its emphasis had shifted. Rather than 'the tragedy of Talbot', which Part One is in Tillyard's words, it became a prelude to Parts Two and Three, in which the various quarrels among the English prepared for the civil war to come.

Lindtberg's adaptation invites comparison with Giorgio Strehler's version of 1975 entitled 'Das Spiel der Mächtigen' (*Il gioco dei potenti*). Since it was transferred to the Burgtheater only after its original run at the Salzburg Festival and, as the subtitle openly acknowledges, was a much freer version 'after *Henry VI* by William Shakespeare', I shall deal with it here only briefly.

Strehler's 'Spiel der Mächtigen', a rather free paraphrase making use of Loek Huisman's rhythmic prose translation, was based on *3 Henry VI* with Act 5 from *2 Henry VI* attached as a prelude, and the first soliloquy from *Richard III* as epilogue. Furthermore, there was a frame in the style of Pirandello with many elements of pastiche from *Henry V* and *Richard II*. Strehler's production started with a prologue by an Actor (strongly reminiscent of a Pirandello figure), whose address to the audience was based on the Prologue and the various Chorus speeches of *Henry V* before Strehler's own writing took over. The Actor then introduced himself as prompter but, in fact, turned out to be a choric figure mentioning some episodes from the first and second parts of *Henry VI*. His words were complemented by short pantomimes suggesting Henry's coronation, the murder of Gloucester, Winchester's death and the Jack Cade rebellion. Furthermore, a soliloquy spoken by the ambitious York was inserted, based on *2 Henry VI* (5.1), and also five lines of dialogue between Henry and Margaret before the actual play began with extracts from Act 5 of the Second Part of *Henry VI*. The Actor then reappeared with a Strehler speech before the beginning of the Third Part, and with a pastiche of Henry's soliloquy from *Henry V*: 'what have kings that privates have not too', before an episode vaguely reminiscent of Act 1, scene 2, of the third part of *Henry VI*.[25] Occasionally, the Actor also commented on the action. Before the episode of Henry's capture by the two Scottish gamekeepers (*3 Henry VI*, 3.1), the Actor combined various monologues from Richard II's deposition scene (4.1) into a single speech ('O that I were a mockery king of snow' (4.1.260), the ensuing dashing of the flattering looking-glass, and 'Now, mark me how I will undo myself' [4.1.203]), while Henry, whose make-up recalled that of a clown, divested himself of his clothes.[26] Against the background of Edward's preparation for his coronation, Henry's burial was prepared in the next scene by two gravediggers, Bevis and Holland, who faintly recalled those from *Hamlet*, although their names derived from the Jack Cade episode in *2 Henry VI* (4.2 and 4.7). They commented on all the corpses they had been burying since the death of Henry V and reasoned: 'The great ones never get enough. The game is never finished; one of them begins again, and then it starts again . . . Craftsmen . . . can find no work, only gravediggers do . . . Prices are rising, but people are falling. Corpses are plentiful, but bread is scarce. And the great ones never have enough – never, never, never.'[27] Although the play reflects the impact of Brecht and thus Strehler's moral concern, this kind of writing or reasoning appears banal, particularly if compared against the richness of Shakespeare's original text, which had been stripped to its bare bones. The pastiche, if not medley, from the histories mixed with passages of Strehler's own, inserted into a simplified version of *3 Henry VI* as well as filtered through Pirandello, is far removed from Shakespeare's original concept.

The most radical change in the artistic policy of the Burgtheater came in 1986 when Claus Peymann, formerly director of the Schauspielhaus, Bochum, was appointed artistic director.[28] In many respects an antithesis to Lindtberg, Peymann introduced the German director's theatre to the Burgtheater – and I mean German not in the sense of our common language but in a political sense. Peymann brought with him his own team of actors and dramaturgs, invited outside directors, preferably from the former German Democratic Republic and, at the same time, refused to employ distinguished members of the traditional company (such as Judith Holzmeister, Inge Konradi and Erika Pluhar, to mention just a few prominent actresses who had contributed to the success of the Lindtberg cycle). Furthermore, Peymann created a climate of confrontation with the elected representatives of the company, which drove some company members to other Viennese theatres, and he even dismissed members of the administrative staff. With all these measures, Peymann very consciously discontinued a long tradition and replaced a style of acting and production which had evolved over two hundred years – admittedly, not without ups and downs. His systematic politicization of the theatre, most obvious in his production of that bitter satire set in Vienna at the time of the 'Anschluß' – Thomas Bernhard's *Heldenplatz* (1988) – was enthusiastically welcomed by the political left and many younger members of the audience, while those who had known the Burgtheater for decades felt that its identity had been lost and that this was itself a kind of artistic 'Anschluß' with Germany.

The most keenly awaited production of Peymann's first season was a Shakespearean history play, *Richard III*. Demonstratively applauded, it showed many hallmarks of his new style.[29] Although generally praised, the production was by no means unproblematic. A positive aspect one ought to mention was Peymann's revival of the Elizabethan custom of doubling minor parts, which avoided Lindtberg's enormous casts; more questionable, however, is the fact that the performance was dragged out to last for four and a half hours – as was also his *Macbeth* of 1992.

The action of *Richard III* was transferred to a timeless present, according to Kurt Kahl in the *Kurier* (7 February 1987), and the political message was made obvious right from the beginning: Richard's close-cut hairstyle, with a wet-hair-parting, immediately recalled Hitler and his period, just as a brief gesture of a raised arm suggested the Hitler salute; his dress in black and leather complemented the impression.[30] These allusions were, however, offset by humanizing and psychologizing tendencies. After his nightmarish dream (5.3), Richard tenderly began to stroke his own hands before uttering the phrase 'Nobody loves me' (instead of the original 'There is no creature loves me' [5.3.201]). His despair when confronted with his own guilt was thus turned into self-pity, which was interpreted by the critic of the *Süddeutsche Zeitung* (Munich) as follows: 'He loves himself, because he was never loved as a boy. He is lonely . . . unloved, expelled . . . a poor pitiable man, worthy of compassion.' In spite, or rather because of, the fascist or Nazi overtones in Richard, such a reading of Shakespeare's merciless villain (who lacks even Aaron's redeeming features) appears highly problematic, if not dangerous.[31]

The central point of focus of the bleak set, above which a vulture circled, was a huge gully. In this gully or cesspit, Richard deposited the corpse of Henry VI after the wooing of Lady Anne, as well as several other corpses; and from it, in the end, all the victims rose again. To Richard, it was implied, killing a fellow human being means no more than throwing a puppet on a scrap heap.[32] Nevertheless, the gully also seemed suggestive of a reductionist tendency and of a propensity to debase both action and characters, which became even more obvious in the textual changes. In order to illustrate Peymann's approach, I shall compare the opening scene of his production to that of Lindtberg.

Lindtberg rigorously cut in the scene, omitting a total of 51 lines (of the original 162) but adhered closely to the original text by employing Schlegel's classic translation; he failed to preserve the sense of Shakespeare's lines in only two instances.[33] Peymann, by contrast, kept most of the lines, cutting only a total of six, but used a modern translation by Thomas Brasch which frequently distorts Shakespeare's text. Although praised by some because it is 'more easily speakable, and also more easily understandable for a modern

Figure 6. Claus Peymann, *Richard III* (Burgtheater, Vienna, 1987). From left to right:
Kirsten Dene as Queen Elizabeth, Gert Voss as King Richard III and Annemarie Düringer
as Duchess of York.

audience' than Schlegel's, 'it is certainly not beautiful'.[34] Others, such as
Otto F. Beer in *Der Tagesspiegel* (19 February 1987) and Bernd Sucher in
the *Süddeutsche Zeitung* (7–8 February 1987), were even more outspoken,
calling it 'coarsening and banal', or pointing to its 'drastic mistakes'. The
following dialogue is a case in point:

> CLARENCE In God's name, what art thou?
> 2 MURDERER   A man as you are.
> CLARENCE But not as I am, royal.
> 1 MURDERER Nor you as we are, loyal.
>   (*Richard III*, 1.4.162–4)

In the Peymann production, the final exchange was rendered as:

> CLARENCE Not as I am. I am of high blood.
> 1 MURDERER My business is with blood as well.[35]

Although this example may be regarded as a very free rendering of the
original, in scene 1 (in 162 lines) there are approximately forty instances

(one quarter of the total), where the meaning of Shakespeare's lines is misrepresented in various degrees: 'merry meetings' (1.1.7), for example, becomes 'triumphant shouts' ('Triumphgeschrei'). 'And if King Edward be as true and just' (1.1.36) becomes 'If King Edward were only half an angel' ('Wenn König Edward nur ein halber Engel wär'). The list can be extended.[36]

More important than these examples from Thomas Brasch's translation, in which the original meaning is not rendered faithfully yet still somehow present, are instances in which nonsense is made of the original text: the 'Tower' of London (1.1.50) is literally translated as 'tower' ('Turm') so that the sense of the specific location is lost; 'by "G" / His issue disinherited should be' (1.1.57) is turned into 'G wrests the inheritance from him with a trick' ('ein G die Erbschaft ihm entreißt mit einem Dreh'); and the original meaning is also lost when 'the world for me to bustle in' (1.1.152) becomes 'down on her knees' ('auf die Knie mit ihr [der Welt]').[37]

Throughout the translation, we can observe a consistent tendency towards exaggeration, coarsening or vulgarization. For example, 'discontent' (1.1.1) becomes 'fury, rage' ('Wut'); 'the Queen's kindred' (1.1.72) becomes 'this pack of the Queen's' ('dieses Pack / der Königin'); 'knave' (1.1.102) becomes 'you dog' ('du Hund'); 'plain Clarence' (118) becomes 'dull or stupid Clarence' ('blöder Clarence').[38] The most striking instance is the consistent replacement of 'villain' by 'shit' ('Dreckskerl') which was also remarked upon by many reviewers.[39]

Conversely, there are instances of trivialization ('farewell' [1.1.107] becomes 'get on well' ['machs gut']), and of debasement or lowering of rank, which are reflected particularly in titles or addresses. Instances of debasement and lowering of rank include: 'what means this armed guard / That waits upon your Grace?' (1.1.42–3), which becomes 'what means the watch by your side' ('was soll die Wache / an Eurer Seite'), losing the irony; and Brakenbury's 'your Graces' (1.1.84) becomes 'you sirs' ('ihr Herrn'), resulting in the loss of class difference. This tendency was also noticed by Lothar Sträter in *Saarbrückner Zeitung*, when he observed that the lords at court are no gentlemen.

A modern production which relies on a translation of this kind in some respects resembles a burlesque or travesty of Shakespeare, with which it shares above all one feature, debasement: characters are lowered in their ranks or social levels, the language is transferred to a present period and milieu with which audiences are intimately familiar and with which they can identify, and the setting of the action is less elevated than that of the original. In addition, they have in common the trivialization as well as the exaggeration, and particularly the debasing of the language of the original to a slangy, coarse and vulgar contemporary idiom. One of the main differences between a Shakespeare burlesque and such a modern translation is that, unlike the author of the travesty, the modern director professes to perform Shakespeare's own play.[40] Yet in spite of the numerous and serious deviations from Shakespeare's text, which have a considerable cumulative effect, Peymann's *Richard III* is, of course, still much closer to Shakespeare than any nineteenth-century burlesque.

What the two productions, in spite of Lindtberg's suggestive style and Peymann's very explicitly political implication, have in common is that each elicited unlooked-for responses, as reviewers associated with them topical events that were never in the minds of the respective directors. In his review of *Richard III* in *Neues Österreich* (10 March 1962), Otto F. Beer, for example, wrote: 'if one watches Richard forcing his way to the throne, one can imagine what is presently going on in the artistic director's office of our State Opera'. And approximately twenty-five years later, reviewing the same play in *Der Falter* (25 February 1987), Franz Schuh observed a striking similarity between Gert Voss as Richard and the then archbishop of Vienna, Hermann Groer (who was accused of paedophile misdemeanour).

Lindtberg's productions with their drastic cuts but faithfulness to the text and their overall suggestiveness definitely came closer to the production style that has been – and still is – prevalent in England; Peymann's – or rather his translator's – radical alterations of the text together with the attempt to modernize the play and rub the audience's nose in its political relevance is characteristic of the German director's theatre. Ultimately, evaluations of productions are, of course, impossible, because of the complexity of the experience and the necessarily personal nature of any response; yet it seems a pity that many modern directors appear not to trust the audience's intelligence to be able to draw parallels and discover associations; neither do they trust the audience's power of imagination, which Lindtberg regarded as one of the liveliest elements of the theatre and to which, so he pleads, theatre ought constantly to appeal. It is a telling detail that both Lindtberg in his essay and Giorgio Strehler in his adaptation quote extensively from the Prologue to and the Chorus speeches in *Henry V*.

Shakespeare's histories have always occupied a prominent position in the repertoire of Viennese theatre, not just at the Burgtheater but also at the Volkstheater and the Theater in der Josefstadt, whose productions I have not considered. At the Burgtheater not only have individual history plays been frequently performed over a period of 150 years but also two complete cycles were staged with great success. Furthermore, the various productions show significant shifts in emphasis: in place of the immediate interest in English history which the plays may have for British audiences, there was lavish visual spectacle in the nineteenth century; the emphasis on universal human problems, the *conditio humana* in Lindtberg's productions; the foregrounding of social questions in Strehler's adaptation; and the undisguised politicization in Peymann's version. Moreover, the various productions reflect general trends and changes in directorial style: Lindtberg's language-oriented productions were faithful also in other respects, since they attempted to recreate essential features and the spirit of the Elizabethan theatre with modern means and for a twentieth-century audience. Claus Peymann's example of the director's theatre ('Regietheater'), by contrast, not only deviated substantially from the original text but also radically modernized the play in idiom and setting in order to appeal directly to younger audiences with less understanding of linguistic and historical intricacies.

The overall success of all these different versions testifies to the timeless appeal in an 'alien' environment even of those plays in the canon whose Englishness is most overt.

NOTES

I am indebted for help, in particular for the generous supply of prompt books, reviews, photographs, Lindtberg's essay and his biography, to Rita Czapka from the Burgtheater archives, and to Claudia Kaufmann-Freßner from the dramaturg's department at the same theatre.

1 W. E. Yates, *Theatre in Vienna: A Critical History, 1776–1995* (Cambridge: Cambridge University Press, 1996), 78.

2 The bill of the complete cycle plus *King John* and *Henry VIII* preserved in the Österreichisches Theatermuseum, Vienna, is unfortunately not dated by the year, but it does give days of the week and the month. In this way it is possible to narrow down the time of Holtei's reading – he frequently came to Vienna and also occasionally stayed there for longer periods – to two years: 1844 and 1850. Because of the quality of the paper and the layout of the bill the most likely year is 1844. For the information on Holtei and the computing of the years I am indebted to Othmar Barnert (Österreichisches Theatermuseum).

3 See Heinz Kindermann in his review of Lindtberg's *Richard III* in *Österreichische Neue Tageszeitung* (10 March 1962).

4 Wilhelm Hortmann's treatment of this seminal theatrical event in his *Shakespeare on the German Stage: The Twentieth Century* (Cambridge: Cambridge University Press, 1998), contains inaccuracies. The performances were 18–22 May 1964, but Hortmann gives '18–22 June 1964' (189) and '16 to 28 May' (222).

5 In François Truffaut's *Jules et Jim* (1961) and *Fahrenheit 451* (1966) he appeared together with Jeanne Moreau and Julie Christie respectively. In Stanley Kramer's *Ship of Fools* (1964) he was an unforgettable Dr Schumann beside Simone

Signoret and Vivian Leigh; and in Martin Ritt's *The Spy Who Came in from the Cold* (1965), his partner was Richard Burton.

6 In a letter dating from 16 March 1961. Information on the actor has been drawn from Robert Dachs, *Oskar Werner: Ein Nachklang* (Vienna: Kremayr & Scheriau, n.d.) and from *Oskar Werner*, edited by Ulrike Dembski and Christiane Mühlegger-Henhapel (Vienna: Christian Brandstätter, 2002).

7 The ensuing paragraph is based upon Erwin Leiser, *Leopold Lindtberg: Schriften – Bilder – Dokumente* (Zurich: Musik & Theater, 1985), which not only gives a biography and lists all his works but also includes Lindtberg's own critical writings and lectures.

8 From 1960 onwards he was also an acclaimed director at the Salzburg Festival.

9 'Leopold Lindtberg [machte] weder auf der Bühne noch in seinen Filmen politische Aussagen auf Kosten der künstlerischen Qualität' (Neither on stage nor in his films did Leopold Lindtberg make political statements at the expense of artistic quality) (Leiser, *Leopold Lindtberg*, 9).

10 'Gegen die Trägheit': 'Die Langeweile kunstfremder Indoktrinierung . . .' (Against indolence: The boredom of indoctrination that is alien to art) (in *ibid.*, 14).

11 'es [ist] . . . unfaßbar . . . zu welcher freiwilligen Liebedienerei und Verleug-nung ihrer selbst er [Richard III] . . . seine Umgebung bringen kann. In diesem Bereich ist "Richard III." ein politisches Lehrstück ohnegleichen' (Richard III can elicit in the people around him an incredible degree of voluntary fawning and self-abasement. In this regard *Richard III* is a piece of political didacticism beyond compare.) See Leopold Lindtberg, *Shakespeares Königsdramen*, Samm-lung Dokumente zur Literatur- und Theatergeschichte 2, edited by Hermann R. Leber and Carlos d'Inclan (Vienna, Stuttgart, and Basel: n.p., 1962), 36. *Shakespeares Königsdramen* was based on a lecture delivered to the Association of Friends of the Burgtheater and Members of the Department of Theatre Studies of Vienna University in May 1962.

12 *Hamlet*, edited by Harold Jenkins, in *The Arden Shakespeare: Complete Works*, edited by Richard Proudfoot, Ann Thompson and David Scott Kastan (London: Thomas Nelson and Sons, 1998), 3.1.114–15.

13 ' "Richard III." braucht nur richtig gespielt zu werden, um den Beweis zu erbrin-gen, daß alle Diktaturen, jede auf ihre Weise, durch seine Schule gegangen sind und daß die Menschen unter ähnlichen Voraussetzungen immer wieder auf ähnliche Art reagiert haben' (*Richard III* has only to be performed in the right way to prove that all dictatorships, each in its own way, have learned from it and that under similar circumstances men have always reacted in a similar way) (Lindtberg, *Shakespeares Königsdramen*, 36–7).

14 See *ibid.*, 40–1.

15 There can be no doubt about the acute political awareness of reviewers and audiences. Nevertheless, in his discussion of Lindtberg, Hortmann claims that postwar 'Viennese . . . spectators were no longer keyed to pitch to catch political innuendoes' (*Shakespeare on the German Stage*, 188).

16 Although every reviewer, of course, brings to bear his or her own ideo-logical and/or political outlook which must colour his judgement, it seems

impossible to pin down how far this influences or even determines a particular review. I have relied on a wide selection of reviews representative of various ideologies and standards, which probably reflect the mixture of views in a theatre audience; and what has struck me has been the frequent congruence of opinions.

17 See Leiser, *Leopold Lindtberg*, 74.

18 Lindtberg was so enthusiastic about his performance that he wrote an extra essay on his Fluellen.

19 See *King Richard III* (edited by Antony Hammond), and *King Henry IV, Part 1* (edited by A. R. Humphreys), in *The Arden Shakespeare: Complete Works*. Further references are to these editions.

20 See Elisabeth Pahl's review in the *Illustrierte Kronen Zeitung* of 20 May 1964 as well as the stage-direction of Lindtberg's prompt book: 'P. [= Pucelle] wird von Mann zu Mann gestoßen . . . Getümmel. Suffolk . . . die Prinzessin Margareta an der Hand führend' (P. [= Pucelle] is kicked from man to man . . . Tumult. Suffolk . . . leading Princess Margaret by the hand) (17).

21 'Gewaltig ragt Shakespeares Welt in unsere Zeit' (20 May 1964).

22 Oskar Werner and many others were able to do justice to this ideal, yet some actors, according to contemporary reviews, fell into declaiming.

23   God, and our good cause, fight upon our side;
        The prayers of holy saints and wronged souls,
        Like high-rear'd bulwarks, stand before our faces.
                                            (5.3.241–3)

24 The 175 lines of 1.1 are drastically cut to 46, the 133 lines of 2.4 are reduced to 82 and of the 200 lines of 3.1 only 99 are retained.

25 *Henry V*, edited by T. W. Craik, in *The Arden Shakespeare: Complete Works*, 4.1.234.

26 For quotations see *King Richard II*, edited by Peter Ure, in *The Arden Shakespeare: Complete Works*.

27 Prompt book, 78–80.

28 He remained in that position until the end of the season 1998–9. For some aspects of the paragraph compare Yates (*Theatre in Vienna*, 238–40), whose view, however, differs in nuance.

29 The prompt book for this production is again supplemented here by numerous contemporary reviews and my personal memory. In contrast to Lindtberg's production, however, no notes by the director are extant.

30 Compare the reviews of Bernd Sucher in the *Süddeutsche Zeitung* of 7–8 February 1987; Benjamin Henrich in *Die Zeit* of 13 February 1987; Kurt Kahl in the *Kurier*; and Alfred Pfoser in the *Salzburger Nachrichten* of 7 February 1987. See also Christoph Hirschmann in the *Arbeiterzeitung*, who associates Richard's unstoppable rise with that of Dr Goebbels (14 February 1987).

31 Hortmann devotes two pages (*Shakespeare on the German Stage*, 337–9) to Peymann's *Richard III* and Gert Voss's performance in the title role. Hortmann, too, concentrates on psychological points ('what emerged [in the end] was the unloved child crying in the night' [338]) and concentrates less on the political implications of the production.

32 'Einen Menschen in den Tod zu schicken, bedeutet ihm nicht mehr, als eine Puppe in den Abfall zu werfen' ('Sending a human being to his death means to him no more than dumping a doll with the waste' [throwing a doll away with the refuse]) (Benjamin Henrichs, *Die Zeit*, 13 February 1987).

33 'Cheated of feature' (1.1.19) becomes 'cheated of education' ('Bildung'), and 'unfinish'd' (1.1.20) becomes 'neglected, uncared for' ('verwahrlost'). One might also mention that in lines 1.1.142–4 he transposes a half line, 'Where is he, in his bed?' from Richard to Hastings, and the next one, 'He is' conversely, but keeps the original sense.

34 Lothar Sträter in *Saarbrücker Zeitung*, 17 February 1987.

35   CLARENCE Nicht wie ich. Ich bin von hohem Blut.
           1 MURDERER Mit Blut hab ich auch was zu tun.

36 Additional examples include the following: 'shap'd' (1.1.14) becomes 'furnished' ('ausgestattet'); 'want love's majesty' (1.1.16) becomes 'not finely cut' ('fein geschnitten nicht'); 'prove' (1.1.28) becomes 'play' ('spielen'); 'libels' (1.1.33) becomes 'insults' ('Beleidigungen'); 'As I am subtle, false, and treacherous' (1.1.37) becomes 'As I am an entire twister of words and people' ('wie ich ein ganzer Wort- und Menschenverdreher bin').

37 Additional examples include the following: 'O, he hath kept an evil diet long, / And over-much consum'd his royal person' (1.1.139) is turned into 'O, would he had restrained himself earlier / Instead of wasting so his royal body' ('O hielt' er sich doch länger schon zurück, / statt seinen Königskörper so zu schinden').

38 Other examples: 'that lour'd' (1.1.3) becomes 'which once meant death' ('die einst hießen Tod'); 'have prevail'd . . . on him' (1.1.131) becomes 'have caused him pain' ('haben Schmerz ihm angetan'); and 'prey at liberty' (1.1.133) becomes 'pursue their unconstrained murderer's course' ('ziehn . . . ihre freie Mörderbahn').

39 See the above reviews by Beer, Sträter (who is disturbed by the term) and Sucher, who refers to it not only in the title of his review ('A Shit: Ugly, Clever, Charming, Lonely') but also summarizes the play's moral as follows: 'A shit becomes a ruler only with the support of (other) shits' ('ein Dreckskerl wird zum Herrscher erst durch Dreckskerle').

40 For the characteristics of nineteenth-century burlesques and travesties see my '"Committing Outrage against the Bard": Nineteenth-Century Travesties of Shakespeare in England and Austria', *Modern Language Review* 88 (1993), 102–9, and 'Nineteenth-Century Burlesques of *Hamlet* in London and Vienna', *Hamlet East–West*, edited by Marta Gibinska and Jerzy Limon (Gdansk: Theatrum Gedanense Foundation, 1998), 64–84. See also Richard W. Schoch, *Not Shakespeare: Bardolatry and Burlesque in the Nineteenth Century* (Cambridge: Cambridge University Press, 2002).

CHAPTER 10

The Spanish premiere of Richard II

Keith Gregor

A year that was cluttered with events designed to mark the centenaries of the loss of Cuba and the Philippines, and of the birth of that national icon, poet and playwright Federico García Lorca, 1998 also saw the launch in Spain of Adrián Daumas's production of *Richard II* at the Cáceres Theatre Festival in the region of Extremadura. The first leg of a tour which would take the play to many of Spain's provinces before culminating in the Community of Madrid, the performance would doubtless have attracted little attention had it not been for the fact that this was the first time the play had been performed in Spain. What were Daumas's motives for wanting to stage for Spanish audiences this seemingly most arcane and intractable of Shakespeare's English chronicles, and how would the director seek to solve the multiple difficulties the play would appear to pose the modern Spanish spectator? Before we offer an answer to these questions, however, it may be worth considering the reasons for the mysterious absence of *Richard II* from Spain's long and enduring love-affair with Shakespeare.

One very important reason for the neglect the play has suffered is suggested in a review of Daumas's production which sought the inevitable comparison with one of *Richard III* by John Strasberg, which happened to be touring at more or less the same time of *Richard II*'s Spanish premiere. 'In some of Shakespeare's tragedies on the saga of England's kings,' wailed the reviewer,

the web of kinship ties is so tangled that at times it is hard to distinguish who is related to whom and how, and it is not uncommon for the spectator to lose the main thread of the action while trying to unravel the arduous problem of genealogy. It is a problem which John Strasberg resolves bravely in his other Richard (the better known one) by sifting the text considerably, a text which only works because the original plot is left intact.[1]

The reaction, which could by no means be said to be restricted to spectators in Spain, has its origins here in a traditional perception by Spanish critics

213

and theatregoers that the tragedy of Richard, Duke of Gloucester is not simply a reflection of medieval English politics and that the Wars of the Roses and their contenders are, thanks largely to the impact of French-based adaptations of the play in the early nineteenth century, viewed as paling beside the enormous stage presence and melodramatic allure of Gloucester himself.[2] Given the phenomenal success and popularity of *Richard III* over the last two centuries, it was thus easy to understand the reaction of another reviewer who would describe Daumas's choice of play as a 'mere caprice', severely short of appeal 'unless you go armed with a history manual'.[3] And though Daumas followed many other European producers of the play in endeavouring to 'prime' his audiences with a programme which included a family tree and short resumé of the main historical action, it was hard not to see the ploy as a kind of admission of failure before the performance began or, in any case, as a mere distraction from the disquieting fact that, as a character, Richard hardly manages to free himself from the tangled web of kinship ties which ensnares even the most informed of audiences.

A further handicap facing even the most imaginative of contemporarizing directors such as Daumas is the play's seemingly insurmountable medieval residue. Though sensitive to the fact that *Richard II* was not intended simply as a way of staging the Middle Ages but rather the transition from the 'rigid, ceremonial and hereditary structure of the Middle Ages to a pragmatic, Machiavellian politics based on convenience, normative control and efficiency, the genesis of modern structures of power', Daumas was still confronted with what for years had been the dominant Spanish approach to the play: the archaeological.[4] The approach, which dates back to the nineteenth century, would find its expression in the middle of the twentieth in Charles David Ley's almost apologetic view of the work as 'a marvel of medieval evocation'.[5] That Ley turned a blind eye to the transitional politics enacted in the play was perhaps more a question of political expediency than of a lack of critical acumen. Writing in the early fifties, barely a decade after General Franco had dissolved the *Cortes* and declared himself *caudillo* of Spain, Ley was understandably reticent about the play's implied critique of despotism;[6] his self-styled introduction to Shakespeare for Spaniards was written near the start of Franco's dictatorship when, significantly, none of the 'Histories', let alone *Richard II*, would be staged at any of the main state-subsidized theatres. More depressing for champions of 'Shakespeare Our Contemporary' is, however, Cándido Pérez Gallego's view in 1993, nearly two decades after Franco's death and with the transition to parliamentary democracy now complete, that the play's status as 'metaphor of the struggle against absolute power in any of its forms', while safely transcending the play's apparent medievalism, is precisely what makes it 'strange and alien' to us today.[7]

To these critical misprisions should be added a conspicuous reluctance to translate the text into any of Spain's main four languages (Castilian, Catalan, Basque or Galician). Up to 1997, in fact, there had been only four Castilian versions of the play, which together with *Pericles, Titus Andronicus, Henry VIII* and all three parts of *Henry VI* was the least translated of all Shakespeare's dramatic works. This situation was in marked contrast to that of other histories such as *Richard III, Henry V, Henry IV* (both parts) and even *King John*, while the deficit in relation to tragedies like *Romeo and Juliet, Hamlet, Macbeth* and *Othello* and comedies like *The Taming of the Shrew* and *A Midsummer Night's Dream* was immense. Seen in this light, the translators' introductory comment in the 1997 edition of *Richard II* under the aegis of the Instituto Shakespeare, that the play's popularity in the English-speaking world 'has quite possibly not been reflected in the Peninsula' is a striking piece of understatement.[8] Of the previous four versions of the play, all part of unfulfilled attempts to produce a Complete Works of Shakespeare in Spanish, the first two were adapted from the French, the third written entirely in prose and the fourth written primarily for reading rather than for performance.[9] The total absence of prose, though a convention of classical Spanish drama, as well as the stylized and at times heavily ritualistic nature of the verse in *Richard II*, had clearly been felt to be major deterrents for both potential readers and spectators of the play.

Both the Instituto's and, a year later, Angel Luis Pujante's translations should thus be seen as bold attempts to redress the imbalance *Richard II* had suffered in relation to Shakespeare's plays in general and to the histories in particular. As well as including critical introductions which take account of recent scholarship on the play, the Instituto's predominantly Q1 and Pujante's F1-based texts are full free-verse versions of the play (Pujante's even respects the play's abundant rhyming lines) which also have an eye to its undeniable performance potential, the Instituto's in a single-minded way which often simplifies the sense of the original, Pujante's in a manner which seeks fidelity 'to the dramatic nature of the [work], the language of the author and the idiom of the reader'.[10] As well as marking a new direction in the translation of Shakespeare's dramas, stage-oriented but also respectful of the plays' formal and, in Pujante's case especially, semantic nuances, both versions can be seen as part of large-scale attempts to bring a representative range of the dramas to a much broader and more knowledgeable reading public than has been possible to date. Both Cátedra and Espasa-Calpe, the mainstream publishers for which these translations were commissioned, publish inexpensive paperback editions of the plays which have proven enormously popular and have provided the play scripts for several important recent productions. It was to the pre-published text of Pujante's translation of *Richard II* that Daumas turned for his stage script.

A constant in Daumas's treatment of the classics, including Shakespeare, has been his effort to adapt them to the idiom and likely referents of a modern stage audience. His theatrical background is virtually unique amongst Spanish directors of any generation in that the bulk of his training was received not in Spain but at the American Repertory Theater's (ART) Institute for Advanced Theater Training at Harvard. It was at Harvard that Daumas assistant-directed *Henry IV, Parts I and II* (1993) with Ron Daniels, and *The Trojan Women* (1995) with Robert Woodruff, as well as producing his own highly acclaimed English-language versions of *Doctor Faustus* (1994) and *Titus Andronicus* (1995). His sole engagement with Shakespeare in Spain to date was a controversial version of *Twelfth Night*, premiered in 1996.[11] Working with casts of predominantly young and relatively untried actors, most of whom are recruited for individual productions on the grounds of motivation and their commitment to the project as a whole rather than on the basis of their ranking in the contemporary Spanish theatrical star system, Daumas has steadfastly sought alternative venues in Madrid's vibrant 'off' scene or, as with *Richard II*, taken his plays to the at times more demanding arena of the provinces and the outskirts of Madrid. In doing so, he has successfully brought mainstream drama to less knowledgeable but more appreciative audiences which, in many cases, are more responsive to the irreverent 'modernity' and subtle experimentation in which his productions generally engage. This very often means a reduction in public subsidies and, in some cases, the reluctance of some theatre managers to take a risk on the productions proposed; on the other hand, the productions offer insights into the classics which, stripped of the pomp and massive budgets of Spain's national companies, address their audiences in a direct and more intimate manner, using the text and its relevance to the present as an immediate point of contact.

In the case of *Richard II* an almost inevitable referent for modern audiences is Spain's own recent transition from the dark days of Francoism to an ostensibly more liberal but at the same time more 'Machiavellian' system based on pragmatism as well as an at times bewildering notion of political compromise coupled with technocratic 'efficiency'. For a whole generation of younger Spanish playgoers, the play thus served as a timely reminder of the conditions and circumstances in which the *transición* took place, as well as effectively chiming in with the state of apathy and disaffection which has emerged as Spaniards try to come to terms with Spain's integration in the modern apparatuses of economic and military power. At the same time, the patriotic rhetoric of a figure like Gaunt, his reference to 'This England' ('Esta Inglaterra') rewritten as an appeal to an unspecified 'Esta tierra' ('This land'), seemed designed to trigger an immediate reaction in an audience which in recent years has witnessed the disintegration of Franco's pre-federal ideal of national unity into a myriad of more or less 'autonomous' communities, each with its particular claims to the notion of a regional 'identity'.

The disintegration of the kingdom was visually announced in Daumas's production by Pedro Moreno's minimalistic stage set which, upstage, featured two imposing vertical structures, the top edges of which sloped away to the left, prefiguring the state's slow slide into dissolution and chaos. Connecting both structures was a narrow horizontal walkway, from which the king surveyed the contenders for the Lists in 1.1, or, in counsel with himself, took the painful decision to banish both in 1.3. A set of strategically placed hand-grips on the right-hand structure enabled the king and his followers to clamber up and down from the walkway as occasion suited or, as in 3.3, provided Richard an imaginary cross from which to drape himself as sacrificial Christ-like victim. The physical difficulty involved in using the hand-grips to descend gave a special resonance to Richard's words in 3.3:

> Down, down, I come; like glistering Phaeton,
> Wanting the manage of unruly jades.
> In the base court? Base court, where kings grow base,
> To come at traitors' calls and do them grace.
> In the base court? Come down? Down, court! Down, king![12]

Richard's reluctance to surrender control and his quite un-Phaeton-like eclipse at the hands of Bolingbroke and his troops were visually and even aurally underlined by the sheer awkwardness of the descent from the position of power. The contrast between high and low, as well as the notion of the spectacle of power the play constantly evokes, was given a further physical reference-point by the presence in the first half of the production of a low central rostrum, almost exclusively reserved for the king and queen, the contenders in the Lists at Coventry or, in 2.1, the Duchess of Gloucester and the moribund Gaunt. As a socially delimited space, the rostrum thus helped mark the 'special' nature of the characters who used it while, in 2.4, the 'intrusion' of Aumerle, Bagot and Green with an empty

Figure 7. Gaunt's dying words. El Foro Espectáculos.

coffer, also stressed the social scandal implied by Richard's sell-out to his cronies.[13] As a theatrical space or, more accurately, stage within a stage, the rostrum also had a distancing effect on the audience, alienating it from the action and interaction of the highest-ranking characters in the first half and stressing the role-play nature of the identities they were, consciously or not, assuming. It was thus an ideal space for the rhetoric of Gaunt's 'This England' speech; passionately delivered at the centre of the rostrum, across the darkened space which ran across the front of the stage and separated the audience from the actors, the speech, as well as the character who delivered it, were given a ritual old-world quality as well as a 'theatricality' which served to emphasize their distance from the present state of things.

If a decadent but rigidly hierarchical and ceremonial state was conveyed in the first half of the production (up to 2.3 in the text), the outbreak of civil strife and the de facto division of the kingdom were signalled by the removal of the central rostrum and the separation of the upstage structures. Gone too was the regal walkway, Bolingbroke's seat of office in 3.3 and 4.1 being a solitary theatrical trunk pushed up against the stage-right vertical, whilst an upturned pallet stage-left suggested the vision of the ruinous, unkempt garden-state advanced in 3.4. As in the first half of the production, the 'tone' of the action was provided throughout by the play of light, also designed by Moreno, especially as it affected the plain cyclorama, with a limited but carefully orchestrated spectrum of colours dominated by gold and ochre in the first two acts and various tones of grey and deepening blue in the last three or, most vividly, blood-red at the conclusion of the production as Richard's bier is borne slowly away.

These delicate tonal variations, coloured by Marcos Conde's eery and menacing musical sounds, were used as complements to the spectacular period costumes worn by both Richard and the queen, costumes which varied from the red and orange of the first half of the production to the blue and purple of the second. As most of the remaining characters, including Bolingbroke, were clad mainly in different shades of grey, black and ochre, this visual highlighting of the king and queen, as well as the spatial deployment of the cast, which tended to leave the actors playing the monarchs at some considerable remove from the rest, seemed deliberately designed to stress both the reluctant protagonism and increasing isolation of the monarchs of the old regime, while hinting that the only characters capable of change or suffering are Richard and Isabella themselves. This process of marginalization would, as I suggest below, culminate in the Pomfret dungeon scene where, now stripped of the trappings of state, a bare-chested Richard was lit by a solitary spotlight, the presence of Exton merely hinted at by some shadowy upstage movements as a prelude to the appearance of the fateful knife which was drawn abruptly across the deposed king's throat. Thereafter, in the final scene, and as if to suggest that the suffering of the deposed sovereign is inevitably transferred to his widow, the final image the play afforded was of a shunned, stunned and grief-stricken Isabella silhouetted against the scarlet cyclorama, wandering aimlessly from one side of the stage to the other. The Gregorian chant which had served as sanctimonious accompaniment to this and other killings in the production was now increased in volume, providing an ambiguous aural 'coda' to the violent process of political transformation enacted throughout.

These technical touches were carefully orchestrated to support a *mise-en-scène* which, as Daumas emphasized in his programme notes, sought to enhance a 'vivacity of rhythm, an accentuation of those elements of the play that are most adapted to our modern-day reality, images full of content and action'. As far as tempo was concerned, the fluid, adaptable stage space, together with the subtle rearrangement of incidents from the plot, were the main agents of the vivacity of rhythm alluded to in the programme. Daumas was at times ruthless in his paring of those textual elements which might be construed as impeding the flow of the action, or, more ambitiously, in his modification of the order of the scenes to generate powerful and innovative juxtapositions.

Two examples of Daumas's cuts are worth highlighting. In the first scene, immediately after a striking dumb-show prologue in which the audience was presented with the assassination of Gloucester, his head plunged into a bowl by two mysterious assassins, the lights went up to reveal Richard on his scaffold ordering his attendants to call Hereford and Mowbray to his presence, thus omitting the imprecation to Gaunt to reveal the motives for his son's challenge. The audience was thus thrust directly into the action, the challenge being inferred as a direct response to the event just enacted. The Lists at Coventry were similarly shorn of much of the contenders' wordy accusations which, as well as cooling the audience's reaction to the dispute, were clearly construed as adding an unwieldy medieval overlay (the chivalric code of honour) to what, instead, came across as a brutal collision between conflicting versions of the same event.[14] Meanwhile, a sense of Richard's isolation was conveyed at the start of 5.5 where, immediately after Exton's vow to rid the new king of his foe, the old king was shown at Pomfret musing, 'For no thought is contented'. As well as side-stepping the awkward comparison of Richard's prison to the world, with its potentially embarrassing identification of the brain as 'the female to my soul; / My soul the father', the cut helped stress the strain of doubt following the deposition, while adding a subtle rejoinder ('Thoughts tending to ambition, they do plot / Unlikely wonders', 5.5.18–19) to the opportunism of the shadowy Lancastrian minion, Exton. The Groom's and the Keeper's interventions were then cut to conclude Richard's reflections abruptly with the entrance of Exton who, equally peremptorily, carries out Bolingbroke's 'instructions' to the full. The absence, meanwhile, of Exton's servants denied Richard even the posthumous glory of having slain two of his executioners, his death thus being underlined as unheroic and ignominious as Gloucester's had been at the start of the production.

This gradual eclipsing of Richard was further effected by the subtle use of montage by which the order of scenes was inverted, or, more strikingly, individual scenes were interrupted by others. This was especially evident in the second half of the production. Bolingbroke and Northumberland's entrance in 2.3 was withheld till after the brief exchange between Salisbury and the Welsh captain in 2.4, thus pointedly stressing the disarray of the troops loyal to Richard, with Salisbury's prophecy:

> Ah, Richard! With the eyes of heavy mind
> I see thy glory, like a shooting star,
> Fall to the base earth from the firmament.
> (*Richard II*, 2.4.18–20)

This served as a prelude to the triumphant entry of the rising star, Henry. 2.3, which commences with Bolingbroke, supposedly in Gloucestershire, asking how far it is to Berkeley, was then followed by 3.2, which commences with Richard asking Aumerle whether the castle in sight is Barkloughly. With no geographical knowledge of England and Wales, the audience could be forgiven for confusing the similar-sounding place names, and this was precisely what the change of scene order seemed designed to encourage. The juxtaposition of both Bolingbroke's and Richard's conflicting fortunes was given further dramatic power by this curious convergence of destinies and destinations. After Richard's confident assertion 'High be our thoughts: I know my uncle York / Hath power enough to serve our turn', 3.2 was then interrupted by Bolingbroke in 3.1 once again gesturing to Bushy and Green 'to wash your blood / From off my hands' before having them murdered in full sight of the audience, only to resume with Sir Stephen Scroop delivering to Richard his 'tidings of calamity'. Though in this case at the expense of strict geographical accuracy, these carefully thought out reorderings not only linked the fates of Richard and his rival in the asymmetrical relation which remained true to the tragic curve of the drama as a whole, but added new and heavily ironic resonances to a play which is, at once, a history full of action and a bitter study of the political and emotional collapse of the king.

Together with the slow build-up to Richard's assassination, Daumas punctuated the generally energetic rhythm with images and tableaux of a quite potent symbolism. Particularly powerful, for example, were the gestural allusions to the religious context of the play, emphasized not just by having the character of the Bishop of Carlisle played by the same actor (Paco Maestre) who had interpreted the 'prophet new inspir'd' Gaunt, but by the numerous occasions on which characters were seen to cross themselves as either marks of contrition or exculpation for political assassination (the killers of Gloucester in the prologue, Exton, and, most strikingly, Bolingbroke on learning of the regicide) or, in King Richard's case in 3.2, recruitment of God for his cause against the rebels. These religious associations were especially evident in Richard's Christ-like pose on the scaffold in 3.3, the numerous invocations in the text to God serving here as pretext for Richard's self-image as immolated Messiah figure. Rather than showing signs of possible strain on Richard as individual, it could be argued that Daumas was paying more than mere lip service here to the Spanish church's own ambiguous relation to power, a relation which is still the subject of debate as Spain's Episcopal Conference examines the part its members played in the 1936–9 Civil War. As if to underline the ambiguity,

Richard's taunting of Bolingbroke as a latter-day Pilate in 4.1, a role which Bolingbroke assumes at the end of the play ('I'll make a voyage to the Holy Land / To wash this blood off from my guilty hand', 5.6.49–50) was imaginatively anticipated in the prologue where Daumas had the murderers cleanse their hands in the same bowl in which they had drowned Gloucester.

The parallelisms were advanced in much of the production's other business and reached maximum force in an imaginative re-presentation of the deposition scene and of the mirror incident in particular. Daumas here took the daring step of producing a mirror with no glass, an empty frame. Holding the mirror to his face, Richard would thus contemplate not his own image but that of Bolingbroke, who was positioned strategically on the other side. This lent a double dimension to the significance of the gesture: on the one hand, Richard's face is ruined less by his own grief than by the political agent of that distress, the 'usurping' king Henry; on the other, as the 'shadow' of Richard's grief, the revelation of Bolingbroke's image on the other side of the 'glass' reminded both Richard and the audience of the inseparable nature of the relation between both men. Bolingbroke, the production suggested, is nothing but Richard's shadow, haunting him throughout the play as his Other until, in this key scene, he takes his place, becomes his double in a tragic reversal of roles which nonetheless ensures a continuation of the Same:

> Was this face the face
> That every day under his household roof
> Did keep ten thousand men? Was this the face
> That like the sun did make beholders wink?
> Was this the face which faced so many follies,
> That was at last outfaced by Bolingbroke?
> A brittle glory shineth in this face.
> As brittle as the glory is the face.
> (*Richard II*, 4.1.271–8)

Richard was thus literally 'outfaced' by Bolingbroke; having already eclipsed him in his self-styled image as Phaeton in 3.3, Bolingbroke's physical face was now thrust at him as the image of his inevitable successor. At the same time, and as the last two lines suggest, Bolingbroke's claim to glory is based on nothing more solid than his decision to 'come but for mine own' (3.3.194) and the political manoeuverings of kingmakers Northumberland and York. Clearly uncomfortable with the implications of Richard's vision, Bolingbroke's 'Go, some of you convey him to the Tower' was spoken with both vehemence and just a hint of shame.

To this dismantling of the oppositional politics which is the play's subtext, Daumas's production also cast an interesting light on the 'sexual politics' which is only hinted at in the play but which has a special relevance to the slowly evolving condition of women in post-Francoist Spain. At first sight, *Richard II* hardly offers fertile soil for a feminist rereading of ancient or modern history, prefacing instead the all-male conflict which is generally regarded as the keynote of Shakespeare's second tetralogy. As one recent Spanish critic has put it, women's roles in the drama are limited to those of 'spouse (the queen), mother (the Duchess of York) and widow (the Duchess of Gloucester) as well as the dramatic function of the supplication and lament'.[15] For his production of the play Daumas dispensed with at least one of these roles by eliminating the Duchess of York from the cast, while the very manly business of war and issuing challenges was softened somewhat by the suppression from Mowbray's gruff speech in 1.1 of the words ''Tis not the trial of a woman's war' (1.1.48). For the role of 'supplicant' Daumas retained the powerful Duchess of Gloucester and gave the character extra weight by having her played by one of the few well-known figures in the cast, the actress Amparo Vega. Her exhortation to Gaunt to 'venge [her] Gloucester's death' was, together with Gaunt's own 'This England' speech, one of the most passionately acted moments in the whole production.

The Duchess's counterpart in the production was the 'sad: so heavy sad' queen Isabella (2.2.30), played by the fragile-looking Claudia Faci. Isabella has very few high points in the play, though Daumas seemed determined to give her the complexity she undoubtedly merits by dispensing with the ladies who, according to the text, accompany her in Langley Garden. This had two effects: on the one hand, to suggest the growing isolation of the queen as, one by one, the king and his followers are either imprisoned, executed or, in the case of York, simply change sides; on the other, and more poignantly, to convey the wretchedness of a woman who, to 'drive away the thought of heavy care' can think of nothing better to do than to talk to herself. The victimization of Isabella reached its climax at the very end of the production with the image described above – the very last image to be engraved on the spectator's mind before the final curtain, 'outfacing' both the removal of Richard's body and Bolingbroke's vow to voyage to the Holy Land.

The insensitivity of both men to the suffering of women was thus highlighted as a rarely explored facet of their characters. Richard in fact was played for most of the play in a detached, self-regarding fashion which, in this and other recent productions, makes his conversion at the end of the play into tragic hero even more improbable than it is in the original text. Eleazar Ortiz's immaculately groomed appearance, including yellow tinged hair, in the early part of the production, the self-consciously clipped and off-hand manner with which he delivered his decisions (as well as some of Shakespeare's finest lines) would always make it difficult for the audience to regard him as anything else but the squanderer of state money and the author of such lines as 'We do debase ourself, cousin, do we not, / To look so poorly and to speak so fair?' (3.3.126–7). The emotionally charged 'graves, worms and epitaphs' speech in 3.2 was delivered in a monotone which seemed to mock the ceremony of such reactions, while like the bulk of Richard's utterances, it was directed at nobody in particular. The effect was unsettling, distancing the audience while increasing their doubts as to whether to applaud the character's equanimity in adversity, or to condemn the actor's failure to rise to the occasions the text and its translation appeared to offer. The impression created, whether intentionally or not, was that of Richard's own sense of the theatricality of the role forced upon him. The impression was enhanced by the manifest relief with which, in the deposition scene, Richard was at last able to lift the 'heavy weight' from his head and hand over the 'unwieldy sceptre', but also by his awareness in Pomfret gaol of his own inescapable condition as Bolingbroke's 'Jack o'the clock', maddened by the measure of Bolingbroke's music, just as, on his way to the Tower, he is tormented by the 'policy' of Northumberland.

In his low-key performance of the role, Ortiz's Richard stood in stark contrast to his shadow Bolingbroke, played with energy and vigour by the swarthy Rafael Rojas. Without the presence of Henry Percy, elided from the dramatis personae, Bolingbroke was called upon virtually single-handedly to sow the chaos feared by York. Bolingbroke's self-crafted status as man of the people ('What reverence he did throw away on slaves, / Wooing poor craftsmen with the craft of smiles' [1.4.26–7]) rendered him the prototype of the modern populist politician, whilst his ability to mould circumstance to his own interests while putting on a face of woe ('They love not poison that do poison need, / Nor do I thee: though I did wish him dead, / I hate the murderer' [5.6.38–40]) made him an early modern champion of realpolitik at its most base and opportunistic. Bolingbroke is also of course fiercely loyal and, in his single-minded ambition to recover what is 'rightfully' his, a reluctant victim of Richard's own brand of state-backed expropriation. But while alert to these nuances, Daumas's production showed another side of Lancaster's character, befuddled and bemused by Richard's 'trick' with the mirror and, despite the exhortations of York and Northumberland's

effective silencing of the renegade Bishop of Carlisle in 4.1, visibly reluctant to ascend the throne vacated by Richard, preferring instead to hold
court from the trunk which had been sitting at the foot of the scaffold which
had served as Richard's literal staircase to power. Apparently aware that, as
the mirror device revealed, his was to be only a 'brittle glory', Rojas's Bolingbroke was, by the end of the production, a hesitant and dubitative successor,
conscious both of the part he had played in the dismantling of Richard's
authority and, despite the omission from the production of the frustrated
Aumerle plot, of his own vulnerability as head of a still divided state.

In her survey of a number of European productions of *Richard II* during
the second half of the twentieth century, Margaret Shewring observed: 'A
number of more recent foreign productions have chosen, as John Barton did
with the RSC in 1973/74, to emphasize the play's discussion of the behaviour
appropriate to someone in a position of authority, and the strains that such
a position places on the individual.'[16] This rather tendentious view of both
Barton's and the three foreign productions which both precede and follow
it has its rationale in the assumption that English history and, in the case
of *Richard II*, the transition from the feudal to the early modern state or
the rise of the Lancastrian faction in late medieval England are per se fairly
barren soil for non-English audiences, and that suffering and the individual are more natural, because more universal, areas to explore. In fact, as
productions such as Daumas's have shown, the depiction of such 'strains'
or of the birth of the notion of the 'individual' itself is not incompatible
with a vision of the play which, though gently toning down its Englishness, does not shirk from foregrounding the wider political 'context' –
the idea of the 'nation', the crisis of the legitimacy of authority, the violent
replacement of one structure of power with another, the brutal masculinism
of war – in which the original work was undoubtedly born and to which,
whatever the context of its reception, it must inevitably refer. As Jonathan
Bate has suggested, these issues can also be described as having their own
brand of 'universality': '"What ish my nation?" What if Shakespeare asked
that question now? I would reply that his has been many nations and can
potentially be every nation, and that is why he matters more than any other
writer there has ever been, and that is why he is a living presence in the
new Europe.'[17] To adapt Shakespeare's plays to the modern and culturally
specific context of post-transitional Spain was Daumas's aim in a production which, though with a relatively inexperienced and low-profile cast and
very little in the way of public subsidies, helped project Shakespeare's 'lesser
known' Richard, however fleetingly, into the national theatrical limelight.

NOTES

The article is part of Research Project PB98-0398: 'La presencia de Shakespeare en España en el marco de la recepción de Shakespeare en la cultura europea', financed by the Dirección General de Enseñanza Superior e Investigación Científica of the Ministry of Education and Culture.

1 Julio A. Máñez, 'Otro Shakespeare', *El País* (13 December 1998). This English translation from the Spanish and all subsequent translations are my own.

2 See especially Alfonso Par and his assessment of the murder of the nephews as the play's 'main theme' for the Romantics, a 'vent for the tender hearts and tearful eyes of our grandparents'. See his *Representaciones shakespearianas en España*, 2 vols. (Madrid and Barcelona: Biblioteca Balmes, 1936), I, 148. So influential was the incident that it actually spawned an offshoot of the play, *Los hijos de Eduardo by Casimir Delavigne*, which was revived on numerous occasions throughout the second half of the nineteenth century.

3 Enrique Herreras, '*Ricardo II* de William Shakespeare. Teatro Rialto'. I have not been able to locate the exact source of this press cutting, which was included in the dossier on the production kindly sent to me by the play's director.

4 Programme notes.

5 In Charles David Ley, *Shakespeare para españoles* (Madrid: Revista de Occidente, 1951), 93.

6 Ley does, nonetheless, address the awkward fact of John of Gaunt's death-bed patriotism, curiously identifying it as a 'sign of the new [*sic*] national spirit which was then in its infancy but which Shakespeare occasionally invokes in his history plays' (*Ibid.*, 96). What the new 'national spirit' might be, however, is left to the reader's imagination.

7 Cándido Pérez Gallego, 'Shakespeare en España: un análisis cultural', in *Shakespeare en España: crítica, traducciones y representaciones*, edited by José Manuel González Fernández de Sevilla (Alicante: Libros Pórtico, 1993), 39–62 (p. 61).

8 Introduction, *Ricardo II* (Madrid: Cátedra, 1997), 58.

9 The four versions mentioned are by Francisco Nacente (1872), Rafael Martínez Lafuente (1915), Luis Astrana Marín (1929) and Jose Mª Valverde (1970).

10 Introduction, *Ricardo II* (Madrid: Espasa Calpe, 1998), 42.

11 See my 'Spanish "Shakespeare-manía": *Twelfth Night* in Madrid, 1996–97', *Shakespeare Quarterly* 49 (1998), 421–31.

12 *Richard II*, 3.3.178–82. All references are to the edition of the play in *Shakespeare: The Complete Works*, edited by Stanley Wells and Gary Taylor (Oxford: Oxford University Press, 1988).

13 Significantly, the Machiavellian gesturings of Northumberland, Ross and Willoughby at Ely House (2.1) took place around the edges of the rostrum, emphasizing a lingering respect for authority and the enormity of their decision to join Bolingbroke and his forces.

14 Mowbray's character perhaps suffered most from the cuts, some of his most important self-justifications (including 'However God or fortune cast my lot, / There lives or dies, true to King Richard's throne, / A loyal, just, and upright

gentleman' [1.3.85–7]) pointedly hacked from the dialogue, thus momentarily diverting the audience's sympathy towards Bolingbroke.

15 Pilar Hidalgo, 'La ideología de la feminidad en las obras históricas de Shake-speare', *Atlantis* 16 (1994), 231–68 (p. 257).

16 Margaret Shewring, *King Richard II*, Shakespeare in Performance (Manchester: Manchester University Press, 1996), 154. The performances discussed are Jean Vilar's *Richard II* for the Avignon Festival, 1947/48; Giorgio Strehler's production at the Piccolo Teatro in Milan, 1948; and Ariane Mnouchkine's production for the Théâtre du Soleil, 1981/82.

17 Jonathan Bate, 'Shakespearean Nationhoods', in *Shakespeare in the New Europe*, edited by Michael Hattaway, Boika Sokolova and Derek Roper (Sheffield: Sheffield Academic Press, 1994), 112–29 (p. 115).

CHAPTER II

Shakespearean history at the Avignon Festival

Dominique Goy-Blanquet

SHAKESPEARE'S RISE TO POWER

Interest in France for Shakespeare's histories as histories came late and grew but slowly. Soon after David Garrick's conquering visit, the Comédie Française added *Richard III* to its repertory in 1781, or, rather, something which tasted like *Richard III* but was in fact a free adaptation of the kind remorselessly staged at the time on both sides of the Channel. French audiences had to wait until 1933 for the first rendering of Shakespeare's play proper in Charles Dullin's production at Théâtre de l'Atelier with himself in the title role. Shakespeare's histories were looked down upon as mere chronicles, probably not even Shakespeare's, and only fit for British consumers. The success of *Richard III* obviously owed more to its attraction to leading actors, and their ability to captivate their audience, than to its metaphysical or political dimension. Since Dullin, the fascination exerted by this character has endured with only few eclipses.

After World War II, interest began to focus on another isolated play, *Richard II*, which opened Jean Vilar's first Avignon festival in 1947, was revived three times to great applause and remembered years later as 'une apogée théâtrale', a theatrical summit.[1] *Richard II* made a hit again in 1971, when Patrice Chéreau raised it to the height of tragedy. Meanwhile, the *Henrys* remained largely ignored, apart from Jean Vilar's single season of *Henry IV* in 1950. Jean-Louis Barrault's *Henry VI* at the Odéon met with barely polite indifference. And Roger Planchon's *Henry IV* never made it to Avignon, though in 1966 he held pride of place there with Michel Auclair in the title roles of both *Richard III* and *Tartuffe*, stressing the powerful seductiveness of evil in both plays. Incidentally, the same two plays would share the top of the Avignon bill in 1995, and, as I will demonstrate below, a few lines in the real news world.

The mid-seventies saw the beginning of a new era. Shakespeare's rise to the zenith of French theatre encouraged more adventurous choices in the canon, and more global views of the 'continent Shakespeare', to use Daniel Mesguich's telling phrase. Integral texts became the rule, replacing shortened or otherwise mutilated versions of the plays. Large frescoes like Denis Llorca's excellent *Kings* (1977–8), which covered the whole range of the Plantagenet saga, kept their audiences spellbound for hours on end. All-powerful directors began to take their time with full versions played out in record-breaking performances. By the time Michael Bogdanov's *Wars of the Roses* came to France in 1987, the public was inured to long-distance Shakespeare. Ariane Mnouchkine had set the norm with four-and-a-half hours of *Richard II* shot *recto tono* at the public with every syllable stressed, soon outdone by Antoine Vitez's complete *Hamlet* in 1983. In those epic years, *in illo tempore*, Avignon spectators wrapped up in rugs and drunk with images saw the dawn rise after a night-long *Mahabharata* (1985) or Vitez's *Soulier de satin* (1987). Nights which joined Vilar's *Richard II* and Gérard Philipe's interpretation of *Le Cid* in the Avignon legend, setting young directors' dreams still farther out of reach, on a level with the stars.

The Avignon Festival, which generally has at least one Shakespeare on the menu, provides a sure measure of the histories' popularity: they may be absent from the programme for ten years running, followed by a season with three or four major productions. The last quarter century has known two high peaks. In 1984, the year when the BBC histories were shown on French television, Ariane Mnouchkine's *Richard II* and *Henry IV* shared the Cour d'Honneur with Georges Lavaudant's *Richard III*. But Mnouchkine's plans to continue the Plantagenet sequence never came to life. Avignon had to wait until 1999, and another batch of histories, for the first French production ever of *Henry V*. Between those two peaks, there were many memorable *Tempests, Hamlets, Dreams* and *Tales*, but again no histories until 1994, when Stuart Seide's three-part *Henry VI* graduated from Poitiers to the Cour d'Honneur, and 1995, when Matthias Langhoff's select audience met history, and Mnouchkine again, at the critical moment of Srebrenica.

It is worth noting that French amateurs developed a taste for the histories thanks to productions which made the least of Shakespeare's texts. Mnouchkine had planned a cycle of six plays, the second tetralogy plus two comedies, concluded by *Henry V*, but never got that far with her company, the Théâtre du Soleil. Her ambitious project, begun in 1981, stopped abruptly in 1984 after *Henry IV, Part One* and the stormy resignation of her star actor, Philippe Hottier, who was playing Falstaff. By then, the public had been totally won over, and the histories, even if seldom performed in fact, established as part of the French repertoire. Faintly evocative of feudal

Japan, actually a free mixture of various foreign elements, Mnouchkine's *Richard II* thoroughly upset the reigning codes of acting and staging, stirred endless arguments between specialists, and converted thousands of amateurs to her unique style. The actors ran in to the beat of drums, sporting fabulous costumes, leaped on to a stage of thick fibre matting and silky backdrops, then stood still in hieratic postures to deliver their lines with maximum energy. In France, the praise for these dramatically superb productions was almost unmitigated. Few critics remembered that their most admired feature, the stylized oriental dancing, had already been used by Dullin for the battle scenes of *Richard III*, and none but scholars complained that the complexities of the plays had been reduced to a timeless conflict between power-hungry warlords.

Beside those of Shakespearean conservatives, a few dissenting voices were raised, questioning Mnouchkine's casual treatment of Asian cultures, 'fake Japanese and fake Shakespeare' in Jan Kott's view, others drawing parallels with capitalist consumerism and round-the-world tourists. Dennis Kennedy was especially outspoken in this regard, pointing to Mnouchkine's domestication of oriental riches as hardly better than the cultural imperialism the West had always perpetrated on the East.[2] Part of Kennedy's criticism and many of his anxieties are undoubtedly justified, yet his censures against artists shopping at the multicultural supermarket should give us pause. However morally sound Kennedy's observations may be, these censures might bring us unpleasantly close to censorship, if we took this path. Ironically, of course, Kennedy's views on the subject of foreign appropriation would equally well apply to Shakespeare's eclecticism: whether pre- or postmodern, he did behave as a shameless tourist with no great concern for cultural authenticity either. Yet if Shakespeare found exotic items at his Southbank market useful in making clear to his audience what their leaders were doing in their name on the world stage, or what was happening just then on their own native ground, should he be restrained? Should he be restricted by law to freedom fries?[3]

What artists say or mean or imply on stage or elsewhere can and should be judged, criticized, torn to pieces if need be, on both aesthetic and political grounds, but one cannot dictate their choice of words or images. Artists are immoral, no less today than in earlier centuries when they were outcasts, and perhaps they had better remain so. Their main problem may be that it is more difficult now than ever before to be a genuine outcast, that too many self-labelled artists are driven by their own consumer appetite for worldly fame and goods rather than by a compulsive need to say something vital at whatever cost to themselves.

First, whatever else may be held against Mnouchkine, she is patently not driven by a personal appetite; indeed, she is the most frugal consumer, paying herself a monthly salary no higher than €1,500. Then, to write that her use of foreign modes tends 'to detach them from *any* political and historical meanings, Elizabethan or contemporary', or accuse her of a 'tendency to abandon political stances' is to substitute unfocused standards of political correctness to her own meaningful record of political fights on specific issues, to isolate her timely interest in Shakespeare from the rest of her highly significant and consistent progress. To read in Mnouchkine's work 'admirable sentiments' conveying a message 'little different from that of global capitalism' is, in fact, to practise at her expense the kind of Shakespearean tourism Kennedy stigmatizes in directors.[4] As to her multi-cultural interests, the themes of her latest productions speak for themselves: *Tartuffe* dealt with Algerian Islamism, *Et soudain, des nuits d'éveil* featured a Tibetan delegation demonstrating against the sale of French planes to China, *Tambours sur la digue* drew on an old Chinese tale to illustrate recent floods and expose the mixed responsibilities in a major ecological catastrophe. Her latest work-in-progress, *Le Dernier Caravansérail*, confronts the Bill of Human Rights with personal narratives of refugees fleeing Afghanistan, Iran or Russia.

By her own admission, Mnouchkine approaches great theatrical texts as ways to other ends, necessary resources for the company's creative energy, and models for techniques to relate political history, give some meaningful form to the present. Shakespeare's treatment of English dynastic wars was to offer guidelines for the subject she was working on, the drawing and quartering of Cambodia. All the lessons learned from *Richard II* served for *Norodom Sihanouk*. Her scriptwriter, Hélène Cixous, would again use a Shakespearean structure for *L'Indiade*, though in this case her loose chronicle form, more akin to *Henry VI*, indirectly exposed Shakespeare's juvenile weaknesses by its mediocre results. Actually Mnouchkine's best tributes to the British poet were her later creations of *Les Atrides*, which showed the maturation of her years of work on *Les Shakespeare*. The enthusiasm for her spectacular achievements, by the way, contradicts the theory that the French have no head for the epic.

The problem diagnosed by Kennedy properly begins when shows designed for home ground and home truths begin to travel abroad. The undisputed fact that Shakespeare is at home everywhere nowadays would seem to make his plays especially well designed for export purposes, the irony being that the greatest artist in the English language can be performed in any idiom around the world, or even without words, and still be understood, or at least appear to be. We all know the story, don't we? Whether our knowledge of the production's original culture will suffice to make clear its director's points is uncertain. Instead of behaving like judges on a theatrical international court of justice, this is perhaps where Shakespeare scholars may be useful, by helping to clarify these issues with side lights on their national contexts.

GLOUCESTER TIME

The 1984 season had confirmed Mnouchkine as Queen Ariane, and made the histories fashionable for a while. Her setting of the plays in a remotely exotic feudal past marked a clean break with the Kott dogma of Shakespeare our contemporary, which partly explains Kott's displeasure with her work. Brechtian suits and boots disappeared from the stage as well as any direct references to current affairs. A no less wide gap opened in less than fifteen years between the two peaks of 1982–4 and 1995–9. Langhoff's *Gloucester Time– Matériau Shakespeare–Richard III*, and Mnouchkine's *Tartuffe* were coupled in the critics' headlines as 'Les machines de guerre', the war machines.[5] If *Les Shakespeare* dealt with power thirst and politics without pointing at any specific target, Mnouchkine's uncompromising stance had often proved disturbing in the past, even to her own allies. In 1979, her *Mephisto* had evinced furious reactions from the Parti Communiste by exposing the German Party's share in the rise of the Nazis. The 1995 *Tartuffe*, set in a Mediterranean climate, was a frontal attack on Arabic fundamentalism and all its European transfers.

Langhoff saw Richard as 'un monstre ordinaire', an ordinary monster, in an age where the whole world limped, where – already – business and the mafia ruled.[6] Richard, he reminded the public, is a very common name in Germany, his native country, where all sorts of deodorants against the smell of blood can now be found on sale. The alliance of criminal gangs and world domination is an old story:

Richard III ou les railleries de Eltsine à la face du monde sur les ruines de Grozny libérée . . . Richard III, un exemple. L'Allemagne, un autre. La Russie à l'abandon, un nouveau.[7]

Richard III or [Boris] Yeltsin's railings in the face of the world, on the ruins of liberated Grozny . . . Richard III, one example. Germany, another. Russia, left to drift on her own, a new one.

Martial di Fonzo Bo played Richard as a common street tough. The innocent victims were Langhoff's own sons, Anton and Caspar, in the parts of the young princes. Clones of Milosevic careered up and down wob-bly staircases of Langhoff's own making, while a voice off delivered an exhaustive lecture on the Plantagenet wars and genealogies, removing that Shakespearean rag at some safe distance from the actual show. The actors in battledress read out loud from *The European, Libération, The Financial Times,* quoted General Norman Schwarzkopf or Clausewitz, and relaxed between two massacres with slides of 'Desert Storm' operations in the Gulf, or a cartoon, *Tintin au Pays des Soviets.*

When Srebrenica, a security zone 'protected' by UNO troops fell to the Serbs, Langhoff's actors led by Bo cancelled a performance of *Richard III,* but the *Tartuffe* company chose to play on, and called their audience to a meeting in front of Palais des Papes the following day. Should the Festival stop? Would not continuing the show make them '*collabos*'? In Mnouchkine's view, shared by other artists, this was absurd: 'Ce n'est pas les combattants du beau qu'il faut arrêter mais les supplétifs de la mort' (Not those who fight on the side of beauty, but the auxiliaries of death should be stopped).

Faced with the crowd's patent dismay – what else is there to do? was the general cry – she rose to the duties of her acknowledged position as queen of the theatrical community by taking the lead of a more resolute protest.[8] Silence was no answer, but performing was not enough, even militant shows like hers, she felt. The wars fought on stage must be grounded in reality: 'Nous ne voulons pas risquer la peau d'un autre, mais nous devons trouver le moyen de risquer la nôtre, de trouver une arme d'intimidation.'[9] (We do not want to put at risk someone else's skin, but we must find a way to risk our own, find some weapon of intimidation).

This was the signal for a hunger strike harboured in her home base, the Cartoucherie de Vincennes, which she undertook with the young director Olivier Py and three other artists.[10]

The histories' second peak really began then, as the 1999 season would make retroactively clear, when the assault on Kosovo awoke cruel memo-ries of ethnic purification in Bosnia, inspiring Olivier Py to produce his *Requiem pour Srebrenica.* The 1999 Avignon Festival at which it premiered was obsessed with war, looking back on the past hundred years, and more particularly the last ten, with a heavy sense of guilt. The approaching millen-nium called for a general 'examen de conscience', self-examination, which showed a terrifying record of barbarity for the twentieth century. As to why Shakespeare's histories were thought fit for the purpose, and why the *Henrys* fitter than the rest, several factors combined. Jean-Louis Benoit and Philippe Torreton, who wanted to do a war epic together, had originally planned a production of *Le Cid*, but had to cancel it when Bernard Faivre d'Arcier commissioned one from Declan Donnellan, and turned to *Henry V* instead, a plan which met with official approval. The play had never been done in French before, it was unseemly to end the century with this major omission. *Henry V* would be the central event of the Festival, eked out by Yann-Joël Collin's *Henry IV*, an eight-hour production which had won critical applause at its creation in Strasbourg the year before, and various minor attempts at *Richard II*.

Politics undoubtedly played a leading role in the artists' choices. However, this renewed popularity of the histories certainly owed something as well to Al Pacino's *Looking for Richard*, while the multiplication of films drawn from Shakespeare's plays no doubt contributed to the vogue, recalling the success of Branagh's *Henry V* with young audiences. The marked absence of this play from our repertoire is often imputed to its epic form, long thought incompatible with the French '*génie*', spirit. Today a renewed interest in the epic is in the air among intellectuals, but whether it blows as far as the stage is another matter, and in this case it may be more a coincidence than a decided revolt against the dry minimal style which has dominated the French theatre for several years. The complaints of intolerable boredom from weary audiences have grown in numbers without yet inducing a clean revolution of its methods and repertoire. 'Nous n'en pouvons plus de nous emmerder au théâtre!,' 'to hell with boredom in the theatre', was Benoit's provocative war cry, quoted before the first night of *Henry V* by a journalist with this comment: 'Il le dit, il le fait. Depuis trente ans, Jean-Louis Benoit chasse l'ennui . . . Cet été il réveille la cour d'honneur à grand renfort de Shakespeare'. 'He says it, he does it. For thirty years, Jean-Louis Benoit has chased away boredom . . . This summer he wakes up the cour d'honneur with large dollops of Shakespeare.'[11]

THE SHAKESPEARE JOKER

Faivre d'Arcier, Chairman of the Festival, met with ironic reactions from the press when he came to announce the 1999 programme: 'What will it be this year? More Shakespeare?' It may be another coincidence, if a thought-provoking one, that some of Avignon's most exciting events took place on Shakespeareless years, the Molière season of Vitez in 1978, Peter Brook's *Conférence des oiseaux* and Mnouchkine's *Mephisto* in 1979, Vitez again with Claudel's *Soulier de satin* in 1987. Could it be that Shakespeare has become the last straw clutched by directors in want of inspiration? The uninventive programmes of too many Maisons de la Culture and other subsidized theatres seem to point that way. Vitez's ideal of 'un théâtre élitaire pour tous', an elite theatre for all, a reformulation of Vilar's 'grand théâtre populaire', great popular theatre, has only one answer: public money, and lots of it. What used to be a glamorous and influential mode of artistic expression has suffered a continuous decline since Vitez ruled the Comédie Française, recruiting former students like Philippe Torreton and Yann-Joël Collin, who would give the *Henrys* pride of place in 1999. Both have resigned from the Comédie since, Collin after one year and Torreton after nine. Perhaps the decline began when the most rebellious and inventive creators invested in the citadels of established theatre, and lost much of their talent inside.

As productions of Shakespeare multiplied, many directors seemed less interested by what the poet had to say, and their motives for 'doing a Shakespeare' more and more confused. Unfamiliar plays like *Pericles, Two Gentlemen of Verona, Cymbeline* were chosen for no better reason than that no one had done them yet. In this regard the histories should have come high on their lists, but for one major drawback: they are full of history, and increasingly difficult to make intelligible, let alone attractive. Most directors prove keenly aware of this, even when they address English speakers. Various devices like inserting blackboard diagrams, dumb shows, scenes from other plays are used to convey the stuff of history, or just the gist of the story, to the unlearned. Collin's *Henry IV* began with the murder of Richard II, performed under the stage while Henry magnanimously forgives Aumerle above. Torreton first appeared as Hal, half-naked in bed with two prostitutes, then re-entered in sober kingly robes with a clean haircut. In *Gloucester Time*, each new character was introduced by a voice off delivering scholarly information, quite as boring as the dustiest lecture. Al Pacino's subtler method in *Looking for Richard* was to seek answers for his own ignorant questions. Back in 1977, Llorca had hit on a more theatrical way of giving information, by representing the York family tree with swords planted like crosses in a graveyard.

If the histories obviously require some rough knowledge of the past, few directors will own that this is true of any play by Shakespeare, and that they have little trust in their ability to bring his world, language, beliefs, morals, learning, rhetoric close enough to our interests and sympathy. In other words, little trust is left in the virtues of his texts. 'Je n'ai pas l'intention d'assommer les gens avec trois heures de Shakespeare' – 'I do not mean to bore people stiff with three solid hours of Shakespeare,' said Benoit, who vowed to keep his *Henry V* under two hours, and waved his scissors whenever the pace lagged:

Figure 8. Laure Bonnet as the Chorus in *Henry V*. Festival d'Avignon 1999.

Trop bavard. Pas de rythme. Y a que du texte. Faut dégraisser. Prendre le temps de jouer. Aller à l'essentiel. Couper. Faire apparaître ce que Peter Brook appelle les 'mots rayonnants'. Au théâtre, rien que le texte, c'est toujours moins que le texte.[12]

Too wordy. No rhythm, only text. You have to diet it. Take time to act. Go straight to essentials. Cut. Show up Brook's 'radiating words'. In the theatre, nothing but the text always means less than the text.

Words, then, are unwanted fat – although Brook's theory of 'radiating words' never advised playing those only – acting is the muscle, and derision a common way of escape from the poet's lofty scene. Just as he ignored the grandiose facade of Palais des Papes towering above him in favour of a miniature cardboard castle, Benoit adopted a cartoon-like style of performance, soldiers armed with improbable wooden swords shaking like the fearful Romans of *Asterix*. Its best feature was the Chorus, a cross between Gavroche and Saint-Exupéry's Petit Prince, endearingly played by Laure Bonnet. In the last act, a model village was rolled up like a carpet to uncover the image of war, a floor strewn with corpses. The initial plan was to organize space around three moments – preparations, confrontation, reconciliation – and use three different codes of acting: tragedy around Henry V, comedy for the French court, farce for the popular scenes. But the comic element developed at the expense of the rest, down to a no-nonsense Henry who made his followers wipe their feet before entering Harfleur, and whose bluff courting mode had the young spectators in stitches.

Farce was equally important to Yann-Joël Collin, whose references were Alfred Jarry's Ubuesque kingdom and the late Coluche, a very popular French comedian.[13] His integral *Henry IV*, 'monstrueusement comique', monstrously comical, was devoured by the appetites of a Falstaff who swelled to the limits of the stage until the prince, identified with history, put an end to the comedy. A company of twelve actors embodied some forty-five characters, with a will to make the doubling meaningful. Lady Percy, who wanted to follow her Harry to the wars, returned as a soldier in his army. When killed, he took on the part of Pistol, and she shared in his fall by playing Doll the prostitute. All bustled on a stage too small for them, built or dismantled the scenery with tremendous energy, fought for space and eventually turned the set into a waste land, from which sprang at last a new order. 'Exit le bouffon', was Collin's comment. 'Mort du théâtre. Le reste, *Henry V*, est littérature' – 'Exit the clown. Death of the theatre. And the rest, *Henry V*, is literature.'[14]

PRIDE AND PREJUDICE

On top of the usual arguments against foreign history or the epic genre, it is commonly alleged that *Henry V* must be particularly distasteful to the French, showing up as it does their alleged foibles, and utter defeat at the hands of their despised enemies. The same objections would apply as well, if not better, to *Henry VI*, which has much more foreign history, and casts worse slurs on the French in the person of their favourite heroine Joan of Arc, yet both Denis Llorca and Stuart Seide had managed to hold their audiences' attention for nine hours. Collin's *Henry IV*, nine hours long as well and more foreign still, France having no place in the plays, stole the show from what was to be the great event of the season. British productions of *Henry V*, Bogdanov's which came to Paris in 1987 or Branagh's film, had been very well received. True, they treated the French with a restraint probably exercised in anticipation of continental touring. Much more delicate than Benoit, who felt no need to spare his own compatriots, and did not raise any indignant protest among them with his caricatures. After much gloating from the press, statements from all concerned in the company, and harrowing tales of their feverish ten weeks' rehearsals, the first French *Henry V* finally defeated all expectations and turned out very unlike what it promised to be in countless interviews.[15] The critics' disapproval was as great as the hopes they had raised. In fact all anticipations of a major clash were disappointed: the Agincourt scandal was a non-event.

This is where our two countries contrast most vividly, if not violently. When the new Globe opened with this play (1997), the Dauphin and his pals were booed in merrily chauvinistic fashion, with the actors' ready excuse of wishing to recreate a truly Elizabethan atmosphere. It is not only in England that *Henry V* is used, or misused, as an apt vehicle for strong national feelings. Other nationalisms have recognized themselves in it since the German *Shakespeare mit uns* of the First World War. A British Navy officer was heard to quote the famous Saint Crispin speech on television before sailing to the Gulf War, while both President Bush Senior and Saddam Hussein had provided their troops with copies of the plays.[16] For all its alleged arrogance, and Torreton's own confession that 'ce défaut-là nous est propre', 'this is a typical fault of ours', France displayed no such aggressive patriotic fibre.[17] Public reactions around the country were entirely correct, even outside sophisticated Avignon. In Amiens, for instance, an audience of mostly young people were moved to tears by the final romance which reconciled the old enemies like a happy-ending *Romeo and Juliet*. Obviously it projected an image of youth as they liked it. They did not pay much attention to its political ironies, and met the national defeat with resigned indifference.

Is it going too far to read in this surprising mildness the first intimations of the French 'pacifism' that would so incense President Bush Junior's war-mongers just five years later, and could the centuries of delay in presenting Shakespeare's firebrand to French audiences account for it? None of our native playwrights ever led us to believe that 'God fought for us'. This, Gary Taylor claimed in a provocative article in the *Guardian* (April 2003), is precisely what Shakespeare did for the English-speaking world: *Henry V* calls for 'plain shock' and 'awe' in so many words. So, Taylor declares, 'if our illegal invasion of Iraq appals you, blame Shakespeare'. In support of this theory, Taylor, editor of the Oxford *Henry V*, points to manipulations of the sources, casualty figures and so on, observing that 'even CNN would have trouble surpassing Shakespeare's breathtaking falsification'. It was this bellicose poet who shaped the consciousness of the English-speaking empire for centuries. If Henry could and still can be relied upon to inflame armies of theatregoers, it is because 'Shakespeare could make carnage sing'.[18]

Carnage cannot sing so beautifully in the French tongue, as all translators of Shakespeare would tell you. A French *Henry V* was not originally Benoit's idea but the actor's, who wanted to explore the mind of a warrior intoxicated with the spirit of war. Torreton recalls how he fell in love with Branagh's film, though he disagrees with his interpretation of the character whom he reads as more impulsive, jealous, war-loving, whereas the film expressed a strong anti-war feeling directly opposed to Laurence Olivier's patriotic hymn. Torreton's interest in the play was wholly political: history as the legitimizing weapon of warmongers. Henry V, who owes his throne to an inherited crime and wakes up dormant hostilities by going back way before Charlemagne to justify his invasion of France, reminded him of Milosevic basing his visions of Greater Serbia on territorial claims as old as the year 500:

Je ne peux m'empêcher de penser à l'actualité et à l'argumentation des Serbes du Kosovo, qui pratiquent les pires horreurs au nom d'une histoire dont ils se sentent les héritiers. Avec ce principe-là, tout le monde doit faire la guerre à tout le monde.[19]

I cannot but think of current events, of the positions defended by Kosovo Serbs, who exercise the most cruel horrors in the name of a history they feel heirs to. With that kind of principles, the whole world should fight everybody else.

How is it that war even today, at the dawning of the twenty-first century, seems the most beautiful experience in a man's life? was Torreton's haunting question. Even if the recent answer of round-the-world, in particular round-Europe, opinion against war in Iraq to world leaders may not be a direct development of theatrical soul-searching, obviously Torreton's position is gaining ground.

At the time, there were plain disagreements on these issues between Torreton and his director, Jean-Louis Benoit, for whom Shakespeare's play has little resonance nowadays apart from a constant meditation on power and responsibility.[20] But despite a professed wish to denounce war, both wanted a hero, and neither could resist the temptation to gratify the public with one.[21] Subtleties disappeared on the way somewhere between rehearsals and the provinces. The farcical scenes which had not greatly amused the critics at the Festival evinced much warmer responses, encouraging them to develop. The sombre side of Henry, so sensitively stressed in Torreton's early interviews, was erased on stage, where the king was seen to believe in his own heroic speeches. The Crispin address was delivered not to an unwilling army of tired men but in private, with intense emotion, to his brother. Henry's order to kill the French prisoners was originally spoken in its proper place, before the raid on the English camp, but the order of the two scenes was reversed in later performances, probably in response to the sympathy of the public for the character.

FACTA EST FABULA

Unlike Langhoff's straight quotations from the first Gulf war in *Gloucester Time–Richard III* four years earlier, the 1999 histories did not spell out any parallels with the outside world, yet these were all around, at their barest in a new genre entitled 'théâtre-document', document theatre. The programme was split between Shakespeare's *Henrys* and various journalistic collages. This new schizophrenia, fabled history on one side and *real* politics on the other, will require delicate analysis before any theory can be advanced. Olivier Py's *Requiem pour Srebrenica* denounced the media's treatment of the massacres through a text made up of quotations from General Philippe Morillon, François Mitterand, the TV newsreader Bruno Masure and other agents of the tragedy. In *Rwanda 1994*, the Belgian Jacques Delcuvellerie gave television and various media the parts of full characters, supported by a chorus of the dead interpreted by a Kigali dance company. On the page next to Torreton's interview, *Le Monde* showed a photograph of Rwandan corpses which could have been the model for the killing fields of *Henry V*.[22] Reviewing the artists' shows, most critics stressed their involvement but also the ambiguities of a festival like that of Avignon dedicated to the charnel houses of Europe while governed by the principle of pleasure:

On balkanise sur tous les tréteaux, et on connaît le Kosovo comme sa poche . . . Un rien de jouissance se paie toujours d'une vague nécessaire de culpabilité.[23]

The Balkans are on every stage, and every one knows Kosovo like the back of one's hand . . . an ounce of pleasure must always be paid for by a necessary expanse of guilt.

This sense of guilt overspilled in the newspapers and televised interviews, but it brought no deep vibrations to the stage, despite its best carpenters' efforts to hammer down the planks.

In his survey of the year 1995, the drama critic of *Le Monde*, Olivier Schmitt, evoked the origins of the theatre and 'les devoirs de la représentation', its moral commitment, since Aeschylus' *Persians*: 'dire le vrai sous l'apparence du faux, prévenir et guérir les maux de la communauté des hommes, élever chacun d'eux à la dignité de la parole'[24] (tell the truth under the guise of falsehood and heal the diseases of the community, raise each man to the dignity of speech).

He did not seem aware of the distance we have travelled from this ideal, how irrelevant it has been made by other forms of talk show. That Shakespeare has ceased to be our contemporary is nowhere more obvious than in the staging of his histories. Showing up the world as a stage was meant to clarify its ways, and the directors who had read Jan Kott were all ready with mirrors to face reality. But the worn-out metaphor found an unprecedented meaning with the Gulf crisis, when all the world's television screens became the battlegrounds of virtual warfare, power play stations for wanton gameboys. Journalists eager to draw parallels between the world stage and the staged world are less prone to discuss their own oblique indictment. After Matthias Langhoff and Peter Sellars, who imported cameras, screens and news torn to shreds on stage to expose the politics of show business, a number of directors registered the pregnant influence of the media on their own medium, and questioned the role of these new actors of the war, beginning with the manipulative press. They have good cause. The theatre seems to have lost all confidence, sensing a perversion of its own subversive codes, and groping to redefine its proper marks. Their claims that it contains all reality, including these new agents, sound like self-reassuring statements that it still makes sense. The repeated appearance of TV sets on stage no doubt points to the origin of the malaise, even if it does little more to analyse it in depth. What happens when the virtual is the only reality? What is there left for the theatre to represent once it is confused with the very fact of representation? We have yet to see whether the latest world news will shake the theatre scene out of its self-absorbed trance and make the stage hold grim mirrors to embedded journalists.

NOTES

1 Jean Tortel, 'Vilar à Avignon ou la permanence du héros', *Cahiers du Sud*, 373–4 (1963), 232.
2 Dennis Kennedy, 'Shakespeare and the Global Spectator', *Shakespeare Jahrbuch* 131 (1995), 50–64.
3 To mark their anger over France's stance against George W. Bush's invasion of Iraq, White House cafeterias changed the name 'French fries' to 'freedom fries'.

4 *Ibid.*, 55, 63, 69.

5 Odile Quirot, *Le Nouvel Observateur*, 20–6 July 1995. The phrase 'une cinglante machine de guerre', a scathing war machine, had just been used by J.-P. Thibaudat, *Libération*, 10 July 1995, to sum up Matthias Langhoff's production.

6 'Un nouvel ordre mondial de mafia et d'affaires', in J.-P. Thibaudat in *Libération*, 10 July 1995.

7 Matthias Langhoff, 'L'heure d'Humphrey ou ce dont je crois qu'il s'agit', *Carnet de voyage 2*, Théâtre Gérard Philipe (1995), 14–15.

8 I was in Avignon to review *Tartuffe* for the *TLS* and saw the play on the night Srebrenica fell, when the actors explained why they had decided to perform, and called for a demonstration the following day, which led to the solemn Declaration d'Avignon.

9 Olivier Schmitt quoted in *Le Monde*, cahier Avignon 95, 14 July 1995.

10 They began their strike on 4 August. The group of strikers included Ariane Mnouchkine, Maguy Marin, Olivier Py, François Tanguy and Emmanuel de Véricourt.

11 Pierre Notte, *L'Evénement*, 8–14 July 1999.

12 Journal of the rehearsals (reportage Jean-Claude Raspiengeas) in *Télérama* 2582 (7 July 1999), 18.

13 Marion Thébaud, *Le Figaro*, 10–11 July 1999.

14 *Le-Maillon*, Théâtre de Strasbourg, press release for Festival d'Avignon, 11–17 July 1999.

15 'Récit haletant de dix semaines de gestation fiévreuse', 'Breathless account of a ten-week feverish gestation', was the caption in *Télérama*.

16 See Balz Engler, 'Shakespeare in the Trenches', *Shakespeare Survey* 44 (1992), 105–11. When he delivered his paper at the 1990 Stratford Conference, participants of all origins came up with similar examples from their own countries.

17 *Le Nouvel Observateur*, 8–14 July 1999.

18 Gary Taylor, 'Cry havoc', the *Guardian*, 5 April 2003.

19 Interviews with Jérôme Garcin and Odile Quirot, in *Le Nouvel Observateur*, 8–14 July 1999, and with Zoé Lin in *L'Humanité*, 9 July 1999.

20 Jean-François Bouthors in *La Croix*, 8 July 1999.

21 Brigitte Salino, reviewing the production for *Le Monde*, 11–12 July 1999, notes that Jean-Louis Benoit 'vise l'efficacité première: offrir un héros au public. Gagné: Philippe Torreton est avec lui . . . Le comédien voulait jouer un héros . . . Beau projet de comédien désireux d'en découdre avec la mythologie d'Avignon, la fureur de la Cour, les 2,200 spectateurs.' (Benoit's concern was one of efficiency: give the public a hero. Done: Philippe Torreton is with him . . . The actor wanted to play a hero . . . The noble design of an actor eager to challenge the Avignon mythology, the awesome courtyard, the 2,200 spectators.) I agree with her opinion that his performance avoided all the shadowy areas of the character, though not with her reading of the play, and of this production, as a glorification of war.

22 This photograph of April 1994 by Gilles Peress, taken from 'Le Silence' (Zurich: Scalo Verlag, 1995), illustrates Jean-Michel Delacomptée's article on Kosovo and the staging of violence in *Le Monde*, cahier Avignon 99 (July 1999), x.

23 Pierre Notte, *L'Evénement*, 8–14 July 1999.

24 'Treize personnages en quête d'histoire: L'objection de conscience culturelle', *Le Monde*, 3 January 1996.

CHAPTER 12

Two Flemings at war with Shakespeare

Ton Hoenselaars

It is a truth almost universally acknowledged that a theatre director presenting Shakespeare's English history plays will at some stage be tempted to adapt or reshape the available material, whether in England or abroad. The common procedure of modifying the 'Histories' for performance takes on a special dimension when they are not only adapted to suit contemporary, local or national purposes – as with the omission of the Harfleur speech from Laurence Olivier's *Henry V* – but are also translated into another language. Luk Perceval and Tom Lanoye's 1997 production of *Ten Oorlog* ('To War', 'Into Battle') in Belgium and The Netherlands is typical of the combined process of translation and adaptation which the history plays may undergo: it presents Shakespeare's two tetralogies rolled into a three-part cycle meant to address matters of contemporary concern to Belgium, all this in a language, or, rather, in a range of languages and variants appropriate to the nation's bilingual composition.[1] One aim of this chapter is to investigate the complex process of translation and adaptation that served to capture Belgian anxiety in Shakespearean terms in 1997.[2]

An additional aim of this chapter will be to consider the fortunes of the trilogy on its subsequent foreign tour. As a result of its instant success, the *Ten Oorlog* trilogy was translated into German two years later, and produced as *Schlachten!* ('battles' or 'slaughter') by the Schauspielhaus Hamburg, who presented a preview of the German version (again directed by Luk Perceval) at the Salzburger Festspiele of 1999.[3] Against the background of the fate that Shakespeare's own English histories meet with as they are adapted for productions both at home and abroad, it is intriguing to find that the Flemish epic by Lanoye and Perceval, with its unmistakable national stamp, should have proved so easy to translate into the language of other countries and that unlike Shakespeare's original, the Flemish adaptation seemed to require little or no revision or rewriting. Looking at the play on its foreign tour, I shall try to account for the apparent discrepancy between two facts: on the one hand, that the Shakespearean original should have required a Flemish adaptation to suit a specific socio-political objective, and, on the other, that this adaptation of the canonical master should have been adopted nearly verbatim by theatre-makers in other countries.

The Flemish adaptation of *Ten Oorlog* developed out of an initiative by Luk Perceval to stage *Richard III*. It was the attempt to analyse the complexity of Richard of Gloucester and to study his motivation that led Perceval to consider the other history plays, and convinced him that a cogent stage representation of *Richard III* would be impossible without reference to the other English history plays as well. At this stage, Perceval invited the politically committed novelist and poet Tom Lanoye to write an adaptation of both tetralogies. From the outset, Lanoye and Perceval were convinced that the joint English history plays could not be presented in their entirety, 'the dramatic quality [being] too uneven and the storyline too chaotic'.[4] To them, the history plays represented 'a baffling series of conspiracies, marriages, murder, and battles; a pandemonium of forty acts, two hundred scenes and three hundred characters'.[5] They did not, like Michael Hattaway, reinterpret the scattered and episodic quality of the histories as a postmodern virtue, and were not prepared, like Horatio, to conceive of history as a mere conjunction

> Of carnal, bloody, and unnatural acts,
> Of accidental judgements, casual slaughters,
> Of deaths put on by cunning and forced cause,
> And in this upshot, purposes mistook
> Fallen on th'inventors' heads.[6]

Instead, like theatre-makers with real rather than academic audiences to address, the solution that Lanoye and Perceval developed for the problem they perceived was an adaptation in the form of 'a three-part theatre poem, about campaigns for power and the struggle for survival . . . told with reference to six entirely different kings'.[7] In the process, they eliminated most other references to English history, since these were considered to distract Belgian and Dutch audiences to whom, as Lanoye put it, the names of Richmond and Kent are suggestive of cigarette brands rather than native, geographical landmarks with a long history.[8] The new text – designed to represent not England but 'a kind of theatrical no-man's-land' ('Jozef de Vos in gesprek', 117) – was approximately half the length of the assembled Shakespeare plays, with contemporary new material added, not merely in Dutch and Flemish, but also in French, Italian, British English and American English.

Part 1 of *Ten Oorlog* is a reworking of *Richard II* and the two parts of *Henry IV*. It focuses on 'warring generations', as the adaptors explain, and takes its patriarchal title – 'In the Name of the Father and the Son' – from the formula accompanying the sign of the cross.[9] Under the title that alludes to Mary's Magnificat (Luke 1: 46–55) – 'Behold the handmaid of the Lord' – Part 2 (also described by the authors as the 'war of the lovers') reworks *Henry V* and the first two parts of *Henry VI*. The final part of *Ten Oorlog* deals with the complete history of Richard the Third, representing 'the war on the Self', and its title completes the religious allusions by quoting the Lord's Prayer: 'And deliver us from evil'.[10]

In many interviews and press statements, Lanoye and Perceval went out of their way to stress the contemporary relevance of their Shakespearean adaptation.[11] On one level, Shakespeare's troubled sequence of English kings was said to rehearse the Belgian apprehension over the monarchy at the sudden death in 1993 of the childless and pious dreamer King Baudouin. Lanoye made no secret of the analogies that he himself recognized between the late Belgian monarch and Shakespeare's Henry the Sixth:

Baudouin: 'le roi triste'. The errant king full of self-pity, unable to father a child. 'Why did I have to become king at such an early age?' Of course he was one of the working models for Perceval. 'Le roi triste' who, as a consequence, near the end of his life became a religious zealot via Zen Buddhism, and at his death had become utterly alienated from the realities of this world.[12]

On another level, the salient strategies adopted by Lanoye and Perceval reveal how consciously the production appealed to a series of interrelated concerns about the political, juridical as well as moral rule and misrule of the Belgian nation following, among other things, the discovery in the mid-1990s of a network of child abuse centring on Marc Dutroux. These preoccupations may be illustrated with reference to various themes and issues brought into focus by the adaptation. For reasons of space, I shall limit myself here to the representation in *Ten Oorlog* of children, and in particular of the relationship between Prince Hal, his father Bolingbroke, and his surrogate parent Falstaff.

One of the notable features of *Ten Oorlog* is the representation of Richard II together with his queen in the early scenes of the first part of the trilogy, 'In the Name of the Father and the Son'. Unlike Shakespeare, who first presents the queen in the famous garden scene where she expresses her apprehensions about the fate of her husband (2.2), Lanoye and Perceval introduce her as *La Reine* in the play's third scene, being a simplified rendering of the events at Coventry. The Flemish adaptors further foreground her by turning Shakespeare's young but mature wife of the homosexually inclined Richard into an infant bride. Interestingly, Lanoye and Perceval rewrite Shakespeare where, for practical reasons, Shakespeare himself departed from his historical source material to profit from an additional, mature female speaker in the play. Their reason for subverting Shakespeare's presentation of history here from the outset and to return to Holinshed is certainly not rooted in any desire for historical accuracy; on occasion, their own departure from Shakespeare's history is even more drastic. Instead, there is little doubt that this manipulation of the queen in the text of *Richard II* serves to align the play more accurately with the disturbing Belgian condition of the late 1990s, following the traumatic discovery of a nationwide practice of child abuse, and increasing evidence of the corruption of state justice. Such a reading of the editorial intervention is inevitable, given the first exchange of words between Richard and his child-queen, shortly before the king corrupts the juridical system at his convenience by hindering divine justice at Coventry. The dialogue rehearses childlike innocence, affection, physicality, and age difference, but also a mode of senior male domination symbolized in the forms of address, which is further supported by the combination of the queen's use of the interrogative and the monarch's choice of the imperative manner:

THE QUEEN (*whispering affectionately in Richard's ear*) Richard, please let me go to the toilet.
RICHARD II (*whispers back*) My dear child, Just wait one little second (*kisses her forehead*).[13]

Matters are equally unambiguous in the second act, where we find the juvenile French queen playing with her doll, as Richard, surrounded by his flatterers, is treated to poetry with allusions of an increasingly homoerotic and scatological nature. Here, on the eve of his departure for Ireland, Richard is also eager to sleep with his child-queen, and the proper stress on the French word 'reine' in this multilingual translation-cum-adaptation poignantly activates the Dutch (as well as German) meaning of 'reine' as 'pure' (1.37). All this does not prepare one for the shock when in the next scene the sexually initiated queen has her first period, while still, childlike, humming a French nursery rhyme (2.3), before speaking her version of Shakespeare's lines about 'Some unborn sorrow, ripe in fortune's womb' (2.2.10), expressing her premonition of Richard's fall and the onset of civil war and national chaos.[14]

Images of children and child abuse of various kinds are echoed at numerous stages in the course of this dynastic soap opera. Henry VI is a child who

spends most of his time reading and playing with tin soldiers, meanwhile
dreaming of Shakespeare's French wars that rage around him on the stage.
He is, as his wife Margaretha di Napoli puts it, an 'eternal child' (2.104). The
infant king's absent-mindedness explains why the frustrated Margaretha
continues her adulterous relationship with Suffolk. Suffolk is beheaded
during his copulation with Margaretha, and Margaretha's resulting preg-
nancy is communicated by the way in which she carries Suffolk's bloody
head under her clothes. Margaretha is cruel at the assassination of the
youngest scion of York, and presents his father with the corpse of his son in
a plastic bag, dripping with blood. In the same vein, her own son, crown
prince Edward – to be played, as the stage direction specifies, by the actor
who plays Suffolk (3.11) – is butchered by Edwaar, Sjors and Risjaar. Also,
there is the famous sequence of the princes' murder in the Tower in the third
part, 'And Deliver Us from Evil'. Lanoye and Perceval invest the sequence
with more than just an expedient expression of disapproval. On the one
hand, Richard/Risjaar's rhetorical polish combined with a Tarantino-based
speech style introduces a note of wry humour. On the other hand, the
adaptors heighten the sense of horror when they have Risjaar devour the
princes' corpses on stage. To Risjaar, as Lanoye sees it, the two nephews
are his greatest source of humiliation, the most painful reminder of his
wickedness, of his hideous exterior, of his unloved state, and hence they
are also the true agents of his disintegration, a process whose lowest point
is reached when Risjaar eats them in full view of the audience. It is an
image that recalls the paintings of Francis Bacon, but which seems to have
been inspired no less by Tom Lanoye's own childhood experiences as the
son of the local butcher: 'In the Tower. Risjaar – crowned, fully adorned –
snorts, clutches, and drubs and sucks two children's corpses, much of which
has already been devoured, and from which the ribs stick out.' At the end of
Shakespeare's first tetralogy, Henry Richmond is introduced as the champion of the new Tudor rule. In *Ten Oorlog*, no such auspicious future is
envisaged as 'the Duchess of York leads in a gorgeous naked and unblem-
ished child, slightly older than a toddler, wearing a paper hat',[15] a child
who ends the production with a nursery rhyme. At the point where Henry
Richmond enters as an infant, vulnerable like the Princess of France in
the opening scenes of *Ten Oorlog*, and, like her, sings a nursery rhyme,
one becomes aware that the cycles of violence that constitute history, by
definition, have no ending.

One of *Ten Oorlog*'s central relationships bearing on child abuse and
the political course of the nation is that between Prince Hal, his father
Bolingbroke and his surrogate parent. No doubt the most drastic, and

Figure 9. Wolfgang Pregler as Hal (left) and Roland Renner as La Falstaff (right) in
Schlachten! at Salzburger Festspiele (1999). Dir. Luk Perceval.

also the most inventive revision of the play with reference to the Belgian
predicament, is that involving the character of Falstaff. In *Ten Oorlog*,
Falstaff, renamed La Falstaff, is a transvestite, the crown prince's 'friend'
and 'substitute mother'.[16]

La Falstaff is introduced in the opening scene of the material based on
Henry IV. In this scene, with its sharp dual focus, we find Bolingbroke
at prayer in the royal chapel, while a subversive La Falstaff, stroking the
crown prince's head, chants a Latin 'Hail Mary'.[17] This counterpoint is
appropriate considering the religious allusions in the subtitles of *Ten Oorlog*,
and its quotation from the Lord's Prayer in the subtitle to the third part,
'And Deliver us from Evil'. Through the maternal prayer, La Falstaff is
directly gendered feminine, and, through its Latin rendering, also as the
foreign other. The spiritual allusions persist, as Hal and La Falstaff exchange
wedding vows while the king is still at prayer:

LA FALSTAFF (*arm in arm with Henk, smiling blissfully*) Will you, Henk, son of
    Henry IV, take the named La Falstaff to your lawful, wedded wife?
HENK (*dead serious*) Yes.
LA FALSTAFF (*delighted*) Really and truly?
HENK Really and truly. (*La Falstaff hugs him.*)

(1.78)

From the outset, the licentious relationship between La Falstaff and Hal is set off against the austere, right-wing policy of the king. Mounting the pulpit after his prayer, Henry expresses the political belief that not only rebellion and high treason undermine national security and order, but also sexual licence and moral decline (1.79). From the pulpit, therefore, Henry preaches discipline: 'Order liberates, since it subjects anarchy' (1.79). Traditional family values should be restored to their original condition, with clear gender distinctions in place:

> No man is a man without Fatherhood,
> The woman not woman without Motherhood.
>
> (1.80)

These right-wing views left no room for the effeminate Richard II, and leave no room now for the substitute motherhood of La Falstaff. It is certainly symbolic that La Falstaff, as the stage directions tell us, is to be played by the same actor who played Richard II. With La Falstaff as the punitive reincarnation of Richard, Bolingbroke's political views cannot prevent the fact that La Falstaff washes and indiscreetly fondles young Hal, cuts his hair, daubs his lips red, and 'breastfeeds' him as he confesses his feelings of guilt at the slaughter committed at the Battle of Shrewsbury.

The issue of Hal's homosexual leanings inevitably surfaces during his several interviews with Henry IV. The king wants his son to be a man, and leave off his 'inferior urges' (1.86). It is worth everything to know his son is like himself; it is even worth his life. This appears from his invitation to his son, steeped in intertextual echoes from *Julius Caesar*, to stab him:

> Look how vulnerable I stand here with my back to you,
> A position that you are not unfamiliar with . . .
> Stab! 'You too, my son!' Make sure to enjoy it.
> What are you waiting for? Show yourself a man.   (1.87)

In the end, Lanoye and Perceval's crown prince indeed kills his sick father. The one-time prodigal son's assassination of his frail and ailing progenitor is an unadulterated display of hatred, but it is also the best fate Henry himself finds he could meet with. As the son curses his sinful father, the latter only encourages him: 'Release that hatred, realize your strength' (1.109). When Hal forcefully stops Henry's mouth, to silence and suffocate him, he really ratifies his father's philosophy, negating the existence of a feeble, but in the present case also satisfied old man.

Ten Oorlog appropriates the troubled relationship between Henry IV, La Falstaff and Hal, in order to position right-wing rule and sexual licence as the twin poles of a socio-political conflict. The carnal excesses and crimes of the Dutroux affair were by many seen as the political and juridical failure of the Christian Democrats. This climate of opinion worked in favour of the Flemish right-wing party which launched a renewed assault on the permissive society which accepted pornography and homosexuality. The Flemish League's exploitation and manipulation of Dutroux's crimes to boost its xenophobic as well as homophobic programme, is an analogy to *Ten Oorlog*'s La Falstaff in Henry IV's eyes, a form of state corruption in need of being ostracized. In accordance with this view, the play's sole alternative to the unorthodox friendship between Hal and La Falstaff is Henry V's rejection of his former friend with a right-wing rigour that glorifies virility, male authority and reactionary views of the family as the cornerstone of society.[18]

As soon as Hal has identified with his father, the rejection of Falstaff is imminent. Falstaff with his real love and affection loses out to the opportunistic Hal, now taken up by the Grand Mechanism. But love and loyalty continue to reside with La Falstaff, who becomes the enamoured Chorus introducing the events of Shakespeare's *Henry V*:

> Grant me your imagination.
> When I sing of Henry, see him before you,
> Ready to take ship across the Channel.
> His jawbone, sharper than the edge of swords;
> His eyes, bluer than the sea in summer;
> His mouth, more savoury than Constantinople.
> His kiss, more thrilling than a cock fight . . .
> See him. And never forget that you saw him.
> This was my Henry when he left me.   (2.9–10)

In a sequence of events followed by La Falstaff, Henry V (by Lanoye called The Fifth Henry) develops into the conqueror of France, and, with a deft gesture of acknowledgement to the Shakespearean metaphor of the 'maiden cities' in *Henry V*, Lanoye and Perceval's Hal also becomes the mindless heterosexual hero, performing a copulation olympiad to the encouraging cheers of the joint peace council at Troyes. It is certainly symbolic that in Lanoye and Perceval, an exiled and upstaged La Falstaff dies of a broken heart as Henry and Katharine are engaged in an act of banal lovemaking.

Ten Oorlog is unique for a number of reasons, not least because of the various ways in which, by appropriating Shakespeare's two tetralogies, Lanoye and Perceval manage deftly to address the plight of Belgium in the 1990s, both in terms of the unexpected death of King Baudouin, and of the far-reaching political repercussions of the exposure of a network of child abuse. However, as we witness the plays with stunning ease being converted into fables for contemporary history, it is worth recognizing also that several relevant analogies and allusions have their origin in Belgium's own medieval history, in its shared past with England. The issue of native and foreign tongues which features in all the plays, easily translates into this sequence of events bearing on the contemporary Belgian situation, not just with the perennial tug of languages between the Flemish and the Walloons, but also with the Francophone bourgeoisie of Flanders occupying the dubious middle region.[19] On another level, Henry V's famous military victory over the French, with surprising ease becomes the Battle of the Golden Spurs, fought at Courtrai in 1302, the military encounter which, in Flemish cultural memory, is the equivalent to the battle of Agincourt as a historical and literary prop for a sense of national self-identity.[20]

Seen from the perspective of Belgian history, Shakespeare's John of Gaunt (or Ghent) comes home in *Ten Oorlog* as he is made to speak the language of the Flemish he used to represent as the son of Edward III after the latter married into the Hainault line. Also the rebellion under Henry IV gains a familiar ring, when the contenders are defined in terms that are recognizably Belgian:

> The dad of Bolingbroke was John of Gaunt
> The fourth in a line of seven sons
> That issued from the stem of Edward the Third.
> His third son was Lionel of Antwerp –
> Mortimer's grandfather, by the father's side,
> So he stems from the third in line;
> He who is king stems only from the fourth.
>
> (1.85)

As presented by Lanoye and Perceval, Shakespeare's tetralogies really also shed light on the history of England when the continent of Europe and the possessions held there still mattered. *Ten Oorlog* achieves this ambivalent focus with such clarity that one is tempted to consider whether, to the 1997 Flemish premiere audience of *Ten Oorlog* in the city of Ghent, the Shakespearean cycles actually represented foreign history in the first place. Appropriation here was really a case of reappropriation.

Against the background of *Ten Oorlog*'s explicit references to the Belgian situation, contemporary as well as historical, it might come as a surprise that the trilogy should so readily have embarked on an international career when the Schauspielhaus Hamburg decided to stage the plays in German under the title of *Schlachten!*, and chose first to present their mammoth project at the Salzburger Festspiele of 1999. In the event – as Lanoye realized his dream of one day becoming 'a literary multinational'[21] – the Salzburg premiere initiated a serious row when the Austrian authorities banned children under sixteen years of age from attending the performance. By their prohibition, the right-wing Austrian authorities suggested that a play that problematized sexual licence also represented a questionable instance of the same.[22] Insensitive to Lanoye and Perceval's original concerns, the authorities really re-enacted right-wing Hal's banishment of La Falstaff in *Ten Oorlog/Schlachten!* After several days of negotiations, the ban on the trilogy was lifted. However, this could not take away the impression that the scandal had eclipsed any reflection on the trilogy's original concern with the crisis that had rocked the Belgian state, and had inadvertently exposed the fissures of an Austrian politico-cultural climate increasingly marked by extreme right-wing tendencies.[23]

In his survey of the German reviews, Maik Hamburger classified *Schlachten!* as 'the event of the year', leaving a profound impression on reviewers, but also dividing opinion.[24] With regard to the trilogy's political commitment, Hamburger reported that some reviewers admired the bleak power struggles taken over from Shakespeare, struggles conducted not for a specific purpose but pursued for their own sake. As one reviewer had it: 'Lanoye and Perceval's interest in Shakespeare's history plays is not so much with the image of medieval Britain as with the anatomy of power in its own right'.[25] Yet, Hamburger emphasized that it would be wrong to think that Shakespeare had been 'politicized' ('politisiert') in any way. In fact, the contrary was the case: 'Politics as a social category, as the totality of decision-making mechanisms through which public interests are co-ordinated, has been severely alienated from the production. One would almost think that there is more political material in every single history play by the Elizabethan playwright than in the entire trilogy.'[26] With reference to Heiner Müller and Jan Kott, Hamburger observed that Shakespeare's history plays are unique in conveying, together with the personality of the royal protagonist, an image of the commonwealth. This, he argued, was lacking in the German Lanoye/Perceval trilogy. In this connection, one understands the verdict of the *Frankfurter Allgemeine Zeitung*: 'A little more of Marx again would not be a bad thing, certainly where kings are concerned.'[27]

If the German reviewers missed what might be termed a serious and explicit political engagement, what did they admire? Paradoxically, what appealed to German theatre-makers and their audiences in this

Shakespearean adaptation was its iconoclastic verve, as well as the project's bold representation of language, sex and gender. As the reviewer for *Die Zeit* put it: 'How refreshing, how terrifying, how destructively entertaining is this wild show of war and slaughter about the royal squabbles among the Plantagenets; at last we have confrontation instead of harmony; at last we have spectacle instead of fidelity to the text; at last we are offered the destruction of plays instead of stale pedagogical theatre.'[28] For a proper sense of the comparative impact of *Ten Oorlog* and *Schlachten!*, and, beyond, of the foreign reception of Shakespeare and his English history plays during the late 1990s, it is worth assessing the proper nature of this iconoclasm.

Critics generally agree that the creative investment that produced *Ten Oorlog* was to a large extent rooted in Tom Lanoye's avowed love–hate relationship with Shakespeare. This relationship is explicitly brought into focus by the quotations which adorn the various parts of *Ten Oorlog*. At the beginning of Part 1, we read Camille Paglia's dictum: 'By approaching our classics with a critical eye and removing the dust, we can both corrupt and liberate them.' That Shakespeare is one of these classical authors is evidenced by the quotations that head the other parts of the adaptation. At the beginning of Part 2, the Flemish adaptors quote Goethe: 'For budding talent it is dangerous to read Shakespeare; he invites them to reproduce him, and they imagine they are producing themselves.' Part 3 begins with the statement by Frank McCourt to the effect that 'Shakespeare is like mashed potatoes. You can never get enough of him.'

These conflicting attitudes towards the power of Shakespeare and the consequently creative act of destroying his work, return like Lanoye's fingerprints in the adaptation of the trilogy. A case in point occurs in the third part of *Ten Oorlog*, focused on the career of Richard III. After killing his brother, George of Clarence, earlier in the play, the Flemish Richard addresses the audience with the words:

> One thing I'll teach de wereld, willens nillens;
> There is tremendous poetry in killings. (3.74)

Given the fact that the original idea for *Ten Oorlog* developed during work on *Richard III*, these lines seem to capture the original fascination with Shakespeare's history and Shakespeare's language as well as the paradoxical justification for the fully passionate act of demolition that is entitled *Ten Oorlog*.

Another illuminating instance of the way in which the Belgian trilogy seems to inscribe its own poetics in the nature of its deviation from the Shakespearean original, is the novel representation of the bond between Hal and Bolingbroke. Just as Prince Hal symbolically blocks his father's mouth in an attempt to kill the old man and to perpetuate the family's rule over England, so Lanoye and Perceval, in a contemporary history play of their own making, drown out Shakespeare's voice with the aim briefly to rule in the cherished realm of literature. Just as in this scene Prince Hal achieves the crown of England by means of a combined act of patricide and regicide, so Lanoye and Perceval attain their own crown of laurels by iconoclastically leaving the sacrosanct but allegedly confused Shakespeare text behind, and rewriting history as well as Shakespeare in their own image. On one level, these fingerprint analogies in the trilogy help us to recognize *Ten Oorlog* as an example of oedipal anxiety over Shakespeare which has been countered with a 'sledge hammer' and 'chain saw' approach to adaptation ('Jozef de Vos in gesprek', 113). On another level, we are witnessing an instance of patricide, of regicide, an attempted theatrical *coup* with the aim of ruling the international stage.

Perhaps the clearest indication that in the case of the trilogy's German reception any interest in Shakespeare, the Shakespearean history play or its socio-political concerns were secondary to the actual act of destroying and rewriting the history plays, is that the transfer of *Ten Oorlog* from the Low Countries to Germany and Austria involved the nearly verbatim adoption of the Flemish text, rather than an adaptation geared to any specific German predicament. Although as part of the translation process, some of the canonical Belgian verse was replaced by canonical German verse, the original dramatic constellation was thoroughly respected, as becomes clear from a brief comparison of *Ten Oorlog* and the German text edition entitled *Schlachten!* Unlike the *Ten Oorlog* text, which does not explicitize its bold departures from the Shakespeare 'original', *Schlachten!* is curiously annotated: square brackets indicate where passages from the Flemish master text were cut or rearranged in the German production; endnotes per scene indicate where certain actors could or should double; there is a revised allocation of speeches to certain characters; we are informed that Falstaff's washing of Hal is no longer accompanied by the canonical Flemish poetry by the paedophilic, Catholic priest Guido Gezelle (1830–99), but by Johann Wolfgang von Goethe's 'Erlkönig', an appropriate poem since in it the fairy king tempts the child away from its father (*Schlachten!*, 64).

What we witness here is that *Ten Oorlog*, lauded for its iconoclastic zeal vis-à-vis the literary canon, was eventually, under the pressure of Western market forces and the rule of copyright to which Shakespeare himself is not entitled, endowed with canonical status in its own right, edited and annotated to preserve and protect Lanoye and Perceval's intellectual property.

Paradoxically, the secure literary status that the two Flemish adaptors denied the Shakespearean 'original' was, with the annotated *Schlachten!* transferred to *Ten Oorlog* itself. Audiences came to see not Shakespeare, but Lanoye and Perceval. Audiences came to see not the history plays in a foreign guise, but applauded the dismantled version of the original Shakespearean drama.

Fortunately, there is sufficient reason to assume that with their adaptation, and even more with its translation into German, Lanoye and Perceval did not consciously plan or perpetrate a *coup de théâtre* in personal terms. Although Lanoye's sharp commercial sense occasionally recalls Shakespeare's, it is likely that the original ambitions and ideals were only at a later stage overtaken by considerations of a mercantile nature.[29] Also, these original ambitions and ideals never really succumbed altogether. After all, even with their international success, Lanoye and Perceval were prepared to produce a reduced version of their epic. Following the successful run of performances in the Low Countries, Lanoye and Perceval truncated their own truncated version of Shakespeare even further and produced *Ten Oorlog: De Solo*, a one-man show of under two hours for Dutch and Flemish theatres, in which Lanoye introduced, explained and acted out his favourite speeches and scenes. In this *reductio* of *Ten Oorlog*, performed by Lanoye as a consummate cabaret artist – dressed like a boy in short trousers secretly reading *Ten Oorlog* as one of the most intriguing books found in his father's library[30] – Shakespeare's kings followed one another in even more rapid succession, though without ever becoming absurd. The consequential socio-political realities of Belgium had to make way for a cabaret-style political satire of more topical matters. These included the Dutch queen's decision to go on a skiing holiday in Austria precisely at the time when Europe was in crisis over the elections that brought Jörg Haider and his extreme right-wing party to power; and the Dutch crown prince's plans to marry Máxima, the daughter of Jorge Videla's one-time Minister of Agriculture, Jorge Zorregieta. Both events were alluded to within the context of *Henry IV* and *Henry V* as presented in *Ten Oorlog*, where the monarchy displays fascistoid, reactionary tendencies. The discussion of the monarchy in our time here was made to extend to the role of La Falstaff whose monologue as the Prologue to *Henry V*, now delivered by Lanoye himself with nostalgia, admiration, suffering, hostility, as well as love, became an explicit instance of the writer's profound personal commitment to and concern with the political fate of Belgium. Naturally, *Ten Oorlog: The Solo*, too, was motivated by gain, but it did not compromise the deepest beliefs of *Ten Oorlog*. There was a clear sense here that La Falstaff-as-chorus as delivered by Lanoye himself represented the author's own challenged political position in a Belgium whose

Figure 10. Tom Lanoye: the man who would be 'king'.

right-wing elements attempt to subvert his rights as an avowed gay writer.[31] It seemed a logical next step that, soon after, Lanoye was to enter active Belgian politics in search of an additional stage on which to confess his beliefs.

This chapter has looked at the process by which Lanoye and Perceval adapted Shakespeare's two tetralogies to the Belgian predicament of the 1990s. Contemporary political concerns of some magnitude marked the adaptation and in part accounted for its huge success in the Low Countries. Against this background, it became apparent that German reviewers were fascinated by this adaptation of Shakespeare, concentrating on its deft handling of language, language variants and styles, as well as its bold representation of sex and gender, but rather surprisingly agreeing that the trilogy was deficient in political commitment. This international reputation of the play revealed that beyond the trilogy's involvement with specific Belgian concerns, it was also Lanoye's oedipal relationship with Shakespeare, a combined case of Shakespearomania and bardophobia, that determined the course of events. In this sense, the adaptation was really an attempt briefly, if not permanently, to dethrone King Shakespeare. It is between Lanoye and Perceval's political engagement (lost on German-speaking audiences) and the bold, author-centred appropriative urge (applauded in the Low Countries and elsewhere) that part of the fate of Shakespeare's history plays abroad comes into focus; between, on the one hand, the fluctuating political relevance of Shakespeare's chronicles, and, on the other, the struggle between Shakespeare and his successors sensing the need to adapt, renew and destroy the inventor's model plays as their own contribution to history.

NOTES

I am grateful to Sylvia Zysset (University of Basel) for generously sharing with me her extensive review file of the German-speaking production of *Ten Oorlog*, entitled *Schlachten!* I also owe a great debt to my Utrecht colleague Paul Franssen, whose many suggestions for stylistic changes I have followed blindly. Also, his sharp insight into contemporary Belgian politics has opened my eyes to much of value in *Ten Oorlog*.

1 For an assessment of the merits of the translation, see Ton Naaijkens, 'Ten Oorlog met Tom Lanoye: Stof voor een eerste vertaalbeschrijving', *Folio* 5:1 (1998), 17–39. See also his *Lof van de verandering* (Bussum: Uitgeverij Couthino, 1988), 24–5.

2 For a detailed analysis of the production see Jozef de Vos, '*Ten Oorlog*: The History Plays Recycled in The Low Countries', *Folio* 5:1 (1998), 7–16; see also '*Ten*

Oorlog' Doorgelicht, edited by Jozef de Vos, special issue of *Documenta: Tijdschrift voor theater* (Ghent), 16:2 (1998); Joost Houtman, *Allen treft eenzelfde lot: 'Ten Oorlog' een verhaal over macht en mens* (Louvain: Uitgeverij van Halewyck, 1999); and Jozef de Vos, 'Shakespeare's History Plays in Belgium: Taken Apart and Reconstructed as "Grand Narrative"' in *Four Hundred Years of Shakespeare in Europe*, edited by Angel Luis Pujante and Ton Hoenselaars (Newark: University of Delaware Press, 2003), 211–22.

3 For an account of the translator's experience, see Klaus Reichert, 'Ein Shakespeare aus Flandern', *Shakespeare Jahrbuch* 137 (2001), 100–14.

4 Quoted from the cover of the original box set containing the three volumes of the adaptation. See Tom Lanoye and Luk Perceval, *Ten Oorlog*, 3 vols. (Amsterdam: Prometheus, 1997).

5 Cover of original box set of *Ten Oorlog* (1997).

6 *Hamlet, Prince of Denmark*, edited by Philip Edwards, The New Cambridge Shakespeare (Cambridge: Cambridge University Press, 1985), 5.2.360–4. See also *The Third Part of King Henry VI*, edited by Michael Hattaway, New Cambridge Shakespeare (Cambridge: Cambridge University Press, 1993), 4.

7 From the cover of the original box set of *Ten Oorlog*.

8 Lanoye: 'Voor ons is Richmond of Kent een merk van sigaretten, maar voor Engelsen is dat een bestaand graafschap met een grond van historische waarheid.' See '*Ten Oorlog* doorgelicht: Jozef de Vos in gesprek met Tom Lanoye en Luc Joosten', in special issue of *Documenta: Tijdschrift voor theater* (Ghent), 16:2 (1998), 111–28 (pp. 116–17).

9 All English translations of *Ten Oorlog*, titles as well as quotations, are my own.

10 The three parts have various subtitles that refer to the main characters staged. The manipulation of names and titles represents an attempt to break through the apparent anonymity of the Shakespearean originals: *Richaar Deuzième* (*Richard Deuzième*), *Hendrik Vier* (*Heinrich IV* in German), *Hendrik de Vijfden* (*Der Fünfte Heinrich* in German), *Margaretha di Napoli*, *Edwaar the King* (*Eddy the King* in *Schlachten!*), and *Risjaar Modderfokker den Derde* (aka *Dirty Rich Modderfocker der Dritte*).

11 See 'Jozef de Vos in gesprek', 111–28. This interview formed the basis of the German interview reproduced in *Schlachten!* Even the typographical design of the original edition of *Ten Oorlog* had borrowed the colour, font and larger design of official Belgian war posters. On the original box set, as a combined product of book design and applied art, see Pascal Verbeken, 'Aannemersbedrijf Lanoye, alle façades en buitenwerken', in *Naamloze vennootschap* LANOYE, edited by Bart Vanegeren (Amsterdam: Prometheus, 1998), 29–43 (p. 37).

12 'Boudewijn, "le roi triste". De dolende koning die zich beklaagt en die maar geen kind kan verwekken. "Waarom ben ik op zo'n jonge leeftijd koning moeten worden?" Natuurlijk was dat bij hem één van de werkmodellen. "Le roi triste" die van de weeromstuit, bijna op het einde, via het zenboeddhisme in een godsdienstwaanzin schiet, en in een complete wereldvervreemding eindigt' ('Jozef de Vos in gesprek', 122–3).

13 Tom Lanoye and Luk Perceval, *Ten Oorlog*, 1.21.

14 The queen's appearance at the beginning of 2.3 was omitted from the German version of the play (*Schlachten!*, 30).

15 *Ten Oorlog*, 3.94. The graphic nature of the stage direction was toned down in the German translation, which does not have the final phrase: 'much of which has already been devoured, and from which the ribs stick out' (*Schlachten!*, 284). See also Tom Lanoye's first novel, *Een Slagerszoon met een brilletje* ('A butcher's son, wearing spectacles') (Amsterdam: Bert Bakker, 1985).

16 There is no indication that Lanoye and Perceval are indebted here to any of the arguments in recent Shakespeare studies concerning the gender of Falstaff. John Dover Wilson introduced the surrogate father theory in *The Fortunes of Falstaff* (Cambridge: Cambridge University Press, 1943). Valerie Traub challenged the gender of Falstaff's parenthood in *Desire and Anxiety: Circulations of Sexuality in Shakespeare* (New York and London: Routledge, 1992). See also *Engendering a Nation: A Feminist Account of Shakespeare's English Histories* (New York and London: Routledge, 1997), chapters on *Henry IV* and *Henry V*.

17 The 'Hail Mary' was omitted from the German acting version of the play.

18 Tom Lanoye, *Columns: tekst en uitleg/Toespraken: woorden met vleugels* (Amsterdam: Prometheus, 2001), 19–23.

19 Dieter Lesage discusses Lanoye, Belgium's bilingual structure and the sense of Flemish national self-identity in 'Een slow met Eric van Rompuy', in *Naamloze vennootschap LANOYE*, 85–93.

20 The nineteenth-century novel boosting the national status of the Battle of the Golden Spurs is Hendrik Conscience, *De Leeuw van Vlaanderen* ('The Flemish Lion') of 1838.

21 Bart Venegeren, 'Tom Lanoye, seismograaf', in *Naamloze vennootschap LANOYE*, 109–30 (p. 128).

22 Franz Wille described the Salzburg incident (allegedly touched off by the fact that Edward IV, in a manner meant to recall the Clinton/Lewinski scandal, was given an onstage blow job) as an unfortunate misunderstanding, but he also felt that it would not be inappropriate to reconsider the limits of such games with Shakespearean materials. See *Theater heute* 10 (1999), 14–19 (p. 17).

23 See '*Schlachten!* in Salzburg niet voor jongeren: "Eerste teken fascisme"', *NRC/Handelsblad*, 2 August 1999; 'Jeugd mag toch naar *Schlachten!*', *NRC/Handelsblad*, 3 August 1999; Kester Freriks, 'Lanoye: "Misschien moet ik blij zijn met de rel"', *NRC/Handelsblad*, 3 August 1999; and '"My fokking Krone für ein Pferd!"' *NRC/Handelsblad*, 6 August 1999.

24 Maik Hamburger, 'Salzburger Schlachteplatte', *Shakespeare Jahrbuch* 136 (2000), 209–12 (p. 209). Translations from the German are my own.

25 *Ibid.*, 211. 'An Shakespeares Königsdramen interessierten Lanoye und Perceval weniger das mittelalterliche Brittanien als die Anatomie der Macht an sich.'

26 *Ibid.*, 212. 'Es wäre ein Irrtum zu meinen, Shakespeare wäre *politisiert* worden. Eher ist das Gegenteil wahr. Politik als eine gesellschaftliche Kategorie, als die Gesammtheit der Entscheidungsmechanismen, durch welche öffentliche Belange geregelt werden, is rigorös entfernt worden. Es liegt die vermutung

nahe, daß in jedem einzelnen Geschichtsdrama des Elisabethaners mehr politischer Stoff steckt als in diesem ganzen Reigen.'

27 *Ibid.* 'Ein bißchen mehr Marx täte vielleicht mal wieder gut. Wenigstens wenn es um Könige geht.' See also Klaus Dermutz who, in 'Das Gehirn der Schlächter', notes that Lanoye and Perceval are not interested in the 'Erforschung der ökonomischen Strukturen' ('analysis of economic structures'), in *Theater der Zeit* (September/October 1999), 50–1 (p. 51).

28 Hamburger, 'Salzburger Schlachteplatte', 211. 'Wie erfrischend, wie erschreckend, wie mörderisch belebend ist diese wüste Kriegs- und Metzel-Show über die Königskabalen im Hause Plantagenet: endlich Konfrontation statt Harmonie, endlich Spektakel statt Werktreue, endlich ein bisschen Stückezertrümmerung statt muffigen Bildungstheaters.'

29 Bert Vanegeren: 'With every new book, Lanoye manipulates the media until he himself and his product are hot news.' See *Naamloze vennootschap* LANOYE, 110. In 1992, Lanoye founded the limited liability company L.A.N.O.Y.E. Its aim was to produce literary texts of all kinds and for all purposes, to organize the publicity of this material in the various media and on various stages. On the various objectives, see *Naamloze vennootschap LANOYE*, 9–12. In 'Het verschil tussen biblioseksualiteit', Luc van Peteghem describes an expensive limited edition of *Ten Oorlog* (*Naamloze vennootschap* LANOYE, 69).

30 For a more detailed discussion of *De Solo* see Paul Franssen and Ton Hoenselaars, '*Ten Oorlog – De Solo*', *Folio* 7:1 (2000), 37–9.

31 In his autobiographical novel, *Kartonnen Dozen* ('Cardboard Boxes'), Lanoye presents a scene in which he, as a child in front of his parents, his aunts and his sister, impersonates the baroness from a popular Dutch cabaret song. Drag here is an integral part of Lanoye's memory and self-identity. It reads like a precursor of La Falstaff in *Ten Oorlog*. With the emphasis in the novel on having to 'repeat' the successful 'act', this incident also foreshadows Lanoye's cabaret skills in *Ten Oorlog: De Solo*. See Tom Lanoye, *Kartonnen Dozen* (1991. Rpt. Amsterdam: Ooievaar Pockethouse, 1995), 28–9.

Shakespeare's history plays: select bibliography

Alter, Jean. 'Decoding Mnouchkine's Shakespeare (A Grammar of Stage Signs)'. In *Performing Texts*. Edited by Michael Issacharoff and R. F. Jones. 75–85. Philadelphia, PA: University of Pennsylvania Press, 1988.

Arai, Yoshio. '*Henry VI* in Japan'. In *Henry VI: Critical Essays*. Edited by Thomas A. Pendleton. 57–66. New York, NY: Routledge, 2001.

Bablet, Marie-Louise, and Denis Bablet. *Le Théâtre du Soleil ou la quête du bonheur*. Ivry: CNRS/SERDDAV, 1979.

Baker, David J. *Between Nations: Shakespeare, Spenser, Marvell, and the Question of Britain*. Stanford, CA: Stanford University Press, 1997.

'"Wildehirissheman": Colonialist Representation in Shakespeare's *Henry V*'. *English Literary Renaissance* 22 (1992): 37–61.

Barton, John, and Peter Hall. *The Wars of the Roses: Adapted for the Royal Shakespeare Company from William Shakespeare's 'Henry VI Parts I, II, III' and 'Richard III'*. London: BBC, 1970.

Bate, Jonathan. *Shakespearean Constitutions: Politics, Theatre, Criticism, 1730–1830*. Oxford: Clarendon Press, 1989.

'Shakespearean Nationhoods'. In *Shakespeare in the New Europe*. Edited by Michael Hattaway, Boika Sokolova, and Derek Roper. 112–29. Sheffield: Sheffield Academic Press, 1994.

Bate, Jonathan, ed. *The Romantics on Shakespeare*. Harmondsworth: Penguin, 1992.

Beauman, Sally, *The Royal Shakespeare Company: A History of Ten Decades*. Oxford: Oxford University Press, 1982.

The Royal Shakespeare Company's Production of 'Henry V' for the Centenary Season at the Royal Shakespeare Theatre. Oxford: Pergamon Press, 1976.

Beaurline, L. A., ed. *King John*. Cambridge: Cambridge University Press, 1990.

Belsey, Catherine. 'Making Histories Then and Now: Shakespeare from *Richard II* to *Henry V*'. In *Uses of History: Marxism, Postmodernism and the Renaissance*. Edited by Francis Barker, Peter Hulme and Margaret Iversen. 24–46. Manchester: Manchester University Press, 1991.

Bingham, Dennis. 'Jane Howell's First Tetralogy: Brechtian Break-out or Just Good Television?' In *Shakespeare on Television: An Anthology of Essays and Reviews*. Edited by J. C. Bulman and H. R. Coursen. 221–9. Hanover, NH: University Press of New England, 1988.

Bloom, Harold. *Shakespeare: The Invention of the Human.* New York: Riverhead Books, 1998.

Boas, Frederick S. '*Hamlet* and *Richard II* on the High Seas'. In Frederick S. Boas, *Shakespeare and the Universities, and Other Studies in Elizabethan Drama.* 84–95. Oxford: Basil Blackwell, 1923.

Bogdanov, Michael, and Michael Pennington. *The English Shakespeare Company: The Story of 'The Wars of the Roses', 1986–1989.* London: Nick Hern Books, 1992.

Bradshaw, Brendan, Andrew Hadfield and Willy Maley, eds. *Representing Ireland: Literature and the Origins of Conflict, 1534–1660.* Cambridge: Cambridge University Press, 1993.

Bragaglia, Leonardo. *Shakespeare in Italia.* Rome: Trevi Editore, 1973.

Branagh, Kenneth. *Beginning.* London: Chatto & Windus, 1989.
  '*Henry V' by William Shakespeare: A Screenplay Adaptation.* London: Chatto & Windus, 1989.

Braunmuller, A. R. '*King John* and Historiography'. *English Literary History* 55 (1988): 309–32.

Brockbank, Philip. 'Shakespeare: His Histories, English and Roman'. In *New History of Literature, III: English Drama to 1710.* Edited by Christopher Ricks. 141–81. New York: Bedrick, 1987.

Brook, Peter. *The Empty Space.* Harmondsworth: Penguin Books, 1968.

Brown, John Russell. 'Foreign Shakespeare and English-speaking Audiences'. In *Foreign Shakespeare: Contemporary Performance.* Edited by Dennis Kennedy. 21–35. Cambridge: Cambridge University Press, 1993.

Bulman, Joan. *Strindberg and Shakespeare: Shakespeare's Influence on Strindberg's Historical Drama.* 1933. Rpt. New York: Haskell House Publishers, 1971.

Burden, Dennis. 'Shakespeare's History Plays: 1952–1983'. *Shakespeare Survey* 38 (1985): 1–18.

Cahill, Patricia A. 'Nation Formation and the English History Plays'. In *A Companion to Shakespeare's Works: Volume II – The Histories.* Eds. Richard Dutton and Jean E. Howard. 70–93. Oxford: Blackwell, 2003.

Cairns, David, and Shaun Richards. *Writing Ireland: Colonialism, Nationalism and Culture.* Manchester: Manchester University Press, 1988.

Calderón de la Barca, Pedro. *The Schism in England (La cisma da Inglaterra).* Translated by Kenneth Muir and Ann L. Mackenzie. Edited by Ann L. Mackenzie. Warminster: Aris & Phillips, 1990.

Campbell, Oscar James. *The Position of the 'Roode en Witte Roos' in the Saga of King Richard III.* 1919. Rpt. New York: AMS, 1971.

Candido, Joseph, ed. *King John.* Shakespeare: The Critical Tradition. London and Atlantic Highlands, NJ: Athlone, 1996.

Charney, Maurice. 'Shakespearean Anglophilia'. *Shakespeare Quarterly* 31 (1980): 287–92.

Christensen, Peter G. 'Eisenstein's *Ivan the Terrible* and Shakespeare's Historical Plays'. *Slavic and East-European Arts* 6:2 (1990): 124–38.

Cohen, Walter. *Drama of a Nation: Public Theater in Renaissance England and Spain*. Ithaca, NY: Cornell University Press, 1985.

Cohn, Albert. *Shakespeare in Germany in the Sixteenth and Seventeenth Centuries: An Account of English Actors in Germany and The Netherlands and of the Plays Performed by Them during the Same Period*. 1865. Rpt. New York: Haskell House Publishers, 1971.

Coursen, H. R. 'Theme and Design in Recent Productions of *Henry VI*'. In *Henry VI: Critical Essays*. Edited by Thomas A. Pendleton. 205–18. New York, NY: Routledge, 2001.

Cousin, Geraldine. *King John*. Shakespeare in Performance. Manchester: Manchester University Press, 1994.

Curren-Aquino, Deborah T., ed. *'King John': New Perspectives*. Newark: University of Delaware Press, 1989.

Danson, Lawrence. '*Henry V*: King, Chorus, and Critics'. *Shakespeare Quarterly* 34 (1983): 27–43.

    Shakespeare's Dramatic Genres. Oxford Shakespeare Topics. Oxford: Oxford University Press, 2000.

David, Richard. 'Shakespeare's History Plays: Epic or Drama'. *Shakespeare Survey* 6 (1953): 129–39.

Dean, Paul. 'Shakespeare's *Henry VI* Trilogy and Elizabethan "Romance" Histories: The Origins of a Genre'. *Shakespeare Quarterly* 33 (1982): 34–48.

Delabastita, Dirk. 'A Great Feast of Languages: Shakespeare's Multilingual Comedy in *King Henry V* and the Translator'. *The Translator* 8:2 (2002): 303–40.

Dessen, Alan C. 'Staging Shakespeare's History Plays in 1984: A Tale of Three Henrys'. *Shakespeare Quarterly* 36:1 (1985): 71–9.

Dobson, Michael. 'Falstaff after John Bull: Shakespearean History, Britishness, and the Former United Kingdom'. *Shakespeare Jahrbuch* 136 (2000): 40–55.

    The Making of the National Poet: Shakespeare, Adaptation and Authorship, 1660–1769. Oxford: Clarendon Press, 1992.

Dollimore, Jonathan, and Alan Sinfield. 'History and Ideology: The Instance of *Henry V*'. In *Alternative Shakespeares*. Edited by John Drakakis. 206–37. London: Methuen, 1985.

Dollimore, Jonathan, and Alan Sinfield, eds. *Political Shakespeare: New Essays in Cultural Materialism*. 1985. Rev. edn. Manchester: Manchester University Press, 1994.

Drakakis, John, ed. *Alternative Shakespeares*. London: Methuen, 1985.

Dutton, Richard, and Jean E. Howard, eds. *A Companion to Shakespeare's Works: Volume II – The Histories*. Oxford: Blackwell, 2003.

Edwards, Philip. *Threshold of a Nation: A Study in English and Irish Drama*. Cambridge: Cambridge University Press, 1979.

Engler, Balz. 'Shakespeare in the Trenches'. *Shakespeare Survey* 44 (1992): 105–11. Rpt. in *Shakespeare and Race*. Edited by Catherine M. S. Alexander and Stanley Wells. 101–11. Cambridge: Cambridge University Press, 2000.

Ewbank, Inga-Stina. 'European Cross-currents'. In *Shakespeare: An Illustrated Stage History*. Edited by Jonathan Bate and Russell Jackson. 128–38. Oxford: Oxford University Press, 1996.

Faulkener, John. '*Edward II* and *Richard II*: The Grand Tour of the Prospect Company'. *TABS* 28:1 (1970): 4–16.

Foakes, R. A. 'Shakespeare's Other Historical Plays'. In *The Cambridge Companion to Shakespeare's History Plays*. Ed. Michael Hattaway. 214–28. Cambridge: Cambridge University Press, 2002.

Forker, Charles R., ed. *Richard II*. Shakespeare: The Critical Tradition. London and Atlantic Highlands, NJ: Athlone, 1997.

  'Shakespeare's Chronicle Plays as Historical-Pastoral'. *Shakespeare Studies* 1 (1965): 85–104.

Franck, Martine, and Claude Roy. *Le Théâtre du Soleil: Shakespeare*. Paris: SNEP, 1982.

Gaby, Rosemary. '"What ish my nation?": Reconstructing Shakespeare's Henriad for the Australian Stage'. *Shakespeare Bulletin* 18:1 (Winter 2000): 43–6.

Garstenauer, Maria. *A Selective Study of English History Plays in the Period between 1960 and 1977*. Salzburg: Institut für Anglistik & Amerikanistik, Universität Salzburg, 1985.

Goy-Blanquet, D. 'Pauvres Jacques: Chroniques et spectacles en Angleterre au XVIe siècle'. In *Figures théâtrales du peuple*. Edited by Elie Konigson. 49–74. Paris: Éditions du Centre National de la Recherche Scientifique, 1985.

  Shakespeare et l'invention de l'histoire: Guide commenté du théâtre historique de Shakespeare. Brussels: Le Cri, 1997.

  Shakespeare's Early History Plays: From Chronicle to Stage. Oxford: Oxford University Press, 2003.

Grady, Hugh. 'Professionalism, Nationalism, Modernism: The Case of E. M. W. Tillyard'. In Hugh Grady, *The Modernist Shakespeare: Critical Texts in a Material World*. 158–89. Oxford: Clarendon Press, 1991.

Grange, William. 'Shakespeare in the Weimar Republic'. *Theatre Survey* 28 (1987): 89–100.

Greenblatt, Stephen. 'Invisible Bullets'. In Stephen Greenblatt, *Shakespearean Negotiations: The Circulation of Social Energy in England*. 21–65. Oxford: Clarendon Press, 1988.

Grene, Nicholas. *Shakespeare's Serial History Plays*. Cambridge: Cambridge University Press, 2002.

Grennan, Eamon. 'Shakespeare's Satirical History: A Reading of *King John*'. *Shakespeare Studies* 11 (1978): 21–37.

Habicht, Werner. 'Shakespeare and Theatre Politics in the Third Reich'. In *The Play Out of Context: Transferring Plays from Culture to Culture*. Edited by Hanna Scolnicov and Peter Holland. 110–20. Cambridge: Cambridge University Press, 1989.

Hadfield, Andrew. '"Hitherto she ne're could fancy him": Shakespeare's "British" Plays and the Exclusion of Ireland'. In *Shakespeare and Ireland: History, Politics, Culture*. Edited by Mark Thornton Burnett and Ramona Wray. 47–67. Houndmills: Macmillan, 1997.

Halio, Jay L. 'Alternative Action: The Tragedy of Missed Opportunities in *King John*'. *Hebrew University Studies in Literature and the Arts* 11:2 (1983): 254–69.

Hamburger, Maik. 'Salzburger Schlachteplatte'. *Shakespeare Jahrbuch* 136 (2000): 209–12.

Hankey, Julie, ed. *Richard III*. Plays in Performance. London: Junction Books, 1981.

Hart, Jonathan. *Theater and the World: The Problematics of Shakespeare's History*. Boston: Northeastern University Press, 1992.

Hattaway, Michael. 'Shakespeare's Histories: The Politics of Recent British Productions'. In *Shakespeare in the New Europe*. Edited by Michael Hattaway, Boika Sokolova and Derek Roper. 351–69. Sheffield: Sheffield Academic Press, 1994.

Hattaway, Michael, ed. *The Cambridge Companion to Shakespeare's History Plays*. Cambridge: Cambridge University Press, 2002.

Hawkes, Terence. 'Aberdaugleddyf'. In Terence Hawkes, *Shakespeare in the Present*. Accents on Shakespeare. 46–65. New York and London: Routledge, 2002.

'Bryn Glas'. In Terence Hawkes, *Shakespeare in the Present*. Accents on Shakespeare. 23–45. New York and London: Routledge, 2002.

Hawley, William M. *Critical Hermeneutics and Shakespeare's History Plays*. New York: Peter Lang, 1992.

Healy, Tom. 'Past and Present Shakespeare's: Shakespearian Appropriations in Europe'. In *Shakespeare and National Culture*. Edited by John J. Joughin. 202–32. Manchester: Manchester University Press, 1997.

'Remembering with Advantages: Nation and Ideology in *Henry V*'. In *Shakespeare in the New Europe*. Edited by Michael Hattaway, Boika Sokolova and Derek Roper. 174–93. Sheffield: Sheffield Academic Press, 1994.

Heinemann, Margot. 'How Brecht Read Shakespeare'. In *Political Shakespeare: Essays in Cultural Materialism*. Edited by Jonathan Dollimore and Alan Sinfield. 202–30. Manchester: Manchester University Press, 1985.

Helgerson, Richard. *Forms of Nationhood: The Elizabethan Writing of England*. Chicago: University of Chicago Press, 1992.

'Writing Empire and Nation'. In *The Cambridge Companion to English Literature, 1500–1600*. Edited by Arthur F. Kinney. 310–29. Cambridge: Cambridge University Press, 2000.

Hirst, David L. *Giorgio Strehler*. Cambridge: Cambridge University Press, 1993.

Hodgdon, Barbara. *The End Crowns All: Closure and Contradiction in Shakespeare's History*. Princeton, NJ: Princeton University Press, 1991.

Henry IV, Part Two. Shakespeare in Performance. Manchester: Manchester University Press, 1993.

'Making It New: Katie Mitchell Refashions Shakespeare-History'. In *Transforming Shakespeare: Contemporary Women's Re-Visions in Literature and Performance*. Edited by Marianne Novy. 13–33. New York, NY: St Martin's Press, 1999.

'*The Wars of the Roses*: Scholarship Speaks on the Stage'. *Shakespeare Jahrbuch* (1972): 170–84.

Hoenselaars, A. J. 'Shakespeare and the Early Modern History Play'. In *The Cambridge Companion to Shakespeare's History Plays*. Ed. Michael Hattaway. 25–40. Cambridge: Cambridge University Press, 2002.

Hoenselaars, Ton. 'Recycling Shakespeare in the Low Countries'. *The Low Countries* 6 (1999): 203–11.

'Shakespeare for "the People": François-Victor Hugo Translates *Henry V*'. *Documenta* (Ghent) 13:4 (1995): 243–52.

Holderness, Graham. *Shakespeare: The Histories*. New York: St Martin's Press, 1999.

Shakespeare's History. Dublin: Gill and Macmillan, 1985.

Shakespeare's History Plays: 'Richard II' to 'Henry V'. New Casebooks. Basingstoke and London: Macmillan, 1992.

Shakespeare Recycled: The Making of Historical Drama. New York: Harvester Wheatsheaf, 1992.

Holderness, Graham, ed. *The Shakespeare Myth*. Manchester: Manchester University Press, 1988.

Holderness, Graham, Nick Potter and John Turner. *Shakespeare: The Play of History*. Basingstoke: Macmillan, 1988.

Holland, Peter. *English Shakespeares: Shakespeare on the English Stage in the 1990s*. Cambridge: Cambridge University Press, 1997.

Homem, Rui Carvalho. 'Of Negroes, Jews and Kings: On a Nineteenth Century Royal Translator'. *The Translator* 7:1 (2001): 19–42.

Hopkins, Lisa. 'Neighbourhood in *Henry V*'. In *Shakespeare and Ireland: History, Politics, Culture*. 9–26. Edited by Mark Thornton Burnett and Ramona Wray. Houndmills: Macmillan, 1997.

Hortmann, Wilhelm. *Shakespeare on the German Stage: The Twentieth Century*. Cambridge: Cambridge University Press, 1998.

Shakespeare und das deutsche Theater im xx. Jahrhundert. Mit einem Kapitel über Shakespeare auf den Bühnen der DDR von Maik Hamburger. Berlin: Henschel Verlag, 2001.

Houtman, Joost. *Allen treft eenzelfde lot: 'Ten Oorlog' een verhaal over macht en mens*. Louvain: Uitgeverij van Halewyck, 1999.

Howard, Jean E., and Phyllis Rackin. *Engendering a Nation: A Feminist Account of Shakespeare's English Histories*. London and New York: Routledge, 1997.

Humphreys, A. R. 'The English History Plays'. In *Shakespeare: Select Bibliographical Guides*. Edited by Stanley Wells. 239–83. New York and London: Oxford University Press, 1973.

Hunter, G. K. *English Drama, 1586–1642: The Age of Shakespeare*. Oxford: Clarendon Press, 1997.

'Notes on the Genre of the History Play'. In *Shakespeare's English Histories: A Quest for Form and Genre*. Edited by John W. Velz. 229–40. Binghamton, NY: Medieval & Renaissance Texts & Studies, 1996.

'The Royal Shakespeare Company Plays *Henry VI*'. *Renaissance Drama* 9 (1978): 91–108.

Iser, Wolfgang. *Shakespeares Historien: Genesis und Geltung*. Konstanz: Universitätsverlag Konstanz GMBH, 1988.

Staging Politics: The Lasting Impact of Shakespeare's Histories. Translated by David Henry Wilson. New York: Columbia University Press, 1993.

Ivic, Christopher. '"Our inland": Shakespeare's *Henry V* and the Celtic Fringe'. *Ariel* 30:1 (1999): 85–103.

Jackson, MacD. P. '*The Wars of the Roses:* The English Shakespeare Company on Tour'. *Shakespeare Quarterly* 40:2 (1989): 208–12.

Jenkins, Harold. 'Shakespeare's History Plays: 1900–1951'. *Shakespeare Survey* 6 (1953): 1–15.

Jorgenson, Paul A. 'Accidental Judgments, Casual Slaughters, and Purposes Mistook: Critical Reactions to Shakespere's *Henry the Fifth*'. *Shakespeare Association Bulletin* 22 (1947): 51–61.

Kastan, David Scott. '"Proud Majesty Made a Subject": Shakespeare and the Spectacle of Rule'. *Shakespeare Quarterly* 37 (1986): 459–75.

'Shakespeare and English History'. In *The Cambridge Companion to Shakespeare*. Edited by Margreta de Grazia and Stanley Wells. 167–82. Cambridge: Cambridge University Press, 2001.

'"To Set a Form Upon that Indigest": Shakespeare's Fictions of History'. *Comparative Drama* 17 (1983): 1–16.

Kennedy, Dennis. *Looking at Shakespeare: A Visual History of Twentieth-Century Performance*. 1993. 2nd edn. Cambridge: Cambridge University Press, 2001.

'Shakespeare and the Global Spectator'. *Shakespeare Jahrbuch* 131 (1995): 50–64.

Kennedy, Dennis, ed. *Foreign Shakespeare: Contemporary Performance*. Cambridge: Cambridge University Press, 1993.

Kernan, Alvin B. 'From Ritual to History: The English History Plays'. In *The Revels History of Drama in English* III: 262–99. London: Methuen, 1975.

Kewes, Paulina. 'The Elizabethan History Play: A True Genre?' In *A Companion to Shakespeare's Works: Volume II – The Histories*. Eds. Richard Dutton and Jean E. Howard. 170–93. Oxford: Blackwell, 2003.

Kiernander, Adrian. *Ariane Mnouchkine and the Théâtre du Soleil*. Cambridge: Cambridge University Press, 1993.

'The Orient, the Feminine: The Use of Interculturalism by the *Théâtre du Soleil*'. In *Gender in Performance: The Presentation of Difference in the Performing Arts*. Edited by Laurence Senelick. 183–94. Hanover, NH: University Press of New England, 1992.

Knowles, Ric. 'The First Tetralogy in Performance'. In *A Companion to Shakespeare's Works: Volume II – The Histories*. Eds. Richard Dutton and Jean E. Howard. 263–86. Oxford: Blackwell, 2003.

Kott, Jan. *Shakespeare Our Contemporary*. Translated by Bolesław Taborski. London: Methuen, 1964.

Labriola, Albert C. '"This sceptered isle": Kingship and the Body Politic in the Lancastrian Tetralogy'. In *Shakespeare and English History: Interdisciplinary Perspectives*. Edited by Ronald G. Shafer. 45–64. Indiana: Indiana University of Pennsylvania, 1976.

Lanoye, Tom, and Luk Perceval. *Schlachten! Nach den Rosenkriegen von William Shakespeare*. Translated from the Flemish by Rainer Kersten and Klaus Reichert. Frankfurt am Main: Verlag der Autoren, 1999.

Ten Oorlog, 3 vols. Amsterdam: Prometheus, 1997.

Leech, Clifford. *William Shakespeare: The Chronicles*. London: Longmans, Green, 1962.

Leggatt, Alexander. 'Henry VIII and the Ideal England'. *Shakespeare Survey* 38 (1985): 131–43.

Shakespeare's Political Drama: The History Plays and the Roman Plays. London: Routledge, 1988.

Leiter, Samuel L. ed. *Shakespeare Around the Globe: A Guide to Notable Postwar Revivals*. New York: Greenwood Press, 1986.

Lerner, Laurence. 'King John, König Johann: War and Peace'. *Shakespeare Survey* 54 (2001): 213–22.

Limon, Jerzy. *Gentlemen of a Company: English Players in Central and Eastern Europe, 1590–1660*. Cambridge: Cambridge University Press, 1985.

Limon, Jerzy, and Jay L. Halio, eds. *Shakespeare and His Contemporaries: Eastern and Central European Studies*. Newark, NJ: University of Delaware Press, 1993.

Lindenberger, Herbert. *Historical Drama: The Relation of Literature and Reality*. Chicago: University of Chicago Press, 1975.

Loehlin, James N. '"Wish Not a Man From England": Henry V Outside the United Kingdom'. In James N. Loehlin, *Henry V*. Shakespeare in Performance. 146–69. Manchester: Manchester University Press, 1996.

Loftis, John. *Renaissance Drama in England and Spain: Topical Allusion and History Plays*. Princeton, NJ: Princeton University Press, 1987.

Maley, Willy. 'The Irish Text and Subtext of Shakespeare's English Histories'. In *A Companion to Shakespeare's Works: Volume II – The Histories*. Eds. Richard Dutton and Jean E. Howard. 94–124. Oxford: Blackwell, 2003.

'Shakespeare, Holinshed and Ireland: Resources and Con-texts'. In *Shakespeare and Ireland: History, Politics, Culture*. Edited by Mark Thornton Burnett and Ramona Wray. 27–46. Houndmills: Macmillan, 1997.

'"This Sceptred Isle": Shakespeare and the British Problem'. In *Shakespeare and National Culture*. Edited by John J. Joughin. 83–108. Manchester: Manchester University Press, 1997.

Marder, Louis. 'History Cycle at Antioch College'. *Shakespeare Quarterly* 4 (1953): 57–8.

Maynard, Katherine. 'Shakespeare's Georgic Nationalism'. *History of European Ideas* 16:4–6 (1993): 981–7.

McEachern, Claire. *Poetics of Nationhood, 1590–1612*. Cambridge: Cambridge University Press, 1996.

McKellen, Ian. 'The Czech Significance'. In *A Night at the Theatre*. Edited by Ronald Harwood. 103–8. London: Methuen, 1982.

McMillin, Scott. *Henry IV, Part One*. Shakespeare in Performance. Manchester: Manchester University Press, 1991.

Merrix, Robert P. 'Shakespeare's Histories and the New Bardolators'. *Studies in English Literature* 19 (1979): 179–96.

Moseley, C. W. R. D. *Shakespeare's History Plays: 'Richard II' to 'Henry V'*. London: Penguin, 1988.

Murphy, Andrew. *But the Irish Sea Betwixt Us: Ireland, Colonialism, and Renaissance Literature*. Lexington: The University Press of Kentucky, 1999.

'Shakespeare's Irish History'. *Literature and History* 5:1 (1996): 38–59.

Myers, Norman J. 'Finding "a Heap of Jewels" in "Lesser" Shakespeare: *The Wars of the Roses* and *Richard Duke of York*'. *New England Theatre Journal* 7 (1996): 95–107.

Neill, Michael. 'Broken English and Broken Irish: Nation, Language, and the Optic of Power in Shakespeare's Histories'. *Shakespeare Quarterly* 45:1 (1994): 1–32.

Nichols, Nina da Vinci. '*Henry VI* '. *Shakespeare Bulletin* 15 (1997): 10–12.

Odell, George C. D. *Shakespeare from Betterton to Irving*. 2 vols. 1921. Rpt. New York: Dover, 1966.

Olivier, Laurence. *Henry V*. London: Lorrimer, 1984.

Orgel, Stephen, and Sean Keilen, eds. *Shakespeare and History*. New York: Garland Publishers, 1999.

Ornstein, Robert. *A Kingdom for a Stage: The Achievement of Shakespeare's History Plays*. Cambridge, MA: Harvard University Press, 1972.

Patterson, Annabel. *Reading Holinshed's Chronicles*. Chicago and London: University of Chicago Press, 1994.

Pearlman, E. *William Shakespeare: The History Plays*. New York: Twayne Publishers, 1992.

Pearson, Richard. *A Band of Arrogant and United Heroes: The Story of the Royal Shakespeare Company Production of the Wars of the Roses. (Adaptation of the Three Parts of 'Henry VI' plus 'Richard III')*. London: Adelphi Press, 1990.

Pendleton Thomas A., ed. *Henry VI: Critical Essays*. New York and London: Routledge, 2001.

Piesse, A. J. '*King John*: Changing Perspectives'. In *The Cambridge Companion to Shakespeare's History Plays*. Ed. Michael Hattaway. 126–40. Cambridge: Cambridge University Press, 2002.

Pieters, Jürgen. 'Vervreemding en herkenning: Shakespeare als tegenspeler'. In Jürgen Pieters, *De honden van King Lear: Beschouwingen over hedendaags theater*. 50–68. Groningen: Historische Uitgeverij, 1999.

'The Plantagenets': Adapted by the Royal Shakespeare Company from William Shakespeare's 'Henry VI' Parts I, II, III and 'Richard III' as 'Henry VI', 'The Rise of Edward IV' and 'Richard III, His Death'. With an introduction by Adrian Noble. London and Boston: Faber and Faber, 1989.

Potter, Lois. '*2 Henry IV* and the Czech Political Context'. *Shakespeare Worldwide: Translation and Adaptation* 14–15 (1995): 252–5.

'Bad and Good Authority Figures: *Richard III* and *Henry V* since 1945'. *Shakespeare Jahrbuch* (1992): 39–54.

'Recycling the Early Histories: "The Wars of the Roses" and "The Plantagenets"'. *Shakespeare Survey* 43 (1991): 171–81.

'The Second Tetralogy: Performance as Interpretation'. In *A Companion to Shakespeare's Works: Volume II – The Histories*. Eds. Richard Dutton and Jean E. Howard. 287–307. Oxford: Blackwell, 2003.

Potter, Nicholas. "'Like to a Tenement or a Pelting Farm": *Richard II* and the Idea of the Nation'. In *Shakespeare in the New Europe*. Edited by Michael Hattaway, Boika Sokolova and Derek Roper. 130–47. Sheffield: Sheffield Academic Press, 1994.

Prior, Moody E. *The Drama of Power: Studies in Shakespeare's History Plays*. Evanston, IL: Northwestern University Press, 1973.

Pugliatti, Paola. 'Shakespeare's Histories as a Genre'. *Il confronto letterario* 1:1 (1984): 29–52.

Shakespeare the Historian. New York: St Martin's Press, 1996.

Rackin, Phyllis. *Stages of History: Shakespeare's English Chronicles*. Ithaca, NY: Cornell University Press, 1990.

Reese, M. M. *The Cease of Majesty: A Study of Shakespeare's History Plays*. London: Arnold, 1961.

Reichert, Klaus. 'Ein Shakespeare aus Flandern'. *Shakespeare Jahrbuch* 137 (2001): 100–14.

Ribner, Irving. *The English History Play in the Age of Shakespeare*. 1957. Rev. edn. Princeton: Princeton University Press, 1965.

Richmond, Hugh M. *King Richard III*. Shakespeare in Performance. Manchester: Manchester University Press, 1989.

'The Resurrection of an Expired Form: *Henry VIII* as Sequel to *Richard III*'. In *Shakespeare's English Histories: A Quest for Form and Genre*. Edited by John W. Velz. 205–28. Binghamton, NY: Medieval & Renaissance Texts & Studies, 1996.

Riehle, Wolfgang. *Shakespeares Trilogie 'King Henry VI' und die Anfänge seiner dramatischen Kunst*. Heidelberg: Carl Winter Universitätsverlag, 1997.

Rutter, Carol Chillington. 'Fiona Shaw's *Richard II*: The Girl as Player-King as Comic'. *Shakespeare Quarterly* 48 (1997): 314–24.

Ryan, Kiernan. 'The Future of History: *1* and *2 Henry IV*'. In Kiernan Ryan, *Shakespeare*. 2nd edn. 40–69. London and New York: Prentice Hall / Harvester Wheatsheaf, 1995.

Saccio, Peter. *Shakespeare's English Kings: History, Chronicle, and Drama*. 2nd. edn. Oxford and New York: Oxford University Press, 2000.

'The Historicity of the BBC History Plays'. In *Shakespeare on Television: An Anthology of Essays and Reviews*. Edited by J. C. Bulman and H. R. Coursen. 208–13. Hanover, NH: University Press of New England, 1988.

Sanders, Norman. 'American Criticism of Shakespeare's History Plays'. *Shakespeare Studies* 9 (1976): 11–24.

Sarlos, Robert K. 'Dingelstedt's Celebration of the Tercentenary: Shakespeare's Histories as a Cycle'. *Theatre Survey* 5 (1964): 117–31.

Schabert, Ina. 'Shakespeares Geschichtsvision in romantischen Brechungen: Die Rezeption der Historien in England 1800–1825'. In *Das Shakespeare-Bild in Europa zwischen Aufklärung und Romantik*. Edited by Roger Bauer, Michael de Graat and Jürgen Wertheimer. 60–76. Bern: Peter Lang, 1988.

Schenker, Adrien. 'Les Drames historiques de Shakespeare, Schiller et Grillparzer dans l'interprétation de Reinhold Schneider'. In *Les Lettres et le sacré:*

Littérature, histoire et theologie. Edited by Guy Bedouelle. 92–105. Lausanne: L'Age d'Homme, 1994.

Schlegel, August Wilhelm. *A Course of Lectures on Dramatic Art and Literature*, translated by John Black. Revised according to the last German edition by A. J. W. Robertson. London: Henry G. Bohn, 1846.

Schoch, Richard W. *Shakespeare's Victorian Stage: Performing History in the Theatre of Charles Kean*. Cambridge: Cambridge University Press, 1998.

Scolnicov, Hanna, and Peter Holland, eds. *The Play Out of Context: Transferring Plays from Culture to Culture*. Cambridge: Cambridge University Press, 1989.

Shaughnessy, Robert. *Representing Shakespeare: England, History, and the RSC*. New York: Harvester Wheatsheaf, 1994.

Sheen, Erica. 'The Pannonians and the Dalmatians: Reading for a European History in *Cymbeline*'. In *Shakespeare in the New Europe*, edited by Michael Hattaway, Boika Sokolova and Derek Roper. 310–20. Sheffield: Sheffield Academic Press, 1994.

Sher, Antony. *The Year of the King*. London: Methuen, 1986.

Shewring, Margaret. 'The Politics and Aesthetics of Theatrical Languages: *Richard II* on the European Stage'. In Margaret Shewring, *King Richard II*. Shakespeare in Performance. 154–79. Manchester: Manchester University Press, 1996.

Shirley, F. A., ed. *'King John' and 'Henry VIII': Critical Essays*. New York: Garland, 1988.

Siegel, Paul N. 'Tillyard Lives: Historicism and Shakespeare's History Plays'. *Clio* 9 (1979): 5–23.

Siemon, James. '"Perplex'd Beyond Self-Explication": *Cymbeline* and Early Modern/Postmodern Europe'. In *Shakespeare in the New Europe*. Edited by Michael Hattaway, Boika Sokolova and Derek Roper. 294–309. Sheffield: Sheffield Academic Press, 1994.

Smidt, Kristian. *Unconformities in Shakespeare's History Plays*. London and Basingstoke: Macmillan, 1982.

Snyder, Susan. 'The Genres of Shakespeare's Plays'. In *The Cambridge Companion to Shakespeare*. Edited by Margreta de Grazia and Stanley Wells. 83–97. Cambridge: Cambridge University Press, 2001.

Speaight, Robert. *Shakespeare on the Stage*. London: Collins, 1973.

Sprague, Arthur Colby. *Shakespeare's Histories: Plays for the Stage*. London: The Society for Theatre Research, 1964.

Steene, Birgitta. 'Shakespearean Elements in Historical Plays of Strindberg'. *Comparative Literature* 11 (1959): 209–20.

Stříbrný, Zdeněk. '*Henry V* and History'. In *Shakespeare in a Changing World*. Edited by Arnold Kettle. 84–101. New York: International Publishers, Inc., 1964.

Shakespeare in Eastern Europe. Oxford: Oxford University Press, 2000.

Suerbaum, Ulrich. 'Die frommen Häretiker: John Barton in Zusammenarbeit mit Peter Hall, *The Wars of the Roses*'. In *Anglo-Amerikanische Shakespeare-Bearbeitungen des 20. Jahrhunderts*. Edited by Horst Priessnitz. 31–43. Darmstadt: Wissenschaftliche Buchgesellschaft, 1980.

Swander, Homer D. 'The Rediscovery of *Henry VI*'. *Shakespeare Quarterly* 29 (1978): 146–63.

Symington, Rodney T. K. *Brecht und Shakespeare*. Bonn: Bouvier, 1970.

Szaffkó, Péter. 'Under the Spell of Shakespeare's Histories: English Historical Drama in Criticism from the Renaissance to Irving Ribner'. *Hungarian Journal of English and American Studies* 1:1 (1995): 13–44.

Tarsitano, Marie. 'Sturua's Georgian *Richard III*'. *Theatre History Studies* 9 (1989): 69–76.

Taylor, Gary. *Reinventing Shakespeare: A Cultural History from the Restoration to the Present*. London: The Hogarth Press, 1990.

Taylor, Gary, ed. *Henry V*. The Oxford Shakespeare. Oxford: Oxford University Press, 1982.

Teetgen, Alexander. *Shakespeare's 'King Edward the Third', Absurdly Called, and Scandalously Treated as, a 'Doubtful Play': An Indignation Pamphlet. Together with an Essay of 'The Poetry of the Future'*. London: Williams and Norgate, 1875.

Tennenhouse, Leonard. *Power on Display: The Politics of Shakespeare's Genres*. New York: Methuen, 1986.

Tillyard, E. M. W. *Shakespeare's History Plays*. London: Chatto & Windus, 1944.

Traversi, Derek. *Shakespeare from 'Richard II' to 'Henry V'*. London: Hollis & Carter, 1958.

Utterback, Raymond V. 'Dramatic Perspectives on Shakespeare's History Plays: A Review Article'. *Studies in the Literary Imagination* 5:1 (1972): 141–62.

Vaughan, Virginia Mason. 'Between Tetralogies: *King John* as Transition'. *Shakespeare Quarterly* 35 (1984): 407–20.

Velz, John W., ed. *Shakespeare's English Histories: A Quest for Form and Genre*. Medieval and Renaissance Texts and Studies, 133. Binghamton: Medieval and Renaissance Texts and Studies, 1996.

Vos, Jozef de. 'Shakespeare's History Plays in Belgium: Taken Apart and Reconstructed as "Grand Narrative"'. In *Four Hundred Years of Shakespeare in Europe*. Edited by Angel Luis Pujante and Ton Hoenselaars. With a Foreword by Stanley Wells. Newark: University of Delaware Press, 2003, 211–22.

'*Ten Oorlog*: The History Plays Recycled in The Low Countries'. *Folio* 5:1 (1998): 7–16.

Vos, Jozef de, ed. *'Ten Oorlog' Doorgelicht*. Special theme issue of *Documenta* (Ghent) 16:2 (1998).

Warren, Roger. 'Comedies and Histories at Two Stratfords, 1977'. *Shakespeare Survey* 31 (1978): 141–53.

Watson, Donald G. *Shakespeare's Early History Plays: Politics at Play on the Elizabethan Stage*. Athens: The University of Georgia Press, 1990.

Watson, Nicola J. 'Kemble, Scott, and the Mantle of the Bard'. In *The Appropriation of Shakespeare: Post-Renaissance Reconstructions of the Works and the Myth*. Edited by Jean I. Marsden. 73–92. Hemel Hempstead: Harvester Wheatsheaf, 1991.

Wells, Robin Headlam. 'The Fortunes of Tillyard: Twentieth-Century Critical Debate on Shakespeare's History Plays'. *English Studies* 66:5 (1985): 391–403.

Wharton, T. F. *Text and Performance: Henry the Fourth Parts 1 and 2.* London: Macmillan, 1983.

Whitton, David. *Stage Directors in Modern France.* Manchester: Manchester University Press, 1987.

Wickham, Glynne. 'The Dramatic Structure of Shakespeare's *King Henry the Eighth*: An Essay in Rehabilitation'. In *Proceedings of the British Academy: Volume 70, 1984.* 149–66. London: Oxford University Press, 1985.

Wikander, Matthew H. *The Play of Truth and State: Historical Drama from Shakespeare to Brecht.* Baltimore and London: Johns Hopkins University Press, 1986.

Wilders, John. *The Lost Garden: A View of Shakespeare's English and Roman History Plays.* London and Basingstoke: Macmillan, 1978.

Williams, David, ed. *Collaborative Theatre.* The Théâtre du Soleil Sourcebook. London and New York: Routledge. 1999.

Williams, Simon. *Shakespeare on the German Stage. Vol. 1: 1586–1914.* Cambridge: Cambridge University Press, 1990.

Wilson, J. Dover, and T. C. Worsley. *Shakespeare's Histories at Stratford 1951.* London: Max Reinhardt, 1952.

Womersley, David. 'The Politics of Shakespeare's *King John*'. *Review of English Studies* n.s. 40 (1989): 497–515.

Wright, Daniel L. *The Anglican Shakespeare: Elizabethan Orthodoxy in the Great Histories.* Vancouver, WA: Pacific Columbia, 1993.

Zander, Horst. 'Bearbeitungen von Historien: John Barton / Peter Hall, *The Wars of the Roses;* John Barton, *Richard II*; John Barton, *King John*'. In Horst Priessnitz, *Anglo-Amerikanische Shakespeare-Bearbeitungen des 20. Jahrhunderts.* 44–63. Darmstadt: Wissenschaftliche Buchgesellschaft, 1980.

Shakespeare 'bearbeitet': Eine Untersuchung am Beispiel der Historien-Inszenierungen 1945–1975 in der Bundesrepublik Deutschland. Tübingen: Narr, 1983.

Index